The Contemporary Relevance of Carl Schmitt

What does Carl Schmitt have to offer to ongoing debates about sovereignty, globalization, spatiality, the nature of the political and political theology? Can Schmitt's positions and concepts offer insights that might help us understand our concrete present-day situation? Works on Schmitt usually limit themselves to historically isolating Schmitt into his Weimar or post-Weimar context, to reading him together with classics of political and legal philosophy or to focusing exclusively on a particular aspect of Schmitt's writings. Bringing together an international, and interdisciplinary, range of contributors, this book explores the question of Schmitt's relevance for an understanding of the contemporary world. Engaging the background and intellectual context in which Schmitt wrote his major works – often with reference to both primary and secondary literature unavailable in English – this book will be of enormous interest to legal and political theorists.

Matilda Arvidsson and **Leila Brännström** are based at Lund University, Sweden; **Panu Minkkinen** is at the University of Helsinki, Finland.

The Contemporary Relevance of Carl Schmitt

Law, Politics, Theology

Edited by
Matilda Arvidsson,
Leila Brännström and
Panu Minkkinen

a GlassHouse Book

First published 2016
by Routledge
2 Park Square, Milton Park, Abingdon, Oxon, OX14 4RN

and by Routledge
711 Third Avenue, New York, NY 10017

a GlassHouse Book

Routledge is an imprint of the Taylor & Francis Group, an informa business

© 2016 Editorial matter and selection: Matilda Arvidsson, Leila Brännström and Panu Minkkinen
Individual chapters: the contributors

The right of Matilda Arvidsson, Leila Brännström and Panu Minkkinen to be identified as editors of this work has been asserted by them in accordance with sections 77 and 78 of the Copyright, Designs and Patents Act 1988.

All rights reserved. No part of this book may be reprinted or reproduced or utilised in any form or by any electronic, mechanical, or other means, now known or hereafter invented, including photocopying and recording, or in any information storage or retrieval system, without permission in writing from the publishers.

Trademark notice: Product or corporate names may be trademarks or registered trademarks, and are used only for identification and explanation without intent to infringe.

British Library Cataloguing in Publication Data
A catalogue record for this book is available from the British Library

Library of Congress Cataloging-in-Publication Data
A catalogue record for this book has been requested

ISBN: 978-1-138-82293-1 (hbk)
ISBN: 978-1-315-74224-3 (ebk)

Typeset in Baskerville by
FiSH Books Ltd, London

Contents

About the authors vii

Editors' introduction 1
MATILDA ARVIDSSON, LEILA BRÄNNSTRÖM AND PANU MINKKINEN

PART I
Law 17

1 Carl Schmitt's definition of sovereignty as authorized leadership 19
LEILA BRÄNNSTRÖM

2 Carl Schmitt and the problem of constitutional guardianship 34
LARS VINX

3 Political community in Carl Schmitt's international legal thinking 50
MARKUS GUNNEFLO

4 Carl Schmitt and the tyranny of values 64
JUHA-PEKKA RENTTO

5 A law without the political: Carl Schmitt, romanticism, and Friedrich Dürrenmatt's *The Execution of Justice* 78
PANU MINKKINEN

6 Social acceleration, motorized legislation and framework laws 91
CARL-GÖRAN HEIDEGREN

PART II
Politics 105

7 Law, decision, necessity: shifting the burden of responsibility 107
JOHANNA JACQUES

8 Representation and the unrepresentable: Ernst Jünger,
Carl Schmitt and the limits of politics 120
MÅRTEN BJÖRK

9 Rethinking the concept of the political: Derrida's reading of
Schmitt's 'The Theory of the Partisan' 134
JACQUES DE VILLE

10 Eschatology and existentialism: Carl Schmitt's historical
understanding of international law and politics 147
WALTER RECH

11 Carl Schmitt and the new world order: a view from Europe 165
MASSIMO FICHERA

PART III
Theology 179

12 'Im Kampf um Rom': Carl Schmitt's critique of Rudolph Sohm
and the post-secular turn 181
HJALMAR FALK

13 Processes of order and the concreteness of the sacred: on the
contemporary relevance of Carl Schmitt's critique of nihilism 195
JON WITTROCK

14 Beyond the jurist as a theologian of legal science: the question
of Carl Schmitt and the international legal order 208
PETER LANGFORD AND IAN BRYAN

15 From teleology to eschatology: the *katechon* and the political
theology of the international law of belligerent occupation 223
MATILDA ARVIDSSON

Index 237

About the authors

Matilda Arvidsson is Lecturer and Doctoral Candidate in International Law at Lund University, Sweden.

Mårten Björk is Doctoral Candidate in Theology and Religious Studies at the University of Gothenburg, Sweden.

Leila Brännström is Senior Lecturer in Jurisprudence at Lund University, Sweden.

Ian Bryan is Senior Lecturer in Law in the Law School, University of Lancaster, United Kingdom.

Jacques de Ville is Professor of Law at the University of the Western Cape, South Africa.

Hjalmar Falk is Postdoctoral Researcher in the History of Ideas and Science at the University of Gothenburg, Sweden.

Massimo Fichera is Lecturer in European Studies at the Network for European Studies, University of Helsinki, Finland.

Markus Gunneflo is Lecturer and Postdoctoral Researcher in Public International Law at Lund University, Sweden.

Carl-Göran Heidegren is Professor of Sociology at Lund University, Sweden.

Johanna Jacques is Lecturer in Law at Durham University, United Kingdom.

Peter Langford is Senior Lecturer in Law in the Department of Law and Criminology, Edge Hill University, United Kingdom.

Panu Minkkinen is Professor of Jurisprudence at the University of Helsinki, Finland.

Walter Rech is Postdoctoral Researcher at the Erik Castrén Institute of International Law and Human Rights, University of Helsinki, Finland.

Juha-Pekka Rentto is Adjunct Professor (Docent) in the Philosophy of Law at the Universities of Helsinki and Turku, Finland.

Lars Vinx is Assistant Professor of Philosophy at Bilkent University in Ankara, Turkey.

Jon Wittrock is Senior Lecturer in Political Science at Södertörn University, Sweden.

Editors' introduction

Matilda Arvidsson, Leila Brännström and Panu Minkkinen

In 2000, Gopal Balakrishnan suggested that: 'In the English-speaking world [Carl Schmitt] *is terra incognita*, a name redolent of Nazism, the author of a largely untranslated *oeuvre* of short texts forming no system, coming to us from a disturbing place and time in the form of scrambled fragments' (Balakrishnan 2000: 1). Indeed, fifteen years on Balakrishnan's observation appears dated. The lion's share of Schmitt's books, articles, and lectures is now available in English editions (for full bibliographical information on Schmitt's publications, see Benoist 2003).[1] The amount of secondary literature dealing with different aspects of Schmitt's thinking, or with his *oeuvre* in general, is constantly growing (for a selection, see, for example, Vinx 2014). And even though Schmitt's explicit intellectual support for and active involvement with National Socialism continues to cast doubts on the value and significance of his thought, the reception of his works has moved beyond a discussion in which commentators either adopt the role of his prosecutors or his apologists. At this moment in time people of diametrically opposite political allegiances seem to find Schmitt's ideas on sovereignty, dictatorship, political theology, legality and legitimacy, the nature of the legal order, the concept of the political and international law and order worthy of attention and engagement or even immediately useful.

But what exactly is the added value of engaging with Schmitt? In which ways is his *oeuvre* relevant from a contemporary point of view? These are questions that the contributions in the present volume attempt to answer.

Before discussing the 'Schmitt revival' of the last few decades in slightly more detail as well as positioning the present volume more precisely within the landscape of recent secondary literature, a short account of Schmitt's

---

1 Important works that have been translated into English between 2000 and 2015 include *The Nomos of the Earth* (Schmitt 2003), *Legality and Legitimacy* (Schmitt 2004a), *On the Three Types of Juristic Thought* (Schmitt 2004b), *Theory of the Partisan* (Schmitt 2007b), *Constitutional Theory* (Schmitt 2008a), *Political Theology II* (Schmitt 2008b), *Dictatorship* (Schmitt 2014), and *The Guardian of the Constitution* (Schmitt 2015).

life and career is apposite (for comprehensive and detailed biographical accounts, see Mehring 2014; Balakrishnan 2000; for a shorter introduction, see, for example, Vinx 2014).

Schmitt was born in 1888 to a Catholic family of modest means in the predominantly Protestant provincial town of Plettenberg in North Rhine-Westphalia. He studied law in Berlin, Munich and Strasbourg, where he earned his degree in 1910. Schmitt embarked immediately on the path of becoming an academic lawyer. As Schmitt entered the academic field of jurisprudence, criticism against the hegemony of 'statutory positivism' was on the rise (cf. Stolleis 2004: 17–19). German statutory positivism, often associated with the name of Paul Laband, suggested that a system of legal norms could cover all concrete instances sufficiently, and it prescribed 'dogmatic', that is, a logical and value-free, exegesis of statutory texts in terms of legal method (see, for example, Caldwell 1994; Paulson 2007). Schmitt's publications before World War I (Schmitt 1910; Schmitt 1969; Schmitt 1914), still not available in English, deal with issues that emerged out of the then ongoing destabilization of the cornerstones of statutory positivism: the inability of legal norms in controlling judgment in concrete cases, the management of indeterminacy by the legal order, the nature of state authority and the relation between law and factual power. These are issues that Schmitt would come back to again and again over time.

Schmitt was exempted from service on the front line during the war because of back injuries he suffered in training. Instead he worked for the regional martial law administration in Munich. After the war and the period of acute disorder that followed it, Schmitt was released from his official duties and returned to academia. He taught during a short period at a business school in Munich before becoming Professor of Public Law in Greifswald in 1922 and, later the same year, in Bonn. In 1928 Schmitt finally moved to the *Handelshochschule* in Berlin, an independent business academy. By then he had already made a name for himself.

Schmitt's first publication after World War I, the 1919 *Political Romanticism* (Schmitt 2011a), was a polemical intellectual history criticizing the attitude of the early nineteenth-century German romantics, which Schmitt described as an indecisive voyeurism detached from ongoing actual political conflicts, an attitude that was underpinned by the belief in the absolutism of the individual. Schmitt's critique of such a withdrawal from politics into aesthetics could be read as a notice about the direction his work would soon take. Over the next few years Schmitt took on issues immediately related to the political crises and conflicts in the Weimar Republic.

Schmitt's Weimar era publications deal with the law and politics of exceptional circumstances, emergency powers and sovereign authority (for example, *Dictatorship* from 1921, Schmitt 2014; *Political Theology* from 1922, Schmitt 2005), with the make-up, ethos and viability of parliamentary government and constitutional liberalism (for example, the 1923 *The Crisis of Parliamentary Democracy*, Schmitt 2000; *Legality and Legitimacy* from 1932, Schmitt 2004a) and with the notions of 'state', 'constitution' and 'the political' (for example, *The Concept of the Political* from 1927, revised and republished in 1932, Schmitt 2007a; *Constitutional Theory* from 1928, Schmitt 2008a). Schmitt did not only work with these issues and notions theoretically but also as they applied to the interpretation of the Weimar constitution (see, for example, Schmitt 2008a; the 1931 *The Guardian of the Constitution*, Schmitt 2015).

Another theme that figured prominently in Schmitt's works during the early part of the Weimer era was theology and the role of Catholicism. *Roman Catholicism and Political Form* (Schmitt 1996a), Schmitt's most overtly theological work, was published in 1923, a year after the influential *Political Theology* in which Schmitt had contended that all significant concepts of the modern theory of state are secularized theological concepts. In the 1923 book Schmitt elaborates on his understanding of the Catholic Church's political mission in the contemporary world and suggests that only the substantive, juridical orientation of Catholicism allows humanity to confront the moral dilemmas of the twentieth century. Schmitt's views about the political role of the Catholic Church were, however, soon to change. Although political and intellectual considerations might have motivated Schmitt's change of mind, a conflict with the Church over a rather personal matter could also constitute an ingredient. Schmitt had married in 1916 and when he, a few years later, tried to have the marriage annulled by the Church, his request was rejected. As he went through with a new (civil) marriage in 1926, the Church excommunicated him. Although there is little consensus on what links there are between Schmitt's religious or metaphysical concepts and ideas concerning the nature of political and action (cf., for example, Meier 1998 with Scheuerman 1999), it is clear that the Catholic Church, even after Schmitt's break with it, continued to represent a model for the exercise of worldly authority in Schmitt's writings (cf., for example, Schmitt 2004b: 60).

Schmitt's career took a practical turn during the political and constitutional crisis of the final years of the Weimar Republic when his theory of presidential dictatorship was used to legitimize the President's repeated use of extraordinary powers. Schmitt's involvement in the concrete *Realpolitik* of the Weimar Republic peaked in 1932 when the right-wing government of the *Reich* appointed him its legal representative before the *Staatsgerichtshof*, a forerunner to the Federal Constitutional Court, to defend the constitutionality of the presidential decrees which had been used to dismantle the Social Democrat-dominated coalition government in Prussia, the most vigorously anti-Nazi state government at the time (for a detailed account, see Dyzenhaus 1997).

Although Schmitt had not displayed sympathies with the Nazis before, he joined the party when they seized power in January 1933 and quickly obtained an influential position in the legal profession. He came to be perceived as the 'Crown Jurist' of National Socialism but his position of power was weakened in 1936 after a feud with elements of the *Schutzstaffel* (SS) (see Mehring 2014: 275–405). There is considerable debate about the causes of Schmitt's association with the Nazi regime. Whereas some point to Schmitt's overly ambitious and opportunistic character (see, for example, Schwab 1989), others suggest that Schmitt's anti-liberal jurisprudence, as well as his anti-Semitism, disposed him to support the Nazi regime (see, for example, Scheuerman 1999).[2] Be that as it may, Schmitt's work during the 1933–36 era consists of short tracts, breathing Nazism and anti-Semitism, that are usually taken to represent 'the moral and scientific nadir of his career' (Teschke 2011: 74). Schmitt's 1934 *On the Three Types of Juristic Thought* (Schmitt 2004b), which introduces 'concrete-order thought' as a jurisprudential doctrine, is something of an exception, as it has attracted, and continues to attract theoretical interest (see, for example, Böckenförde 1984; Günther 2011; Croce and Salvatore 2013).

Throughout the later Nazi period, Schmitt's work centred on questions related to international law and order. Although he seemed to be driven by the immediate motive to justify Nazi expansionism (see, for example, Schmitt 2011b), Schmitt was also theoretically interested in the history and the foundations of international law and order. He was convinced that 'the turn towards liberal cosmopolitanism in 20th century international law would undermine the conditions of stable and legitimate international legal order' (Vinx 2014). Schmitt's engagement with international law culminated in *The Nomos of the Earth*, a lengthy monograph written in the early 1940s, but published only a decade later (Schmitt 2003).

Owing to his support for and involvement with the Nazis, Schmitt was detained and interrogated at the end of the war as a potential defendant in the Nuremberg trials. He was released in 1946 after more than a year in American internment, after which he resettled in his hometown Plettenberg. Schmitt could not return to an academic position as he refused every attempt at de-Nazification and rehabilitation but he remained an important background figure on the West German conservative intellectual scene and enjoyed a considerable degree of clandestine influence elsewhere (Scheuerman 1999: 183–251; Koskenniemi 2004). Schmitt died in 1985 at the age of 96. His post-war writings mostly dealt with issues related to international law and order (for example, *Theory of the Partisan* from 1963, Schmitt 2007b) but he also published works in which

---

2   Reinhard Mehring has made a list of no less than forty-two possible reasons for Schmitt's decision to back National Socialism (Mehring 2014: 282–5).

he re-thought and re-worked his most basic ideas and concepts such as 'the political' and 'political theology (for example, his last publication *Political Theology II* from 1970, Schmitt 2008b).

So why Schmitt today?

The ongoing revival of Schmitt scholarship can, perhaps, best be depicted as three overlapping waves of scholarship that all feed into each other. The first wave started as an approach from the left as a critique of liberalism and parliamentary democracy mainly inspired by *The Concept of the Political* (Schmitt 2007a). The work of Chantal Mouffe comes immediately to mind (for example, Mouffe 2005; also Bendersky 1983; Kennedy 2004; Marder 2010). This wave can be seen as extending to different variations of agonistic political theory (for example, Schaap 2009). The second wave, originating in the wake of the events of September 2001 and the subsequent bombings in Europe as well as the military interventions in Afghanistan and Iraq (see, for example, Stirk 2005), was a focus on emergency powers and their constitutional framework mainly in the light of Schmitt's *Political Theology* (2005). The perhaps best-known body of work within this second wave is Giorgio Agamben's *Homo Sacer* project (for example, Agamben 1998, 2005), following which was a large volume of secondary literature (for example, Zartaloudis 2010; Frost 2013). The third and, chronologically speaking, latest wave draws together Schmitt's work from a wider set of sources and, correspondingly, includes at least three focal points, namely the theory of popular sovereignty (for example, Lindahl 2007; Kalyvas 2008: 79–186; Loughlin 2010: 209–37; Kahn 2011; Minkkinen 2013; Vinx 2013a), Schmitt's conception of international order (for example, Odysseos and Petito 2007; Slomp 2009; Legg 2011; Benhabib, 2012; Vinx 2013b) and his theory of law (for example, Croce and Salvatore 2013; Neumann 2015).

One outcome of this revival of interest in Schmitt's work and the way in which scholars from divergent academic disciplines have made use of Schmitt is an ever-expanding secondary literature characterizing Schmitt as a representative of one academic discipline or another. So depending on the perspective adopted Schmitt may appear as a constitutional lawyer, a legal theorist, a political philosopher, or other. But attempts have also been made to understand Schmitt's work in interdisciplinary contexts. In November 2011, a group of Swedish scholars across the fields of legal studies, philosophy, intellectual history, political science, sociology and theology gathered in Gothenburg to take stock of Schmitt's legacy in their respective fields and to assess the significance of the new waves of Schmitt scholarship outlined above. The symposium resulted in a well-received anthology (Wittrock and Falk 2012). The same group met in June 2013 in Helsinki together with Finnish and international colleagues with the aim of further exploring the relevance of Schmitt's legal and political thought from a distinctly interdisciplinary and contemporary perspective. What does Schmitt have to offer to ongoing debates on questions relating to sovereignty, globalization, spatiality, the nature of the political, and political theology? Can Schmitt's positions and concepts offer insights that would help us understand our concrete present-day situation?

The collection at hand is the result of this interdisciplinary and international collaboration. Its uniqueness lies in its focus on Schmitt's relevance for an understanding of our contemporary world. Existing collections usually limit themselves to either historically isolating Schmitt into his Weimar or post-Weimar contexts (for example, Dyzenhaus 1998), to reading him together with classics of political and legal philosophy (for example, Tralau 2010) or to focusing uniquely on a particular aspect of Schmitt's overall production (for example, Odysseos and Petito 2007). This collection also sheds light on the background and intellectual context in which Schmitt wrote his major works, often with reference to both primary and secondary literature unavailable in English. Its specific aim, however, is to critically assess the explanatory potential of Schmitt's various theoretical interventions from a contemporary perspective. What is the *contemporary* relevance of Carl Schmitt?

The fifteen chapters of the present collection are divided into three interlinked parts. The first part focuses primarily on Schmitt's writings on law, from both domestic and international perspectives. The second part broadens the discussion to include political perspectives. The third part examines Schmitt's views on theology and how they configure in his legal and political theory. The sections bring together the ways in which Schmitt saw law, politics and theology as interconnected: not thought of as separate phenomena, but necessarily related. If, for Schmitt, law requires thinking through the political, then conversely theology, in Schmitt's view, is at the core of the political. In other words, the chapters included in the sections address the contemporary conditions of our world in these terms showing how Schmitt's thinking is and can be made relevant to us today. While one can identify Schmitt's thoughts on law, politics and theology throughout this volume, each section brings together chapters that either address or depart from one of the three.

Brännström's contribution (Chapter 1) revolves around Carl Schmitt's (in)famous definition in *Political Theology* that the sovereign is the one 'who decides on the exception'. More specifically, Schmitt suggests that the defining characteristic of sovereignty is the authority to decide whether an extreme emergency situation is at hand, and if so, to do whatever is required, including suspending all legal norms, to secure a normal situation. Reading *Political Theology* against the background of Schmitt's later developed concrete-order approach to law, which places its ultimate foundation and legitimacy in a given way of life in a community, Brännström argues that Schmitt's decision must not be understood as an a-legal, extra-legal or illegal, law-and-order-creating decision *ex nihilo* but as a legal decision (re)interpreting the character of the already existing socio-legal order. The trouble with Schmitt's notion of sovereignty, Brännström suggests, is not that it violates or transgresses the law, but rather that it presupposes a hierarchical structure of authority, the function of which is to control who can speak in the name of the people and negotiate the character of the socio-legal order. Schmitt's notion of sovereignty can be useful from a contemporary perspective only if it is reformulated and purged of its preference for hierarchy and leadership.

In 'Carl Schmitt and the Problem of Constitutional Guardianship', (Chapter 2) Vinx critically examines Schmitt's constitutional theory, which is currently having a revival. Conceptualizing the constitution as a form of concrete social and political ordering that results from a popular constituent decision, Schmitt suggests that allowing a constituted power to change the basic structure of a constitution, by way of amendment or judicial review, would amount to a usurpation of constituent power. Instead, Schmitt proposes that the popularly elected head of the executive should be the guardian of the constitution and should settle non-trivial disputes about a society's form of social and political ordering through executive dictatorship. To Schmitt, such an arrangement is compatible with popular sovereignty since plebiscitary leadership is taken to represent the unity of the people. Vinx argues that Schmitt's constitutional scheme is ultimately designed to silence or remove those who do not fully concur with the order ensuing from the founding decision and who are therefore cast as aliens and enemies not properly belonging to the people whose unity is represented by the guardian of the constitution. Schmitt's constitutional theory is therefore not only objectionable because it fails to provide adequate safeguards to individuals and minorities, but also because of the anti-democratic implications of the notion of popular sovereignty that justifies it.

Gunneflo's 'Political Community in Carl Schmitt's International Legal Thinking' (Chapter 3) also works on the presumption that Schmitt's legal, political and ethical thinking is underpinned by the overriding concern to secure the survival of the political community, in the sense of a particular way of life. Gunneflo's attention is, however, directed at Schmitt's thinking on international law and order. Gunneflo demonstrates how Schmitt's commitment to political community explains his evaluation of European international law and its demise, of the use of force, of various forms of exercising influence beyond state borders, and of different kinds of partisans. Regarding all these issues, Schmitt pitches the defence of a concrete form of political existence against a universalizing form of imperialism, which acts in the name of liberal values and in the interests of world economy. Gunneflo also shows that the tension between these opposing rationales still haunts contemporary post-Westphalian international law and order. Although the notion of exercising power and using force in the name of a universal right has steadily gained ground, the defence of political community retains significant potency in international law which is visible, for example, in the legal asymmetry maintained between the state and its non-state enemy or in the fact that the 'inherent right of self-defence' ultimately remains subject to state auto-interpretation.

Rentto's 'Carl Schmitt and the Tyranny of Values' (Chapter 4) is an engagement with Schmitt's post-war tract *The Tyranny of Values* (Schmitt 1996b). In this piece, Schmitt criticizes the notion that the basic rights of the German Basic Law are an expression for even more fundamental values, such as human dignity, which not only provide the ultimate standard for the legitimacy of the Constitution, but also lend themselves to being used as supposedly objective criteria for interpreting its provisions. Rentto brings into view that Schmitt's criticism in *The Tyranny of Values* is in line with his earlier criticism of the legalism of the liberal constitutional state. In both cases, the existential evaluative decision, which constitutes political existence and makes a choice for a concrete set of values, is evaded or veiled. Rentto points out that for Schmitt human beings only have qualities, interests and rights as members of some concrete order and that 'human rights' and 'human dignity' are but abstract, empty and non-committal notions which can be used as sham justifications for desired interpretations. Siding with Schmitt, Rentto, suggests that those speaking the abstract and universal language of human rights do not know 'how to distinguish between well-founded distinction and arbitrary discrimination'.

Minkkinen's 'A Law without the Political' (Chapter 5) centres on 'juridical romanticism', a romantic stance in relation to law that, in its logic, follows the main lines of Carl Schmitt's definition of political romanticism. 'Juridical romanticism', Minkkinen suggests, is not only a strain in contemporary legal scholarship, but also to be found for example in the appeal of transitional justice. Schmitt described romanticism as the attitude of someone who is above all seeking emotional experience and therefore suspends reality in order to imagine other, more emotionally stimulating, possibilities. The 'political romanticist', more specifically, suspends the reality of antagonism and instead of choice and decision resorts to a third, more appealing, but fictional, alternative. Drawing on Schmitt, Minkkinen suggests that the juridical romantic is a an apolitical figure who refuses to see law, or 'justice' which is the term preferred by romantics, as a set of crude oppositions such as legal and illegal, right and wrong, or even just and unjust on which one has to decide. The chapter illustrates the theme of juridical romanticism through Friedrich Dürrenmatt's late novel *The Execution of Justice*, in which the main protagonist denies the reality of the legal opposition between guilty and innocent and instead approaches it as a constellation of infinite possibilities that can be played with.

In 'Social acceleration, motorized legislation and framework laws',

(Chapter 6) Heidegren fleshes out the notion of 'the motorized legislator', which Schmitt coined in the lecture *The Plight of European Jurisprudence* from 1944. Schmitt used the notion in relation to a broad historical trend: the ever-increasing size and speed of new legislation on the one hand, and the delegation of authority from the legislative body to the executive and administrative bodies on the other hand. According to Schmitt these developments were on the one hand due to the increasing ambitions of planning and steering on the part of the state, and on the other, to the rapid changes and growing complexity of modern society. Heidegren points out that the two causal factors that Schmitt identified have also been the main driving forces behind the extensive use of framework legislation in Sweden since 1945. He argues that the use of framework legislation, which enacts open-ended laws that are to be specified and concretized at a later point in time and by a different authority, can be seen a strategy for handling social complexity and social acceleration by way of temporalization and delegation. Heidegren finally suggests that Schmitt's notion of 'the motorized legislator', far from being dated, is rather of considerable current interest in relation to the issue of the changing preconditions for politics in a high-speed society, and calls for detailed analysis of the dynamics behind the phenomenon at which Schmitt only hinted.

In 'Law, Decision, Necessity' (Chapter 7) Jacques's investigates what it might mean to act politically by analyzing a tension in Schmitt's account of the sovereign, political decision: on the one hand, the choice of words implies that the decision is triggered and concluded by the necessities of existential self-preservation, leaving no agency to the decision maker, on the other hand the decision on the exception is presented as discretionary, stressing the agency and freedom of the subject of decision. Fleshing out Schmitt's notion of political existence, Jacques suggests that necessity as a force that determines action has no place in Schmitt's theory of the political. The defence of political existence is a matter of a choosing between alternative ways of life in the conditioning but not determining context of an existing order, the character of which is at stake. Drawing on Max Weber's ethics of responsibility, Jacques argues that although the correctness of the political decision ultimately remains uncertain, the decision maker must assume responsibility for its consequences. By restoring to Schmitt's decision its aspects of freedom and independence, Jacques's chapter outlines a positive role for the political decision maker that goes beyond that of the law-abiding subject, arbitrary dictator or the helpless victim of higher forces.

In 'Representation and the Unrepresentable' (Chapter 8) Björk contrasts Carl Schmitt's and Ernest Jünger's political and philosophical thinking, focusing on the way in which Jünger and Schmitt use symbols, in particular the symbols of the 'ship' and the 'forest'. In the rare cases in which the works of the two 'radical conservatives' have been read in conjunction, the similarities between their proto-fascist ideologies have been highlighted. Björk, in contrast, attends to their dissimilarities and in particular their different views on the human being and on political existence and its limits. Björk suggests that whereas for Schmitt individuals are always already subsumed by the life and offices of the state and have no real life outside of it, for Jünger the corporeal human being cannot be reduced to a political animal and human life cannot be adequately represented by the life in the state. Jünger insists that there is something anarchic and 'unurban' about the human ape, which cannot be politically represented and which has the possibility to defy the binary opposition between friend and enemy and reach for freedom and peace. Björk suggests that the explored differences between the two theorists might indicate why Schmitt endorsed National Socialism whereas Jünger avoided it, and why Schmitt lamented the crises of the nation state, while Jünger casted it as a potential move towards a more peaceful world order.

In 'Rethinking the Concept of the Political' (Chapter 9) De Ville analyzes Jacques Derrida's (1997) reading of 'The Theory of the Partisan' in *Politics of Friendship*, with the purpose of exploring its implications for the concept of the political. De Ville argues that Derrida's reading of Schmitt can only be understood if one takes into account Derrida's transformation of Freud's psychoanalysis. It is in view of this transformed psychoanalysis that Derrida understands Schmitt's criteria for determining the true partisan, his mention of the abyss and the Acheron, his recognition of the brother as absolute enemy, and his silence about women in the context of partisan warfare. De Ville suggests that Derrida's reading of Schmitt results in a concept of the political that has lost its identity and is characterized by a force of self-destruction as its condition of possibility.

In 'Eschatology and Existentialism' (Chapter 10) Rech scrutinizes Schmitt's philosophy of history in relation to international law and order. Rech also investigates whether Schmitt's ideas are suitable for rethinking international law and relations, and in particular, the contemporary relations between the USA and China. In the 1950s, Schmitt suggested that the quest for universal hegemony pursued by the Soviet Union and the USA was driven by a belief in utopian historical progressivism. In opposition to such a view of history, which he associated tightly to hegemonic aspiration, Schmitt submitted that human history consists of a succession of independent paradigms within which all major civilizations establish a particular and 'concrete' international order. He also contended that 'concrete' international order could only arise from the multipolar balance of power of equally strong political entities, be they national states or 'large spaces'. Rech points out that Schmitt's views and arguments are in many respects problematic and untenable, but that his critique of progressivism – of belief in technology, technocratic rule and economic rationalism – remains extremely topical. Schmitt's existentialist emphasis on the meaningfulness of historical existence and his insistence on context as opposed to progressive metanarrative also make an insightful alternative to both realist and Foucaultian accounts of international affairs.

Although critical of many of Schmitt's presuppositions, Fichera employs his writing in the area of international law in 'Schmitt and the New World Order' (Chapter 11) to shed light on the international ambitions of the European Union. Fichera points out that the Union deals with security problems, broadly defined, by expanding externally through exporting a model of regional integration based on the rule of law. At the same time, it tries to assert itself on the global scene by emerging as a space that promotes liberal/Western values. Fichera proposes that it is fruitful to configure the European Union's imperial ambitions in terms of an effort to establish a Schmittian 'large space'. What distinguished the large space for Schmitt was the technique of domination at work: not the occupation of territory, but the proclamation of a zone of non-intervention coupled with a right of intervention for the dominant state in the large space. However, differently from what Schmitt had in mind, the European Union is not striving for military influence, but is instead assuming geopolitical influence by offering peace, stability, prosperity and wellbeing.

Falk's '*Im Kampf um Rom*' (Chapter 12) enquires into the largely ignored intellectual relation between Schmitt and the German jurist and legal scholar Rudolph Sohm, in order to shed light on the character of Schmitt's Catholicism. In his work on the organization of the original Christian congregation, Sohm (1912) claimed that the *Urgemeinde* knew no law and was instead governed directly by God's exceptional grace as materialized in *charismata*, a gift of grace unequally distributed within the congregation. Falk argues that even if the reception of Schmitt's political theology has been dominated by something akin to Sohm's thoughts, it took form in opposition to Sohm's idea of exceptional grace. For Schmitt, it is not charisma that constitutes office, but the office that confers charisma. What Schmitt transferred to state theory from Christianity was the worldly organization of the Catholic Church, its character as a legal order which can answer the question: who decides? Schmitt's Catholicism, Falk argues, was political. By investigating Schmitt's engagement with Sohm's ideas, Falk is also able to position Schmitt in relation to the contemporary field of so-called post-secular thought. In contrast to several proponents of post-secular thought, Schmitt accords a positive, relatively autonomous existence to 'the secular'. For Schmitt, the rationality of worldly jurisprudence is not *identical* with theological reason. It is *analogous* to it. Falk suggests that it is exactly the structural analogy that makes Schmitt's theological perspective useful today: the theological tradition can offer a resource for critical perspectives on contemporary theory.

In Chapter 13, Wittrock explores Carl Schmitt's critique of nihilism in 'Processes of Order and the Concreteness of the Sacred'. Schmitt defined nihilism as the disconnection of order from sacred orientation. For Schmitt an order consists at the most basic level in the appropriation, distribution and production of resources and it is these processes that are supposed to be tied, in a non-nihilistic order, to a sacred orientation. Wittrock argues that, for Schmitt, the sacred and corresponding categories represent the ultimately ungraspable, transcendent, metaphysical exception, within the immanent world of human, everyday life and activities. Sacred orientation is the counter-pole to the 'spirit of technicity' and partly functions by withdrawing certain domains, both spatial and temporal – be it natural objects, artefacts, sites, temporal intervals, animals or people – from ordinary usage and circulation. When order is disconnected from sacred orientation, everything is approached as resources to be exploited. Wittrock's essay ties Schmitt's polemic concerning nihilism and the sacred to three themes of contemporary relevance: the role of political symbols and rituals, the fragmentation of an oscillating movement between the division of labour and a festive coming together beyond it, and a reflection on the sacred as entailing the establishment of exceptional relations to certain persons, objects, sites or temporal intervals. A reading of Schmitt's critique thus invites further reflection on the role of these themes in relation to processes of the appropriation, distribution and production of resources in the contemporary world.

In 'Beyond the Jurist as a Theologian of Legal Science', (Chapter 14) Langford and Bryan read Schmitt's post-1945 writings on international law and order focusing on the position and identity that he cuts out for the jurist as the theologian of legal science. Langford and Bryan highlight that, for Schmitt, spatial appropriation is the force in history, which constitutes legal order. This force produces a history of subsequent processes of appropriation attaching to orders of distribution and production. According to Schmitt, the role of the jurist is to demarcate the *nomoi* of the earth and render the parameters of these configurations intelligible. Langford and Bryan suggest that the notion of the common, that is a space which is always already common, allows us to imagine what precedes law as something other than the creation and division of space by violence, appropriation and preservation. They also establish that the notion of the common opens the possibility of reconceiving the role of the jurist beyond the one assigned by Schmitt: to interrogate law in relation to the experience of injustice.

In 'From Teleology to Eschatology' (Chapter 15), Arvidsson draws on Schmitt's famous claim that 'all significant concepts of the modern theory of the state are secularized theological concepts' to inquire into the temporal structure of the laws of occupation. In line with Schmitt's brief notes on this field of law, Arvidsson understands it as an exception within the international legal order, which renders the non-sovereign governance of territories *legal.* Arvidsson highlights the way in which the non-progressive temporality of this field of law is an anomaly within contemporary international law, which encompasses notions such as progress, development, and prosperity for all of human kind. The laws of occupation do not deliver any redemptive promise beyond the 'now' for people under belligerent occupation. Instead, they superimpose a temporary and emphatically non-democratic form of governance while an end and a return of, or a turn towards, law and sovereignty in its full sense is awaited. For Arvidsson, this field of law embodies the figure of the *katechon* within international law's eschatology.

Acknowledgements

The editors would like to thank Martin Loughlin, who delivered the keynote of the 2013 seminar (published as Loughlin 2014) and generously commented on early versions of the chapters, and everyone at Routledge for their hard work. Finally, we would like to acknowledge the support of the Centre of Excellence in the Foundations of European Law and Polity, University of Helsinki, and the Swedish-Finnish Cultural Foundation.

Bibliography

Agamben, G. (1998) *Homo Sacer. Sovereign Power and Bare Life.* Trans. D. Heller-Roazen. Redwood City, CA: Stanford University Press.
Agamben, G. (2005) *State of Exception.* Trans. K. Attell. Chicago, IL: University of Chicago Press.
Balakrishnan, G. (2000) *The Enemy. An Intellectual Portrait of Carl Schmitt.* London: Verso.
Benhabib, S. (2012) 'Carl Schmitt's Critique of Kant: Sovereignty and International Law', *Political Theory*, Vol. 40, No. 6: 688–713.
Bendersky, J. W. (1983) *Carl Schmitt, Theorist for the Reich.* Princeton, NJ: Princeton University Press.
Benoist, Alain de (2003) *Carl Schmitt. Bibliographie seiner Schriften und Korrespondenzen.* Berlin: Akademie Verlag.
Böckenförde, E. W. (1984) 'Ordnungsdenken, konkretes', p. 1312–15, in J. Ritter and K. Gründer (eds), *Historisches Wörterbuch der Philosophie*, Vol. 6. Basel: Schwabe Verlag.
Caldwell, P. (1994) 'Legal Positivism and Weimar Democracy', *American Journal of Jurisprudence*, Vol. 39, No. 1: 273–301.
Croce, M. and A. Salvatore (2013) *The Legal Theory of Carl Schmitt.* Abingdon: Routledge.
Derrida, J. (1997) *The Politics of Friendship.* Trans. G. Collins. London: Verso.
Dyzenhaus, D. (1997) 'Legal Theory in the Collapse of Weimar: Contemporary Lessons', *American Political Science Review*, Vol. 91, No. 1: 121–34.
Dyzenhaus, D. (ed.) (1998) *Law as Politics. Carl Schmitt's Critique of Liberalism.* Durham, NC: Duke University Press.
Frost, T. (ed.) (2013) *Giorgio Agamben: Legal, Political and Philosophical Perspectives.* Abingdon: Routledge.

Günther, F. (2011) 'Ordnen, gestalten, bewahren. Radikales Ordnungsdenken von deutschen Rechtsintellektuellen der Rechtswissenschaft 1920 bis 1960', *Viertalsjahrshefte für Zeitgeschichte*, Vol. 59, No. 3: 353–84.
Kahn, P. W. (2011) *Political Theology: Four New Chapters on the Concept of Sovereignty*. New York: Columbia University Press.
Kalyvas, A. (2008) *Democracy and the Politics of the Extraordinary. Max Weber, Carl Schmitt, and Hannah Arendt*. Cambridge: Cambridge University Press.
Kennedy, E. (2004) *Constitutional Failure. Carl Schmitt in Weimar*. Durham, NC: Duke University Press.
Koskenniemi, M. (2004) *The Gentle Civilizer of Nations: The Rise and Fall of International Law 1870–1960*. Cambridge: Cambridge University Press.
Legg, S. (ed.) (2011) *Spatiality, Sovereignty and Carl Schmitt: Geographies of the Nomos*. London: Routledge.
Lindahl, H. (2007) 'The Paradox of Constituent Power. The Ambiguous Self-Constitution of the European Union', *Ratio Juris*, Vol. 20, No. 4: 485–505.
Loughlin, M. (2010) *Foundations of Public Law*. Oxford: Oxford University Press.
Loughlin, M. (2014) 'Politonomy', in J. Meierhenrich and O. Simons, *The Oxford Handbook of Carl Schmitt*. Oxford: Oxford University Press (forthcoming).
Marder, M. (2010) *Groundless Existence. The Political Ontology of Carl Schmitt*. London: Continuum.
Mehring, R. (2014) *Carl Schmitt: A Biography*. Trans. D. Steuer. Cambridge: Polity.
Meier, H. (1998) *The Lesson of Carl Schmitt: Four Chapters on the Distinction between Political Theology and Political Philosophy*. Trans. M. Brainard. Chicago, IL: University of Chicago Press.
Minkkinen, P. (2013) 'Political Constitutionalism versus Political Constitutional Theory: Law, Power and Politics', *International Journal of Constitutional Law*, Vol. 11, No. 3: 585–610.
Mouffe, C. (2005) *On the Political*. Abingdon: Routledge.
Neumann, V. (2015) *Carl Schmitt als Jurist*. Tübingen: Mohr Siebeck
Odysseos, L. and F. Petito (eds) (2007) *The International Political Thought of Carl Schmitt. Terror, Liberal War and the Crisis of Global Order*. Abingdon: Routledge.
Paulson, S. L. (2007) 'Statutory Positivism', *Legisprudence*, Vol. 1, No. 1: 1–30.
Schaap, A. (ed.) (2009) *Law and Agonistic Politics*. Aldershot: Ashgate.
Scheuerman, W. E. (1999) *Carl Schmitt. The End of Law*. Lanham: Rowman and Littlefield.
Schmitt, C. (1910) *Über Schuld und Schuldarten: eine terminologische Untersuchung*. Breslau: Schletter'sche Buchhandlung.
Schmitt, C. (1914) *Der Wert des Staates und die Bedeutung des Einzelnen*. Tübingen: J. C. B. Mohr.
Schmitt, C. (1969) *Gesetz und Urteil: Eine Untersuchung zum Problem der Rechtpraxis* [1912], 2nd ed. Munich: C. H. Beck.
Schmitt, C. (1996a) *Roman Catholicism and Political Form* [1923]. Trans. G. L. Ulmen. Westport: Greenwood.
Schmitt, C. (1996b) *The Tyranny of Values* [1959]. Trans. S. Drahici. London: Plutarch.
Schmitt, C. (2000) *The Crisis of Parliamentary Democracy* [1923]. Trans. E. Kennedy. Cambridge, MA: MIT Press.
Schmitt, C. (2003) *The Nomos of the Earth in the International Law of the Jus Publicum Europaeum* [1950]. Trans. G. L. Ulmen. New York: Telos.

Schmitt, C. (2004a) *Legality and Legitimacy* [1932]. Trans. J. Seitzer. Durham, NC: Duke University Press, 2004.
Schmitt, C. (2004b) *On The Three Types of Juristic Thought* [1934]. Trans. J. Bendersky. Westport: Praeger.
Schmitt, C. (2005) *Political Theology: Four Chapters on the Concept of Sovereignty* [1922]. Trans. G. Schwab. Chicago, IL: Chicago University Press.
Schmitt, C. (2007a) *The Concept of the Political* [1932], Expanded ed. Trans. G. Schwab. Chicago, IL: Chicago University Press.
Schmitt, C. (2007b) *Theory of the Partisan: Intermediate Commentary on the Concept of the Political* [1963]. Trans. A. C. Goodson. New York: Telos.
Schmitt, C. (2008a) *Constitutional Theory* [1928]. Trans. J. Seitzer. Durham, NC: Duke University Press.
Schmitt, C. (2008b) *Political Theology II. The Myth of the Closure of any Political Theology* [1970]. Trans. M. Hoelzl and G. Ward. Malden: Polity.
Schmitt, C. (2011a) *Political Romanticism* [1919]. Trans. G. Oakes. Cambridge, MA: MIT Press.
Schmitt, C. (2011b) 'The *Großraum* Order of International Law with a Ban on Intervention for Spatially Foreign Powers: A Contribution to the Concept of Reich in International law' [1939–1941], p. 75–124, in C. Schmitt, *Writings on War*. Trans. T. Nunan. Cambridge: Polity.
Schmitt, C. (2014) *Dictatorship: From the Beginning of the Modern Concept of Sovereignty to the Proletarian Class Struggle* [1921]. Trans. M. Hoelzl and G. Ward, Cambridge: Polity.
Schmitt, C. (2015) *The Guardian of the Constitution* [1931], p. 79–173, in L. Vinx (ed.), *The Guardian of the Constitution: Hans Kelsen and Carl Schmitt on the Limits of Constitutional Law*. Trans. L. Vinx. Cambridge: Cambridge University Press.
Schwab, G. (1989) *The Challenge of the Exception. An Introduction to the Political Ideas of Carl Schmitt Between 1921 and 1936*. 2nd edn. Westport: Greenwood Press.
Slomp, G. (2009) *Carl Schmitt and the Politics of Hostility, Violence and Terror*. Basingstoke: Palgrave Macmillan.
Sohm, R. (1912) *Wesen und Ursprung des Katholizismus*. Berlin: Teubner.
Stirk, P. M. R. (2005) *Carl Schmitt, Crown Jurist of the Third Reich. On Preemptive War, Military Occupation and World Empire*. Lewiston: Edwin Mellen.
Stolleis, M. (2004) *The History of Public Law in Germany, 1914–1945*. Trans. T. Dunlap. Oxford: Oxford University Press.
Teschke, B. (2011) 'Decisions and Indecisions: Political and Intellectual Receptions of Carl Schmitt', *New Left Review*, Vol. 67: 61–95.
Tralau, J. (ed.) (2010) *Thomas Hobbes and Carl Schmitt. The Politics of Order and Myth*. Abingdon: Routledge.
Vinx, L. (2013a) 'The Incoherence of Strong Popular Sovereignty', *International Journal of Constitutional Law*, Vol. 11, No. 1: 101–21.
Vinx, L. (2013b) 'Carl Schmitt and the Analogy between Constitutional and International Law: Are Constitutional and International Law Inherently Political?', *Global Constitutionalism*, Vol. 2, No. 1: 91–124.
Vinx, L. (2014) 'Carl Schmitt', in *The Stanford Encyclopedia of Philosophy* (Winter 2014 edn). E. N. Zalta (ed.). Available online at http://plato.stanford.edu/archives/win2014/entries/schmitt (accessed 8 April 2015).

Wittrock, J. and H. Falk (eds) (2012) *Vän eller Fiende. En antologi om Carl Schmitts politiska tänkande*. Gothenburg: Daidalos.

Zartaloudis, T. (2010) *Giorgio Agamben. Power, Law and the Uses of Criticism*. Abingdon: Routledge.

Part I

Law

Chapter 1

Carl Schmitt's definition of sovereignty as authorized leadership

Leila Brännström

Introduction

Political Theology from 1922 begins with Carl Schmitt's definition of the sovereign as the one 'who decides on the [state of] exception' (Schmitt 1996a: 13/2005: 5). This definition is usually read as an attempt to point out the essential predicate of sovereignty and is made use of for identifying sovereignty's historical instantiations and discussing its contemporary resurgence, waning or displacement (cf., for example, Butler 2004: 59; Bartelson 2014: 49–57). In such readings, 'decisionism' is taken as the 'signature characteristic of sovereignty' in the sense of a political act unrestrained by any legal considerations, which owing to its concrete effectiveness 'renders a political subject into a legitimate sovereign' (Brown 2010 a: 22–3; Kahn 2004: 263; Kahn 2011: 32; Croce and Salvatore 2013: 5, 17–18; cf. also, for example, Bartelson 2014: 41–49, Gross 2000: 1851; Bates 2006: 415–16).

The tendency to emphasize the a- or extra-legality of Schmitt's sovereign decision, influential though it is, appears not to sit well with the fact that Schmitt characterizes his definition of sovereignty *juristic* and opens *Political Theology* with a criticism of approaches to law which are unable to offer legal answers in the face of 'decisive' questions of state and constitution, such as whether a state of emergency is at hand (Schmitt 1996a: 9, 13/2005: 4, 6). Schmitt also insists that the 'fundamental problem of the concept of sovereignty' is 'the connection of actual power with the legally highest power' and that 'power proves nothing in law' (Schmitt 1996a: 26/2005: 17–18). In fact, a key argument in *Political Theology* is that the decision on the state of exception is a legal decision if made by the authorized subject. Schmitt maintains that it is only from the point of view of 'constitutional liberalism [*rechtsstaatlichen Liberalismus*]', which assumes that 'a decision in the legal sense' must be 'derived entirely from the content of a norm', that the test of whether an emergency exists appears as a non-juristic one (Schmitt 1996a: 13–14/2005: 5–6).

One of the purposes of this chapter is to bring into view that a major concern in *Political Theology* is to suggest a conceptualization of law, which is not only capable of encompassing answers concerning extremely exceptional circumstances, but also of accurately describing the way in which the legal order operates. Rather than pitching sovereignty against law, *Political Theology* advances a particular understanding of law. However, while Schmitt devotes much effort to highlight the shortcomings and inconsistencies of the 'liberal constitutional' conception of law, he only gestures towards a different understanding which does not equate law with what can be derived from the body of legal norms and which can account for sovereign decisions. Instead of a fully fleshed-out alternative notion, Schmitt speaks of what is not derived from legal norms but is 'accessible to jurisprudence [*im Rahmen des Juristischen*]' (Schmitt 1996a: 19/2005: 12) or is to be understood 'in the juristic or the legal sense [*im Rechtssinne, im juristischen Sinne, im rechtlichen Sinne*]' (Schmitt 1996a; 14, 18, 38/2005: 6, 12, 32). Despite the lack of conceptual clarity, it is only by distinguishing the different conceptions of law concurrently at work in the text that an apparent paradox in *Political Theology* can be resolved: a decision can be within and beyond the bounds of law simultaneously because what is a- or extra-legal from a liberal constitutional point of view can be anchored in the legal order from a different understanding of law.

Schmitt is only able to offer a clear alternative to the liberal constitutional conception in his *On the Three Types of Juristic Thought* (hereinafter *Three Types*, Schmitt 2004) published more than a decade later, in 1934. In *Three Types*, Schmitt advances a 'concrete-order approach [*konkretes Ordnungsdenken*]' to law, which places its ultimate foundation and legitimacy in a given form of life in a community, in 'a set of standards and models that are produced by social institutions in everyday life' (Croce and Salvatore 2013: 158).

Although the understanding of law, politics and sovereignty that we find in *Three Types* is often seen as a turn away from the decisionism expressed in *Political Theology* (cf., for example, Croce and Salvatore 2013: 1, 13–29; Bates 2006: 415; Ungureanu 2008: 295), this chapter suggests that it is rather a clarification and development of it and that Schmitt's notion of sovereignty in *Political Theology* is already inflected by concrete-order thinking.[1] This

---

1 Croce and Salvatore (2013) have convincingly demonstrated that Schmitt's concrete-order perspective retains strong elements of decisionism. This chapter, in reverse, is drawing attention to the way in which concrete-order thinking infuses Schmitt's decisionism in *Political Theology*. Despite our different readings of *Political Theology*, I completely agree with Croce and Salvatore's proposition that Schmitt's work on politics, law and the relation between these two spheres should in general be read through the lens of *Three Types*. Croce and Salvatore themselves pointed out the presence of concrete-order thinking in *Constitutional Theory* (Schmitt 2008; Croce and Salvatore 2013: 25–9) and David Bates (2006) has done that in relation to *Roman Catholicism and Political Form* (Schmitt 1996b).

mode of thinking is implicit in the text and the structure of the argument and it is only by taking this approach into account that an ambiguity in *Political Theology* can be clarified. For Schmitt, it is only when the authorized subject of sovereignty makes an effective decision on the state of exception that 'actual power' and 'the legally highest power' come together. This, however, presupposes that the authorized subject can be identified prior to the decision. Even if Schmitt suggests that the question about the proper subject of sovereignty is 'the whole question of sovereignty', he does not clarify how this subject is to be localized (Schmitt 1996a: 14/2005: 6–7). The concrete-order approach gives us the key to this puzzle.

The aim of this chapter is, however, not only to highlight that Schmitt's sovereign decision is underpinned by concrete-order thinking and is not an, a-legal, extra-legal or illegal, law-and-order-creating decision *ex nihilo*. The purpose is also to read Schmitt's definition as an intervention in a dispute about the future of the political rather than as an attempt to identify the essential attribute of sovereignty.[3] Looked at from this angle, Schmitt is offering us the conceptual resources for a particular way of arranging political life and community, which, if influential enough, would constitute sovereignty in the way defined. Two questions that are addressed in this chapter are therefore the following: which way of approaching and ordering the political world is Schmitt promoting when offering his definition of sovereignty? What might be useful or appealing in Schmitt's offering from a contemporary point of view?

This chapter proceeds with a short exposition of Schmitt's notion of concrete-order thinking, after which *Political Theology* is read in light of this viewpoint, to clarify how Schmitt can present the sovereign as simultaneously standing inside and outside the legal order. Following this, Schmitt's account of the decision on the state of exception is analyzed to shed light on how, and in what sense, sovereign decisions are claimed to be legal. Next, the chapter moves on to explore the particular way of ordering the political community, which Schmitt's notion of sovereignty advances. And finally, Schmitt's agenda is critically examined and its contemporary relevance is briefly discussed. It is suggested that the truly problematic feature of Schmitt's notion of sovereignty, is not its purported a-, extra- or illegality, but the hierarchical structure of authority presupposed by it, the function of which is to control who can speak in the name of the people and negotiate the character of the socio-legal order.

2   In addition, the preface to the second edition of *Political Theology* indicates that concrete-order thinking should be taken into account when reading the book (cf. Schmitt 1996a: 8–9/2005: 2–4).
3   Such a reading also seems in line with Schmitt's claim in *The Concept of the Political* that political concepts such as sovereignty 'have a political meaning' (Schmitt 1963: 31/2007: 30–1; on Schmitt's definitions more generally, see Croce and Salvatore 2013: 64).

Concrete-order thought

Despite the centrality of the concept, 'concrete order' remains underdeveloped and under-theorized in *Three Types*. What can be gathered is that it is an institution that is not constituted by legal fiat, but is established through repetitions of standardized conduct that the members of a social group *de facto*, maintain or are, at least, expected to maintain (see further Croce and Salvatore 2013: 30–45; Böckenförde 1984). Marriage, family, office, state bureaucracy, and the army, are some of the concrete orders mentioned in *Three Types*.

The most important feature of a concrete order is the sustaining of a 'normal situation'. Concrete orders maintain stable normal situations by providing sedimented norms of conduct, which are usually complied with (cf. Schmitt 1934: 10–11, 19–24, 56/2004: 45–6, 53–7, 88). If a public servant, for instance, wants to be a normal and good public servant, she needs to do what is customary for her role (for the 'normal figure'), which means that she has to act in accordance with established praxis in various 'normal situations' (cf., for example, Schmitt 1934 42–3/2004: 75–76). Normality, according to Schmitt, makes up the 'legal substance [*rechtliche Substanz*]' of the concrete order and offers an answer to the legal question of what should be considered fair, reasonable or required in various contexts (Schmitt 1934: 20, 50/2004: 54, 81). The function of the legal order is to crystallize, stabilize and protect the legal substance of concrete orders. Thus, the concrete-order perspective takes the norms of conduct in concrete orders as *legally normative* guidelines for legislative and judicial decision making.

The legal substance of concrete orders cannot be anything but underdetermined, however. Such legal content can no more establish its own practical meaning in concrete historical situations than can a legal norm. To avoid or solve conflicts about the meaning of socio-legal normative content, a leadership principle (*Führergedanken, Führergrundsatz*) must be in place. Every concrete order has, or is tied to, a hierarchy of authority that ascends to a personal leader to whom the members of the order are meant to show loyalty and obedience (cf. Schmitt 1934: 50–2, 63–4/2004: 81–3, 94–5). In a concrete order, there is no strict separation between norm-based jurisdiction and actual leadership (cf. Schmitt 1934: 50–2/2004: 81–3). The role of the leader is to maintain and develop the legal substance of the concrete order. The decision making of the authority figure is legitimized and guided, although never completely, by the legal substance, at the same time as the concrete orders and their normality are renewed through the decisions. The decision rests on the order at the same time as the decision (re)creates the order: order and decision are thus the two intertwined poles within the concrete-order framework (cf. Schmitt 1934: 15–16/2004: 50–1).

The state is, in Schmitt's words, 'the institution of institutions' and 'the concrete order of orders' (Schmitt 1934: 45–8, 57/2004: 78–9, 88). The state is an overarching institution, standing above and incorporating the civil society of concrete orders, under the auspices of which other institutions can be given protection and uphold their own order (cf. Schmitt 1934 45–8, 57/2004: 76–80, 88). The state is neither engendered through a sovereign decision nor constructed by legal norms. Like other institutions, the state is a concrete social and historical formation. And the authority to decide in the name of the state, in the form of law, cannot simply be derived from legal norms but must stem from concrete, personal nominations (Schmitt 1934: 15–17/2004: 50–1). We will come back to the role cut out in this scheme for the leader heading the concrete order of the state, the sovereign.

Law in *Political Theology*

The primary target of *Political Theology*, as well as that of *Three Types*, is the conception of law that Schmitt labelled 'liberal constitutionalism' in the first book and '19th century juristic positivism' in the second, and which nowadays often travels under the rubric of 'statutory positivism' (cf., for example, Vinx 2016, Chapter 2 in this volume; Caldwell 1994). Schmitt's criticism of this conception centres on the idea that law is a system of positively given norms, which can be interpreted and applied to concrete cases without taking the real organization of social life or law's conditions of realization into account (cf. Schmitt 1934: 29–40/2004: 63–71). Schmitt argues that liberal constitutionalism denies the protean quality of social and political life and is undergirded by faith in the possibility of control by means of systems of abstract propositions (cf., for example, Schmitt 1996a: 14/2005: 7; cf. Prozorov 2005: 87). Liberal constitutionalism replicates a 'pattern of thinking characteristic of the natural sciences', presents the legal order as a 'machine [that] runs itself', 'attempts to banish from the realm of the human mind every exception' and, as a consequence, fails to apprehend 'the independent meaning of the decision' (Schmitt 1996a: 13, 52/2005: 5, 41–2, 48).

For Schmitt the juridical decision has an independent meaning for logical and ontological reasons. Legal norms cannot identify the concrete events to which they are applicable, nor can they pass judgments on whether or not they have been correctly applied in concrete cases.[4] Norms are mediated by judgement in their transition to social reality and

---

4 Schmitt was certainly not he first one to call attention to this fact (cf., for example, Kant 1998: 267–70 [A 131–6/B 169–75]).

mediation adds something to the general idea or norm (cf. Schmitt 1996a: 36–7/2005: 30–1). Even though the question of how 'correct' legal decisions are arrived at is not dealt with in depth in *Political Theology*,[5] Schmitt makes two things clear: norms gain their actual meaning from a 'normal everyday frame of life' and the correct decision is the one made by the responsible jurisdictional authority (Schmitt 1996a: 19/2005: 13).

In *Political Theology* as well as in *Three Types*, Schmitt emphasizes that the validity of a norm depends on the existence of a normal situation presupposed by it (Schmitt 1996a: 19/2005: 13; 1934: 23, 33–4/2004: 56–7, 66). The dependency of legal norms on normality is, however, elaborated more fully in *Three Types*. Here Schmitt suggests that outside 'functionalistic' areas of life such as the traffic or the market, the generally formulated conditions of applicability that a norm provides (the factual requisites), that is the description of the factual situation in which the norm is applicable, are implicitly tied to socially established normal situations (Schmitt 1934: 10–24/2004: 46–57). If the normal situation presupposed by the norm becomes abnormal or disappears, the norm loses its field of application and becomes obsolete and invalid (Schmitt 1934: 23/2004: 56).

In routine cases, when the circumstances in a case match both the factual requisites provided by the legal norm and the social normal situation presupposed by the norm, legal decision making approaches the limit of pure repetition and it appears *as if* norm application can dispense with judgment and mediation. In the atypical case, however, a rift opens up between the factual requisites (taken in their literal meaning) and the normality prescribed in the type situation presupposed by the norm; that is to say, circumstances correspond to the factual requisites, but deviate relevantly from the normal situation presupposed by the norm (or vice versa). In such exceptional cases, 'the power of real life breaks through the crust of a mechanism that has become torpid by repetition' (Schmitt 1996a: 21/2005: 15). The decision on the exception, 'suspends', to use Schmitt's vocabulary, the norm in relation to the atypical case, and reconstitutes the proper field of application of the norm, and thus its *raison d'être* and

---

5   Schmitt's early work, *Gesetz und Urteil* (Schmitt 1969) from 1912, is devoted to the question of how to distinguish the correct legal decision. Schmitt's rather abstract answer is that a judicial decision is correct if it can be assumed that another judge would have decided in the same way. The correct judicial decision is thus not distinguished by being derived from the body of established positive norms but neither is it an arbitrary decision. In a legal order adhering to the rule of law, the correct judicial decision is the one that satisfies the expectations placed on the legal order (see, further, Jacques 2016, Chapter 7 in this volume).

meaning.[6] Schmitt argues that from the perspective of the legal norms regulating a situation, and thus from the perspective of liberal constitutionalism, the constitutive legal dimension of the decision on the exception is 'new and alien' and appears as if it 'emanates from nothingness' (Schmitt 1996a: 37–8/2005: 31–2). However, from the concrete-order perspective, the decision is not 'new and alien' but guided by the normative parameters, behavioural patterns and expectations that are attached to the relevant normal situation. In other words, the decision is faithful to the legal substance of the concrete order in which the case unfolds. For Schmitt, both judicial decisions and legal norms are intrinsically related to the social fabric within which they have emerged and in which they operate.

As already mentioned, the legal substance of concrete orders cannot be anything but underdetermined, which means that the question of faithfulness in concrete cases can be open to reasonable disagreement. At this point the leadership principle enters the scene. Schmitt stresses that differences in judgment are ultimately settled by jurisdictional competence (Schmitt 1996a: 38–40/2005: 33–4). A decision made by the authoritative body has a legal significance that surpasses the substantive reasons given for the correctness of the decision, which might not be more convincing than alternative reasons pointing to a different solution. In contrast to other bids on correct judgment, however, the decision of the jurisdictionally competent body takes the form of law and enters into force (Schmitt 1996a: 37, 40/2005: 31, 34; cf. also Gehring 2003). For Schmitt, taking on the form of law means that an actually effective formation such as the state, bridges the gap between normative content and its realization (Schmitt 1996a: 35/2005: 28).

The sovereign decision and the state of exception

In *Political Theology* Schmitt speaks of 'the exception [*die Ausnahme*]' in four different senses and no consistent terminology is used to distinguish them. The exception signifies the 'atypical case', as well as the suspension of a legal norm in response to it. The 'exception' in these two senses, which are by no means exceptional in the ordinary workings of a legal order, have

---

6   The legislator can anticipate the atypical case and suspend the norm in relation to it in advance. The examples that Schmitt offers relate to the anticipation of states of occupation and emergency in constitutions and the attribution of extraordinary powers. A simple example would be a norm stating the prohibition of motorized traffic on a specific road but allowing such traffic in cases of medical emergency, as expectations of normal behaviour are different in this atypical case (cf. Schmitt 1996a: 20/2005: 14). Schmitt does not always describe the relation between suspension of a norm and an exception from it in this way (cf. Vinx 2016, Chapter 2 in this volume).

been discussed above. In addition, 'exception' also signifies the 'state of exception'; that is, the suspension of all legal norms and their normal application, and finally, also the factual situation, 'the extreme emergency', which triggers a decision on the state of exception.[7]

According to *Political Theology*, the defining characteristic of sovereignty is the authority (*die Kompetenz, die Befugnis*) to decide on the state of exception; that is, the monopoly to decide if the extreme emergency is at hand and, if so, to do whatever is required to secure a normal situation in which legal norms can be effective (Schmitt 1996a; 13, 18–19/2005: 5, 12–13). Quite consistent with the concrete-order approach, Schmitt establishes in *Political Theology* that order must be present for 'a legal order to make sense' (Schmitt 1996a; 19/2005: 13). In the same way that the validity of a single norm depends on the presence of a presupposed normal type situation, Schmitt suggests that the body of legal norms as such; that is, the legal order in the liberal constitutional sense, loses its field of application if the normal kind of social order presupposed by this body is unsettled. Because the decision on the state of exception involves a judgment on whether the factual condition of applicability of the ordinary legal order is present, this state is 'a general concept in the theory of the state' and not a 'construct applied to any emergency decree or state of siege' or any 'extraordinary measure' (Schmitt 1996a: 13, 18/2005: 5, 12).

Schmitt contends that the whole question of sovereignty is about the proper subject of sovereignty (Schmitt 1996a: 14/2005: 6). As a general norm can neither conclusively settle whether the prevailing normal order is sufficiently threatened, nor what should be done if that is the case, the key question is who has the authority to judge. As already mentioned, *Political Theology* consistently presents the sovereign as somebody already invested with supreme authority (cf., for example, Schmitt 1996a: 14, 18/2005: 7, 18). Just like any ordinary (limited) jurisdictional competence, the authority to suspend the entire body of laws is ultimately anchored in the actual hierarchy of the concrete order of the state and cannot necessarily be derived from legal norms. The authority of the sovereign subject therefore remains intact even when 'law recedes' in the state of exception (Schmitt 1996a: 18/2005: 12). The state also retains its legal substance after the suspension of the normally valid legal order. Schmitt insists that the state of exception is something different than anarchy and chaos and that 'order in the juristic sense still prevails' even if it is not a *Rechtsordnung;* that is to say, not a legal order of the kind liberal constitutionalism imagines (Schmitt 1996a: 18, 20/2005: 12, 14). As long as the organization of the

---

7   Schmitt indicates, although inconsistently, the exception in the third sense by using the expressions 'the state of exception [*der Ausnahmezustand*]' or 'the total exception [*die absolute Ausnahme*]' and in the fourth sense by using the expressions 'the real exception [*der echte Ausnahmefall*]' or 'the extreme emergency [*der extreme Notfall*]'.

state continues to be effective, and as long as social order has not turned 'abnormal', sovereign authority is valid and in force, even if legal norms are not.

Does the lingering order, in Schmitt's structure, limit the field of possible actions that the sovereign can take? Whereas it is clear in Schmitt's construction of sovereignty that legal norms in their normal meaning put no restrictions on the sovereign, the relation of order and decision remains undecided in *Political Theology*. On the one hand, Schmitt claims that every order ultimately rests on a decision, which gestures towards a decision unrestricted by order; on the other hand, he insists that the sovereign 'belongs' to the normally valid legal order (Schmitt 1996a: 14, 16, 18–19, 26/2005: 7, 10, 12–13, 18). What are the implications of the sovereign's attachment to the normally valid legal order? *Three Types*, presenting, as we have seen, order and decision as standing in a relation of induction to each other, sheds light on this.

In the preface to the second edition of *Political Theology*, published shortly before *Three Types*, Schmitt argues that isolated concrete-order thinking can lead to a feudal type of pluralism without sovereignty (Schmitt 1996a: 8/2005: 3). Under historically volatile conditions, an overarching order, the state, with a supreme leader, needs to uphold/re-establish normal living conditions, in which the concrete orders of a community can subsist and co-exist. The state is to guarantee the stability and coordination of the social order in its totality. This is the legal substance of the institution of the state. Schmitt's reference to Fichte in *Three Types*, in a statement that is reminiscent of his own way of defining the state in *The Concept of the Political* (Schmitt 1963: 20, 26–7/2007: 19, 26), that is, that the state is a concrete-historical political unit that can tell apart friend and foe, summarizes the role of the state as the steward and developer of a political community's order as a whole (Schmitt 1934: 44/2004: 77). The telling apart of the friend and foe is not only a matter of the survival of a community as an entity, but is also an assurance that the character of the community, its way of life, is cultivated (cf. Schmitt 1963: 27/2007: 27; also Schmitt 1970: 3–11/2008: 59–66; Jacques 2016, Chapter 7 in this volume).

The sovereign is the ultimate guarantor of the overarching condition of normality – the one who is to ensure that the separate elements of the community form a body (cf. Gunneflo 2016, Chapter 3 in this volume). In its capacity as the leader of the political community the sovereign ultimately judges which concrete orders and which notion of normality deserve the support and protection of the law and the state, which can be tolerated, and which should be eliminated (cf. Schmitt 1934: 8–13, 43–4/2004: 44–9, 76; cf. also Vinx 2016, Chapter 2 in this volume). Because the sovereign embodies the 'concrete qualities of an order', its decisions are not capricious or subjective, but a construal of the legal substance of the concrete social order of the community (Schmitt 1934: 15/2004: 50).

'The core of the political idea', Schmitt writes, 'is the exacting moral decision', and the sovereign make such decisions against the background of the way of life already prevalent in a community (Schmitt 1996a: 69/2005: 65).

The objective to re/establish the specific normal order of a particular political community, which is the product of time and history, guides the decisions of the sovereign on, and in, the state of exception. The decision is thus not arbitrary or subjective, even if it is not conditioned by positive legal norms or control mechanisms (cf. Schmitt 1969: v). From the concrete-order perspective, the decision is also legal, even if its 'ultimate' correctness, just like decisions on exceptions in ordinary legal decision making, could be called into question, and is in the last instance given by the authority of the decision maker. The sovereign decision is the exercise of authorized leadership in a concrete order and cannot abolish the existing social order and constitute a wholly new one, but like the ordinary exercise of jurisdictional authority, the decision will *re*constitute law and order. For this reason, the relationship between decision and order unavoidably remains unstable in Schmitt's definition of sovereignty. The sovereign of *Political Theology* is neither the commissarial dictator (an extraordinary magistrate who is authorized to temporarily suspend certain legal barriers to be able to efficiently protect the constitutional order) nor the sovereign dictator (who establishes a completely new legal and political order) of *Dictatorship* (Schmitt 1994a/2014a). S/he is the leader who revitalizes an existing concrete order by re/interpreting its legal substance.

The agenda implied by Schmitt's notion of sovereignty

Three Types presents the Germany of 1934 as on its way to being reshaped by concrete-order thinking and as already recognizing a supreme *Führer*.[8] Be it as it may with Germany in 1934, *Political Theology* is set in a context in which no one is entrusted with unrestricted authority.[9] The book speaks to, or against, what Schmitt took to be the current of the jurisprudential thought of the time, which did not see any need for legal recognition of unlimited final authority. *Political Theology* stressed that a community committed to surviving and cultivating its way of life must recognize the

---

8   It is noteworthy that the passages in *Three Types* that praise National Socialism and how it establishes a new concrete social order are more characterized by pure decisionism than by concrete-order thinking (cf. Schmitt 1934: 52, 63–4/2004: 82–3, 94–5). This shows that establishing concrete-order thinking in a society not already recognizing hierarchies of authority and the leadership principle cannot be achieved by concrete-order thinking: it will require revolutionary decisionism.

9   Schmitt was, however, also engaged in convincing others that the Weimar constitution in actual fact did invest the president with unlimited authority (see Vinx 2016, Chapter 2 in this volume; also Schmitt 1994b/2014b).

need for an 'exacting moral decision' and a supreme leader because irresolvable conflicts about how life in common should be ordered, that is the possibility of an extreme emergency, cannot be eliminated through optimistic 'philosophical ... convictions' (Schmitt 1996a: 14, 69/2005: 7, 65).

There is, however, a difference between the need for an 'exacting moral decision' and the need for an authorized 'master' of that decision. In *Political Theology* Schmitt merges the two together and argues that the people, apart from the constituent power of which no ultimate authority is acknowledged in modern democracies, is not the kind of subject who is able to decide conclusively between opposing interests and coalitions (Schmitt 1996a: 53–5/2005: 49–51). Only if personified in a leader will the people be able to take legitimate and effective decisions in cases of conflict. By identifying the people with a leader, a move that will disqualify some members of the community from belonging to the 'people', and by placing an effective state organization at the disposal of the leader, Schmitt is able to reconcile the 'fundamental problem of the concept of sovereignty' that is 'the connection of actual power with the legally highest power' (Schmitt 1996a: 26/2005: 18).

The ultimate authority of the people does not, however, have to be represented by someone embodying the substantive identity of the people, as Schmitt suggests, but could rather be understood as a 'symbolic empty place' testifying to society's, and the people's, non-identity with itself (cf. Vinx 2016, Chapter 2 in this volume; also Lefort 1986a, 1986b). As Paul Kahn has argued, in a society in which no political actor can make an uncontested claim to be sovereign, speaking in the sovereign register (that is to say, representing the people) takes the form of a competition between different political actors, the result of which cannot be settled beforehand (Kahn 2011: 15). In such a non-identitarian order, the ultimate authority to speak in the name of the *demos* can be momentarily occupied by a political actor, but not exhaustively localized in a person or a body (Lefort 1986a, 1986b). The distance between 'the people' as the symbolic ultimate source of power, and any temporary wielder of that power, would necessarily remain open. The authority entrusted to the head of state or government would not exclude the possibility of another subject – the leader of the political opposition, the representative of a popular movement, the chairman of the supreme court, or somebody outside the field of institutionalized politics – taking on the role of the spokesperson for the *demos*, trying to win support for its position and, if successful, putting its decision through. Casting the ultimate authority of the people as a symbolic empty place undermines stable hierarchies of authority and allows the question about a community's way of life to be kept in abeyance and subject to political struggle and contestation for hegemony.

The function of the leadership principle, which underpins both Schmitt's notion of sovereignty and his concrete-order approach, is exactly to suppress society's non-identity with itself and the legitimacy of political struggle. Besides an inability to see the dependence of legal norms on social reality, Schmitt's criticism of liberal constitutionalism concerns its inclination to accept the initiation of legitimate social and legal change by whoever gains enough support. Schmitt, derogatorily, calls such an attitude 'political relativism' and suggests that it is grounded in an unjustified belief in the human capacity to use reason and critical doubt (Schmitt 1996a: 47/2005: 42). Against 'political relativism', Schmitt promotes the idea of a society in which societal development is controlled by a clear hierarchy of authority and respectful of existing social order and the vested interests that go with it. The leadership principle is in place to banish political contestation and struggle and Schmitt's favouring of this principle seems connected to the belief that the human being is a dangerous, potentially evil, creature who needs to be kept in check as to not destroy itself and others (cf., for example, Schmitt 1996a: 59–70/2005: 53–66).

What are we to make of Schmitt's claim that a society without an authorized supreme leader is unable to decide in favour of itself and defend its way of life in face of serious threats? No doubt, commitment to the rules of the game constitutes an outer limit to what can be allowed to prosper in a community devoted to non-identitarian democracy (cf. Mouffe 2000). If forces opposing such an order grow to such an extent that they pose a serious threat to it, the rest of the community will have to 'decide' against it and take action to preserve its way of life. There is, however, no reason to believe that the multi-headed subject 'the people' would not be able to make such a decision, except if too many people lose faith in the non-identitarian order. There is no difference between this possibility and the 'risk' that many people in a community with a recognized leader might turn against the one personifying the people and overthrow him/her. The idea that the risk of irresolvable political conflict can be eliminated by putting in place stable hierarchical relations that suppress disagreement appears as a 'philosophical conviction' of the kind that Schmitt accused the arguments of his adversaries of being based on.

It could, of course, be argued that there are situations that require immediate action and leave no time for the people to arrive at a decision through political struggles for hegemony, and that is why an order dispensing with a supreme leader is not a viable alternative. There is no denying that such situations do arise, but Schmitt's theory of sovereignty is not about decision making under time pressure, but about *who* is entitled to speak for the community in cases of foundational disagreement (Schmitt 1996a: 13–14, 16–17/2005: 6, 9–10). Schmitt is clear that the accuracy of the sovereign decision is not to be questioned *ex post facto* (Schmitt 1996a: 18/2005: 12). It is final and infallible (cf. Schmitt 1996a: 59–70/2005: 53–66).

What use for Schmitt's concept of sovereignty today?

Schmitt's notion of sovereignty is an effort to justify an authoritarian, conservative, leadership principle, which forecloses the space in which political contestation and questioning of the prevalent order can take place. It proposes that a hierarchical structure of authority be put in place, the function of which is to control who can speak in the name of the people and negotiate the character of the socio-legal order. However, Schmitt's notion of sovereignty can be purged of the preference for hierarchy and leadership and reformulated as: sovereign is the social formation speaking in the name of the people and proposing a frame of normality, which gains enough support as to make its decisions effective and trump its alternatives (cf. Kahn 2011).

One of the merits of Schmitt's reformulated notion of sovereignty is that it redirects our attention from legal norms to the foundational qualities of the prevailing normal order animating the norms. Given Schmitt's analysis of the relation of law and social reality, the question at stake in the decision on the state of exception is not whether legal norms should be bypassed or violated but through which frame of normality they should be seen. The extreme emergency is a factual situation in which the overarching inclinations of the socio-legal order, its structural biases as Koskenniemi (2009) puts it, are put into question by a political force strong enough to demand a response. The sovereign decision is the capacity and the claimed authority to bring the meaning of legal norms together with social reality, either by adapting the norms to a new reality or by reversing the 'changes on the ground' and warding off the proponents of change. Thus, the sovereign decision determines whether the prevailing hegemonic sense of normality is to be reinforced or transformed. When the character of the legal order is at stake, it is unproductive to speak the language of legal restrictions and transgressions since the question of legality is contingent upon the chosen frame of normality.

In addition, Schmitt's reformulated notion of sovereignty also implies a particular way of organizing the sociopolitical world which appears appealing in a historical juncture distinguished by the incapacity of the *demos* to control social powers, and in particular, the strongest social force of our time, capital (see, for example, Brown 2010a, 2010b). When purged of the leadership principle, Schmitt's notion is still decisionist in the sense that it implies that the character of the socio-legal order is in the last instance to be settled by wilful political decision-making re/acting on social forces. This, in turn, requires a kind of social organization that enables the transformation of the decisions made by the *demos*, through deliberation or struggles for hegemony, into reality. In other words, in an order of non-identitarian democracy, the decisionism of the political sovereign stands for the potency of the *demos* to set the conditions of its life in common.

Given that, it is perhaps timely to follow Schmitt, although with different motives and objectives, and to call for a stronger element of decisionism on the part of the subject of sovereignty at this moment in history.

Bibliography

Bartelson, J. (2014) *Sovereignty as Symbolic Form*. Abingdon: Routledge.
Bates, D. (2006) 'Political Theology and the Nazi State: Carl Schmitt's Concept of the Institution', *Modern Intellectual History*, Vol. 3, No. 3: 415–42.
Böckenförde, E. W. (1984) 'Ordnungsdenken, konkretes', p. 1312–15, in J. Ritter and K. Gründer (eds), *Historisches Wörterbuch der Philosophie*, Vol. 6. Basel: Schwabe Verlag.
Brown, W. (2010a) *Walled States, Waning Sovereignty*. New York: Zone Books.
Brown, W. (2010b) 'We are all Democrats Now…', p. 44–57, in G. Agamben, A. Badiou, D. Bensaïd, W. Brown, J.-L. Nancy, J. Ranciere, K. Ross and S. Žižek (eds), *Democracy in What State?* New York: Columbia University Press.
Butler, J. (2004) 'Indefinite Detention', p. 50–100, in J. Butler, *Precarious Life: The Powers of Mourning and Violence*. London: Verso.
Caldwell, P. (1994) 'Legal Positivism and Weimar Democracy', *American Journal of Jurisprudence*, Vol. 39, No. 1: 273–301.
Croce, M. and A. Salvatore (2013) *The Legal Theory of Carl Schmitt*. Abingdon: Routledge.
Gehring, P. (2003) 'Kraft durch Form: Rechtsbestimmtheitspostulat und Justizverweigrungsverbot', p. 57–74, in J. Vogl (ed.), *Gesetz and Urteil: Beiträge zu einer Theorie des Politischen*. Weimar: VDG.
Gross, O. (2000) 'The Normless and the Exceptionless Exception: Carl Schmitt's Theory of Emergency Powers and the "Norm-Exception" Dichotomy', *Cardozo Law Review*, Vol. 21, No. 5–6: 1825–67.
Gunneflo, M. (2016) 'Political Community in Carl Schmitt's International Legal Thinking', Chapter 3 in M. Arvidsson, L. Brännström and P. Minkkinen (eds), *The Contemporary Relevance of Carl Schmitt. Law, Politics, Theology*. Abingdon: Routledge.
Jacques, J. (2016) 'Law, Decision, Necessity: Shifting the Burden of Responsibility', Chapter 7 in M. Arvidsson, L. Brännström and P. Minkkinen (eds), *The Contemporary Relevance of Carl Schmitt. Law, Politics, Theology*. Abingdon: Routledge.
Kahn, P.W. (2004) 'The Question of Sovereignty', *Stanford Journal of International Law*, Vol. 40, No. 2: 259–80.
Kahn, P. W. (2011) *Political Theology: Four New Chapters on the Concept of Sovereignty*. New York: Columbia University Press.
Kant, I. (1998) *Critique of Pure Reason* [1781/1787]. Trans. P. Guyer and A. W. Wood. Cambridge: Cambridge University Press.
Koskenniemi, M. (2009) 'The Politics of International Law – 20 Years Later', *European Journal of International Law*, Vol. 20, No. 1: 7–19.
Lefort, C. (1986a) 'The Logic of Totalitarianism', p. 273–91, in C. Lefort, *The Political Forms of Modern Society: Bureaucracy, Democracy, Totalitarianism*. Trans. J. B. Thompson. Cambridge, MA: MIT Press.

Lefort, C. (1986b) 'The Image of the Body and Totalitarianism', p. 292–306, in C. Lefort, *The Political Forms of Modern Society: Bureaucracy, Democracy, Totalitarianism*. Trans. J. B. Thompson. Cambridge, MA: MIT Press.
Mouffe, C. (2000) 'For an Agonistic Model of Democracy', p. 80–107, in C. Mouffe, *The Democratic Paradox*. London: Verso.
Prozorov, S. (2005) 'X/Xs: Toward a General Theory of the Exception', *Alternatives*, Vol. 30, No. 1: 81–111.
Schmitt, C. (1925) *Römischer Katholizismus und politische Form* [1923]. Munich: Theatiner-Verlag.
Schmitt, C. (1934) *Über die drei Arten des rechtswissenschaftlichen Denkens*. Hamburg: Hanseatische Verlagsanstalt.
Schmitt, C. (1963) *Der Begriff des Politischen*. Text von 1932 mit einem Vorwort und Corollarien [1932], 6th ed. Berlin: Duncker and Humblot.
Schmitt, C. (1969) *Gesetz und Urteil: Eine Untersuchung zum Problem der Rechtpraxis* [1912], 2nd edn. Munich: C. H. Beck.
Schmitt, C. (1970) *Verfassungslehre* [1928], 5th edn. Berlin: Duncker and Humblot.
Schmitt, C. (1994a) *Die Diktatur: Von den Anfängen des modernen Souveränitätsgedankens bis zum proletarischen Klassenkampf* [1921], 6th edn. Berlin Duncker and Humblot.
Schmitt, C. (1994b) *Die Diktatur des Reichspräsidenten nach Artikel 48 der Weimarer Verfassung* [1924], p. 211–57, in C. Schmitt, *Die Diktatur: Von den Anfängen des modernen Souveränitätsgedankens bis zum proletarischen Klassenkampf*, 6th ed. Berlin Duncker and Humblot.
Schmitt, C. (1996a) *Politische Theologie. Vier Kapitel zur Lehre von der Souveränität* [1922], 7th ed. Berlin: Duncker and Humblot.
Schmitt, C. (1996b) *Roman Catholicism and Political Form* [1923]. Trans. G. L. Ulmen. Westport, CT: Greenwood.
Schmitt, C. (2004) *On The Three Types of Juristic Thought* [1934]. Trans. J. Bendersky. Westport CT: Praeger.
Schmitt, C. (2005) *Political Theology: Four Chapters on the Concept of Sovereignty* [1922]. Trans. G. Schwab. Chicago, IL: Chicago University Press.
Schmitt, C. (2007) *The Concept of the Political* [1932], Expanded ed. Trans. G. Schwab. Chicago, IL: Chicago University Press.
Schmitt, C. (2008) *Constitutional Theory* [1928]. Trans. J. Seitzer. Durham, NC: Duke University Press.
Schmitt, C. (2014a) *Dictatorship: From the Beginning of the Modern Concept of Sovereignty to the Proletarian Class Struggle* [1921]. Trans. M. Hoelzl and G. Ward, Cambridge: Polity Press.
Schmitt, C. (2014b) 'The Dictatorship of the President of the Reich according to Article 48 of the Weimar Constitution' [1924], p. 180–226, in C. Schmitt, *Dictatorship. From the Origins of the Modern Concept of Sovereignty to Proletarian Class Struggle*. Trans. M. Hoelzl and G. Ward. Cambridge: Polity Press.
Ungureanu, C. (2008) 'Derrida on Free Decision: Between Habermas' Discursivism and Schmitt's Decisionism', *Journal of Political Philosophy*, Vol. 16, No. 3: 293–325.
Vinx, L. (2016) 'Carl Schmitt and the Problem of Constitutional Guardianship', Chapter 2 in M. Arvidsson, L. Brännström and P. Minkkinen (eds), *The Contemporary Relevance of Carl Schmitt. Law, Politics, Theology*. Abingdon: Routledge.

Chapter 2

Carl Schmitt and the problem of constitutional guardianship

Lars Vinx

Introduction

Carl Schmitt's constitutional theory argues for strong counter-majoritarian constraints on the powers of legislative majorities. In Schmitt's view, every constitution has a core of fundamental constitutional principles that are shielded not just from ordinary legislative majorities, but also from the power of constitutional amendment (Schmitt 2008a: 72–4, 79–81, 150–8). Schmitt does not argue, however, that the protection of certain individual interests against legislative interference is an indispensable part of a morally justifiable constitution (Dworkin 1978). Neither does Schmitt hold that strong constitutionalism will stop the people from taking rash and unconsidered decisions (Holmes 1995). His argument appeals to democracy and to popular sovereignty, although these notions are nowadays often deployed against entrenched constitutional restrictions on the legislative powers of a democratically elected parliament (Waldron 2006: 1348–406; Bellamy 2007).

According to Schmitt, basic constitutional principles express a self-determining people's fundamental decision on the concrete form of its political life. They must accordingly be protected against any constituted power, including the power of constitutional amendment (Schmitt 2008a: 150–1). To allow a constituted power to change the basic structure of a constitution, Schmitt argues, would amount to a usurpation of constituent power.

Although Schmitt advocated a constitution that fundamentally restricts the powers of the constituted legislator, he argued against the legitimacy of constitutional review (Schmitt 1958a: 63–109; 2015: 79–120). If the core of the constitution expresses the people's self-chosen political identity, authoritative interpretations of basic constitutional principles must be provided by the constituent power itself or by a political authority speaking in its name, not by a court (Schmitt 2008a: 126). Consequently, Schmitt advocated alternative forms of constitutional guardianship capable of protecting the constitution without resort to constitutional review (Schmitt 2004: 67–94; 2014: 180–226; 2015: 150–73).

This chapter explores whether Schmitt succeeded to develop a form of strong constitutionalism based on popular sovereignty. The question is obviously important: a successful combination of constitutional rigidity with popular sovereignty would solve the common objection that strong constitutionalism must necessarily violate the principle of democratic equality. It would open up the enticing prospect of a middle path between juristocracy and parliamentary sovereignty.

I argue that Schmitt's attempts to develop a democratic conception of strong constitutionalism that does without constitutional review were unsuccessful. The problem can be fleshed out by taking a closer look at Schmitt's conception of constitutional guardianship. As Schmitt would have recognized, talk of constitutional guardianship is ambiguous. It may either refer to the protection of a concrete form of social and political ordering, or it may refer to the protection of rights that are guaranteed by the legal norms contained in a written constitution.

Liberal constitutional theory has a tendency to veil this distinction. If a constitution is understood as a set of codified legal norms that safeguard certain individual or minority interests, the protection of constitutional rights must appear to be the core function of constitutional guardianship. But it is equally possible, as Schmitt's constitutional theory illustrates, to conceive of constitutional guardianship as the protection of a concrete form of social and political ordering. The protection of the constitution, so understood, is no longer tantamount to the protection of rights guaranteed by the written constitution. It may even require that constitutionally protected rights be disregarded (Schmitt 2008a: 156–8).

Schmitt gives the impression that there is a need for both forms of constitutional guardianship but he privileges the second, purely political understanding of constitutional guardianship over the first, even though he relies on a notion of constitutional guardianship as a protection of rights to attack the view that a democratically elected parliamentary majority should enjoy materially unrestricted legislative powers. As a result, Schmitt fails to offer an attractive middle path between judicial rule and unrestrained majority rule. The potential tyranny of a majority in a system with a sovereign parliamentary legislature is simply replaced with the potential tyranny of the Schmittian popular sovereign.

Schmitt's failure does not merely consist of a refusal to take rights seriously enough. The tendency to privilege a purely political understanding of popular sovereignty also undermines the democratic credentials of his constitutional theory. We should therefore be more sceptical towards contemporary attempts to base a democratic constitutional theory on Schmitt (Kalyvas 2008: 79–186; Loughlin 2010; Posner and Vermeule 2010; Kahn 2011; Colon-Rios 2012; Minkkinen 2013).

Schmitt against the legislative state

Schmitt's argument for strong constitutionalism is based on a critique of the 'legislative state', of the liberal constitutional ideal of the nineteenth century (see Schmitt 1985; Schmitt 2004: 3–36; Schmitt 2008a: 181–96, 328–42). In a legislative state, the legislator is a representative assembly, democratically elected, whose members are responsible only to their conscience. The assembly enacts general laws, and only general laws, after careful discussion of legislative proposals. These general laws then govern all administrative and judicial activity. Proponents of the legislative state assume that the democratic election of parliament and the generality of law, together with a principle of administrative legality, are sufficient to protect citizens from arbitrary rule. Further material restrictions on legislative power, enforced by a guardian of the constitution extraneous to parliament, are seen as unnecessary and undemocratic.

Schmitt argues that the ideal of the legislative state has become obsolete. The liberal expectation that legislation by parliament would sufficiently protect individual rights had been based on a picture of parliamentary debate as high-minded, disinterested discussion about the public good. Members of nineteenth-century parliaments, as well as the bourgeois public that observed and discussed their performance, wrongly interpreted the prevalence of agreement among parliamentarians as the natural product of reasonable deliberation. In truth, it had been a function, Schmitt argues, of the shared opposition to a monarchical executive as well as of the social homogeneity of nineteenth-century parliaments.

A number of social and political trends of the later nineteenth and early twentieth centuries exposed the cracks in the ideology of liberal parliamentarianism. As a result of the extension of the franchise and the turn from constitutional monarchy to parliamentary republic, parliaments came to represent greater social diversity, while the absence of a monarch as a shared political adversary reduced the pressure on parliamentarians to find agreement. Consequently, parliament became a battleground for competing social groups that were organized around their own political parties and that tried to exploit the legislative process to impose their factional interests (Schmitt 2015: 125–46; Schmitt 2000). This trend was reinforced by the rise of the administrative state, which blurred the distinction between general laws and particular judicial or administrative decisions and thus eroded the protection afforded by the principle of legality (see Heidegren 2016, Chapter 6 in this volume). Schmitt concludes that the legislative state, under modern social and political conditions, no longer suffices to protect individual citizens against arbitrary rule exercised by parliamentary majority.

Schmitt's ambiguous assessment of the Weimar Constitution finds its explanation in the fact that the Weimar Constitution did, to some extent, depart from the constitutional framework of the legislative state. In his view, however, it did so too hesitantly and without proper concern for constitutional coherence. The prevailing constitutional doctrine of the 1920s and early 1930s, on the other hand, was still influenced by the ideal of the legislative state, and was therefore incapable, according to Schmitt, of making proper sense of the Weimar Constitution.

The Weimar Constitution did hold on to key elements of the legislative state. A parliament composed of elected representatives of the people was made dominant in the process of legislation. At the same time, the Weimar Constitution experimented with a number of institutional devices restricting the legislative power of parliament, such as the powers of the president to dissolve parliament or to refer a legislative proposal to a popular referendum. It also protected a lengthy list of rights-provisions against the ordinary legislator, by requiring a parliamentary supermajority for their repeal or amendment. Finally, it provided for the direct election of the president, who was to form a political counterweight to parliament. The Weimar Constitution thus marked a departure from the framework of the legislative state, but the departure was half-hearted, in Schmitt's view (Schmitt 2008a: 82–8), and was undercut by constitutional incoherence.

The clearest example of such incoherence appeared in the list of basic rights in the second part of the constitution. This list contained a number of provisions protecting classical liberal individual rights. These rights, however, though protected by the constitution's requirement of a legislative supermajority for constitutional change, were explicitly made subject to a *Gesetzesvorbehalt*; that is, they were granted subject to the possibility of restriction on the basis of ordinary statute. The framers of the constitution, in other words, still assumed that a simple principle of legality was sufficient to protect individual rights. At the same time, the constitution gave protection to a number of group privileges that were not made subject to a *Gesetzesvorbehalt*. As a result, the right of public officials to have access to their personnel files, for instance, enjoyed a higher degree of constitutional protection than any of the classical liberal individual rights.

Such absurdities, in Schmitt's view, undercut the constitution's aspiration to move beyond the legislative state. The move beyond the legislative state was also hampered by inadequate constitutional theory. The predominant constitutional theory in Germany at the time is often referred to as 'statutory positivism' (Caldwell 1997: 13–39, 63–84). Statutory positivism was closely wedded to the framework of the legislative state. Statutory positivists advocated a purely procedural and value-neutral conception of the constitution. Law was identified with statute and statute was regarded as the result of the legislative will of the state. The constitution, as a result, came to be understood as the set of laws that identify the legislative will of the state and determine how it is validly exercised. The question of the legitimacy of these constitutional norms, in turn, was treated as a purely political issue of no jurisprudential concern.

Applied to the Weimar Constitution, the constitutional theory of statutory positivism led to the conclusion that the constitution's protections of the classical individual rights were *leerlaufend* or empty, owing to the fact that they were subject to a *Gesetzesvorbehalt*. Gerhard Anschütz, for example, denied that these rights enjoyed more protection under the Weimar Constitution than they had enjoyed in Wilhelmine Germany, since the constitution of the latter had already recognized a principle of administrative legality (Anschütz 1933: 517–20). The Weimar Constitution required a supermajority for the repeal or change of any constitutional provision. However, statutory positivists held that there were no material limits on the power of constitutional amendment exercised by a parliamentary supermajority. Given the requisite supermajority, the Weimar Republic was open to be transformed into a socialist state, even though the constitution appeared to have instituted a liberal-democratic state (Anschütz 1933: 400–8).

According to Schmitt, statutory positivism failed to reflect on the social and political presuppositions that had made the legislative state viable in the nineteenth century (Schmitt 2008a: 62–74). As a result, statutory positivism did not succeed in developing an account of the conditions of the legitimate applicability of constitutional laws and failed to recognize that the ideal of the legislative state, under modern social circumstances, is no longer able to live up to its promises. The refusal to acknowledge this failure, Schmitt argued, served to provide an ideological cover for the 'indirect rule' of parties and factions abusing the legislative mechanisms of the Weimar Constitution for their own partial ends (Schmitt 2008a: 65–77; 2008b). To prevent this reduction of legitimacy to mere legality a new constitutional theory was called for; one that would adequately reflect the constitution's aspiration to move beyond the legislative state and that would allow political practice to overcome the constitution's own deficiencies.

Schmitt's rejection of the legislative state, to sum up, purports to be based on the insight that parliamentary democracy wedded to a principle of legality is not a sufficient safeguard against arbitrary rule exercised by a parliamentary majority. Schmitt is committed, in other words, to the first of the two conceptions of political guardianship distinguished above; that is, to the claim that the constitution must protect individual rights against arbitrary legislative infringement.

As we see in this chapter, Schmitt's own conception of constitutional guardianship fails to follow through on this apparent commitment to the protection of rights, which exposes his critique of the legislative state to a charge of hypocrisy. Schmitt relies on a counter-majoritarian discourse of rights to argue against parliamentary sovereignty but he jettisons strong constitutionalism without hesitation once arguing on the plane of 'the political'. Rights, as we will see, are not supposed to stand in the way of executive action, which raises the question why Schmitt thought it so important to protect them against the legislator in the first place.

Schmitt on the positive concept of constitution

Schmitt develops his alternative to the statutory positivist understanding of constitution, the 'positive concept of constitution', in the first part of the *Constitutional Theory* (Schmitt 2008a: 75–88). Schmitt argues that the shortcomings of the statutory positivist view can be overcome only if we acknowledge a fundamental distinction between the constitution itself and constitutional laws; that is, the particular legal norms contained in a written constitutional document. The constitution itself, according to Schmitt, is not a legal norm or a set of legal norms, but rather a fundamental form of concrete social and political ordering that results from a constituent decision (Schmitt 2008a: 75–6).

The Weimar Constitution, Schmitt's example, resulted from a decision of the German people, taken in the course of the revolution of 1918, for democracy, for a republican form of state, for a federal state, for a parliamentary and representative system of legislation, and for the rule of law; that is, for the protection of the classical liberal individual rights and for the principle of a separation of powers (Schmitt 2008a: 77–8). Schmitt regards the written constitution enacted by the national assembly as a derivative expression of this fundamental choice of the German people for a liberal democratic state. Constitutional laws take their legitimacy from the decision of the constituent power on the form of social and political ordering that they serve to implement (Schmitt 2008a: 78).

Schmitt emphatically insists that a people, in exercising its constituent power, does not alienate its constitution-making authority to the positive constitutional framework it creates. The constituent power always retains the option to initiate a new constitutional start (Schmitt 2008a: 140–1). As Schmitt points out, forms of social and political ordering can change fundamentally even while the state continues to exist. The identity and permanence of a constitution, in other words, is not to be confused with the identity and permanence of the political community whose constitution it is. The latter precedes the former.

A constitution continues to exist and to remain the same as long as a society's present form of social and political ordering continues to persist. Constitutional identity can be broken in a number of different ways, some legitimate and some illegitimate. A people could decide to give itself a new constitution and thus legitimately modify its form of social and political existence. More problematic, from Schmitt's point of view, are cases of constitutional change where a new constitution is imposed on a people by an external force or where a constitutional framework is gradually transformed in such a way as to come to violate the people's original constitutional choice for a certain form of social and political ordering. In both of these cases, the constitution is destroyed illegitimately, since a fundamental constitutional change not brought about by the people itself indicates a loss of the people's constituent power and consequently of its political self-determination (Vinx 2013: 98–100).

The positive concept of constitution implies that a constitution cannot legitimately be changed in ways that violate the people's original choice for a certain form of social and political ordering. Statutory positivists were therefore wrong, in Schmitt's view, to hold that the procedure for amendment of the Weimar Constitution might license a fundamental change of the Weimar Republic, for instance from a liberal to a socialist democracy (Schmitt 2008a: 151–4). In the revolution of 1918, the German people, in Schmitt's view, had not simply initiated the process of the drafting of a written constitution. They had taken a conscious decision for a particular form of social and political ordering. The Weimar Constitution, hence, could not legitimately be used to turn Germany from a liberal democratic state into a state of a fundamentally different political character. Any attempt to employ the amendment procedure for such purposes would have amounted to a usurpation of constituent power on the part of constituted powers.

The ingredients for a democratic constitutionalism, it appears, are now in place. The restrictions that the positive constitution imposes on constituted powers, since they flow from the fundamental choice, on the part of a self-determining people, of its own form of political life, are not incompatible with democracy. Rather, they are the highest expression of the democratic self-determination of a people, which is only imperfectly realized, as Schmitt argues in his critique of the legislative state, in the sphere of constituted politics (Schmitt 1985: 1–17, 22–32; Schmitt 2008a: 302–7).

Schmitt's argument against judicial review

Schmitt's defence of strong constitutionalism, as outlined so far, might appear to provide the basis for a defence of the democratic legitimacy of constitutional review. If a constitutional court was endowed with the authority to preserve and to protect the substance of the constituent choice of the people against the encroachments of constituted powers acting on behalf of sectional interests, then its activity would apparently have to be regarded as democratically legitimate (Ackerman 1993: 9–10).

Schmitt, however, was vehemently opposed to the introduction of constitutional review during the Weimar years (Schmitt 2015: 79–120). In postwar West-Germany, Schmitt attacked the jurisprudence of the Federal Constitutional Court as a 'tyranny of values' (see Rentto 2016, Chapter 4 in this volume). In arguing against the legitimacy of constitutional review,

Schmitt observes that a constitutional court would have to be endowed with the authority to invalidate laws enacted by the legislator, on the ground that these violate either written constitutional laws or the positive constitution. But the question of whether a particular law can really be said to violate the constitution in one of these two senses, Schmitt observes, will typically be open to reasonable disagreement. Constitutional review is therefore going to end up in a simple dilemma: either, a piece of legislation constitutes an obvious violation of a norm of the written constitution, and in this rare case, it will be permissible, Schmitt concedes, for any court not to apply that law, or a more common scenario, it will be claimed that it violates the spirit or integrity of the positive constitution while the question is legally and politically disputed. Here, a court would have to determine the meaning of the positive constitution in the face of political disagreement. Constitutional review would be unnecessary in the first instance, Schmitt argues, and democratically illegitimate, as usurping the constituent power of the people, in the second.

Schmitt's argument against judicial review anticipates arguments against strong constitutionalism that question the democratic legitimacy of judicial rule (Waldron 2006). These contemporary arguments, though, usually propose parliamentary sovereignty as the democratic alternative to judicial rule. Of course, this response to the alleged illegitimacy of judicial review is not open to Schmitt as a critic of the legislative state. So who is to guard the constitution, if it is neither to be the parliament nor the courts?

Schmitt's conception of constitutional guardianship

Schmitt argued that the role of the guardian of the constitution ought to fall to the popularly elected president of the Weimar Republic, or more generally, to the head of an executive endowed with plebiscitary legitimacy (Schmitt 2015: 150–73). This move may seem puzzling at first. If the guardian of the constitution is to enforce constitutional limits on the legislative powers of parliament, a court would appear to be a much more natural fit than the head of the executive. Here, we must remember that the idea of constitutional guardianship can be understood in two different ways: as the protection of the rights enshrined in a written constitution or as the protection of a form of social and political ordering. Schmitt's discussion of presidential guardianship focuses on the second of these two understandings, and it tends to subordinate the protection of constitutional rights to the protection of the positive constitution as a concrete social and political ordering.

This tendency can already be detected in *Constitutional Theory*. On the one hand, liberal rights are portrayed as an essential part of the specific form of social and political ordering – liberal democracy – that was chosen by the German people when it gave itself the Weimar Constitution. It would therefore be unconstitutional, according to Schmitt, for the legislature to try to transform the political ordering of German society in a way that would permanently eliminate any of the classical liberal rights (Schmitt 2008a: 214–15). On the other hand, rights can of course be seen as protections of individual interests against the potentially dominating power of the executive. But as protections of individual interests, the rights enshrined in the Weimar Constitution are open, Schmitt argues, to almost limitless suspension by the executive (Schmitt 2008a: 80–1).

In the later Weimar years, Schmitt's tendency to read down the protective power of constitutional rights became even more pronounced. Schmitt put forward a theory of 'institutional guarantees', according to which many constitutional provisions that appear to protect individual rights merely protect the existence of certain social institutions, and thus do not give rise to legally enforceable individual claims (Schmitt 1958b; Croce and Salvatore 2013: 25–9).

Despite the fact that Schmitt's argument against the legislative state appeals to the liberal fear of a tyranny of the majority, Schmitt's own constitutional theory, on closer inspection, thus turns out to be surprisingly unconcerned with that danger. A genuine liberal constitutionalist would surely want to prevent the executive – as much as the legislature – from riding roughshod over individual interests that, in his view, deserve constitutional protection. Schmitt, by contrast, is more concerned with the danger that the pluralism of the legislative state may turn out to be 'state-destroying' (Schmitt 2015: 125–46). What is to be protected against a parliamentary majority, in imposing restrictions on the parliamentary legislator, is the political unity and identity of the people, as expressed in its constituent choice for a certain kind of social and political ordering. But that unity and identity, Schmitt now suggests, need not be defended against the executive. The latter, rather, is its proper guardian.

We thus arrive at the seemingly paradoxical conclusion that rights are to be shielded from any legislative transformation, even from an exercise of the power of amendment, while they are open, at the same time, to be freely disregarded by the executive, to hold down those who are considered to be inimical to the positive constitution. Schmitt, as other authors have pointed out, wants to preserve a liberal and bourgeois society against the danger of a legislative transformation initiated by a left-wing legislative majority. But he does not want those he perceives to be the constitution's enemies – social democrats and communists – to benefit from the protection afforded by liberal rights and the rule of law should they decide to challenge the content of a positive constitution that, in Schmitt's view, blocks their legislative ambitions (Maus 1980; Cristi 1998; Dyzenhaus 1997: 38–101).

This background explains why Schmitt aims to reserve the function of constitutional guardianship for the president of the Weimar Republic. If the protection of the constitution does not primarily consist in the enforcement of legal norms protecting individual rights, but rather in the defence, against insurrectionary challenges, of a certain form of social and political ordering that has already been declared off-limits to peaceful legislative change, it obviously makes sense to argue that the task of defending the constitution must fall to executive and not to the courts. The head of the executive, after all, is typically the one constitutional organ that is best equipped to perform the task of securing public order.

Schmitt's leading article on presidential guardianship of the constitution confirms this interpretation (Schmitt 2014). Article 48, paragraph 2 of the Weimar Constitution, authorized the president of the Weimar Republic to take dictatorial measures to protect public security:

> In case public safety is seriously threatened or disturbed, the President of the Reich may take the measures necessary to reestablish law and order, if necessary using armed force. In the pursuit of this aim he may suspend the civil rights described in articles 114, 115, 117, 118, 123, 124 and 154, partially or entirely.

On its face, the second sentence of this article claims that the president, in using extraordinary measures to restore public security and order, may infringe on the enumerated constitutional provisions, but not on other constitutional provisions that are not explicitly mentioned. In other words, the enumeration of rights that can be suspended seems to imply a limitation of the president's powers in a state of exception.

Schmitt proposes a different interpretation (Schmitt 2014: 188–200). According to Schmitt, it is necessary to distinguish between a suspension of constitutional provisions and their infringement in particular instances. If a constitutional provision is suspended, it no longer has any legal force. As a result, any administrative agency is entitled to disregard it. Constitutional provisions, however, can also be violated or infringed in particular instances without having first been suspended. There is a difference, Schmitt holds, between suspending a norm and making an exception from the norm. The latter violation implies that the norm is still in force, since the exception presupposes the rule. So what Article 48 really claims, in Schmitt's view, is that the constitutional articles listed in Article 48 are the only ones the president may suspend. But this does not imply that his action in a state of emergency must not infringe upon other, non-enumerated constitutional provisions. The point is merely, Schmitt claims, that infringements of non-enumerated constitutional rights cannot take the form of a suspension. They must, rather, take place in the form of exceptional measures that are directly authorized by the president himself.

This view implies that presidential dictatorship is all but unlimited in terms of the methods it might permissibly use. Schmitt makes a point to cite a statement of one of the members of the constituent assembly to the effect that Article 48 would permit even the use of poison gas to put down public unrest (Schmitt 2014: 214). The protection of individual rights, then, is to be thrown overboard in a state of emergency. While liberal rights are to be preserved as elements of a certain kind of social and political ordering, they are not to stand in the way of dictatorial action in situations of crisis (cf. Dyzenhaus 2006: 35–54).

Schmitt's rejection of constitutional review implies, moreover, that it is up to the president alone to determine what counts as a threat to the positive constitution and to decide what extra-legal measures are necessary to remove any such threat. But these powers, as Schmitt knew well, are powers to authoritatively determine the meaning of the constitution in the face of reasonable disagreement. It would be highly naïve, from a decisionist point of view, to assume that presidential guardianship will be any less constitution making than constitutional review exercised by a constitutional court.

In effect, Schmitt's conception of constitutional guardianship does little more than to transfer the unjustified confidence of the proponents of the legislative state that a democratic parliament can do no wrong to the head of the executive, who – in virtue of his popular election – is uncritically portrayed as representing the unity of the people and as protecting the integrity of its constituent choice (Schmitt 2015: 150–73). Schmitt's concern, we can conclude, is not to protect constitutional rights. It is simply to empower an executive that is more reliably conservative than parliament or the courts to act as the sole arbiter of constitutionality and to employ extra-legal means, whenever it sees fit, to deal with those whom it judges to be enemies of the existing social order.

Democratic legitimacy and executive guardianship of the constitution

Schmitt's constitutional theory appears attractive because it promises to justify a strong constitutionalism on democratic grounds. The promise of the conception was that it would impose democratically legitimate restrictions on legislative majorities while avoiding the danger of judicial rule. It should be clear by now that the way in which Schmitt aims to accomplish this end is highly problematic.

Schmitt's positive concept of constitution, and the notion of executive guardianship that goes along with it, protect an established form of social and political ordering against violent, insurrectionary challenge. This protection, however, comes at a high price. Schmitt's argument for presidential guardianship no longer reflects any genuine concern for the protection of the freedom of the individual or the minority. Though individual rights are to be protected, as we have seen, insofar as they are elements of the social ordering chosen by the constituent power, Schmitt aims to prevent their protective deployment against executive action. Non-trivial disputes about rights, or more generally about a society's form of social and political ordering, are to be settled in a state of exception, through executive dictatorship.

Defenders of Schmitt's constitutional theory are likely to be unimpressed by this critique. They are going to reply that Schmitt is right to give preference to politics over the rule of law, either because they agree with Schmitt's idea that the law is incapable to tame politics or because they think that the constituent decisions of the popular sovereign deserve to take precedence over the protection of individual or minority interests. This reply to the liberal objection to Schmitt, I submit, merely points towards another, equally serious problem with Schmitt's constitutional theory: its highly dubious democratic credentials.

Schmitt's constitutional theory rests on the assumption that the founding decision taken by a people acting as constituent power enjoys a higher degree of democratic legitimacy than any possible outcome of constituted politics. Without this assumption, Schmitt would not be able to defend the claim that the founding decision imposes limits not merely on simple parliamentary majorities, but even on the constituted constitutional legislator. Neither would he be able to justify his conception of constitutional guardianship, which is based on the view that the president's far-reaching dictatorial powers are legitimate because they represent the unity of the people more authentically than courts or parliamentary majorities. Schmitt must explain, then, why the legitimate power to take a decision affecting the identity of the constitution should reside exclusively with a formless constituent power – one that is, in practice, likely to be exercised by an executive that hangs on to the thin reed of plebiscitary legitimacy – and not at all with constituted legislative supermajorities, however inclusive, or with courts, however deeply embedded in a democratic constitutional tradition.

Schmitt's answer to this question is simple. Democracy, he argues, is to be defined as the 'identity of ruler and ruled', and such identity can only obtain under conditions of social and ideological homogeneity (Schmitt 2008a: 255–67). The founding decision, in contrast to any constituted decision, perfectly expresses the democratic identity of ruler and ruled. But the reason why the founding decision expresses identity is simply that it is a decision on the boundaries of political community. The founding decision, of course, is a political decision, in Schmitt's peculiar sense of the term (Schmitt 2007: 25–7; Schmitt 2008a: 76). It brands as enemies all those who do not acquiesce in the form of social and political ordering preferred by the group whose overwhelming power allows it to identify itself with the people. Constitutional guardianship, in turn, consists in using the power of the state to break the resistance of those who do not fully concur with the founding decision, and to do so before the procedural constitution comes into force or while it has been suspended.

The problem with Schmitt's conception of strong constitutionalism, then, is not just that it does not take individual rights seriously enough. Schmitt's strong constitutionalism also conflicts with the democratic principle that all members of a society ought to have an equal say in how it is governed. Schmitt, in effect, denies that the decision about a society's basic social and political ordering should be taken in a way that gives standing to all its members, since those who – in the context of the constituent decision – turn out to disagree with the majority's view are to be treated as aliens, to be silenced or removed by a plebiscitary dictatorship that acts outside of legal restraints. Schmitt confronts the procedural constitution of liberal democracy with a pseudo-democratic pre-legal constituent power precisely because that constitution has had a tendency, at least for the better part of the twentieth century, to politically enfranchise dissident groups, to empower them to contest the existing content of the constitution without having to fear a loss of legal protection, and thus to keep in abeyance the decision on the people's identity that Schmitt thinks must be antecedent to all legal order (cf. Lindahl 2007).

The issue is not merely of antiquarian interest. Schmittian understandings of constitutional guardianship have resurfaced, for example, in recent American discussions on the use of executive power in situations of crisis. Eric Posner and Adrian Vermeule have argued, with explicit reference to the authority of Schmitt (Posner and Vermeule 2010), that it would be futile to try to achieve full legal control of the executive power of the president of the United States. In the modern administrative state, all legal control of executive power exercised in situations of crisis inevitably comes too late, and attempts to impose such control in advance carry the danger of disabling the executive from providing efficient responses to crises. Processes of constitutional change, consequently, must be driven by precedent-setting executive action that can never be fully subject to antecedent legal control. But this is no reason to worry, Posner and Vermeule reassure us, since the exercise of executive power is still subject to political controls that arise from an executive-centred conception of 'popular constitutionalism':

> In our approach, the elites who control the institutions of government effectively decide whether or not to engage in precedent-setting showdowns, but public constitutional sentiment – which may or may not be very popular, depending on circumstances – is both a major political constraint and a major variable in the elites' political calculations. The populace at large exercises an indirect influence over constitutional development, but as a filter that rules out certain elite positions and as an ultimate court of appeal, rather than as a frontline participant. The process of constitutional change is roughly plebiscitary: the people do not propose, but they do dispose.
> (Posner and Vermeule 2010: 82–3)

The last sentence of this quote directly echoes Schmitt, who emphasized that the popular sovereign's capacity to act and decide presupposes plebiscitary leadership (Schmitt 1927: 31–54). But Schmitt at least aimed to restrict executive dictatorship to situations of openly declared emergency that were to be cabined off strictly from normal governance, so as to avoid a normalization of the emergency. Posner and Vermeule repudiate even this modest restriction of executive power. According to Posner and Vermeule, the administrative state has already made the emergency the new normality, a process they take to be justified by the plebiscitary legitimacy of the presidency.

Unlike Schmitt, Posner and Vermeule do not explicitly address the question of how it is decided who belongs to the people that is to dispose of presidential proposals. Presumably, they would not object to executive action that puts individual citizens *hors la loi* (see Posner and Vermeule 2007: 15–57). There is a danger, hence, that their conception of executive power will tend to be afflicted by the same problem of democratic legitimacy that haunt's Schmitt's: if the executive is empowered to interfere with individual rights without being subject to legal control, and if the only safeguard against such interference is the presidency's need for the majority's continued political support, there is a standing threat that the rights of minorities that are perceived as alien to the identity of the community are going to be trampled upon in a way that infringes the integrity of the democratic process. The problem here is not merely that the interests of minority groups may not be given adequate weight in extra-legal executive decision-taking (Posner and Vermeule 2007: 87–129). The problem, rather, is one of domination. The effective exercise of democratic rights of participation, assuming they are not denied in the first place, surely requires that members of a dissident group must not be open to intimidation by the threat of arbitrary executive action that treats them as enemies.

These observations, I submit, cast a critical light on the current revival of Schmittian constitutional theory. The relevant literature typically portrays Schmitt as a heroic defender of popular sovereignty, while his 'normativist' opponents in legal and constitutional theory – who, like Hans Kelsen, refused to derive the constitution's legitimacy from the untrammelled choices of a legally formless constituent power – are painted as undemocratic for failing to recognize the foundational dimension of democracy (Kalyvas 2006; Loughlin 2010: 209–37). Schmitt's reflections on constitutional guardianship make it clear that such assessments rest on a superficial understanding of Schmitt's intentions as well as of the logic of his argument. Those who appeal to the authority of Schmitt in developing modern conceptions of democratic constituent power should be pressed harder to explain how their approaches can avoid the anti-democratic implications of Schmitt's development of the theme.

Bibliography

Ackerman, B. (1993) *We the People 1: Foundations.* Cambridge, MA: Harvard University Press.
Anschütz, G. (1933) *Die Verfassung des Deutschen Reiches vom 11. August 1919.* 14th edn. Berlin: Georg Stilke.
Bellamy, R. (2007) *Political Constitutionalism: A Republican Defence of the Constitutionality of Democracy.* Cambridge: Cambridge University Press.
Caldwell, P.C. (1997) *Popular Sovereignty and the Crisis of German Constitutional Law. The Theory and Practice of Weimar Constitutionalism.* Durham, NC: Duke University Press.
Colon-Rios, J. (2012) *Weak Constitutionalism. Democratic Legitimacy and the Question of Constituent Power.* Abingdon: Routledge.
Cristi, R. (1998) *Carl Schmitt and Authoritarian Liberalism. Strong State, Free Economy.* Cardiff: University of Wales Press.
Croce, M. and A. Salvatore (2013) *The Legal Theory of Carl Schmitt.* Abingdon: Routledge.
Dworkin, R. (1978) *Taking Rights Seriously.* Cambridge, MA: Harvard University Press.
Dyzenhaus, D. (1997) *Legality and Legitimacy. Carl Schmitt, Hans Kelsen and Hermann Heller in Weimar.* Oxford: Oxford University Press.
Dyzenhaus, D. (2006) *The Constitution of Law. Legality in a Time of Emergency.* Cambridge: Cambridge University Press.
Heidegren, C.-G. (2016) 'Social Acceleration, Motorized Legislation and Framework Laws', Chapter 6 in M. Arvidsson, L. Brännström and P. Minkkinen (eds), *The Contemporary Relevance of Carl Schmitt. Law, Politics, Theology.* Abingdon: Routledge.
Holmes, S. (1995) 'Precommitment and the Paradox of Democracy', p. 134–77, in S. Holmes, *Passions and Restraint. On the Theory of Liberal Democracy.* Chicago, IL: University of Chicago Press.
Kahn, P. W. (2011) *Political Theology. Four New Chapters on the Concept of Sovereignty.* New York: Columbia University Press.
Kalyvas, A. (2006) 'The Basic Norm and Democracy in Hans Kelsen's Legal and Political Theory', *Philosophy and Social Criticism*, Vol. 32, No. 5: 573–99.
Kalyvas, A. (2008) *Democracy and the Politics of the Extraordinary. Max Weber, Carl Schmitt and Hannah Arendt.* Cambridge: Cambridge University Press.
Lindahl, H. (2007) 'Constituent Power and Reflexive Identity: Towards an Ontology of Collective Selfhood', p. 9–24, in M. Loughlin and N. Walker (eds), *The Paradox of Constitutionalism. Constituent Power and Constitutional Form.* Oxford: Oxford University Press.
Loughlin, M. (2010) *Foundations of Public Law.* Oxford: Oxford University Press.
Maus, I. (1980) *Bürgerliche Rechtstheorie und Faschismus. Zur sozialen Funktion und aktuellen Wirkung der Theorie Carl Schmitt's.* 2nd edn. Munich: Wilhelm Fink.
Minkkinen, P. (2013) 'Political Constitutionalism versus Political Constitutional Theory: Law, Power and Politics', *International Journal of Constitutional Law*, Vol. 11, No. 3: 585–610.
Posner, E. and A. Vermeule (2007) *Terror in the Balance. Security, Liberty, and the Courts.* New York: Oxford University Press.

Posner, E. and A. Vermeule (2011) *The Executive Unbound: After the Madisonian Republic.* New York: Oxford University Press.
Rentto, J.-H. (2016) 'Carl Schmitt and the Tyranny of Values', Chapter 4 in M. Arvidsson, L. Brännström and P. Minkkinen (eds), *The Contemporary Relevance of Carl Schmitt. Law, Politics, Theology.* Abingdon: Routledge.
Schmitt, C. (1927) *Volksentscheid und Volksbegehren. Ein Beitrag zur Auslegung der Weimarer Verfassung und zur Lehre von der unmittelbaren Demokratie.* Berlin: Walter de Gruyter.
Schmitt, C. (1958a) 'Das Reichsgericht als Hüter der Verfassung' [1929], p. 63–109, in C. Schmitt, *Verfassungsrechtliche Aufsätze aus den Jahren 1924–1954.* Berlin: Duncker and Humblot.
Schmitt, C. (1958b) 'Freiheitsrechte und institutionelle Garantien der Reichsverfassung' [1931], p. 140–173, in C. Schmitt, *Verfassungsrechtliche Aufsätze aus den Jahren 1924–1954.* Berlin: Duncker and Humblot.
Schmitt, C. (1985) *The Crisis of Parliamentary Democracy* [1926]. Trans. E. Kennedy, Cambridge, MA: MIT Press.
Schmitt, C. (2000) 'State Ethics and the Pluralist State' [1930], p. 300–12, in A. J. Jacobsohn and B. Schlink (eds), *Weimar: A Jurisprudence of Crisis.* Trans. B. Cooper. Berkeley and Los Angeles: University of California Press.
Schmitt, C. (2004) *Legality and Legitimacy* [1932]. Trans. J. Seitzer. Durham and London: Duke University Press.
Schmitt, C. (2007) *The Concept of the Political* [1932]. Expanded edn. Trans. G. Schwab. Chicago, IL: University of Chicago Press.
Schmitt, C. (2008a) *Constitutional Theory* [1928]. Trans. J. Seitzer. Durham and London: Duke University Press.
Schmitt, C. (2008b) *The Leviathan in the State Theory of Thomas Hobbes* [1938]. Trans. G. Schwab and E. Hilfstein. Chicago, IL: University of Chicago Press.
Schmitt, C. (2014) 'The Dictatorship of the President of the Reich according to Article 48 of the Weimar Constitution' [1924], p. 180–226, in C. Schmitt, *Dictatorship. From the Origins of the Modern Concept of Sovereignty to Proletarian Class Struggle.* Trans. M. Hoelzl and G. Ward. Cambridge: Polity.
Schmitt, C. (2015) *The Guardian of the Constitution* [1931], p. 79–173, in L. Vinx (ed.), *The Guardian of the Constitution: Hans Kelsen and Carl Schmitt on the Limits of Constitutional Law.* Trans. L. Vinx. Cambridge: Cambridge University Press.
Vinx, L. (2013) 'Carl Schmitt and the Analogy between Constitutional and International Law: Are Constitutional and International Law Inherently Political?', *Global Constitutionalism*, Vol. 2, No. 1: 91–124.
Waldron, J. (2006) 'The Core of the Case against Judicial Review', *Yale Law Journal*, Vol. 115, No. 6: 1348–406.

Chapter 3

Political community in Carl Schmitt's international legal thinking

Markus Gunneflo

Schmitt on the protection of political community in domestic law

A distinctive feature of Carl Schmitt's legal thinking is the pivotal role that he grants political community. Against the background of Schmitt's particular conception of political community and the importance placed on its protection in a *domestic* law setting, this chapter highlights the role of political community in Schmitt's *international* legal thinking. We may have little reason to study – and even less reason to follow – Schmitt's assessment of the legacy of European international law, questions of self-defence, imperialism and partisan warfare, were it not for the fact that political community remains a significant force in international law. Accordingly, this chapter makes a case for the relevance of Schmitt's thinking today, particularly for understanding questions related to the use of force in international affairs.

Political community, for Schmitt, concerns the establishment of a 'boundary that secures the existential survival of a particular way of life' or *Lebensform* (Kennedy 2008: xvi). This is a conception of political community premised on the friend-enemy distinction:

> The specific political distinction to which political actions and motives can be reduced is that between friend and enemy ... The distinction of friend and enemy denotes the utmost degree of intensity of a union or separation, of an association or dissociation.
> (Schmitt 2007a: 26)

Both 'union [*Verbindung*]' and 'association [*Assoziation*]' signify the action of joining separate elements so as to form a whole or a body, or the condition resulting from such action. In his *Three Types of Juristic Thought* (Schmitt 2004) Schmitt commits himself to 'concrete-order thinking'. Here we may note that, as with 'unity' and 'association', the adjective 'concrete', stemming from *concrescere*, implies to grow together, coalesce, or, in other words, to form a whole or body. Similarly, 'constitution [*Verfassung*]', which is the fundamental concept underwriting Schmitt's *Constitutional Theory*, is the arrangement or combination of different parts or elements that determines the nature and character of a specific whole. According to this meaning, Schmitt maintains, 'everything, each man and thing, every business and association, is somehow included in a "constitution"' (Schmitt 2008: 59). If this meaning is limited to the constitution of the *state*, we arrive at 'the concrete, collective condition of political unity and social order of a particular state' (Schmitt 2008: 59). In the same work Schmitt describes the constitution as a 'political being' (singular) (Schmitt 2008: 125).

The contemporary Italian theorist of community, Roberto Esposito, has noted that once community is identified with a property, be it with a people, a territory, or an essence (or a combination thereof), 'the community is walled in within itself and thus separated from the outside' (Esposito 2010: 16). Schmitt presents an exemplary case of such turning of community into its opposite; the turning of the condition of being in relation to the other and the outside into dissociation and defence, or, as Esposito would have it, community into immunity (Esposito 2008, 2010, 2011, 2013).

Schmitt's thoughts about how the protection of political community is to be achieved in a domestic law setting appears to have developed over time.

The first sentence of Schmitt's 1922 *Political Theology* reads: 'Sovereign is he who decides on the exception' (Schmitt 1985: 5). And, as Étienne Balibar (2004: 136) puts it: 'what the sovereign decides on is the necessity of public safety and order: where and when it is in danger, and what means are to be used to preserve it'. This has been read as Schmitt committing to sovereign protection through Hobbesian decisionism. When sovereignty is exercised in this extra-legal monarchical mode it reveals how the sovereign, in Schmitt's words, 'stands outside the normally valid legal system [and] nevertheless belongs to it, for it is he who must decide whether the constitution needs to be suspended in its entirety' (Schmitt 1985: 7). In her contribution to the present volume, Leila Brännström argues against this reading of *Political Theology* in which the sovereign decision is an extra-legal order-creating decision *ex nihilo*, highlighting instead how the sovereign decision is a legally authorized decision defending and maintaining the prevailing social order or political community (see Brännström 2016, Chapter 1 in this volume).

The conception of law underpinning such legally authorized decision making in the context of liberal constitutional states is developed furthest in Schmitt's 1928 *Constitutional Theory*. In this text Schmitt notes that what characterizes the liberal constitutional state is the suppression of extra-legal sovereign power for the benefit of a supposedly all-encompassing rule of law, creating its very own constitutional dynamic that Schmitt refers to as 'apocryphal' (Schmitt 2008: 155–6, 159, 215–16).

Reading *Constitutional Theory* legal theorist and former judge of the German Constitutional Court, Ernst-Wolfgang Böckenförde, describes the *telos* of constitutional law as to facilitate, preserve, and support the state as a political order and unity and to deal with politics in the immediate sense of addressing the existence, form and action of political community (Böckenförde 1997: 8). Lars Vinx refers to how Schmitt privileges a purely political form of constitutional guardianship (see Vinx 2016, Chapter 2 in this volume). This is a deformalized law that is more responsive to demands for the protection of the very political community that is its 'political existence' and only reason for being. The guiding principle of this conception of law is that the existential self-preservation of political community – the 'constitution' in a Schmittian sense – is the ultimate arbiter: 'the protection of the constitution in the positive and substantial sense' must not be 'sacrificed to the protection of the constitutional provision in the formal and relative sense' (Schmitt 2008: 80). Rather, the latter must be made responsive to the demands of the former.

One way of accounting for this constitutional jurisdiction *qua* political jurisdiction is by way of a kind of zero-sum relation, according to which the liberal constitutional state, in permanently closing the 'safety-valve' that the sovereign decision on the exception constitutes, forces the extra-legal powers necessary to maintain political community to find other means of expression. What comes to mind is Schmitt's assertion of how the liberal insistence on an all-encompassing rule of law cannot suppress sovereignty but rather can only leave the question of sovereign authority 'unclear', and how 'for the inevitable sovereign actions, a method for *apocryphal acts of sovereignty* develops' (Schmitt 2008: 155).

Schmitt's eulogy for the era of European international law

During the Second World War Schmitt's thoughts turned from questions of sovereignty and constitutional law to international affairs. This turn to international law has been described in terms of an attempt to justify Nazi expansionism (Vinx 2014) but also as an interest in the question of the foundations of international law and the international legal order (Rasch 2005). While there may be truth in both of these statements, I think that Schmitt's international legal thinking reveals a keen interest in the role of international law for the protection of political community. As seen in this chapter, his assessment of historical periods but also of a number of substantive issues of international law hinges on precisely this issue.

Schmitt sees the First World War, in which US President Wilson had intervened, as a watershed. It began as a conventional war among states along the lines of European international law, and ended as a global civil war (Schmitt 2007b: 95). This transformation can be seen in the guilt placed with the German Kaiser after the war for the *jus ad bellum* 'crime of war', as distinct from *jus in bello* 'war crimes'. In the logic of European international law the first is an unthinkable crime because war was at the disposal of sovereign equals; because heads of state did not pursue war personally but by the state as *justus hostis;* and, finally, because of the principle of *par in parem non habet jurisdictionem* (Schmitt 2006: 262).

One aspect of Schmitt's regret about this shift concerns the consequences of substituting equality for hierarchy in inter-state relations. If European international law was fundamentally characterized by an equality that bound (European) states together and bracketed war between them, with the resurgence of hierarchical relations and war as the suppression of illiberal rebellion, the notion of *justus hostis* and a public concept of enmity was in retreat. This in turn implied 'the intensification of the means of destruction and the disorientation of theaters of war' (Schmitt 2006: 321). Instead of the bracketed 'war as duel' characteristic of European international law, war was put back in pre-Westphalian 'just war', or, conceived differently, the entire world was placed beyond the line in the New World. More fundamentally perhaps, Schmitt's appreciation of the era of European international law (and regret about its demise) is grounded in its sanctioning of the boundary that secures the existential survival of a particular way of life, or, as Esposito would prefer, the immunity it afforded to (European) political community.

Schmitt's *The Nomos of the Earth* (Schmitt 2006) is first and foremost a eulogy for the international legal order that was established through the peace of Westphalia. Schmitt noted that European international law had clear implications for the protection of political community: it forestalled internecine struggle by means of establishing a domestic jurisdiction in which the political was monopolized. It secured the independence to make the distinction between friend and enemy or to remain neutral in foreign affairs (Hooker 2009: 19).

In this framework the border that is sanctioned by European international law represents the protective boundary that deactivates communal exposure, affording identity, security, or, if we follow Esposito, immunity. In fact, Schmitt borrows explicitly from the biomedical sphere in considering the timeless significance of the border: 'often in world history, peoples and empires have sought to isolate themselves from the rest of the world and to protect themselves from an infection by a defensive line' (Schmitt 2006: 295).

European international law was, as the name suggests, Eurocentric. It was the mutually binding law between *European* sovereigns and 'this European core determined the *nomos* of the rest of the earth' (Schmitt 2006: 126). This determination of the *nomos* of the rest of the world proceeded along the lines of a clear distinction between the Old World of Europe and the New World with regard to territorial rights. As has been stressed by Jennifer Beard, in remaining silent about the territorial rights of the peoples of the 'New World' and their territories, the peace of Westphalia enabled European legal theorists to carry forward the older claims of the legitimate rule of the Holy Roman Empire and the Catholic Church into new theories sanctioning pan-European land-appropriation, conquest and colonialism (Beard 2010: 18). Schmitt even suggests that the freedom of European states in the 'New World' was indispensable for the order of Central Europe:

> the designation of a conflict zone at once freed the area on this side of the line – a sphere of peace and order ruled by European public law – from the immediate threat of those events 'beyond the line', which would not have been the case had there been no such zone.
> (Schmitt 2006: 97)

Reading these passages in Schmitt's *The Nomos of the Earth*, Rasch notes that the pacification of Europe is achieved at the expense of the non-European world, against which holy wars – that is, total wars – are directed as a form of release or discharge (Schmitt speaks of *Entlastung*, 'unburdening') of unwanted violence. Europe imports relative peace and prosperity, as it were, by exporting violence (Rasch 2005: 181). Characteristically, Schmitt claims that the proper way to understand this state of affairs is not as an ethical but as a legal problem. He writes that this restriction of law to the land has been:

> characterized sociologically as 'landlocked morality.' In my view, it is simply a matter of the age-old maxim: 'all law is law only in a particular location.' ... Then the idea of amity lines and of an area designated as free of law easily becomes understandable as an antithesis to law in the Old World, i.e., to an old law in a particular location.
> (Schmitt 2006: 98)

Gerry Simpson has showed that there is a case to be made for a certain continuity of claims of legalised hegemony in international law, all the way from the demarcation between Christian/non-Christian, subsequently European/non-European to the *unequal* distribution of *equal* rights between Great Powers and outlaw states in the present era of formal sovereign equality (Simpson 2004). This is particularly so in debates in which the territorial integrity and political independence of outlaw states is diminished, resulting in highly permissive environments in which great powers may legally intervene (Simpson 2004: 325), what Stuart Elden calls 'contingent sovereignty' (Elden 2009).

Although this particular aspect of European international law may still be with us, it is not difficult to see that other aspects of this international legal order has changed drastically since. Accordingly, it is difficult to describe states today as unified, impermeable and self-contained, and exceedingly difficult to describe war as a 'duel'. However, Schmitt's writing on international law not only eulogizes European international law but also provides a number of important perspectives for thinking about the question of protection of political community in what might be termed a post-Westphalian international legal order.

The ban on war and the self-defence exception in international law

In *The Concept of the Political* Schmitt stated that the 1928 Kellogg–Briand Pact's ban on war could not and in fact did not prohibit 'a people which exists in the sphere of the political in case of need ... determin[ing] by itself the friend-enemy distinction' (Schmitt 2007a: 50). Schmitt continues:

> Such a declaration is subject, first of all, to specific reservations which are explicitly or implicitly self-understood as, for example, the reservation regarding the autonomous existence of the state and its self-defense, the reservation regarding existing treaties, the right of a continuing free and independent existence, and so on. Second, these reservations are, according to their logical structure, no mere exceptions to the norm, but altogether give the norm its concrete content. They are not peripheral but essential exceptions; they give the treaty its real content in dubious cases. Third, as long as a sovereign state exists, this state decides for itself, by virtue of its independence, whether or not such a reservation (self-defense, enemy aggression, violation of existing treaties including the Kellogg Pact and so on) is or is not given in the concrete case.
>
> (Schmitt 2007a: 50–1)

After the Second World War, the ban on war was articulated in United Nations (UN) Charter Article 2(4), which proscribed 'the threat or use of force against the territorial integrity or political independence of any state'. Applying Schmitt's analysis of the Kellogg–Briand pact to the international legal order under the UN Charter, one would however be forced to recognize the significance of the exception in Article 51 or the 'inherent right of self-defense'. In this way, Samuel Weber has argued that Schmitt's definition of sovereignty under the UN Charter can be translated as 'the nation state able to decide what constitutes a threat to its survival and thus a situation of self-defense' (Weber 2008: 109).

Armed conflicts in the twentieth century would appear to confirm Oscar Schachter's critical note that 'despite the apparent agreement that self-defense is governed by law, the meaning and validity of that proposition remain open to question' (Schachter 1989: 259). Despite the steps taken since the days of the League of Nations (particularly the mandate of the United Nations Security Council to assert jurisdiction over questions of international peace and security and a few judgments of the International Court of Justice), much as anticipated by Schmitt, the problem still seems to be one of auto-interpretation or self-judging. Accordingly, a Schmittian conception of sovereignty and primacy of the protection of political community continues to haunt the international law of self-defence. A look at doctrinal debates on Article 51 of the UN Charter and the right to self-defence 'if an armed attack occurs' and the substantial disagreement with regard to if this encompasses the protection of nationals abroad, defensive measures against small-scale or 'imminent' attacks, military actions against states engaged in 'indirect aggression', and so on, is not reassuring. Neither are disagreements with regard to the relationship between Article 51 and the prohibition on the use of force 2(4) and the relationship between Article 51 and the customary right of self-defence (see, for example, Ruys 2010).

Greater space assertions of political community and spaceless imperialism in international law

The tendency of states to define spheres of interest and the resulting 'space for exceeding the boundaries of the state proper' in the name of self-defence, had according to Schmitt, caused a strain in the spatial order of European international law (Schmitt 2006: 281). The prime example to which Schmitt refers with regard to such a claim for *Großraum* – literally 'great space' but perhaps more appropriately 'sphere of influence' or 'geopolitical space' (Elden 2011: 93) – is the American Monroe doctrine, articulated in an address by President James Monroe in 1823. Schmitt claims that it contains 'three simple thoughts': 'independence of states in the Americas; non-colonization in this space; non-interference of extra-American powers in this space, coupled with non-interference of America in non-American space' (Schmitt 2011b: 46). Hence, as it was originally conceived, the Monroe doctrine was a specifically Western hemispheric and purely defensive form of regionalism; defensive, that is, in relation to European nations, because from the right to exclude other powers from the Western hemisphere followed the right of the United States to intervene militarily within that territory (Vagts 2001: 846).

Schmitt embraces the original Monroe doctrine as a greater-space assertion of political community and at the beginning of the Second World War he argues for the appropriateness of its application in relation to the *German Reich* and 'the East European space', which he referred to as a *völkischer Großraum* (Schmitt 2011a: 99). This was corroborated by a self-incriminating reference to the declaration by Adolf Hitler in the German parliament on 20 February 1938 that there 'existed a German right of protection for German national groups of foreign state citizenship, all on the foundation of our National Socialist national idea.' The 'völkischness' of this *Großraum* is corroborated through an equally self-incriminating racist argument about the 'political idea for the Central and East European space in which there live many nations and national groups that are, however, not – apart from the Jews – racially alien from one another' (Schmitt 2011a: 99).

The original idea of the Monroe doctrine would be turned into something very different in the hands of US Presidents Theodor Roosevelt and Woodrow Wilson. Schmitt writes that Wilson's announcement in 1917 of what subsequently would become known as Wilsonianism had the meaning of applying the Monroe doctrine to the entire world: 'In this way he sought a justification for his massive interference in non-European areas completely foreign to him and in military conflicts between the European powers' (Schmitt 2011b: 47). This transformation of the Monroe doctrine was made possible 'by the fact that Wilson substituted for the original and true Monroe Principle the ideological idea of liberal democracy and its associated images, especially those of "free" world trade and [a] "free" world market' (Schmitt 2011b: 48).

Schmitt's embrace of the original Monroe doctrine and his contempt for its Wilsonian universalization can be understood in terms of his commitment to political community. While the original Monroe doctrine can be understood as a greater-space assertion of political community, Wilsonianism represents the detachment of the friend–enemy distinction from any concrete form of political existence and its application along the lines of abstract liberal values or the world economy – it replaces a greater-space assertion of political community with spaceless imperialism. Because of the primacy of political community in Schmitt's thinking he embraced the former, but thought the latter reprehensible. Both these forms of imperialism remain crucial tendencies in the international politics of today.

The 2014 crisis and subsequent Russian military intervention in Ukraine may be taken as a reminder of the political currency of *Großraum* thinking, properly speaking. In the English translation of Schmitt's *Nomos*, G. L. Ulmen notes that the term *Großraum* gained currency after the First World War when the isolation of specific forms of energy such as electricity and gas were overcome organizationally in a *Großraumwirtschaft* or great-space economy (Ulmen 2006: 23). This tendency has, of course, only been further accentuated since. The huge dependency of Ukraine on Russian gas and Russia's use of the price of gas for political leverage in its attempt to stave off Ukrainian closer cooperation with the European Union and NATO is a reminder that 'it was no accident that *Großraum* thinking had appeared first in economics, and that the underlying principle might be applicable to a new order of international law since the economy had become political' (Ulmen 2006: 23). It seems to be an increasingly common opinion that a Russian relationship to the post-Soviet space in general and Ukraine in particular is determined by thinking in terms of a sphere of influence or, in other words, *Großraum*. The name 'Ukraine' in itself, from the Slavic *Krajilkrajin* meaning 'borderland', captures this country's liminal status between the European Union and NATO on the one hand and Russia on the other (on Ukraine as geopolitical borderland, see Tunander 1997: 20).

Michael Hardt and Antonio Negri's argument in *Empire* may be used in considering the further development of what Schmitt saw as the perversion of *Großraum*-thinking into spaceless imperialism. They argue that in the waning years and wake of the cold war 'the responsibility of exercising an international police power "fell" squarely on the shoulders of the United States' (Hardt and Negri 2000: 180). Further, the first Gulf War was the first time the United States could exercise this power in its full form but Haiti, Somalia and Bosnia also presented the United States as 'the only power able to manage international justice, *not as a function of its own national motives but in the name of global right*' (Hardt and Negri 2000: 180). All of these examples of the exercise of an international police power were sanctioned by the UN Security Council which shows that legitimization of this order is not merely based on the effectiveness of sanction and the military might to impose it but through the 'production of international juridical norms that raise up the power of the hegemonic actor in a durable and legal way' (Hardt and Negri 2000: 180).

The tellurian and the dislocated partisan in international law

A similar distinction between the protection of political community in a concrete sense and the fight for an abstract cause is at work in Schmitt's embrace of the tellurian partisan, and his rejection of the displaced or globalized Partisan. We will also find in these considerations important insights about the legal asymmetry that international law maintains between the state and its non-state enemies; an asymmetry that we are reminded of in the current war against terrorism.

Theory of the Partisan from 1963 has certainly been read as a rather limited in scope genealogy of irregular warfare. However, it can also be read as a re-articulation of the concept of the political in the face of the continuing disintegration of European international law. The key to such a reading is found in the subtitle *Intermediate Commentary on the Concept of the Political*. The subtitle is explained in the foreword as being related to the simultaneous re-issue of Schmitt's *The Concept of the Political*. Schmitt refers to the theory of the partisan as 'independent' in relation to the concept of the political but also stresses how it 'unavoidably flows into the problem of the distinction between friend and enemy' and thus into the question of political community (Schmitt 2007b: unpaginated foreword).

The partisan is defined by the criteria of: 1) irregularity; 2) mobility and agility; 3) intense political commitment; and 4) tellurian character or deep-rooted attachment to a particular land and space (Slomp 2009: 66). The figure of the partisan, at the same time, challenges and restores the political. Slomp explains that:

> when the state is no longer able to protect, then the partisan emerges: partisan insurgence and partisan groups are, for Schmitt, the symptoms of a 'weak' state: the stronger the political bond of an individual to a group or party, the weaker the state. By choosing their own enemy, partisan groups both challenge the legitimacy of the state and claim legitimacy for themselves.
>
> (Slomp 2009: 66)

One could be forgiven for assuming that the partisan's conviction concerning the justness of her cause would make Schmitt contemptuous towards her because 'it was the absolute commitment to a just cause which he [Schmitt] railed against in *The Nomos*', because of its devastating effects on the bracketed, public wars of European international law (Slomp 2009: 66). However, here, the tellurian element enters and with it an important distinction between different forms of partisanship is introduced (see, further, De Ville 2016, Chapter 9 in this volume). The tellurian character of the partisan assures her defensiveness and 'guard[s] it against the absolute claim of an abstract justice' (Schmitt 2007b: 20). While the tellurian partisan certainly poses a challenge to any given state authority, as long as the defensiveness that the tellurian character guarantees is retained and partisan warfare takes place in the demarcated domains of the Westphalian state system, it is still wielded in protection of political community.

Schmitt considers another form of partisan: the one that has lost the defensiveness guaranteed by the tellurian character, or in other words, the dislocated or global partisan. This was a development driven by ideologies of world revolution as much as by technological developments. In relation to the former, Schmitt in the early 1960s, clearly has Communist world revolution in mind, invoking the writings of Ernesto 'Che' Guevara, among others. In relation to technological developments, Schmitt refers to 'motorization' but also modern weaponry. The dislocation of the partisan makes her something of a non-state equivalent of American imperialism. In his considerations of the distinctly tellurian Spanish civil war, Schmitt quotes a French commandant as saying you have to fight like a partisan wherever there are partisans, evoking the vicious circle of terror and counter-terror of partisan warfare (Schmitt 2007b: 20). Could this expression be adapted to capture how the dislocated partisan and the state that it challenges might become entangled in ever-widening circles of terror and counter-terror such as we have seen with the dislocated form of partisanship that Schmitt analyzed all the way to the present and the allegedly new kind of transnational terrorism of al-Qaeda (Schmitt 2007b: 13)?

The legal relationship between the state and the partisan is the legal hierarchy of civil war, articulated in Common Article 3 of the 1949 Geneva Conventions. Ralph suggests that: 'the intense political commitment of the partisan sets him apart from the common criminal but his actions are still unlawful' (Ralph 2010: 289). One feature, in particular, of the kind of warfare that takes place between the state and its irregular enemy is this ability of the state to invoke its monopoly on legitimate force. The sovereign state is able to adopt the simple and clear position that the law is on its side. This is for instance the stance taken by the Israeli state in the distinctly tellurian Israeli–Palestinian conflict. It is also the position taken by the United States in its distinctly less tellurian conflict with al-Qaeda. This shows how the notion of post-Westphalian international law does not imply an age where nation-state sovereignty is finished or irrelevant (Brown 2010: 21). One aspect that relentlessly conditions the current war on terrorism in Israel, the United States and elsewhere is the legal asymmetry that international law maintains between the state and its non-state enemy. This is so even though the lawfulness of the measures taken by the state is often called into question. For, as Schmitt maintains,

> even the legality that is challenged in the modern state is stronger than any other type of right. That is a manifestation of the decisionistic power of the state and its transformation of right into law ... legality is the irresistible functional mode of every modern state army.
> (Schmitt 2007b: 84)

The increasingly lethal nature of counterterrorism serves as a reminder of how the legality of which Schmitt speaks is able to transform 'the irregularity of the partisan into a deadly illegality' (Schmitt 2007b: 84, on Schmitt and counter-terrorism see Gunneflo 2016).

Carl Schmitt and the force of political community in international law

This chapter has been an attempt to highlight the imperative role of political community in Schmitt's international legal thinking. Political community has this imperative role in Schmitt's eulogy of the era of European international law for its shielding of (European) political community. The same is true for Schmitt's account of the disintegration of European international law and his dismissal of early twentieth-century attempts to ban war as a sham that unavoidably would be determined by the self-defence exception. Further, Schmitt's embrace of *Großraum*, or greater-space assertion of political community, together with his rejection of the spaceless imperialism of American Wilsonianism, can be read along the lines of a defence of political community. The same applies to Schmitt's positive evaluation of the tellurian partisan and his dismissal of the dislocated partisan who has drifted away from deciding on the enemy in a concrete defence of political community. In all of these examples we can see how Schmitt makes the protection of political community the ultimate arbiter – legally, politically and ethically speaking.

It is important to see that Schmitt's thinking here is not the unopposable realism that he would like us to believe. Instead Schmitt's international legal thinking builds on and privileges a conception of political community that we have good reasons to resist. At the same time we are reminded of the continued importance of the question of the protection of political community in international affairs by arguments about the inherent right to self-defence, when greater-space assertions of political community serves as reason for military intervention or when the irregularity of the present-day partisan is turned into deadly illegality in a drone attack. Even though Schmitt's insistence on political community may come across as parochial in present times of globalization, increasing traction of various universalisms and the liberal rule of law, we have not by any means overcome the force of political community in international law.

Bibliography

Balibar, É. (2004) *We, The People of Europe? Reflections on Transnational Citizenship*. Trans. J. Swenson. Princeton, NJ: Princeton University Press.
Beard, J. (2010) 'The International Law in Force', p. 18–28 in F. Johns, R. Joyce and S. Pahuja (eds), *Events: The Force of International Law*. New York: Routledge Cavendish.
Brown, W. (2010) *Walled States, Waning Sovereignty*. New York: Zone Books.
Böckenförde, E.-W. (1997) 'The Concept of the Political: A Key to Understanding Carl Schmitt's Constitutional Theory', *Canadian Journal of Law and Jurisprudence* Vol. 10, No.1: 5–19.
Brännström, L. (2016) 'Carl Schmitt's Definition of Sovereignty as Authorized Leadership', Chapter 1 in M. Arvidsson, L. Brännström and P. Minkkinen (eds), *The Contemporary Relevance of Carl Schmitt: Law, Politics, Theology*. Abingdon: Routledge.
De Ville, J. (2016) 'Rethinking the Concept of the Political: Derrida's reading of Schmitt's 'The Theory of the Partisan', Chapter 9 in M. Arvidsson, L. Brännström and P. Minkkinen (eds), *The Contemporary Relevance of Carl Schmitt: Law, Politics, Theology*. Abingdon: Routledge.
Elden, S. (2009) *Terror and Territory*. Minneapolis, MN: University of Minnesota Press.
Elden, S. (2011) 'Reading Schmitt Geopolitically: Nomos Territory and *Großraum*', p. 91–105, in S. Legg (ed.), *Spatiality, Sovereignty and Carl Schmitt: Geographies of the Nomos*. New York: Routledge.

Esposito, R. (2008) *Biós – Biopolitics and Philosophy*. Trans. T. Campbell. Minneapolis, MN: University of Minnesota Press.
Esposito, R. (2010) *Communitas – The Origin and Destiny of Community*. Trans. T. Campbell. Redwood City, CA: Stanford University Press.
Esposito, R. (2011) *Immunitas – The Protection and Negation of Life*. Trans. Z. Hanafi. Cambridge: Polity.
Esposito, R. (2013) *Terms of the Political – Community, Immunity, Biopolitics*. Trans. R. N. Welch. New York: Fordham University Press.
Gunneflo, M. (2016) *Targeted Killing: A Legal and Political History*. Cambridge: Cambridge University Press (forthcoming).
Hardt, M. and A. Negri (2000) *Empire*. Cambridge, MA: Harvard University Press.
Hooker, W. (2009) *Carl Schmitt's International Thought: Order and Orientation*. Cambridge: Cambridge University Press.
Kennedy, E. (2008) 'Foreword', p. xv–xvi, in C. Schmitt, *Constitutional Theory*. Trans. J. Seltzer. Durham, NC: Duke University Press.
Ralph, J. (2010) 'War as an Institution of International Hierarchy: Carl Schmitt's Theory of the Partisan and Contemporary US Practice', *Millennium: Journal of International Studies*, Vol. 39, No. 2: 279–98.
Rasch, W. (2005) 'Introduction: Carl Schmitt and the New World Order', *South Atlantic Quarterly*, Vol. 104, No. 2: 177–83.
Ruys, T. (2010) *'Armed Attack' and Article 51 of the UN Charter: Evolutions in Customary Law and Practice*. Cambridge: Cambridge University Press.
Schachter, O. (1989) 'Self-Defense and the Rule of Law', *American Journal of International Law*, Vol. 83, No. 2: 259–77.
Schmitt, C. (1985) *Political Theology: Four Chapters on the Concept of Sovereignty* [1922]. Trans. G. Schwab. Cambridge, MA: MIT Press.
Schmitt, C. (2004). *On the Three Types of Juristic Thought* [1934]. Trans. J. W. Bendersky. Westport, CT: Praeger.
Schmitt, C. (2006) *The Nomos of the Earth in the International Law of the Jus Publicum Europaeum* [1950]. Trans. G. L. Ulmen. New York: Telos.
Schmitt, C. (2007a) *The Concept of the Political* [1932]. Expanded edn. Trans. G. Schwab. Chicago, IL: University of Chicago Press.
Schmitt, C. (2007b) *Theory of the Partisan: Intermediate Commentary on the Concept of the Political* [1963]. Trans. G. L. Ulmen. New York: Telos.
Schmitt, C. (2008) *Constitutional Theory* [1928]. Trans. J. Seltzer. Durham, NC: Duke University Press.
Schmitt, C. (2011a) 'The *Großraum* Order of International Law with a Ban on Intervention for Spatially Foreign Powers: A Contribution to the Concept of *Reich* in International law' [1939–1941], p. 75–124, in C. Schmitt, *Writings on War*. Trans. T. Nunan. Cambridge: Polity.
Schmitt, C. (2011b) '*Großraum* Versus Universalism: The International Legal Struggle over the Monroe Doctrine' [1939], p. 46–54, in S. Legg (ed.), *Spatiality, Sovereignty and Carl Schmitt: Geographies of the Nomos*. London: Routledge.
Simpson, G. (2004) *Great Powers and Outlaw States: Unequal Sovereigns in the International Legal Order*. Cambridge: Cambridge University Press.
Slomp, G. (2009) *Carl Schmitt and the Politics of Hostility, Violence and Terror*. New York: Palgrave Macmillan.
Tunander, O. (1997) 'Post-Cold War Europe: A synthesis of a Bipolar Friend-Foe

Structure and a Hierarchic Cosmos-Chaos Structure?' p. 17–44, in O. Tunander, P. Baev and V. I. Einagel (eds), *Geopolitics in Post-Wall Europe*. London: Sage.

Ulmen, G. L. (2006) 'Translators Introduction', p. 9–34, in C. Schmitt, *The Nomos of the Earth in the International Law of the Jus Publicum Europaeum.* Trans. G. L. Ulmen. New York: Telos.

Vagts, D. F. (2001) 'Hegemonic International Law', *American Journal of International Law*, Vol. 95, No. 4: 843–8.

Vinx, L. (2014) 'Carl Schmitt', in *Stanford Encyclopedia of Philosophy* (Winter 2014 edn), E. N. Zalta (ed.). Available online at http://plato.stanford.edu/archives/win2014/entries/Schmitt (accessed 10 April 2015).

Vinx, L. (2016) 'Carl Schmitt and the Problem of Constitutional Guardianship', Chapter 2 in M. Arvidsson, L. Brännström and P. Minkkinen (eds), *The Contemporary Relevance of Carl Schmitt. Law, Politics, Theology.* Abingdon: Routledge.

Weber, S. (2008) 'Rogue Democracy.' *Diacritics*, Vol. 38, No. 1–2: 104–120.

Chapter 4

Carl Schmitt and the tyranny of values

Juha-Pekka Rentto

Cuckoo's eggs

At the same time a metaphysical sceptic, a post-neothomistic Catholic organicist, and a Machiavellian realist ineptly characterized as a twentieth-century Hobbes,[1] Carl Schmitt is an enigmatic political thinker who develops from this unlikely combination of premises a biting criticism of even the most sacred articles of faith in the established political creeds of our time, most importantly the modern liberal democratic–egalitarian theology.[2] Many of Schmitt's works, from *Der Wert des Staates* of 1914 (Schmitt 2004a) to the 1970 *Political Theology II* (Schmitt 2008b/2008c)[3] are aspects on this one grand theme. The task of this chapter is to examine one of its variations, namely Schmitt's post-war criticism of 'the tyranny of values' embodied in the West German constitutional review of laws, which

---

1 Ineptly so, because Schmitt's political theory, unlike that of Hobbes, is not the result of a systematic series of deductions from a metaphysical theory of reality. On the contrary, it purports, like Bentham's, to be based on an observation of facts subjected to unbiased logical criticism.
2 The whole of Schmitt's *Constitutional Theory* (Schmitt 2003/2008a) can be interpreted as a criticism of the political theology, predominant even today, which misleadingly applies the hazy and self-contradictory notions usually connected with ideal liberal democracy as criteria for evaluating real political solutions. The same theme strikes the tone in *The Crisis of Democracy* (Schmitt 1996a/2000), as well. See also *The Concept of the Political* (Schmitt 1963: 24–5, 55, 70–1/1996d: 22–4, 54, 70–2); *Legality and Legitimacy* (Schmitt 2005: 29–30, 40–3, 84–9/2004b: 28–9, 41–4, 87–92); and *State, Movement, People* (Schmitt 1934b: 24–6/2001: 26–8).
3 A double date separated by a slash indicates two editions of the work cited, the first of which is the German edition actually used and the second an English edition. The interpretations brought forward in this essay are based on the German editions. The English editions have been consulted for the benefit of English-speaking readers. All language, including paraphrases and direct quotes, has been rendered into English from the German originals by the author and may therefore deviate from the English editions. Different works cited are separated with a semicolon.

in 1959, he formulated in a privately printed short tract entitled *The Tyranny of Values* (Schmitt 2011a/1996e), later published in 1967 with an added introduction. The target there was the notion that the task of the judiciary is to promote and safeguard purportedly important generally accepted or universally acceptable *values* like, for instance, the value of 'human dignity [*Menschenwürde*]' so often – and, perhaps, hastily – taken to be an unquestioned foundation for so-called human rights. This post-war notion Schmitt seems to place on a level with the political myths that he had criticized in the 1922 and 1934 editions of *Political Theology* (Schmitt 1934a/1985), in *State, Movement, People* (Schmitt 1934b/2001) and in *On the Three Types of Juristic Thought* (Schmitt 2006/2004c), for overlooking the factor of pure *decision* in politics, and in *Der Hüter der Verfassung* (Schmitt 1996b)[4] for yielding a distorted view of the proper role of the judiciary in a state.

But when *The Tyranny of Values* was published, many a reader was astonished at the way in which it now criticized the constitutional review of laws with reference to basic rights (*Grundrechte*). Nevertheless, in the light of Schmitt's argument in the first two parts of his *Constitutional Theory* (Schmitt 2003/2008a), it is probable that even now, thirty years later, his intention was *not* to criticize basic rights as such, as long as they were plainly treated as what they were, namely a necessary ingredient in a *decision* by the people to create a *Rechtsstaat* governed by the Rule of Law, *but* rather the make-believe notion that basic rights are an expression of even more fundamental values which not only provide the ultimate standard for the legitimacy of the constitution but also lend themselves to being used as supposedly objective criteria for interpreting its provisions. For this latter purpose, they are not an appropriate method, owing to what Schmitt now, with reference to Nicolai Hartmann's *Ethics*, called 'the tyranny of values' (see Hartmann 1962: 574–8/1951: 421–5; Schmitt 2011a: 48–51/1996e: 24–6). The very same idea in a slightly different form had already preoccupied his mind in the 1930s when he, addressing a burning problem of the day, had discussed the 'anarchy of general clauses', considered by many a major plague of the German legal system (see Schmitt 2006: 48–50/2004c: 90–2; 1934b: 43–4/2001: 49–50). Both then and now, the crux of the problem was the same: value-laden, vague and contradictory principles, like cuckoo's eggs in the nest of the liberal legal system, once accepted as unquestioned sources of law, will be used as sham justifications

---

4   A translation has recently been published (see Vinx 2015).

for any desired interpretation of the law (Schmitt 2006: 49/2004c: 91).[5] This makes the judiciary a devious lawgiver which pretends not to be making arbitrary decisions when, supposedly acting under the constraint of allegedly self-imposing obligatory values, it actually dilutes that which once was a concrete thing, like a piece of one's property, and then an objective right to the thing, like the right of ownership, to 'a mere value' (Schmitt 2011a: 11/1996e: 2), presumably based on the 'highest value, human dignity', which nevertheless 'remains open' (Schmitt 2011a: 12/1996e: 3), destroying the predictable basis for a 'legally meaningful application of the Law which only permanent rules and clear rulings in a concrete order' can deliver (Schmitt 2011a: 23/1996e: 10).[6] The same argument is made in *Roman Catholicism and Political Form* (Schmitt 1925b: 41–3/1996c: 30–1), with reference to an international tribunal falsely posing as a representative of universal justice.

A standard version of the doctrine of the division of powers holds that the judiciary should not meddle with legislation because the power to give laws properly belongs to the people or its democratically elected representatives. However – as Schmitt, in a quaint footnote to a reference to Montesquieu in his *Constitutional Theory*, lets us understand – the very 'power' of the judiciary is illusory (Schmitt 2003: 184–5/2008a: 222–3). Rather, from what he has to say about constitutional review (*Verfassungsjustiz*) in *Der Hüter der Verfassung* we can gather that the crux of the problem for him is not that the judiciary would thereby usurp powers that properly belong elsewhere. Constitutional review can only be *justice* (*Justiz*; on the German term, see also Minkkinen 2016, Chapter 5 in this volume) when a clear breach of the constitution has been identified, but this can only take place after the fact – whereas in cases in which it is unclear if the constitution has been broken it is not a judgment by law at all but legislation. In the former case, justice comes in too late to be able to put an effective restraint on government, whereas the latter case is not justice at all but a plain *decision* (*Entscheidung*).

---

5 Note, though, that they can be used well, too, if only subjected to the interests of 'the whole people' – and not to those of the liberal individualistic *Verkehrsgesellschaft* ('transaction society'; see also Schmitt 2006: 16–17 / Schmitt 2004c: 53–54), which only turns the State into a huge club where necessary decisions are postponed for endless discussion, (Schmitt 1934a: 76–80 / Schmitt 1985: 60–63; Schmitt 1996a:7–11 / Schmitt 2000: 3–7); the political unity of the people into a waste product of daily compromise (Schmitt 1934b: 24–26 / Schmitt 2001: 26–28); the political process into a *plébiscite de tous les jours* where no one bears the ultimate responsibility for anything (Schmitt 2005: 84–87 / Schmitt 2004b: 88–90); and public authority itself into a demagogy by manipulation and propaganda (Schmitt 1963: 71 / Schmitt 1996d: 72).

6 The English translator, unhappily, gives 'form' for 'order'.

Being a plain decision, in itself, is quite in order, however, since decisions have to be made if the political and juridical system is to work at all – for it is only the irreducible element of *Entscheidung* which constitutes the positive validity (*Geltung*) of any court judgment, right or wrong (Schmitt 1996b: 38–46; 1934a: 42–4/1985: 31–3). What is out of order is that the decision is glossed over by something which is not justice but is posing as justice, thereby raising false expectations.

Now the problem with values for Schmitt is precisely the fact that they can only gain validity if someone chooses them; that is, gives them *Geltung* by positing them for application: 'who says that [values] are valid without someone giving them validity, lies' (Schmitt 2011a: 41/1996e: 21). For this reason the notion that values can be *directly* applied in judicial reasoning will change the judge from the simple carrier of the judicial function of the law he properly is (Schmitt 2004a: 75) into a 'pioneer' (Schmitt 2011a: 11/1996e: 2) and promoter of whatever values he chooses to posit – or a 'romanticist' (Schmitt 1925a: 109–12/2011b: 74–7) – opening up the field for unpredictable and conflicting judgments. What the legal system needs, on the contrary, are clear and stable rules that can be *applied* as they come, just as the army needs commands to *obey* and a moral agent virtues to *practice* – and for this reason the very purpose of law is to provide a predictably applicable *medium* for applying values *indirectly*, so as to avoid the 'terrors of direct positing of values' (Schmitt 2011a: 41, 54/1996e: 21, 28).[7] In his *Nachwort*, appended to the 2011 German edition of *The Tyranny of Values*, Christoph Schönberger thinks that Schmitt makes all too much of Hartmann's 'tyranny of values' because strictly speaking, it only applies to individual morality (Schmitt 2011 a: 74–5). If we take a closer look at Hartmann's train of thought, we see that it actually arrives at similar conclusions to Schmitt's. Therefore it seems that Schmitt's reference to Hartmann is only superficially justified by an incidental agreement on a 'tyranny' they both ascribe to values. What Schmitt really aims at, I think, is the German *Wertphilosophie*[8] at large – Hartmann being its greatest system builder. To understand the issue at stake, it is necessary to examine Hartmann's theory of values in relevant detail.

Values and points

For Hartmann, the value of a thing is a *quale* in it, a perceivable or 'felt' property, with its own validity, independent both of the factual nature of the thing and of the personal characteristics of the subject for whom the thing is an

---

7 The very notion of 'norm' entails, for Schmitt, that it precedes every and any opinion of any individual and, as a consequence, cannot be constituted by even any number of individuals (see Schmitt 2004a: 35–6).
8 *Wertphilosophie* can be translated as 'value philosophy' but, here, we are strictly concerned with the distinctively German school, the most prominent representatives of which were Max Scheler and Nicolai Hartmann.

object (Hartmann 1962: 119–21/1958: 183–5). As such, values are absolute in themselves but at the same time relative, or rather they have an absolute relation not only to the subject who 'feels' them but also to things, which thereby become 'goods' for him, and to other subjects, who thereby become 'persons' for him (Hartmann 1962: 140–1/Hartmann 1958: 207–9). Despite the objectivity of values, a subject can make mistakes about them and can even be blind to them (Hartmann 1962: 156–8/Hartmann 1958: 226–9). Moreover, as different subjects at different times perceive the values from different perspectives, knowledge about values is not progressive in a way that would gradually approach and eventually reach the ultimate level of what is possible to know, but rather keeps 'wandering back and forth', concentrating now on this, now on that area within the rather broad limits of what is possibly valuable (Hartmann 1962: 158–60/1958: 229–31).

Sollen is, according to Hartmann, built into the values in that they present themselves as an end that wants to be actualized by the subject (Hartmann 1962: 170–82/1958: 247–62). As ends cannot actualize themselves, they need the mediation of a subject, who is to *posit* them as a *Seinsollen*; a subject can only posit them for himself, whereby his *Sollen* is strictly personal (Hartmann 1962: 182–9/1958: 262–70). What a subject must posit for himself is in several ways determined by given factors, but he must posit it freely – and it is precisely this that makes him a person – since values cannot posit themselves (Hartmann 1962: 191–200/1958: 273–82). When ends are posited, however, means must also be chosen, and together they appear as a series leading to an end (*Finalreihe*). If you change the end, the entire series changes and alternative means are not indifferent with regard to the posited ends. It follows that not all *Finalreihen* are compatible with each other in a world where the series of different persons intermingle. Therefore, in order for the many to be able to live together, either their personal ends must be harmonized under common ends or their use of means must be organized so that it is possible to use them for different personal ends without conflict. But even then the most fundamental conflict remains irresolvable, namely the conflict between absolute values, which, being objectively perceived, do not depend on being posited but on the contrary determine what is possible for a person to posit and, being originally several and different, allow a radical incompatibility between the ends subjectively posited (Hartmann 1962: 210–14/1958: 297–302). This radical conflict is sharpened, as Schmitt underlines, by the tendency of values always to present themselves as tyrannically overriding any alternative value, no matter the price (Schmitt 2011a: 50/1996e: 25).

Value conflicts between individual spirits are to a degree remedied by the *objective spirit* of a community of persons who recognize each other mutually as 'Thou'. The objective spirit, on the one hand, is created by the individual spirits positing values but, on the other hand, it determines what the individuals can posit (Hartmann 1962: 230–48/1958: 321–44; 1933: 151–3). This results in the individuals being *mutually responsible* for each other: it is not only so that the world is for each individual and makes him what he is but each individual is for the world and is its co-creator and both the pedagogue and the lawgiver of every other person (Hartmann 1962: 424–7/1951: 234–7; 1933: 199–200). To secure everyone access to the lower, vital goods and to make the pursuit of higher values possible, mutual responsibility requires justice, a minimum of morality, which in turn demands to be *objectified* in a system of positive laws, thus placing the foundations for the validity of the rules concerning justice outside every personal spirit. Thereby a piece of *objectified spirit* is created which only can provide an objective, protective *medium* between individual persons in their two capacities as lawgivers and legal subjects (Hartmann 1962: 426–7/1951: 236–7; 1933: 236–9, 269). But the objective spirit is in itself inadequate for creating this medium because it is unconscious and depends on the consciousness of the individual personal spirits that make it up – and the individual consciousnesses are inadequate to themselves, because each individual covers the reality of values only from his limited perspective. Therefore, a political leadership function is necessary, borne by individual spirits which can, in combination with the objective spirit, serve as a vicarious consciousness for it and 'give it the head it lacks'. This 'head' can then posit a working synthesis of the totality of the conflicting personal *Finalreihen* by issuing objectified, positive laws, which, as 'dead spirit' not only prevent individual spirits, including the leaders, from unduly imposing their personal value positions on others but also provide the objective spirit with an incentive to change when the rules thus objectified have lived out their time (Hartmann 1933: 267–322, 445–66).

Hartmann is thus not only quite aware but also in full agreement with Schmitt that his value ethics requires a legal order the application of which is independent of personal valuations. But Schmitt is afraid that subjective valuations will now be reintroduced into the legal order through a direct application of 'basic values' for constitutional review, even if values, due to their economic background, have a logic of their own which makes them particularly unsuitable sources of law. For when, in the nineteenth century, the triumph of natural science shook the foundations of moral theory, many a moral philosopher, in an attempt as desperate as it was vain at saving the status of ethics as a scientific discipline, switched the moral notions of 'good' and 'virtue' for the economic notion of 'value', ostensibly lending itself more readily for objective measurement (Schmitt 2011a: 37–41/1996e: 18–21); cf. *Introduction*, Schmitt 2011a: 21–9/1996e: 9–13).[9]

---

9 That this is Hartmann's purpose can clearly be seen in the initial chapters of his *Ethics*. Noteworthy is also Wilhelm Dilthey's attempt at showing how ethics can surpass the naturalistic consequences of his own view of man as an instinctive animal (see, in particular, Dilthey 1958). Interestingly enough, even G. E. Moore's 1903 *Principia Ethica* (Moore 1951), with its notion of values as non-natural properties of things, in a strange way belongs to the same wave of thought.

In economic exchange, the concept of value is useful as a common measure for incommensurable things when, for example, different products are *evaluated* (*verwertet*)[10] in terms of money. This gives it 'its own logic' for, as a measure of incommensurables, value is, *qua* value, relative to a position (*Stelle*) one assumes, or a viewpoint, and thereby a substitute for other values (*Stellenwert*), interchangeable in that it depends on the variable positions or viewpoints that one can adopt towards the incommensurate goods that one pretends to measure – and a position will seem as good as any for applying the ostensibly common measure to considerations which, in reality, are irreducibly *different* rather than *more or less valuable.*

This may work very well for economics, and for that limited sphere of justice that scholastics called the justice of exchange, comprising just a few fields of civil law, but it has no application in any of those other fields of law in which money is not a consideration. If applied in them, it falsely pretends to measure incommensurables and to provide substitutes for that which cannot be substituted. It is all very well to say, for example, that life, instead of being sacred, has the highest value but the very fact that life is thereby reduced from an absolute consideration to a value ensures that, even if it be the highest, it will nevertheless just be a value among values and consequently a *Stellenwert*, susceptible to both being used as a substitute for and of being substituted by some other value from some other viewpoint. Also, as soon as 'human dignity' becomes a value, it becomes meaningful to ask if a human person is worth being treated for a condition, or, being transported to a location. If not, we can deny him a cure or refuse to sell him a ticket. As the value perspective, much in the same way as utilitarianism, subjects to 'evaluation–exploitation [*Verwertung*]', even that for which exploitation is not at all relevant it is fundamentally incompatible with the very idea of legal order, which presupposes (at least temporarily) rigid and stable rules. But where utilitarianism at least claims to specify objective criteria for choice, *Wertphilosophie* evaluates from a subjective perspective, a particular viewpoint, from which given values appear to impose themselves as overriding considerations. A legal order based on these values is therefore not based on 'categories, principles, or premises' but on 'sheer points', an ever-fluctuating series of changing perspectives (Schmitt 2011a: 12–25, 41–5/1996e: 3–11, 21–2; 2008b: 28/2008c: 52),[11]

---

10 '*Verwerten*' means 'to use', 'to exploit' or 'to convert into money', rather than 'to evaluate' but Schmitt seems to use it even when he clearly refers to simple 'evaluation', perhaps to play on the negative connotation of the prefix '*ver-*', as opposed to the neutral '*be-*'. In order to emphasize these connotations, 'to evaluate–exploit' will be used below.

11 That the Hegelian Alexandre Kojève, in the early 1940s, could in almost identical terms describe the perspectivism of what he calls 'bourgeois' or 'servile' justice (Kojève 1981: 291–7), raises the question of Schmitt's indebtedness to Hegel's view of the inner contradictions of the civil society (*bürgerliche Gesellschaft*) for his own criticism of liberal individualism.

whereas a well-functioning legal order would be based on principles and norms that rest on foundations above all and any purposes or perspectives individuals may have, even above the very idea of evaluating something from such perspectives (see Schmitt 2004a: 39–40, 56–7). Elsewhere (Schmitt 1925a: 109–12/2011b: 74–7) Schmitt offers another graphic description of reality reduced to points and every individual posing as the centrepiece of a subjective system of emanations, characterizing this kind of thinking, as a servant of 'whatever needs', as 'economic' rather than 'juridical' (Schmitt 1925b: 20–45/1996c: 14–33).

Empty humanity

Schönberger wonders (Schmitt 2011a: 79–83) whether Schmitt is inconsequent when he, after the War, appears to uphold the importance of formal legality and therefore to deny the foundational role of values in post-war constitutional review, whereas before and during the War he had always made a point of underlining the fact that formal legality was merely one corollary of liberal democracy which could work only in an historically exceptional state of political conditions in which 'normality' maintained itself without active intervention by the government (Schmitt 2005: 21–6/2004b: 19–24) and had nothing to do with the essential constitution, which consisted of a value-based political *Entscheidung* of the people to constitute itself as a political unit in a given manner.[12] A major problem with the formal legality of liberal democracy is precisely its value neutrality, as it not only destroys the very possibility of distinguishing between materially lawful and unlawful pieces of formally valid legislation (Schmitt 2005: 22–3, 47–53/2004b: 20–1, 47–55) but also undermines the unity that is the most important constitutive characteristic of a people organized into a political entity.[13] Schönberger believes that Schmitt's criticism of *Wertphilosophie* may to some degree be covertly directed against his own earlier, value-positing self (Schmitt 2011a: 77)[14] but despite this, he never changed his mind about the fundamental point that a value-free legality cannot constitute the people into a political unit because values, ever dependent on switching viewpoints, are necessarily plural (Schönberger, at

---

12 This is one of the main themes of *Constitutional Theory* (Schmitt 2003/2008a) as a whole.
13 According to, for example, *State, Movement, People* (Schmitt 1934b: 15–16, 22–6/2001: 15–16, 24–8), a liberal democracy is based upon an irreconcilable dichotomy between the state and the non-state or the 'free civil society', which exists outside the state and is independent of it, and the function of the constitution is to maintain a war of everyone against everyone (cf. Schmitt 2011a: 46/1996e: 23) and to prevent the state from subjecting the civil society to the requirements of a genuine political unity.
14 See footnote 18 below for an indication of why Schmitt, on his own theory, perhaps was able to think that during the National Socialist era, but not at other times, it was quite appropriate to posit and apply values directly.

Schmitt 2011a: 84; cf. Schmitt 2011a: 20, 43/1996e: 8, 22). Schmitt's rejection of the values he perhaps promoted during the National Socialist era does not entail a rejection of the theory according to which a people can only constitute itself as a political unit through an evaluative *Entscheidung*, for the political existence of a people does not require the choice of any specific values. It requires merely a decision, and decision implies choice. Choice, in turn, implies preference for one thing rather than another thing. This, I think, is what Schmitt means when he says that the *Entscheidung* must consist of a decision to distinguish between friend and foe:[15] no matter where the distinction is drawn, the essential thing is simply to distinguish, for the very notion of distinction entails adopting a stance towards one thing – metaphorically regarded as 'friend' – which is not the stance taken towards some other thing implicitly regarded as 'not friend' but 'foe' (Schmitt 2003: 226/2008a: 257–8). Plural values which thrive in conditions tempered by value-free legality are incapable of constituting the people into a political unit by way of such a distinction.

The political impotence of value-free legality is a consequence of 'the universal neutralization' of the values that it engenders, coupled with 'limitless relativism and tolerance' (Schmitt 2011a: 20, 43/1996e: 8, 22). From the neutrality of the state towards values, it follows that the values themselves become neutral: *ne utrum*, 'neither' – neither friends nor foes, all 'equally valued', thereby necessarily indifferent and irrelevant. Such quasi-values cannot provide a basis for any meaningful distinction. Politics will, for one thing, become non-political in that one begins to suppose that political choices cannot be legitimized with reference to specific values but, rather, ought always to be made on the basis of professional expertise (*Sachlichkeit*), acquiring thereby the false pose of being mere technical applications of knowledge and necessary reactions to the pressing demands of the objective facts (Schmitt 1996b: 108–11). For another thing, as indirectly indicated in the *Introduction* to *The Tyranny of Values* (Schmitt 2011a: 11–12/1996e: 2–3), the value of 'human dignity' as a purported foundation for basic rights is 'indeterminate'. This statement must be read in the light of what Schmitt has previously written about egalitarian democracy and liberal individualism as a basis for government. In the last analysis they depend on the notion that the politically relevant aspect of man is his universal humanity as such, and that the fundamental values which the state is to safeguard is their freedom and equality, precisely in their universal capacity of being human. But men, as mere individual members of the human species, appear all the same only because we abstract them thereby from all their different properties and different situations. 'Universal

---

15   'Foe' is used here only to maintain Schmitt's original alliteration, with no regard whatever to any eventual difference between the connotations of 'foe' and 'enemy'.

humanity' is therefore an empty abstraction with no significant content whatsoever, except perhaps *vis-à-vis* the members of some alien species. It follows that it cannot provide any sort of criteria for any kind of *Entscheidung* within the human species, and least of all a political decision, because decision presupposes distinction, and a property shared by all in the relevant class can quite obviously in no way constitute any distinction between its members. The value of 'human dignity' can supply a foundation for a club engaged in an endless discussion on 'human freedom' or 'human equality', but not for a constitution which must distinguish between different parts or aspects of humanity in order to be able to constitute a people into a political unit (Schmitt 2004a: 106–7/1996a: 16–18/ 2000: 10–12/2003: 226–34/2008a: 257–64/1963: 70–1/1996d: 70–71/ Schmitt 1934b: 44/Schmitt 2001: 50–51). 'Who says "humanity", wants to betray' (Schmitt 1963: 55/1996d: 54)[16] or to make believe that a 'hominizing society' can make true what *The Principle of Hope* promises; namely, make Man 'man to man' and create not only this new Man but also the conditions of his very possibility (Schmitt 2008b: 31/2008c: 54).[17]

Order or Utopia

It turns out that Schmitt is indeed a Catholic thinker. If anything significant is to be said about men, it must be said about them as members of some concrete order (*konkrete Ordnung*) and the Catholic Church is a concrete order *par excellence*, as *Roman Catholicism and Political Form* (Schmitt 1925b/1996c) as a whole shows. And as Saint Paul writes to the Corinthians (I Cor. 12), Christian society is not a homogeneous mass but an organic whole, a body whose members have different capacities and therefore different tasks, which must be distinguished. The material content of humanity is provided by the different positions and roles that individual persons occupy in society. The state, again, is based on a real representation of these positions and roles and an individual is, from that perspective, nothing but an accidental carrier of a function of state (Schmitt 2004a: 86–94; for a conceptual clarification of, and a slightly different emphasis on, Schmitt's notion of 'representation', see Falk 2016, Chapter 12 in this volume).

A possibility for meaningful social representation would also seem to be a necessary prerequisite for a genuine distinction between friend and foe. In a state based on an 'economic' rather than a 'juridical' rationality, like

---

16 In *Roman Catholicism and Political Form* (Schmitt 1925b: 45–9/1996c: 33–6), the appeal to 'humanity', in a sharp analysis of Mozart's *Zauberflöte*, is presented as a devious stratagem of elitist revolutionaries who think they know what is best for the people better than the people themselves.
17 The reference to *The Principle of Hope* is to Ernst Bloch's (1995) psychoanalytical Utopia.

the liberal bourgeois or the Marxist proletarian state, there will, in the end, be nothing to represent against anything different (see Schmitt 1925b: 26–8/1996c: 18–20) and consequently, no basis whatever for any meaningful political distinction. An obvious further application of this view to 'the human rights', inasmuch as they are conceived of as something like pieces of private property owned by abstract individuals, is that they are nothing but void abstractions, unsusceptible of distinction and incapable of meaningful representation. Rights can only truly be held in a real relationship between persons representing their real interests within a concrete order. In different words, they are fundamentally objective, rather than subjective, rights to remain in a right relationship to others (that this is a by and large Catholic view of rights; see, for example, Henle 1981 and Pizzorni 1993).

To sum up, an existential value-based decision which distinguishes between friend and foe is what essentially constitutes the people as a state. A central function of this self-constitution of the people is to provide a safeguard against a direct imposition of arbitrary values by individual subjects on each other. The legal order provides therefore a predictable medium which only allows values to have an indirect effect through relatively stable and permanent rules. To base the application of the law directly on values is to open a broad avenue for the members of the judiciary to posit their different and ever changing personal convictions as sources of law, thereby undermining the very capacity of the legal order to perform its mediating function.[18] Most dangerous of all is the now so fashionable appeal to the value of 'human dignity', to 'human rights', to 'human equality' or to 'human freedom', to 'the universal value of humanity' at large, because all these notions are empty and non-committal (*nichtssagend*). Lacking the courage to treat 'the unequal unequally' (Schmitt 1934b: 32/2001: 36), they pretend to treat the equal equally, hiding from sight the fact that the very concept of 'treatment' implies a decision to treat in one way, rather than in some other way, which again presupposes a distinction – which, in turn, can only be made between unequals. Thus, the distinction between friend and foe which is an essential prerequisite of the existence of a people as a political community, is diluted to the point of obfuscating the very purpose of the state for its constituent members. In Schmitt's 'normal conditions' this can, perhaps, go on indefinitely, but only as long as the people can be deceived into believing that a direct application of values to

---

18 Values, readily posing as timeless notions, are too unspecific to perform this mediating function in a time when they are not self-evident. Conversely, an immediate application of values can work in a time in which they are immediately evident – and thereby timeless – to all those whom the state represents (see Schmitt 2004a: 75, 80–1, 107).

legal judgment is not what it is, namely a devious cover for the exercise of naked political power. In the end the scales will fall off the eyes of the people, the 'normal conditions' will need to be redefined and perhaps another *Movement*, as in 1933, will help the people to constitute itself anew along the lines of a different set of values.

However, if values, as Schmitt argues, are as dysfunctional to the working of human society as they are necessary for its political constitution, what can we do, and should we care? The sheer fact that mankind has not gone under yet may show that the fictive and mythical notions, values and value-laden principles, which it is our instinct to entertain, despite their being almost invariably rationally unfounded, mysteriously serve our practical needs, and that history is a cemetery of *élites*, each promoting its own myths and fallacies, until the next one takes over (cf. Pareto 1923/1935, as a whole and in particular chapter XI: § 2002–XIV). In the 1920s and the 1930s, the *élites* in question were the liberal egalitarian democrats at large and the daydreaming constitutional formalists in particular. In the 1950s, they were the lemurs hanging freedom values in the gum tree of Karlsruhe for us to worship in the name of basic rights (Schönberger at Schmitt 2011a: 87). In the 1960s they were the proponents of an 'untheologized', 'value free' political science which would create a new mankind without distinctions – thus creating a nothing, *ne utrum*, not even *tabula rasa* but a tablet untableted even of its emptiness, an un-unned self-creating process–progress which feeds on what it can evaluate–exploit (*verwerten*) and discards or destroys what it has no use for on its unending way to nowhere, a Utopia of novelty (Schmitt 2008b: 96–8/2008c: 127–30).[19]

Were Schmitt alive today, in the new millennium, he would surely pay the attention they deserve to those greening human rights-stricken sprouts of this process–progress who now no longer know how to distinguish between well-founded distinction and arbitrary discrimination.

---

19 Schmitt leaves us to guess what this 'process–progress' consists of. An indication of what he quite arguably has in mind can be found in Hannah Arendt's analysis of the modern 'progressing process' which, in order to maintain a self-feeding motion of unending economic growth, transforms 'action' and 'work' into an automatic process of 'labour', reduces men to replaceable units of production and consumption, and occupies the 'public realm' of political action with merely 'private activities displayed in the open'. Distinction by class and specialization will be replaced by a division of undifferentiated labour and the public political community of citizens will yield to a welfare 'society', which merely households the private needs of its clients in public (Arendt 1958: 105–35, 294–325).

Bibliography

Arendt, H. (1958) *The Human Condition*. Chicago, IL: Chicago University Press.
Bloch, E. (1995) *The Principle of Hope*. Volumes 1–3 [1954–1959]. Trans. N. Plaice, S. Plaice and P. Knight. Cambridge, MA: MIT Press.
Falk, H. (2016) '*Im Kampf um Rom*': Carl Schmitt's Critique of Rudolph Sohm and the Post-secular Turn', Chapter 12 in M. Arvidsson, L. Brännström and P. Minkkinen (eds), *The Contemporary Relevance of Carl Schmitt. Law, Politics, Theology*. Abingdon: Routledge.
Dilthey, W. (1958) *System der Ethik. Gesammelte Schriften. X. Band*. Stuttgart: B. G. Teubner.
Hartmann, N. (1933) *Das Problem des geistigen Seins. Untersuchungen zur Grundlegung der Geschichtsphilosophie und der Geisteswissenschaften*. Berlin: Walter de Gruyter.
Hartmann, N. (1951) *Ethics. Vol. Two: Moral Values* [1932]. 2nd edn. Trans. S. Coit. New York: Macmillan.
Hartmann, N. (1958) *Ethics. Vol. One: Moral Phenomena* [1932]. 2nd edn. Trans. S. Coit. New York: Macmillan.
Hartmann, N. (1962) *Ethik* [1926]. 4. unveränderte Aufl. Berlin: Walter de Gruyter.
Henle, R. J. (1981) 'A Catholic View of Human Rights: A Thomistic Reflection', p. 87–93, in A. S. Rosenbaum (ed.), *The Philosophy of Human Rights: International Perspectives*. London: Aldwych.
Kojève, A (1981) *Esquisse d'une phénoménologie du droit. Exposé provisoire*. Mayenne: Gallimard.
Minkkinen, P. (2016) 'A Law Without the Political: Carl Schmitt, Romanticism, and Friedrich Dürrenmatt's *The Execution of Justice*', Chapter 5 in M. Arvidsson, L. Brännström and P. Minkkinen (eds), *The Contemporary Relevance of Carl Schmitt. Law, Politics, Theology*. Abingdon: Routledge.
Moore, G. E. (1951) *Principia Ethica* [1903]. Cambridge: Cambridge University Press.
Pareto, V. (1935) *The Mind and Society* [1916]. Trans. A. Bongiorno and A. Livingston, with J. H. Rogers. New York: Harcourt, Brace.
Pareto, V. (1923) *Trattato di sociologia generale* [1916]. 2:a edizione. Firenze: G. Barbèra.
Pizzorni, R. M. (1993) 'Persona umana e diritti dell'uomo', *Persona y Derecho*, Vol. 28: 85–119.
Schmitt, C. (1925a) *Politische Romantik* [1919]. 2. Aufl. München: Duncker and Humblot.
Schmitt, C. (1925b) *Römischer Katholizismus und politische Form* [1923]. München: Theatiner-Verlag.
Schmitt, C. (1934a) *Politische Theologie. Vier Kapitel zur Lehre von der Souverenität* [1922]. München: Duncker and Humblot.
Schmitt, C. (1934b) *Staat, Bewegung, Volk. Die Dreigliederung der politischen Einheit* [1933]. 2. Aufl. Hamburg: Hanseatischer Verlagsanstalt.
Schmitt, C. (1963) *Der Begriff des Politischen*. Text von 1932 mit einem Vorwort und Corollarien [1932]. 6. Aufl. 4. Nachdruck der Ausgabe von 1963. Berlin: Duncker and Humblot.
Schmitt, C. (1985) *Political Theology. Four Chapters on the Concept of Sovereignty* [1922]. Trans. G. Schwab. Cambridge, MA: MIT Press.

Schmitt, C. (1996a) *Die geistesgeschichtliche Lage des heutigen Parlamentarismus* [1923]. 8. Aufl. Berlin: Duncker and Humblot.
Schmitt, C. (1996b) *Der Hüter der Verfassung* [1931]. 4. Aufl. Berlin: Duncker and Humblot.
Schmitt, C. (1996c) *Roman Catholicism and Political Form* [1923]. Trans. G. L. Ulmen. Westport, CT: Greenwood.
Schmitt, C. (1996d) *The Concept of the Political* [1932]. Trans. G. Schwab. Chicago, IL: Chicago University Press.
Schmitt, C. (1996e) *The Tyranny of Values* [1967]. Trans. S. Draghici. Washington, DC: Plutarch.
Schmitt, C. (2000) *The Crisis of Parliamentary Democracy* [1923]. Trans. E. Kennedy. Cambridge, MA: MIT Press.
Schmitt, C. (2001) *State, Movement, People* [1933]. *The Triadic Structure of the Political Unity* [1933]. *The Question of Legality* [1950]. Trans. S. Draghici. Washington DC: Plutarch.
Schmitt, C. (2003) *Verfassungslehre* [1928]. 9. Aufl. Berlin: Duncker and Humblot.
Schmitt, C. (2004a) *Der Wert des Staates und die Bedeutung des Einzelnen* [1914]. 2. Aufl. Berlin: Duncker and Humblot.
Schmitt, C. (2004b) *Legality and Legitimacy* [1932]. Trans. J. Seitzer. Durham, NC: Duke University Press.
Schmitt, C. (2004c) *On the Three Types of Juristic Thought* [1934]. Trans. J. Bendersky. Westport, CT: Praeger.
Schmitt, C. (2005) *Legalität und Legitimität* [1932]. 7. Aufl. Berlin: Duncker and Humblot.
Schmitt, C. (2006) *Über die drei Arten des rechtswissenschaftlichen Denkens* [1934]. 3. Aufl. Berlin: Duncker and Humblot.
Schmitt, C. (2008a) *Constitutional Theory* [1928]. Trans. J. Seitzer. Durham, NC: Duke University Press.
Schmitt, C. (2008b) *Politische Theologie II. Die Legende von der Erledigung jeder politischen Theologie* [1970]. 5. Aufl. Berlin: Duncker and Humblot.
Schmitt, C. (2008c) *Political Theology II. The Myth of the Closure of any Political Theology* [1970]. Trans. M. Hoelzl and G. Ward. Malden, MA: Polity.
Schmitt, C. (2011a) *Die Tyrannei der Werte* [1967]. 3. korrigierte Aufl. mit Nachwort von Christoph Schönberger. Berlin: Duncker and Humblot.
Schmitt, C. (2011b) *Political Romanticism* [1919]. Trans. G. Oakes. Cambridge, MA: MIT Press.
Vinx, L. (ed.) (2015) *The Guardian of the Constitution. Hans Kelsen and Carl Schmitt on the Limits of Constitutional Law.* Trans. L. Vinx. Cambridge: Cambridge University Press.

Chapter 5

A law without the political
Carl Schmitt, romanticism, and Friedrich Dürrenmatt's *The Execution of Justice*

Panu Minkkinen

Apolitics

The protagonist of Friedrich Dürrenmatt's (1921–1990) late novel *The Execution of Justice* from 1985 (Dürrenmatt 1990/1985; see also Henry 2007)[1] is a young and unaccomplished lawyer called Felix Spät. Shortly before his final downfall, Spät contemplates on his predicament in the following way:

> I needed a bottle of whiskey ... I realized that I couldn't live without whiskey, the panic-stricken fear overcame me that I wouldn't be able to get hold of any whiskey, while everything in me rebelled against drinking anything but whiskey, wine, say, or beer or schnapps or even the hard cider that clochards drink here (which is why they have bad livers but no rheumatism), some remnant of human dignity in me demanded that I drink only whiskey, for the sake of justice, which was destroying me.
> (Dürrenmatt 1990: 171/1985: 134)

How does justice destroy Spät? Can justice destroy anyone? By addressing these questions, this chapter attempts to formulate a response by making a claim about the relationship between law and politics that draws on Carl Schmitt and by illustrating how that Schmittian claim configures in Dürrenmatt's novel.[2] The chapter first discusses Schmitt's notion of

---

1 All quotes are from the English edition. References to the German original have also been given. Bernhard Auge has written a thorough analysis of the novel (see Auge 2004) and it has also been adapted into a film by the German director Hans Geißendörfer (Geißendörfer *et al.* 1993).

2 In terms of the conventional ways of pairing thinkers together, there is no evidence of Dürrenmatt and Schmitt having ever met or known of each other's work. Dürrenmatt's second wife, the German documentarist Charlotte Kerr (1927–2011), was, however, acquainted with the German author Ernst Jünger who, in turn, was a close friend of Schmitt (on Schmitt and Jünger, see Junger and Schmitt 1999; see also Björk 2016, Chapter 8 in this volume). These distant relations of acquaintance may, then, suggest a certain intellectual kinship.

political romanticism and its relationship to law. Schmitt argues that a genuinely legal position is by necessity antithetical in relation to romanticism, but in this chapter, I also attempt to flesh out an apolitical position in relation to law that will be called 'juridical romanticism'. Next the chapter depicts how the position of the lawyer protagonist in Dürrenmatt's novel sways between the political and the apolitical during the course of the plot. Finally, after the special case of a 'romantic politics' as a form of Quixotism has been considered, the chapter concludes with more general remarks on how Schmitt's definition of romanticism can help us understand the political deadlocks of legal liberalism.

Romanticism and law

There is a strain in contemporary legal scholarship that I propose to call 'juridical romanticism'. Although the expression is not altogether satisfactory, it attempts to portray a legal variant of Schmitt's definition of political romanticism. Its essential feature is to assume that, despite the evidence, there is always something more to law than meets the eye, something perhaps intangible and yet feasible (on law and romanticism from a more conventional perspective, see Hewitt 2007). In juridical romanticism, this something includes within itself a potential redemption, a positive possibility that is suspended and banished into a limbo from where it cannot actualize itself. Nor is it meant to be actualized, because it should only remain a possibility. This type of juridical romanticism is often expressed with the vocabulary of 'justice'.

Here the chapter takes its cue from Schmitt's short and rather muddled 1919 pamphlet *Political Romanticism* (Schmitt 1986/1998).[3] The book can well be called 'muddled' because the literature that it deals with polemically (for example, political scientist and economist Adam Müller) is esoteric at best and is certainly not drawn from the canon of modern political philosophy. From this literature Schmitt extracts several commonly held assumptions about romanticism from which he then moves towards a definition.

According to one such assumption, certain objects and notions are regarded as romantic in themselves. This inherent romantic quality would then be independent of the position that one takes on the object or notion

---

3   In the first edition (Schmitt-Dorotič 1919), Schmitt uses his first wife's supposedly aristocratic Serbian surname alongside his own. Later Pawla Dorotič was exposed as a fraud and the couple divorced. Although the book is one of Schmitt's less influential, John P. McCormick provides an excellent contextualization, especially in relation to Weber (McCormick 1997: 46–53). Kierkegaard is a major influence (see Ryan 2011). Reinhard Mehring's biography also provides a good intellectual contextualization (Mehring 2014: 84–96; see also Mehring 2006). I would like to thank Heike Jung for bringing this to my attention.

in question. A piece of music (for example, Brahms) or lines of lyric poetry (for example, Goethe) would accordingly be regarded as romantic because they induce particular emotions, moods and sentiments. Schmitt's view is quite different. Things are not romantic in themselves. Romanticism is always a stance or an attitude that one can have in relation to practically anything. The romantic sentiment is, then, in the 'eye of the beholder'. It is this attitude that Schmitt then proceeds to explicate in more detail and especially in relation to politics (Schmitt 1986: 104–5/1998: 110–11).

For the romantic genius as Schmitt understands it, an object or a notion has no objective qualities. It exists only as something that can serve an aesthetic interest, and it is 'real' only in so far as it provides an occasion for an emotional experience. Schmitt pinpoints the birth of the romantic genius as coinciding with the demise of God as the ultimate metaphysical principle (see also Schmitt 1996/2008). In the post-Cartesian world, God is replaced by two new demiurges. One is a revolutionary; the other a conservative. One is a constituent force that creates; the other restores or conserves what has been created (Schmitt 1986: 59–64/1998: 68–75). The romantic world becomes possible in the tension between the two. As society disintegrates into atomized individuals, the aesthetically productive romantic genius can shift the intellectual centre of the world on to itself. For Schmitt, such a world is a bourgeois world where the individual is isolated in the domain of the intellectual and becomes its own point of reference:

> In this society, it is left to the private individual to be his own priest. But not only that. Because of the central significance and consistency of the religious, it is also left to him to be his own poet, his own philosopher, his own king, and his own master builder in the cathedral of his personality. The ultimate roots of romanticism and the romantic phenomenon lie in the private priesthood.
> (Schmitt 1986: 20/1998: 20–1)

Romanticism in Schmitt's sense does not deny the existence of a more objective reality for that would require the recognition of an alternative objectivism which would destroy the very foundation of the romantic attitude. So romanticism does not replace reality with an alternative but it suspends it allowing the romantic genius to exercise its imagination within the universe of infinite possibilities that is left in the suspended space.

The romantically inclined will, for example, not renounce the existence of a legal reality, for romanticism has no ontological grounds for doing so. Instead, the romantic allows her or his imagination to suspend that reality, to push it into the distance, so that she or he can freely pursue her or his aesthetic objectives. This type of juridical romanticism is essentially about aestheticizing the law. As a result, the theoretical and practical contradictions that make up the reality of law are reduced to mere aesthetic contrasts that imply neither choice nor decision but only the possibility to stir pleasurable emotions. When the romantic encounters poverty, to take another example, she or he will not deny its existence. But the romantic attitude, intent on seeking emotional stimulation, will paraphrase the implied opposition of wealth and poverty in aesthetic terms and elevate it into reconciled notions such as the Arcadian myth of the ennobling quality of simple peasant life or the 'dignified humility' of the deprived working class. And so the romantic does not have to confront reality but neither does she or he have to deny its existence.

Similarly, the juridically romantic cannot see the law merely as a set of oppositions such as legal and illegal, right and wrong, or even just and unjust. For the romantic, 'justice' can never be reduced to a simple choice or decision between what is just and what is unjust. Justice is always something more than these crude oppositions suggest. It is a 'third', a sublimated reconciliation beyond the dichotomy of just and unjust that suspends the legal reality of politically relevant choices leaving the romantic imagination free to entertain itself with aesthetically more pleasing alternatives. Justice is never here and now. It will, for instance, remain 'to come', like Jacques Derrida's '*à-venir*', but in a truly messianic sense, without the paradox created by the simultaneous urgency of an immediate decision (see Derrida 1992: 26–7/1994: 60–1; on Derrida and Schmitt, see De Ville 2016, Chapter 9 in this volume, and the literature quoted therein).

For Schmitt, law is, in fact, antithetical in relation to romanticism:

> Any relationship to a legal or moral judgement would be incongruous here, and every norm would seem to be an antiromantic tyranny. A legal or a moral decision would be senseless and it would inevitably destroy romanticism. This is why the romantic is not in a position to deliberately take sides and make a decision.
> (Schmitt 1986: 124/1998: 126)

Thus, in Schmitt's definition, romanticism essentially implies the absence of a politically relevant decision. In a way, the terms 'political romanticism' and 'juridical romanticism' are both oxymorons. If the key characteristic of politics is a decision, and romanticism, by definition, rules a decision out, then 'political romanticism' would be an apolitical politics, a politics without the political. And in Schmitt's terms, law is always political.

The fiction

How can we identify these themes in Dürrenmatt's novel? There should be no doubt that the Swiss author's satirical prose is by nature political, at least in the more conventional sense of the term (on Dürrenmatt's politics, see Federico 1989). The politics of the novel can be viewed on three different albeit overlapping levels. *The Execution of Justice* is, firstly and perhaps for the most part, a political intervention in relation to literature and writing. Apart from its law-related main theme, much of the novel is a contemplation on the complex relationship between literature and reality. But like most of Dürrenmatt's plays and novels, it is also a critique of Swiss society and of bourgeois life and values more generally. Although Dürrenmatt was politically often pragmatic in his views, he was a member of the progressive writers' guild Gruppe Olten together with his more radical compatriots like Max Frisch and Peter Bichsel (on Dürrenmatt's and Frisch's strained friendship, see Frisch and Dürrenmatt 2011). Lastly, and this would be the level emphasized here, beyond Zürich or Switzerland, the book is also a critique about apolitical positions in general.

More specifically, the law-related theme in Dürrenmatt's novel can be seen as a critique of the type of 'juridical romanticism' outlined above.[4] But its potential does not lie in the hidden poetic qualities of the text that need to be extracted by hermeneutic close readings. In fact, it has much more to do with the plot and how that plot animates the relationship between the novel's two main characters. The story unfolds in three diachronically arranged parts. The first part sets the scene, while the second weaves the net into which the first-person narrator gets tangled. Both are recounted by Spät himself as 'an orderly report' (Dürrenmatt 1990: 3/1985: 5), as a written record of his account of the events, and they are addressed to the public prosecutor as a sort of testament to be read after Spät has exonerated himself by committing suicide. The third and last part, written later and seemingly signed by Dürrenmatt himself, attempts to tie together the loose ends in Spät's confused and porous account but without much success. This second narrator can only be 'seemingly' the author of the novel because a first-person Dürrenmatt commenting on the report written by a fictive character that the author himself has created is, of course, a fictive character himself.

The novel begins, as many novels about law do, with a crime. And it is an audacious crime at that. One spring evening in 1955, Doctor *honoris causa* Isaak Kohler, or simply 'Dr. h.c.' as Spät often abbreviates him, canton deputy *emeritus* and affluent businessman, pulls up in his chauffeured Rolls Royce in front of the restaurant Café Du Théâtre where the *Zürcher*

---

4   Many of Dürrenmatt's main works touch upon themes related to law and justice (see, for example, Crockett 1998: 80–103; Daviaua 1982), most famously, perhaps, his 'existential detective novels' *The Judge and His Hangman* (1950) and *Suspicion* (1951–2) (both available in English as Dürrenmatt 2006a; see also Gillis 1962). The play 'The Visit' (1956) and the essay 'Monster Lecture on Justice and Law, with a Helvetian Interlude' (1968) are available in English in the first and third volumes, respectively, of his selected works (Dürrenmatt 2006b).

bourgeoisie is just beginning dinner. As he enters the restaurant, he takes a quick look around the dining room, then walks directly towards Professor Adolf Winter, a Germanist and liberal arts scholar and author of the two-volume treatize *Carl Spitteler and Hesiod, or Switzerland and Greece: A Comparison*,[5] and shoots him dead with a revolver in plain sight. In his account Spät suggests that writing such a preposterous piece of academic rubbish would be quite enough to get anyone shot, but this is apparently not the case here. Kohler murders his victim calmly, 'not without having first greeted him amiably' (Dürrenmatt 1990: 11/1985: 11), as the novel tells us. He then walks composedly out of the restaurant, gets back into his Rolls Royce, and drives off.

Kohler is later brought into custody and tried. Although the public cannot quite comprehend why a distinguished member of society would commit such a brutal crime, especially as he never volunteers a motive for his actions, the overzealous and generally disliked prosecutor Jämmerlin manages to convince the court that Kohler is an amoral monster that murders merely for the thrill of it. Kohler does nothing to rebut this depiction and accepts the verdict and sentence thanking fervently the prosecutor and all five appellate court judges for the professionalism with which they have tried his case. And so, as the novel tells us, 'the rolling wheels of justice had set an exceptional example, and as he [Kohler] was led away, the curtain seemed to have fallen on an unambiguous, though not thoroughly elucidated, affair' (Dürrenmatt 1990: 37/1985: 30). The original German title of the novel is *Justiz* and, although the etymology would suggest some affiliation with 'justice' understood as '*iustitia*', it is actually these procedural 'rolling wheels' to which the title refers; hence the English translation *The Execution of Justice*.

While serving his sentence, Kohler summons Spät, the young lawyer that he has once briefly met a few years earlier, to visit him in prison. Spät is initially intrigued because he hopes that such a notorious criminal would instruct him to prepare an appeal. But instead Kohler has quite a different kind of request: 'You are to reinvestigate my case under the presumption that I was not the murderer ... You are to create a fiction, nothing more' (Dürrenmatt 1990: 50/1985: 40).

Spät is suspicious of this unusual and legally meaningless instruction because it is so obviously clear who the murderer is. So Kohler explains:

> You see, my dear Spät, we know very well what reality is, that's why I'm in here weaving baskets, but we hardly know what possibility is. Possibility is something almost limitless, while reality is set within strictest limits, since, after all, only one of all those possibilities can

---

5 Carl Spitteler (1845–1924) was a Swiss poet and Nobel laureate 1919.

become reality. Reality is only an exception to the rule of possibility, and can therefore be thought of quite differently too. From which follows that we must rethink reality in order to forge ahead into possibility.

(Dürrenmatt 1990: 50/1985: 41)

Although Spät initially regards Kohler's instruction as a 'pact with the devil' (Dürrenmatt 1990: 51/1985: 41) and declines, he is later too fascinated to resist. What could Kohler be up to? Spät could also use the rather handsome fee that Kohler is prepared to pay. And so the young lawyer accepts Kohler's offer.

During the course of his investigations, Spät visits Kohler's residence. He sees a billiard table and a library full of books on natural science. Kohler's motive for the murder comes to Spät like an epiphany. It was neither lust nor love as it usually is. No, Kohler's motive was scientific:

> He loved billiards not as a game for itself but because it served him as a model of reality. As one of its possible simplifications ... Kohler busied himself with natural science and mathematics for the same reason. They, too, offered him 'models of reality'. Except that these models were not enough for him, he had to move on to murder in order to create a new 'model'. He was experimenting by using a crime, murder was merely a method.
>
> (Dürrenmatt 1990: 73/1985: 59; see also Wright 1981)

As Spät continues his investigations, he comes to realize that by accepting the offer, he has been lured into a sinister fabrication of the truth. Spät, of course, knows that his client is guilty and so should the justice system too. But an accumulation of wishful thinking, public sentiments and rumours to which Spät's investigations have contributed in a significant way, have manufactured an alternative possibility: Kohler was, in fact, wrongly convicted and the real murderer is a certain Dr. Benno, former Swiss champion in pistol shooting and excellent marksman, whom most of the *Zürcher* bourgeoisie would much prefer to see convicted as the murderer. And so Kohler is acquitted and Benno is tried for the murder.

Involvement in Kohler's acquittal contrary to the facts triggers Spät's own downfall as he indulges in excessive drinking and frequent visits to prostitutes. Now, as a member of the *demimonde*, he must also reassess what justice means to him. For Spät, the only way to redeem himself is to undo the false reality that he has participated in creating. Under these extraordinary circumstances, it can only be achieved by murdering the guilty Kohler after which Spät himself must commit suicide. Mocking his own drunken literary pathos, Spät summarizes the existential significance of his situation:

perhaps the answer to the question lies lurking behind it all, perhaps it will unexpectedly break out of each conceivable human situation and constellation, like an assault from an ambush. The answer will be the judgement spoken upon us, and the carrying out of that judgement, the truth. I want to believe that. Passionately and steadfastly. Not for the sake of the exquisite society in which I vegetate, not for the sake of these intolerable relics that surround me, but for the sake of justice, for the love of which I act, must act, in the hope of preserving my last scrap of humanity ... Therefore I have no other choice ... but to drink, to whore, to report, to register my doubts, to punctuate with question marks, and to wait, to wait, until truth reveals itself, until that cruel goddess unveils herself ... That will not happen on these pages, the truth is not a formula that can be jotted down, it lies outside every attempt at speech, outside all poesy, only when justice bursts upon us, only when justice carries out its own eternal execution of justice, will it take effect, only then will we surmize it. Truth will be when one day I stand before Dr. h.c. Kohler, eye to eye, when I effect justice and execute its judgement.

(Dürrenmatt 1990: 119–20/1985: 92–3)

A law without the political

How can, then, the relationship between the two main protagonists of Dürrenmatt's novel be characterized with reference to the juridical romanticism outlined above?

Kohler's position in relation to the legal significance of his own actions is evidently romantic. For him, legal reality is merely an imposition on the possibilities that are available to him in his romantic play. Kohler's world unfolds as a constellation of infinite possibilities where the romantic genius can find delight in making the unexpected happen. Even one of the key metaphors of the novel is playing billiards '*à la bande*', manipulating the game with inventive strokes off the cushion.[6] Neither does Kohler view his own predicament in terms of legal oppositions as, for example, just and unjust or guilty and innocent. Instead, his romantic position fuses these oppositions into a counterfactual 'third', an acquittal that addresses neither justice nor guilt. Kohler is not freed because he is decidedly innocent but because Dr. Benno steps into his place regardless of the former's undeniable guilt. This replacement is a kind of paraphrased option, a romantic reconciliation beyond the either-or oppositions of the law.

Spät's position, on the other hand, is more complicated. His original attitude is reflected in his legally motivated reluctance to accept Kohler's

---

6   The manipulation of reality is a recurrent theme in Dürrenmatt; it is also the title and theme of Ulrich Weber's (2006) analysis.

offer and this would seem to correspond with the anti-romantic position of formal legalism with its rigid conceptualism and decisionism that Schmitt also endorses. But as Spät accepts the offer and is lured into Kohler's world, he also aligns himself with his client's romantic attitude. Even though he cannot see what the point of his instruction is because there is no doubt about Kohler's guilt, he willingly participates in the fabrication of the fiction, if only to satisfy his own curiosity. In the end, he tries to redeem himself by destroying the fiction he has created: 'Justice can be restored only by a crime' (Dürrenmatt 1990: 4/1985: 6).

But Spät never quite manages to find his way back into his original anti-romantic legalism. Perhaps his relentless commitment to the execution of justice can be described as a romantic politics, a position that Schmitt was keen to distinguish from what he understood as political romanticism. And for Schmitt, the archetypal representative of such romantic politics is Don Quixote:

> When enthusiasm for his ideal of chivalry and an indignation over supposed injustice drove the poor knight to senseless disregard of external reality, still he did not withdraw aesthetically into his own subjectivity, composing complaints for a criticism of the present. His sincere zeal brought him into situations in which the romantic sense of superiority became impossible. His battles were fantastically absurd. But they were still battles in which he exposed himself to personal dangers, not battles of the higher sort ... He had the enthusiasm of a real knight for his rank, not the enthusiasm of a bourgeois for the impressive image of an aristocracy.
> (Schmitt 1986: 147–8/1998: 153)

Not being able to accomplish his task, Spät describes his own Quixotism in the following way:

> Executing justice is something different from having to live in the expectation of executing it. I feel like some frenzied madman. My drinking like this is simply an expression of my absurd position; it's as if I were drunk on justice. The feeling of being in the right is destroying me. Nothing is more horrifying than this feeling. I am executing myself, because I cannot execute old man Kohler.
> (Dürrenmatt 1990: 84/1985: 67; see also Bühler 2011)

Thus, in the end, justice destroys Spät because the plot carries him from his original politically relevant legalism first to the romantic position of his client and, finally, motivated by a desire to retract to a third position, a dislocated romantic legalism that has all the makings of a politics but is too much at odds with the surrounding world to be regarded as anything other than absurd.

Schmitt's notion of romanticism is undoubtedly simplistic (see e.g. Löwy and Sayre 2001: 2–3) and one could well claim that it reduces a complex historical, cultural and political phenomenon into a few catchy sound bites. But perhaps Schmitt's focus is not really romanticism in itself. And its aim is certainly not historical description. If we situate *Political Romanticism* within the scope of Schmitt's 'pamphleteering' over the next few decades, then it would be fairly safe to assume that the target of the book goes beyond romanticism understood in any precise narrow sense. And here we may also draw some parallels to Dürrenmatt's novel.

Firstly, political romanticism in Schmitt's meaning can also be a metonymic expression for liberalism in general or for a particular 'aestheticizing' aspect of liberalism (see, for example, Galli 2000). In this way, Schmitt's metonymic object of critique would roughly correspond with the lives and times of the *Zürcher* bourgeoisie that Dürrenmatt uses as a springboard for his own critique. Secondly, Schmitt's confrontation with romanticism is highly polemical and antagonistic, and his scornful style of writing is at times closer to literary satire than to the traditions of academic writing. Taking into account Schmitt's own definition of politics outlined in *The Concept of the Political* (Schmitt 2007/1991) less than ten years later, it is, then, no surprise that Schmitt identifies romanticism with the absence of politics: 'Where political activity begins, political romanticism ends' (Schmitt 1986: 160/1998: 178) Politics, on the other hand, is only possible through the polemical identification of an enemy. And if Schmitt intended his own critique of romanticism to be political, then the antagonistic confrontation is unavoidable. This politicization is, then, not an insincere 'methodological abuse' (see, for example, Müller 1999), but an inevitable and necessary feature of Schmitt's own metapolitical position.

Schmitt's pamphlet enters into confrontation with a particular aspect of liberalism, namely its tendency to avoid political antagonisms and to defuse them into consensual deliberation. In today's legal landscape, the most obvious example of such a law-related romanticism would be the appeal of transitional justice as an antidote to the limitations of legal formality (see Minkkinen 2007). The individual institutions of transitional justice are usually introduced as attempts to resolve particular historical deadlocks, the South African Truth and Reconciliation Committee being the most obvious example (for a critical account, see, for example, Wilson 2001). But juridical romanticism has also adopted the inherent themes of forgiveness and reconciliation as a more general ethos of human rights applicable in other transformative environments (Teitel 2003; more generally, see, for example, Williams *et al.* 2012).

The resulting penumbral vocabulary of 'mainstreamed' human rights (Koskenniemi 2010) conveys the issues at hand beyond the either–or choices of a politically relevant law. The victimizer is never entirely 'guilty' but neither is the victim 'innocent' in any legally significant way. Conflicts are 'resolved' by 'parties' rather than 'decided upon' by 'authorities'. Because no decision is taken, endless deliberations will follow. In fact, deliberative democracy provides an excellent example of the apolitical romantic position (see, for example, Mouffe 2000). The allegedly democratic outcome of deliberation is not a decisive choice between possibly irreconcilable options but neither is it the agreement that may have been reached through negotiation. It is, rather, the sentiment of communal belonging that the act of deliberating and the consensual compromize produce amongst the participants involved (see also Rentto 2016, Chapter 4 in this volume).

In the family of legal liberalism, the position identified here as juridical romanticism is the twin sister of the rule of law. The latter conceals the law's political element by banishing the factual decision beyond the formality of the norm, while the former achieves a similar effect by sublating the formal oppositions into inoperable 'thirds' and by postponing the decision indefinitely. In both cases, the outcome is a law where the political element is either weak or non-existent; that is, a law without the political.

Bibliography

Auge, B. (2004) *Friedrich Dürrenmatts Roman "Justiz": Entsehungsgeschichte, Problemanalyse, Einordnung ins Gesamtwerk*. Münster: LIT Verlag.

Björk, M. (2016) 'Representation and the Unrepresentable: Ernst Jünger, Carl Schmitt and the Limits of Politics', Chapter 8 in M. Arvidsson, L. Brännström and P. Minkkinen (eds), *The Contemporary Relevance of Carl Schmitt: Law, Politics, Theology*. Abingdon: Routledge.

Bühler, P. (2011) 'A Hermeneutical Approach to Text-Image-Interactions: Friedrich Dürrenmatt's Reception of Don Quixote', p. 139–52, in D. Pezzoli-Olgiati and C. Rowland (eds), *Approaches to the Visual in Religion*. Göttingen: Vandenhoeck and Ruprecht.

Crockett, R. A. (1998) *Understanding Friedrich Dürrenmatt*. Columbia, SC: University of South Carolina Press.

Daviaua, D. G. (1982) 'Justice in the Works of Friedrich Dürrenmatt', *Kentucky Foreign Language Quarterly*, Vol. 9, No. 4: 181–93.

Derrida, J. (1992) 'Force of Law: The "Mystical Foundation of Authority"', p. 3–67, in D. Cornell, M. Rosenfeld and D. G. Carlson (eds), *Deconstruction and the Possibility of Justice*. New York: Routledge.

Derrida, J. (1994) *Force de loi. Le 'fondement mystique de l'autorité'*. Paris: Galilée.

De Ville, J. (2016) 'Rethinking the Concept of the Political: Derrida's reading of Schmitt's 'The Theory of the Partisan', Chapter 9 in M. Arvidsson, L. Brännström and P. Minkkinen (eds), *The Contemporary Relevance of Carl Schmitt: Law, Politics, Theology*. Abingdon: Routledge.

Dürrenmatt, F. (1985) *Justiz*. Zürich: Diogenes.

Dürrenmatt, F. (1990) *The Execution of Justice* [1985]. Trans. J. E. Woods. London: Picador.

Dürrenmatt, F. (2006a) *The Inspector Barlach Mysteries: The Judge and His Hangman and*

Suspicion [1952–1953]. Trans. J. Agee. Chicago, IL: University of Chicago Press.
Dürrenmatt, F. (2006b) *Selected Writings. Vols 1–3 (Plays, Fiction, Essays)*. Trans. J. Agee. Chicago, IL: University of Chicago Press.
Federico, J. A. (1989) 'The Political Philosophy of Friedrich Dürrenmatt', *German Studies Review*, Vol. 12, No. 1: 91–109.
Frisch, M. and F. Dürrenmatt (2011) *Correspondence*. Trans. B.S. Duarte. London: Seagull Books.
Galli, C. (2000) 'Carl Schmitt's Antiliberalism: Its Theoretical and Historical Sources and Its Philosophical and Political Meaning', *Cardozo Law Review*, Vol. 21, No. 5–6: 1597–617.
Geißendörfer, H. W. [producer and director], R. Santschi [producer] and T. Wommer [producer] (1993) *Justiz* [motion picture]. Germany: Bayerischer Rundfunk (BR)/GFF/Saarländischer Rundfunk (SR)/Schweizer Fernsehen (FS)/Triluna Film AG.
Gillis, W. (1962) 'Dürrenmatt and the Detectives', *German Quarterly*, Vol. 35, No. 1: 71–4.
Henry, P. (2007) 'Friedrich Dürrenmatt, *Justice*', p. 75–88, in F. Jongen and K. Lemmens (eds), *Droit et Littérature*. Louvain-la-Neuve: Anthemis.
Hewitt, R. (2007) 'Romanticism and the Law: A Selective Introduction', *European Romantic Review*, Vol. 18, No. 3: 299–315.
Jünger, E. and C. Schmitt (1999) *Briefe 1930–1983*. Stuttgart: Klett-Cotta.
Koskenniemi, M. (2010) 'Human Rights Mainstreaming as a Strategy for Institutional Power', *Humanity*, Vol. 1, No. 1: 47–58.
Löwy, M. and R. Sayre (2001) *Romanticism Against the Tide of Modernity*. Trans. C. Porter. Durham, NC: Duke University Press.
McCormick, J. P. (1997) *Carl Schmitt's Critique of Liberalism: Against Politics as Technology*. Cambridge: Cambridge University Press.
Mehring, R. (2006) 'Überwindung des Ästhetizismus. Carl Schmitts selbstinquisitorische Romantikkritik', *Athenäum*, Vol. 16: 125–47.
Mehring, R. (2014) *Carl Schmitt: A Biography*. Trans. D. Steuer. Cambridge: Polity.
Minkkinen, P. (2007) '*Ressentiment* as Suffering: On Transitional Justice and the Impossibility of Forgiveness', *Law and Literature*, Vol. 19, No. 3: 513–31.
Mouffe, C. (2000) *The Democratic Paradox*. London: Verso.
Müller, J. (1999) 'Carl Schmitt's Method: Between Ideology, Demonology and Myth', *Journal of Political Ideologies*, Vol. 4, No. 1: 61–85.
Ryan, B. (2011) 'Carl Schmitt: Zones of Exception and Appropriation', p. 177–207, in J. Stewart (ed.), *Kierkegaard's Influence on Social-Political Thought*. Farnham: Ashgate.
Schmitt, C. (1986) *Political Romanticism* [1919]. Trans. G. Oakes. Cambridge, MA: MIT Press.
Schmitt, C. (1991) *Der Begriff des Politischen. Text von 1932 mit eimen Vorwort und drei Corollarien* [1927]. 3. Aufl. der Ausgabe von 1963. Berlin: Duncker and Humblot.
Schmitt, C. (1996) *Roman Catholicism and Political Form* [1923]. Trans. G. L. Ulmen. Westport, CT: Greenwood Press.
Schmitt, C. (1998) *Politische Romantik* [1919]. Sechste Auflage. Berlin: Duncker and Humblot.
Schmitt, C. (2007) *The Concept of the Political* [1927]. Expanded edn. Trans. G. Schwab. Chicago, IL: University of Chicago Press.

Schmitt, C. (2008) *Römischer Katholizismus und politische Form* [1923]. 5. Auflage. Stuttgart: Clett-Kotta.

Schmitt-Dorotič, C. (1919) *Politische Romantik*. München: Duncker and Humblot.

Teitel, R. (2003) 'Transitional Justice Genealogy', *Harvard Human Rights Journal*, Vol. 16, No. 1: 69–94.

Weber, U. (2006) *Friedrich Dürrenmatt oder von der Lust, die Welt nochmals zu erdenken*. Bern: Haupt.

Williams, M. S., R. Nagy and J. Elster (eds) (2012) *Transitional Justice*. New York: New York University Press.

Wilson, R. (2001) *The Politics of Truth and Reconciliation in South Africa: Legitimizing the Post-Apartheid State*. Cambridge: Cambridge University Press.

Wright, A. M. (1981) 'Scientific Method and Rationality In Dürrenmatt', *German Life and Letters*, Vol. 35, No. 1: 64–72.

Chapter 6

Social acceleration, motorized legislation and framework laws

Carl-Göran Heidegren

Introduction

In his essay, *The Plight of European Jurisprudence* from 1950 (Schmitt 1990),[1] Carl Schmitt makes use of the suggestive notion of 'the motorized legislator', by which he means the increasing volume and speed of introduction of new legislation, as well as the delegation of authority from the legislative to the executive and administrative bodies. In the following text the concept of social acceleration as developed within contemporary social theory is first introduced. Thereafter, the line of argumentation in parts of Schmitt's above-mentioned essay is reconstructed. This section also casts a glance at an earlier article by Schmitt on the issue of legislative delegations. Next, Schmitt's problematic is related to the practice of framework legislation (*ramlagstiftning*) in Sweden since 1945. Finally, the text touches upon the issue of the changing preconditions for politics in a high-speed society and how the use of framework laws fits into that picture.[2]

Social acceleration

The German historian Reinhart Koselleck (2009) has argued that a trend towards social acceleration is discernable in the western world even before the industrial revolution. Improvements in road networks and channels started to increase the speed of inland travelling and transportation, and the new clipper ships speeded up the movement of men and commodities at sea. The railway, when it was introduced some decades later, became a symbol of speed. It was often compared to a projectile moving through the landscape at an unprecedented velocity. Towards the end of the nineteenth

---

1   In this chapter, however, I follow the translation of relevant sections in Rosa and Scheuerman's collection (Schmitt 2009).
2   The text is very much inspired by Scheuerman's and Rosa's work (Scheuerman 2004; Rosa 2013). My contribution is mainly to bring the practice of framework legislation in Sweden since 1945 into the discussion. I thank the editors of this volume for very helpful comments on the text.

century, new and fast means of transportation such as the bicycle (four times faster than walking), the electric tram, the subway, and finally, the automobile and the aeroplane were introduced (Kern 2003). At the same time, the telephone, the wireless telegraph and the high-speed rotation press revolutionized communication and the transmission of news over long distances. The motion picture, as well as new musical styles such as ragtime and jazz, conveyed a feeling of a way of life in high tempo. Also, in the inter-war years 'fast' cigarettes became popular at the expense of 'slow' cigars.

The trend towards social acceleration has not diminished since then; rather, it has continued at an ever-increasing speed and effectiveness. For some time this has been a growing concern of the social sciences (Eriksen 2001; Rosa and Scheuerman 2009).

To begin with, social acceleration is defined as an increase in quantity per unit of time. It can be the number of kilometres covered in an hour, the number of Darlecarlian horses (small carved toys) produced in a day or the number of different jobs that someone has during a working life. Furthermore, a distinction is made between three major forms of social acceleration (Rosa 2013). Firstly, there is *technological* acceleration, clearly visible in the areas of transportation, communication and production. Examples of this are innovations such as the internet and high-speed trains. Secondly, there is an increased speed of *social change* to be seen, for example, in the fast and, so it seems, ever faster shifts in fashion, life styles, family constellations, occupations, working conditions, terms of employment, and so on. Important changes nowadays occur not between two generations but several times within one and the same generation. Thirdly, there is the speed-up of the *tempo of life*. The number of definable episodes in terms of actions and experiences increases per unit of time, for example in a day. Multi-tasking, reducing pauses and empty time, sleeping less, eating faster, and so on, are strategies we use for speeding up or, rather, for keeping up with the pace of life. Subjectively, this tends to generate feelings of chronic scarcity of time, of constantly being hurried and under stress. We run as fast as we can to stay in the same place. Rosa calls this the slipping slopes syndrome.

In sum, we are living today in what can be characterized as a high-speed society, in which processes of social acceleration are manifest. The islands of slowness handed over from the past are diminishing and becoming increasingly marginalized, and the various protest movements that gather under the banner of slowing down have thus far generally proved to be inefficient (Cittaslow, Slow Food, Slow Money, and so on).

The motorized legislator

As mentioned above, Schmitt (1950) uses the very suggestive notion of 'the motorized legislator' in a short essay entitled *The Plight of European*

Jurisprudence, published a few years after the end of the Second World War. This section focuses mainly on this notion, whereas Schmitt's overall argument is less in focus. Schmitt's diagnosis of the contemporary situation is first presented, followed by his views on the causes of this situation.

Schmitt's text, including a version in French, was presented as a lecture in 1943/44 to the faculties of law at several European universities. It was to be published in a *Festschrift* in honour of Schmitt's close friend Johannes Popitz, Secretary of State in Prussia. However, Popitz was executed on 2 February 1945 because of his involvement in the attempted coup of 20 July 1944. According to Werner Weber, a former pupil and long-time friend of Schmitt, the text published in 1950 is identical to the one from before 1945 (Mehring 2009: 433–4, 693 fn. 50). This statement is supported by the fact that there is no reference in Schmitt's essay to any publication from later than 1944.

The broad historical trend that Schmitt diagnoses is:

> Since 1914 all major historical events and developments in every European country have contributed to making the process of legislation ever faster and more summary, the path to realizing legal regulation ever shorter, and the role of legal science ever smaller.
>
> (Schmitt 2009: 65)

Schmitt's diagnosis is two-fold: the ever-increasing size and speed of new legislation on the one hand and the delegation of authority from the legislative body to the executive and administrative bodies on the other.

Firstly, Schmitt talks about an increasing statutorification of law (*Vergesetzlichung des Rechts*): new laws are made at an increasing speed and in a more summary way.[3] This tendency he describes in terms of 'the growing motorization of the legislative machinery' (Schmitt 2009: 71). Motorization and machinery are words that stand for something that is fast and at the same time mechanical, in contrast to something that is the object of careful deliberation and discussion. 'The legislative machine [has] increased its tempo to a hitherto unimaginable extent' (Schmitt 2009: 67). This increasing statutorification brings forth the triple danger of 'mechanization, technicization, and termiticization' (Schmitt 2009: 71, translation altered). I interpret the very unusual word formation, *Termitisierung*, which Schmitt uses in terms of a process of corruption and destruction that comes from within.[4] This is what happens when the

---

3   The notion of 'statutorification' has been in use since some time in American legal scholarship to designate 'a dramatic increase in the quantity of legislative statutes and a no less considerable boost in the tempo with which legislative bodies promulgate them' (Scheuerman 2004: 127).
4   The English translation uses the word 'corruption', thereby making Schmitt's idiosyncratic choice of terminology invisible.

question of legitimacy is watered down into a question of formal legality as in legal positivism; hence his reference to 'the idea of deadly legality on which governments and people die' (Schmitt 2009: 72) that came up in France shortly before the revolutionary upheavals of 1848.

Secondly, Schmitt draws attention to new forms of legislative delegation, to what he calls 'the structural transformation of the legislative process' (Schmitt 2009: 66). He points, to begin with, to the increasing use of Enabling Acts (*Ermächtigungsgesetze*) in Germany and other European countries, beginning on the eve of the First World War and becoming common in the inter-war period.[5] The general form of delegation is that the legislative body authorizes the government and administrative bodies to issue decrees (*Verordnungen*) and orders (*Anordnungen*), in order to speed up the legislative process. According to Schmitt, the decree has been called 'the motorized law' and the order, 'as the most elastic form of legislation', can in turn be called 'the motorized decree' (Schmitt 2009: 67–8). With the latter development the process of 'simplification and acceleration' reaches its 'pinnacle' (Schmitt 2009: 67) thus far. What characterizes the order is that, among other things, it is 'changeable without further ado' (Schmitt 2009: 68, translation altered).[6] Furthermore, this development has had the following consequences: 'Law is transformed into an instrument of planning, the administrative act into an act of steering' (ibid.). As a further consequence, and this is what worries Schmitt, the legal profession is becoming ever more marginalized in the process of legislation. In 'the age of motorized law and motorized decree' (Schmitt 2009: 72), legal scholarship has lost much of its traditional role in law making.

Such kinds of delegations, it should be noted, were foreign to the founding fathers of the theory of liberal democracy. 'The legislative cannot transfer the power of making laws to any other hands, for it being but a delegated power from the people, they who have it cannot pass it over to others' (Locke 1978: 189). Alluding to Locke, Schmitt lays down that 'in the end legislative bodies are called upon by the constitution to make laws themselves, not to empower other agencies to legislate' (Schmitt 2009: 65).

So far Schmitt's diagnosis of the situation a few years after the end of the Second World War has been analyzed. But what are his views on the causes of this historical trend? Schmitt hints at two broad tendencies as being responsible for the increasing motorization of law and decree. Firstly, he

---

5   However, Schmitt does not mention the notorious Enabling Act of 24 March 1933, which spelled the end of the Weimar Republic and the beginning of his own alliance with the Nazi regime (Mehring 2009: 304–6; on the extensive use of economic emergency powers in the twentieth century, see Scheuerman 2004: 107–17).

6   Here a serious mistranslation in the English text occurs: '*ohne weiteres abänderbar*' (Schmitt 1950: 20) does not mean 'without possibility of further amendment' but, rather, the opposite.

points to 'the pressure to adapt legal provision to rapidly changing circumstances' (Schmitt 2009: 67) as being far too strong and irresistible. In a rapidly changing society severe pressure is put upon the political sphere to speed up the legislative process, so that the law is continuously adapted to the new circumstances. Thus, rapid social change tends to bring about the motorization of the legislator. Secondly, Schmitt points to the fact that 'new accelerations have resulted from market regulation and state direction of the economy' (ibid.). This is a somewhat specified rehearsal of the first argument. The speeding-up of the internal dynamics of the market economy on the one hand and the practice of state intervention in the economy on the other hand both tend to give rise to an increasing number of laws and legal regulations as well as to the speeding up of the process of legislation by means of delegation. In particular, an interventionist state, with far-reaching planning and steering ambitions, will have to speed up the process of law making. These two hints at causal connections are incidentally mentioned in Schmitt's text. However, no attempt is made to work out this explanation in any detail. Instead Schmitt, in the end, rounds up his usual suspects: legal positivism, which introduced the rift between legitimacy and legality, and the multiparty system of parliamentary democracy. Nevertheless, Schmitt's diagnosis from the mid-twentieth century has been considered as highly accurate from today's perspective:

> Recent empirical research confirms Schmitt's temporal diagnosis: most debate in the halls of parliament is now rushed and hectic, legislatures are busily streamlining their activities in accordance with the temporal demands of our high-speed society, and legal regulation decreasingly accords with classical liberal models.
> (Scheuerman 2004: 106)

Before turning to the practice of framework legislation in Sweden, let us say a few words about Schmitt's interest in social acceleration, and also take a look at an article by Schmitt from 1936 on contemporary forms of legislative delegations.

Schmitt seems to have had a keen eye for, and an interest in, phenomena of social acceleration. According to Günter Maschke (see the commentary in Schmitt 1995: 507), this interest was in part influenced by his reading of the American historian and essayist Henry Adams (1838–1918), who formulated what he called 'a law of acceleration' in his autobiography from 1907 (Adams 2009). This was boldly conceived as an all-embracing historical law but became particularly clearly observable from about the beginning of the nineteenth century. In a short essay from 1952, entitled '*Die Einheit der Welt*', Schmitt compares the stage of technical development reached in the mid-nineteenth century – the railway, the steamship and the telegraph – with that of a hundred years later –

aeroplanes, electric waves, and atomic energy. 'The planet contracts' (Schmitt 1995: 497), he lays down, arguing that the various means of transportation and communication have become so much faster, and that the world has thus, to the same degree, become smaller. Schmitt is here primarily reflecting upon technological accelerations, whereas the thesis of the fast and ever faster pace of new legislation rather pinpointed an important aspect of the speeding up of social change. Furthermore, Schmitt's ideas of a 'space revolution [*Raumrevolution*]' and a new 'order of large spaces [*Großraumordnung*]', which he presented in several versions during and after the Second World War, was also in part inspired by the fact that the world is contracting; that is, it is becoming smaller because of the development of faster means of transportation and communication (Schmitt 2006; see also Fichera 2016, Chapter 11 in this volume).

In an article from 1936, Schmitt presents an overview of the strong tendencies towards legislative delegations that could be observed in many countries, especially since the time of the First World War. The end of the war and demobilization had in no way meant a return to standard procedure when it came to the process of legislation: 'No state on Earth can today evade the necessity of a "simplified" legislation' (Schmitt 1940: 227). The constitutional implication of this is, according to Schmitt, that the separation between the legislative and the executive tends to become blurred. This step, he further argues, was definitely taken in Germany with the Enabling Act of 24 March 1933, by which the Führer and the government were turned into legislators. In Schmitt's interpretation, the whole constitutional tradition centred on the doctrine of the separation of powers, and dating back to Locke and Montesquieu, is now approaching its end. The time has come, he argues, for new conceptions of constitution and law.

Schmitt hints in the article at three causes for this general trend towards legislative delegations (Schmitt 1940: 214). Firstly, inflation and deflation after the war have made exceptional legislative measures increasingly necessary. Secondly, several states have started practising more or less ambitious forms of state intervention – in the form of planning and steering – in the economy. Furthermore, the order of production and the market economy have demanded new forms of judicial regulation. This is part of the argument that we found in Schmitt's essay from 1950, discussed previously. Thirdly, increasing obligations relating to international law may also have implied pressure in the direction of simplified forms of legal regulation.

In the article from 1936, Schmitt welcomes the practice of Enabling Acts as a necessary step in the direction of governmental legislation (*Regierungsgesetzgebung*) and new conceptions of constitution and law. In the essay published in 1950, but probably written before 1945, he is deeply worried about the increasing use of decrees and orders, the process of legislation becoming ever faster and more summary and the role of legal science becoming ever smaller; a remarkable turncoat manoeuvre performed by Schmitt. However, his views about the general causes for this development remain more or less the same in the two texts: the increasing ambitions of planning and steering on the part of the state, and the rapid changes and growing complexity of modern society.

Framework legislation as a downward delegation of authority

A core idea in the tradition of liberal democracy has been the separation of powers as a system of checks and balances. From the beginning a certain temporality or temporal dimension was built into the idea of a separation of powers (Scheuerman 2004). The legislative power was seen as future oriented and its task as consisting of making clear and stable laws to give guidance to the state and its citizens in their future action. The judicial power, on the contrary, is retrospective and decisive in legal disputes on the basis of already existing law and comparable previous cases. The executive power, finally, takes action in the present by implementing new laws and upholding existing law, as well as reacting quickly in situations of sudden crisis; for example, a conflict with a foreign power. Of the three powers the legislative is the one that is characterized by 'the virtues of slow-going, freewheeling deliberation' (Scheuerman 2004: 40). The legislator must never be in a hurry, whereas the executive must have the ability to act quickly. The judicial power, finally, must in its workings combine careful consideration and effectivity. With this backdrop let us now turn to some developments in Swedish legislative practice.

Framework legislation is an example of the practice of the downward delegation of authority. My suggestion is that this practice can be partially (not solely) understood as a response to social acceleration; that is, to the social processes which led Schmitt to introduce his notion of the motorized legislator. Framework legislation can be seen as an attempt at reducing complexity by temporalizing it and thereby managing scarce resources of time. Instead of laying down a detailed legislation all at once, the legislative body enacts open-ended laws that are to be specified and concretized at a later point in time and by a different authority. In this way, the parliament is relieved from being overburdened by issues demanding a decision within a limited span of time. Something that is relatively firm and constant over time, a framework, is established in the form of overall goals and guidelines but which at the same time is highly flexible in its adaptations and adjustments to rapidly changing circumstances. The driving forces considered to be behind the use of framework legislation are similar to those that Schmitt singled out as being behind the trend towards motorized legislation.[7]

---

7 In an article on framework legislation from 1989, the Swedish jurist Torsten Bjerkén, in passing, refers to Schmitt's notion of the motorized legislator (Bjerkén 1989: 131).

Since 1945, a number of the laws issued by the Swedish parliament, as the legislative body, have been so-called framework laws (*ramlagar*). This has been done with increasing frequency, especially since the 1960s and 1970s: 'The number of framework laws is unknown, but probably very big' (Esping 1994: 16).[8] The word *ramlag* was coined in the 1970s and 'framework laws are the most important phenomenon in modern legislative technique' (Sterzel 1993: 333). For example, the Social Services Act, the Health and Medical Services Act, the Occupational Safety and Health Act and the Environmental Protection Act are generally considered to be framework laws.

In order to be more precise about what is new about framework legislation the Swedish jurist Fredrik Sterzel makes a distinction between general clauses, whose substantial content is decided on in court, portal paragraphs (programmatic statutes), which are of a more or less ornamental character and what he calls 'goal-rules'. The latter indicate goals, possibly operative guidelines, intended to serve as guidance in practice (Sterzel 1993: 343–6). All three of the aforementioned are often subsumed under the headline of framework law. Insofar as the focus is on what is new, the designation framework law should, according to Sterzel, be reserved for goal-rules. However, in practice the three forms are closely related.

What characterizes framework legislation is that a delegation of authority downwards in the hierarchy of decision takes place: from the parliament to the government, to central public administrative authorities, and to local governments, and so on. At the same time, new legislation, rather than being a codification of the sense of justice (*rättsmedvetandet*), to an increasing extent, becomes an instrument for social planning and steering. The social democratic politician Carl Lidbom, the Minister of Justice in the 1970s, once stated: 'Laws are not to be looked upon with subservient respect. They are working tools that we make use of in order to reach political goals' (quoted in Esping 1994: 36).

What are the driving forces behind the extensive use of framework legislation since 1945? Let us begin by presenting a somewhat longer quote from a bill in the Swedish parliament submitted by six representatives of one of the parliamentary parties. The bill ('Framework legislation and the rule of law') is from 2001 and formulates:

> The laws that the Swedish Parliament decides on are to an ever-greater extent so-called framework laws, i.e. they describe in outline the meaning of the law and delegate the more detailed instructions to the Government … Is the framework law necessary or is it a way in which to transfer the legislative power from the Parliament to the

---

8   All translations from Swedish are mine (C.-G. H.).

Government? ... One of the arguments for creating framework laws to an ever-greater extent is that we live in an increasingly internationalized society and that this sometimes demands *fast* adaptations and adjustments. The traditional legislative process, in which the Parliament lays down the valid law in relation to the citizen, is considered to take *too long time* ... Against the consideration of effectivity stand the demands for democracy, predictability and the rule of law.

(Motion 2001/02: K246, Sveriges riksdag, Ramlagstiftning och rättssäkerhet; emphasis added)

Two causes are explicitly hinted at: the traditional legislative process is considered to be too slow, and living in an increasingly internationalized society demands fast adaptations and adjustments; that is, a capacity to cope with social complexity and changing circumstances.

In a report from 1984, Håkan Hydén, sociologist of law, points to the same general causes: 'The growth of framework laws is generally considered to be due to the fact that various conditions in modern society are changing relatively quickly and that the formation of norms and standards (*normgivning*) has to adapt to these societal changes.' He goes on to say: 'Another causal factor is considered to be the growing complexity in the organization of society' (Hydén 1984: 2). Thus, the relatively fast pace of social change on the one hand, and the growing societal complexity on the other, are singled out as the main causes for the increasing use of framework legislation.

Another sociologist of law, Antoinette Hetzler, being very positive towards the use of framework legislation, argues that detailed legislation was relevant in a society in which 'change only came slowly and was predictable' (Hetzler 1988: 12). However, this kind of society now belongs to the past. In a modern welfare society, with a comprehensive system of social welfare rights, a legislative technique is needed that can 'adapt to changes and which has a "reflexive" character, i.e. a good learning ability' (ibid.). Thus, framework legislation is considered to be the appropriate legislative technique of societies that undergo rapid changes in unpredictable directions, and which need constantly to relearn as a way of adapting to ever-new circumstances.

Finally, Hans Esping, also a sociologist of law, draws attention to what he considers to be two general causes (Esping 1994: 19–34). First, he points to the rationalization of public decision making. Through delegation the law becomes more flexible, as compared with detailed legislation, in relation to new experiences and changed circumstances, and thus more responsive to and capable of handling them. The parliament and the government are relieved from much decision making by delegating downwards in the hierarchy. Secondly, Esping also mentions the growing complexity of modern society. He particularly points to the fast changes taking place in the sectors of science and technology as well as within the economic sphere. These give rise to the need for more legislation and thus decision making. To this can be added, perhaps as a third causal factor, the growing ambitions of the state at political steering, which in turn can be seen as an answer to the growing need for social security among citizens.

To sum up, confronting the danger that rapid social change and growing societal complexity render existing law outdated and irrelevant, a new type of law has been introduced, namely a type of law that lays down overall goals and guidelines, is open ended and, in general, presupposed to be specified and concretized by other bodies than the legislative, thus giving rise to an extensive so-called secondary legislation in the form of decrees, orders, precedents, instructions and recommendations. As a consequence, it is only after a concretization has taken place that the precise meaning and implications of the law can be known. Another consequence is that the classical dividing line between future-oriented law making and past-oriented law application becomes blurred. Furthermore, in the interpretation and application of the law, non-judicial expertise, rather than the legal profession, often plays a prominent role. The latter being a consequence of the delegation of authority downwards was already pointed out by Schmitt, talking about 'the growing volume of practical commentaries composed by practitioners or ministerial experts' (Schmitt 2009: 67).

High-speed society

The fast pace of social change in modern societies as well as their growing complexity, due to the speeding-up of the internal dynamics of the market economy and the practice of state intervention in the economy, were the two causes that Schmitt hinted at in his diagnosis of the motorized legislator. As we have seen, the very same two factors are generally considered in the literature to be the main driving forces behind the extensive use of framework legislation in Sweden since 1945. The major aim of this text has been to draw attention to this parallel and thus to highlight an embryonic argument to be found in Schmitt that has lost none of its relevance. However, in neither case is any detailed analysis of the dynamics of the suggested causal connection worked out. This also amounts to saying that the use of framework legislation in Sweden and elsewhere needs to be further analyzed from this perspective. Here the legal sciences have an important task. In this concluding section, some further remarks are made about the changing preconditions of politics and legislation in a high-speed society, before once again returning to the practice of framework legislation.

The notion of high-speed society neither implies that everything changes at the same pace nor that different social sub-systems undergo the same process of social acceleration (Rosa 2013: 259–67). On the contrary, it can be argued that a growing desynchronization is taking place between fast changing sub-systems like science and technology and the economy, and slower changing sub-systems like politics and law. The latter, so the argument goes, are less capable of speeding up their way of working. At the same time, the fast pace of scientific and technological innovation and economic change puts severe pressure on modern democratic politics to speed up its processes of decision making and legislation. But democratic politics is, in many ways, inherently time consuming. However, the time available for political decisions tends to decrease, the number of decisions that have to be made, on the contrary, to increase, while at the same time it becomes more and more difficult to foresee the future. Furthermore, the long-term consequences of the decisions tend to increase (consider genetic engineering), at the same time as the need to plan for the future is becoming ever more urgent (consider the pension system or environmental influence), while the socio-cultural common ground for decision making seems to be eroding. Many difficult and time-consuming issues must be dealt with democratically within a diminishing span of time. In such a situation politics tends to become what Rosa calls *situationalist* or *situational*; that is, reactive and stuck in a short-term perspective. As an example of how politics has become reactive, we may quote the former Swedish Prime Minister Göran Persson, who before the elections in 2002 stated: 'What we do promise is that every time something unforeseen happens, we will handle the situation energetically and in accordance with our values' (quoted in Gustavsson 2004: 114).

The growth of framework legislation in Sweden since 1945 must be seen in the context of the political ambitions of the modern welfare state to plan and steer society in the direction of certain overarching goals on the one hand, and as a way of dealing with the time pressures and speeding-up imperatives put on the legislative and executive bodies by a society undergoing processes of social acceleration on the other hand. However, there is a dangerous tendency for democratic politics to increasingly get out of step with fast-changing societal sub-systems like science and technology and the economy. As politics becomes situationalist, it more and more abdicates from the ambition of long-term planning and steering as well as from having guiding visions of a better society. Situational politics flourish in a society without a political vision for the future. Muddling through, as the primacy of the short-term, becomes the *modus vivendi* for this kind of politics (on the positive potentialities of speed for democratic pluralism on a scale transcending the nation-state, see Connolly 2009).

The use of framework legislation can be seen as an attempt from the side of politics to come to grips with social complexity and social acceleration. Seen in this perspective, it is a strategy for reducing complexity by way of temporalizing it. A framework law is supposed to provide a stable frame in terms of goals and guidelines, which at the same time allows for a rather high degree of flexibility in its concretization and application. In a Swedish government official report from 2005 it is laid down:

> One reason for retaining the technique of framework legislation is that it has been in use for a long time without having been changed in any essential respect. Instead the activities of local governments and public administration authorities have been adjusted.
> (SOU 2005: 34, 83)

It is a political and judicial technique for delegating authority from the slower legislative body, the parliament, to supposedly faster political and administrative bodies. One of the consequences of this delegation is the rapid growth of secondary legislation, which as such is difficult to overview and is sometimes seen as a threat to the rule of law. Another consequence is the growing importance of not popularly elected experts and officials, which can be interpreted as a democratic deficit (Hydén 1984: 8–17; Sterzel 1993: 349–52; Esping 1994: 52–4). It has also been pointed out that the success of framework legislation relies on the existence of a community of values within which those who are to interpret and apply the law are included, concerning the overall goals to be achieved (Hetzler 1988: 14). The question is whether such a consensus in terms of values exists today and will exist in the future.

Scheuerman has voiced some hesitation about delegation as a way of handling the pressure put on the legislative in a high-speed society: 'Forcing administrative actors to rush their decisions is sure to generate irrational and undesirable results no less than in the case of overhasty legislatures' (Scheuerman 2004: 53). If this is correct, the downward delegation of authority will rather be a case of termiticization in the sense of Schmitt; that is, a kind of corruption that comes from within the system of legislation itself. Instead, Scheuerman suggests that so-called reflexive law, as a form of regulated self-regulation, might do better in handling law making in a high-speed society, without sacrificing democratic legitimacy. However, he acknowledges that, on this issue, 'empirical confirmation is still needed' (Scheuerman 2004: 217).[9] According to Hetzler, framework legislation can be seen as a form of reflexive law. With the Social Services Act in mind, she writes that 'the application of the law is not decided in advance, but shall be designed in close consultation with the individual' (Hetzler 1988: 11)

---

9   The concept of reflexive law, as developed by the German sociologist of law Günther Teubner in the early 1980s, favours decentralization before central planning or deregulation and procedural orientation before result orientation: 'Instead of taking over regulatory responsibility for the outcome of social processes, reflexive law restricts itself to the installation, correction, and redefinition of democratic self-regulatory mechanisms' (Teubner 1983: 239).

who is affected by it. If this is a reasonable interpretation, framework legislation could be an empirical test case for Scheuerman's suggestion. Thus, there is good reason to take a closer look at the technique and practice of framework legislation, its potentials as well as its problems, from a temporal perspective or, to be more precise, from the perspective of social acceleration.

In conclusion, the downward delegation of authority can take on many forms: framework legislation is one of them. The reasons and social forces behind the use of framework legislation are likewise manifold. This text has focused on social acceleration, rather than on the need for flexibility and expertise or the wish to bring decisions closer to those who are affected by them. Framework legislation is, and will probably continue to be, an important feature of complex high-speed societies undergoing further social acceleration. A social pressure in the direction of a motorization of legislation will most probably likewise be a persistent feature of such societies. Moreover, as long as this is the case, Schmitt's casual remarks and hints at causal connections in his essay from 1950 will be of relevance as an early reaction to certain trends that are still with us.

Bibliography

Adams, H. (2009) 'A Law of Acceleration' [1918], p. 33–40, in H. Rosa and W. E. Scheuerman (eds) *High-speed Society: Social Acceleration, Power, and Modernity*. University Park, PA: Pennsylvania State University Press.
Bjerkén, T. (1989) 'Ramlagarna och förvaltningen', *Tidskrift för rättssociologi*, Vol. 6: 123–35.
Connolly, W. E. (2009) 'Speed, Concentric Cultures, and Cosmopolitanism', p. 261–85, in H. Rosa and W. E. Scheuerman (eds) *High-speed Society: Social Acceleration, Power, and Modernity*. University Park, PA: Pennsylvania State University Press.
Eriksen, T. H. (2001) *Tyranny of the Moment: Fast and Slow Time in the Information Age*. London: Pluto.
Esping, H. (1994) *Ramlagar i förvaltningspolitiken*. Stockholm: SNS Förlag.
Fichera, M. (2016) 'Carl Schmitt and the New World Order: A View From Europe', Chapter 11 in M. Arvidsson, L. Brännström and P. Minkkinen (eds), *The Contemporary Relevance of Carl Schmitt. Law, Politics, Theology*. Abingdon: Routledge.
Gustavsson, K. (2004) *Socialismens liv efter döden*. Stockholm: Atlas.
Hetzler, A. (1988) 'Ramlagar – det moderna samhällets styrteknik', p. 6–17, in *Blickpunkten. Tidskrift från forskningsdelegationen om den offentliga sektorn*. Stockholm: Civildepartementet.
Hydén, H. (1984) *Ram eller lag? Om ramlagstiftning och samhällsorganisation*. Departementsserie C 1984:12. Stockholm: Riksdagens offsetcentral.
Kern, S. (2003) *The Culture of Time and Space 1880–1918*. With a New Preface [1983]. Cambridge, MA: Harvard University Press.
Koselleck, R. (2009) 'Is There an Acceleration of History?' [2000], p. 113–34, in H.

Rosa and W. E. Scheuerman (eds) *High-speed Society: Social Acceleration, Power, and Modernity*. University Park, PA: Pennsylvania State University Press.

Locke, J. (1978) *Two Treatises of Government* [1690]. London: Dent.

Mehring, R. (2009) *Carl Schmitt: Aufstieg und Fall*. München: C. H. Beck.

Rosa, H. and W. E. Scheuerman (eds) (2009) *High-speed Society: Social Acceleration, Power, and Modernity*. University Park, PA: Pennsylvania State University Press.

Rosa, H. (2013) *Social Acceleration: A New Theory of Modernity*. Trans. J. Trejo-Mathys. New York: Columbia University Press.

Scheuerman, W. E. (2004) *Liberal Democracy and the Social Acceleration of Time*. Baltimore, MD: Johns Hopkins University Press.

Schmitt, C. (1940) 'Vergleichender Überblick über die neueste Entwicklung des Problems der gesetzgeberischen Ermächtigungen: "Legislative Delegationen"' [1936], p. 214–29, in C. Schmitt, *Positionen und Begriffe im Kampf mit Weimar – Genf – Versailles 1923–1939*. Hamburg: Hanseatische Verlagsanstalt.

Schmitt, C. (1950) *Die Lage der europäischen Rechtswissenschaft*. Tübingen: Internationaler Universitäts-Verlag.

Schmitt, C. (1990) 'The Plight of European Jurisprudence' [1950], *Telos*, No. 83: 35–71.

Schmitt, C. (1995) 'Die Einheit der Welt' [1952], p. 496–512, in C. Schmitt, *Staat, Großraum, Nomos. Arbeiten aus den Jahren 1916–1969. Herausgegeben, mit einem Vorwort und mit Anmerkungen versehen von Günter Maschke*. Berlin: Duncker and Humblot.

Schmitt, C. (2006) *The Nomos of the Earth in the International Law of the Jus Publicum Europaeum* [1950]. Trans. G. L. Ulmen. New York: Telos.

Schmitt, C. (2009) 'The Motorized Legislator' [1950], p. 65–73, in H. Rosa and W. E. Scheuerman (eds), *High-speed Society: Social Acceleration, Power, and Modernity*. University Park, PA: Pennsylvania State University Press.

SOU (2005). *Socialtjänsten och den fria rörligheten*. No. 2005: 34. Stockholm: Statens Offentliga Utredningar.

Sterzel, F. (1993) 'Ramlagarna – nytt och gammalt', p. 333–52, in E. Nerep and W. Warnling-Nerep (eds) *Festskrift till Jacob W. F. Sundberg*. Stockholm: Juristförlaget.

Teubner, G. (1983) 'Substantive and Reflexive Elements in Modern Law', *Law and Society Review*, Vol. 17, No. 2: 239–85.

Part II
Politics

Chapter 7

Law, decision, necessity
Shifting the burden of responsibility

Johanna Jacques

Introduction

If Carl Schmitt's concept of the political is still to contribute today to the question that 'never ceases to reverberate in the history of Western politics', namely, 'what does it mean to act politically?' (Agamben 2005: 2), it is essential to clarify the relation of the political decision to necessity. For regardless of how one may frame the primacy of the political in theoretical terms; that is, how one explains why it is necessary to take a political *decision* at all (rather than, for example, follow a moral code), once practical necessity is thought to apply, the decision loses all meaning: action becomes *re*-action, and the sovereign decision falls victim to necessity's force.

An example of a reading that has this practical effect is that of Leo Strauss. Strauss wonders how Schmitt can defend the primacy of the political without recourse to moral reasons and concludes that Schmitt's theory of the political represents a 'liberalism with the opposite polarity' (Strauss 1995: 117). According to this liberal stance, Strauss explains, all political decisions are equally valid as long as they are based on '"*serious*" convictions'; that is, they are 'decisions oriented towards the real possibility of *war*' (Strauss 1995: 117). Having confirmed the freedom of the political decision, Strauss thus immediately qualifies this freedom by reference to war – qualifies, because war is only too easily associated with necessity, and necessity negates the freedom to decide. Harvey Lomax, for example, finds that the serious situation or '*Ernstfall*' (Schmitt 1963: 30) on which Schmitt premises war as a state of exception 'refers to a state of emergency in which everything important is at stake, a matter of life and death' (Meier 1995: 132). Accordingly, the term is rendered 'dire emergency' by Lomax himself (Meier 1995: 132), 'exigency' by Gary Steiner (Löwith 1995: 147) and 'the extreme case' by George Schwab (Schmitt 1996a: 30). Whether intended or not, the suggestion in each of these cases is that there is a situation that *necessitates* war.

Schmitt's own choice of words appears to confirm this finding of necessity. For example, in *Political Theology*, Schmitt links the state of exception to an existential danger threatening the state: 'The exception can ... be characterized as a case of extreme peril, a danger to the existence of the state, or the like' (Schmitt 2005: 6). Schmitt also refers to Jean Bodin as justifying the sovereign's breach of duty to the people only 'under conditions of urgent necessity' (Schmitt 2005: 8), calls the exception '*extremus necessitatis casus*' (Schmitt 2005: 10) and bases the state of exception on the state's 'right of self-preservation' (Schmitt 2005: 12). In *The Concept of the Political*, Schmitt then defines the political in such a way as to seemingly equate politics with self-defence; the political is the recognition of the enemy and the enemy is he who attacks (Meier 1995: 18–19).

These references to necessity – *existential* necessity – are surprising, given that the latter is incompatible with the notion of the decision, being neither based on a decision nor allowing for a decision to be made. This incompatibility could be resolved by claiming, as Agamben does, that an objective state of necessity is a 'naive conception' and that 'obviously the only circumstances that are necessary and objective are those that are declared to be so' (Agamben 2005: 30). However, this view can only lead to two possible conclusions, and neither is helpful in drawing out a constructive meaning of political action. If one were to adopt Agamben's view, the whole problematic of the state of exception would either reveal itself as a *legal* phenomenon in the first place; that is, law's attempt to establish a fictitious state of nature as its own presupposition (Agamben 2005: 33), leaving no independent role for the sovereign to play. Or, if the sovereign *were* recognized as independent of the legal order and free to decide on its suspension, an Agamben-inspired critique would merely focus on the sovereign's false *claim* of existential necessity, leaving the underlying assumption of the sovereign's absolute freedom to decide intact. Between these two poles of systemic determination and absolute freedom, a constructive role for the sovereign actor can hardly be made out.

In contrast, this chapter takes the possibility of objective necessity seriously, even if only to show that it has no place in Schmitt's theory of the political. This raises the question of what Schmitt means by the term 'existential' if not existential *necessity*. The ensuing analysis discovers the creative role of the sovereign in giving meaning to the state's existence, a role in which the sovereign stands not only 'outside' the legal system, but also 'belongs' to it (Schmitt 2005: 7). This belonging, it is argued, is composed of two active aspects: the sovereign's orientation towards the legal order and his responsibility in taking the decision – responsibility not as a *response* (to law, to God, to the Other, to necessity) and thus as *subsumption* and potential accountability (see, for example, Kahn 2011: 89) but, as a unilateral *assumption* of the work the decision sets itself.

Necessity and the decision on the exception

Necessity, conceived as a force that determines action (rather than as a particularly compelling reason for an action aimed at a certain outcome), is incompatible with the notion of the decision. When something is necessary in the absolute sense, it is more than merely possible or persuasive or the only option for achieving a certain aim. It simply must be done. As such, necessity leaves no scope for deliberation and decision on the part of the subject. It is for this reason that necessity is said to 'have no law [*necessitas legem non habet*]'; that is, that no legal responsibility is said to attach to necessary action. Law's self-distinction from force is premised on the subject's capacity to decide, to choose between lawful and unlawful action. Law takes into consideration 'the contrary will of the legal subject [*den entgegenstehenden Willen eines Rechtssubjekts*]', as Schmitt would say (Schmitt 1978: XVII).[1] As soon as this capacity is removed by the force of necessity, law can no longer hold the actor responsible without losing its claim to right. Necessity, on the other hand, is not premised on the possible acquiescence of the subject. On the contrary, as force, necessity acts directly on the subject, leaving it no choice in how to act.

However, the absence of choice *on the part of the subject* is not the only way in which necessity excludes the decision. This absence of choice also applies to necessity itself, which is not made but simply arises. As a source of right, necessity thus has no alternatives, no outside. Not only does it not allow for a decision, it is not based on one. Schmitt explicitly contrasts law to such a natural theory of right by claiming that 'every legal order is based on a decision' (Schmitt 2005: 10). His main point here is not to show that sometimes law needs to create an exception to its own processes of apportioning responsibility because necessity has removed the subject's capacity to decide (in which case law would end where necessity begins, with no role for the decision to play), but that there is a point of view outside and independent of law from which law's borders are established by a decision. This decision must evade all normative determination, whether by law, morality or necessity, if it is to be an origin rather than a subject of right. To claim that necessity governs such a decision therefore makes no sense.

1   This phrase is cited from the German edition because it has not been captured by the English translation. The following is the German original: '*Grade aus dem, was sie rechtfertigen soll, wird die Diktatur zu einer Aufhebung des Rechtszustandes überhaupt, denn sie bedeutet die Herrschaft eines ausschließlich an der Bewirkung eines konkreten Erfolgs interessierten Verfahrens, die Beseitigung der dem Recht wesentlichen Rücksicht auf den entgegenstehenden Willen eines Rechtssubjekts, wenn dieser Wille dem Erfolg hinderlich im Wege steht; demnach die Entfesselung des Zweckes vom Recht*' (Schmitt 1978: XVI–XVII). Compare this to the English translation: 'Paradoxically, dictatorship becomes an exception to the state of law by doing what it needs to justify; because dictatorship means a form of government that is genuinely designed to resolve a very particular problem. That problem is the successful defence of a case to which the opponent's will is diametrically opposed. Thus there is an unfettering of the means from the law itself' (Schmitt 2014: xlii).

Indeed, Schmitt leaves no doubt that it is a decision that establishes when the legal order 'needs' to be suspended: 'By his own discretion, the extraordinary lawmaker determines the presupposition of his extraordinary powers (danger for public security and order) and the content of the "necessary" measures' (Schmitt 2004: 69). Here, the need for a decision should be distinguished from the need to make a *particular* decision. While circumstances may be such as to create a perceived need for a decision, it does not follow that the content of the decision itself is therefore governed by necessity. 'Necessity', Bernard Williams (1981: 126) writes, 'is not the same as decisiveness'. War, in this view, is not something that is triggered, something into which one is forced, but is decided upon: 'What always matters is the possibility of the extreme case taking place, the real war, and the decision whether this situation has or has not arrived' (Schmitt 1996a: 35).

Political existence

If this is the case, then why does Schmitt nevertheless write about the political decision in terms that appear to imply existential necessity? For example, in *The Concept of the Political*, Schmitt explains that the political sphere is set apart from other spheres by its distinction between friend and enemy (Schmitt 1996a: 26). He then stipulates two criteria for the enemy; namely, that 'he is, in a specially intense way, *existentially* something different and alien' and that this existential difference is such 'that in the extreme case conflicts with him are possible' (Schmitt 1996a: 27, emphasis added). Such conflicts, to the extent that they entail the right of the sovereign to suspend the normal legal order and demand the 'sacrifice of life' from citizens (Schmitt 1996: 35), are furthermore justified only by *existential* threats:

> There exists no rational purpose, no norm no matter how true ... which could justify men in killing each other for this reason. If such physical destruction of human life is not motivated by an existential threat to one's own way of life, then it cannot be justified.
> (Schmitt 1996: 48–9)

One might want to conclude from this that war, and its associated state of exception, is a matter of existential necessity, of 'encounter[ing] an objective, external force ... that makes a life-and-death claim' (Meier 1995: 15). However, as Schmitt himself warns in *The Age of Neutralizations and Depoliticizations*, care must be taken when interpreting concepts whose meaning will depend on their specific use at the time: 'All essential concepts are not normative but existential. If the center of intellectual life has shifted in the last four centuries, so have all concepts and words' (Schmitt, 1996b: 85).

For the meaning of 'existential' itself, it is significant that in this context Schmitt opposes norms to *existence*, given his opposition of norms to *decisions* elsewhere in his work. Indeed, in *Constitutional Theory*, Schmitt not only links political existence to a decision ('political will') but finds this will itself to have an 'existential character':

> The constitution-making power is the political will, whose power or authority is capable of making the concrete, comprehensive decision over the type and form of its own political existence. The decision, therefore, defines the existence of the political unity in toto ... In contrast to any dependence on a normative or abstract justice, the word 'will' denotes the essentially existential character of this ground of validity.
> (Schmitt 2008: 125, footnote and emphasis omitted)

Accordingly, what justifies war is not a threat to bare existence but to the *type and form* of existence; that is, one's political organization. 'Each participant is in a position to judge whether the adversary intends to negate his opponent's *way of life* and therefore must be repulsed or fought in order to preserve one's own *form* of existence' (Schmitt 1996a: 27, emphasis added).

Such a threat may still lead to a situation of necessity, albeit now artificially construed in terms of the 'life or death' of the political form. However, even this necessity does not adequately capture Schmitt's understanding of the decision on the exception. After all, it is not the case that a decision about the form of political existence is taken and then defended in war, but that the decision that determines the form of political existence is *itself* the decision to go to war.

Perhaps one therefore ought to begin one's inquiry elsewhere and ask what role the claim of necessity plays in relation to the decision on the exception. In this respect, Williams's observations on necessity are again helpful:

> To arrive at the conclusion that one must do a certain thing is, typically, to make a discovery – a discovery which is, always minimally and sometimes substantially, a discovery about oneself ... The incapacities [that limit the field of options for actions] are ones that help to constitute character, and if one acknowledges responsibility for anything, one must acknowledge responsibility for decisions and action which are expressions of character – to be an expression of character is perhaps the most substantial way in which an action can be one's own.
> (Williams 1981: 130)

Thus, the declaration of enmity is part of the continuing struggle to define one's own character; a struggle that, *because* it involves claims of necessity, is thereby not defensive but *productive* of meaning. This struggle is an active process for which one cannot but assume responsibility. Therefore, when Schmitt writes that the exception 'confirms not only the rule but also its existence' (Schmitt 2005: 15), 'existence' here should be understood as the meaning conveyed by having been chosen amongst a number of possibilities – in this case, by having been chosen as the rule that one is ready to defend with one's life – and not just as the bare fact of existence. In war, one struggles against an enemy identified as representing the antithesis to what one aspires to be. This makes the enemy valuable for the process of self-constitution. 'Do not speak lightly of the enemy', Schmitt (1950: 90) warns: 'One classifies oneself through one's enemy. One rates oneself through that which one recognizes as enmity'.

Paradoxically, therefore, the 'defence of one's existence' through war is what makes life into something 'serious', something more than mere existence. In risking one's life in war, one takes control, *works* on one's identity and therefore *lives* in an enriched sense. As Karl Löwith writes, in Schmitt 'a real state of mutual enmity gets portrayed not as a naturally given reality but rather as an essential possibility of political existence, as a capacity-for-Being rather than as a naturally determined Being-thus' (Löwith 1995: 148).

From this perspective, it is unsurprising that Schmitt finds that it is with real wars of existence that this possibility of *political* existence ends. When war is conducted as self-defence, one is no longer struggling for meaning, but is merely defending one's life against forces beyond one's control: 'A life which has only death as its antithesis is no longer life but powerlessness and helplessness' (Schmitt 1996b: 95). Similarly, when war is conducted in the name of universal values (that is, values thought to be *necessary*) it requires the eradication of the enemy (Rasch 2004a: 12) and thus destroys any future possibility of struggle.

Necessity as a force that determines action therefore has no place in Schmitt's theory of the political, not only because it would negate the notion of the decision but also because it would spell an end to political existence. What is necessary is neither war nor values, both of which are chosen and thus subject to a decision, but the continuing *possibility* of contestation, of struggle for meaning. This possibility is represented by a plural order in which differences co-exist, as only such an order can contain the continuing possibility of enemies being made, meaning being worked out, and life being something more than mere existence: '[L]ife struggles not with death, spirit not with spiritlessness; spirit struggles with spirit, life with life, and out of the power of an integral understanding of this arises the order of human things' (Schmitt 1996b: 96). Political existence therefore cannot be governed by necessity. On the contrary, in such an order it is necessary that nothing becomes necessary.

Orientation

Once the 'facade of necessity' (Rasch 2000: 1682) has been removed from the political decision, the question once again returns to the decision's freedom. Is it true, as Slavoj Žižek writes, that the decision is a merely arbitrary instance of the sovereign's will?

> The concrete content of the imposed order is arbitrary, dependent on the Sovereign's will, left to historical contingency ... modern conservatism, even more than liberalism, assumes the lesson of the dissolution of the traditional set of values and/or authorities – there is no longer any positive content which could be presupposed as the universally accepted frame of reference.
> (Žižek 1999: 18–19; see, however, Brännström 2016, Chapter 1 in this volume)

Žižek may be right in saying that Schmitt's theory of the political is no longer dependent on a universally accepted frame of reference, but it does not follow that the decision is therefore arbitrary. Just because it is free in the sense that it is not predetermined by norms – '[e]very concrete juristic decision contains a moment of indifference *from the perspective of content*' (Schmitt 2005: 30, emphasis added) – it does not mean that the decision is also indifferent *to* its content. After all, Schmitt characterizes the decision not only as the 'pure decision not based on reason and discussion and not justifying itself ... an absolute decision created out of nothingness' (Schmitt 2005: 66) but also as 'the exacting moral decision' (Schmitt 2005: 65). Arbitrariness suggests whim or the throwing of dice, a lack of interest on the part of the decision maker. The sovereign, however, seeks to establish meaning; he seeks to do the 'right' thing, whatever that may be. This becomes clear when one considers that already in 1919, Schmitt criticizes political romanticism for its lack of political commitment (Schmitt 1986). In *The Concept of the Political*, he then contrasts the 'meaningful antithesis' of the friend–enemy distinction with merely 'interesting antitheses and contrasts, competitions and intrigues of every kind' (Schmitt 1996a: 35). The political, in other words, requires a commitment from the decision maker that the expression of a merely private preference does not.

In her foreword to *Political Theology*, Tracy Strong remarks that the concept of sovereignty 'looks in two directions, marking the line between that which is subject to law ... and that which is not' (Strong 2005: xxi). To situate the sovereign as *oriented* in a certain way is helpful, as orientation entails neither the passivity of subordination (to law, to God, to the Other, to necessity) nor a potentially arbitrary freedom. When one is oriented, one assumes an active, directed stance.

The active aspect of orientation also manages to avoid that other passivity of which Schmitt has sometimes been accused; namely, occasionalism. Löwith, for example, sees the sovereign decision as merely caused by a particular set of factual circumstances (the concrete order) and concludes that this causation removes the need for a separate concept of the decision altogether: 'For it is simply a consequence of decision, which in itself is empty, if from what occurs *de facto* politically, decision happens to derive the sort of content which deprives decisionism as such of an object' (Löwith 1995: 158). To counter this argument, one needs to show that the 'genuine' (Schmitt 2005: 3) decision serves neither merely as an order's means to establish *itself*, nor as the means for the realization of an independent and *arbitrary* will.

In this respect, one could enlist the help of Schmitt's 1912 work *Gesetz und Urteil*, in which he first attempts to situate judicial decisions between the immanence of legal order and an arbitrary transcendence. Looking back over his work in 1968, Schmitt explains in the preface to the second edition of *Gesetz und Urteil* how his 'thought of the independence of the decision ... lead to a definition of state sovereignty as political decision' (Schmitt 1969). He then expresses his hopes that the new edition of *Gesetz und Urteil* may help to clear up the misunderstanding of the decision (*Dezision*) as 'a fantastic act of arbitrariness' and of decisionism (*Dezisionismus*) as a 'dangerous world view' (Schmitt 1969).

In *Gesetz und Urteil*, Schmitt claims that the rightness of a decision arises not from the subsumption of an individual case under a general rule but from the production of this rule through the individual, exceptional case. In this production, the judge orients himself towards a prevailing conception of normality. This normality, however, is not normality as it arises from a common practice of judging (which would once more entail a subsumption of the judge to this practice) but as the common *expectation* inherent in such a practice. Schmitt thus writes: 'A judicial decision is correct today when it can be assumed that another judge would have decided the same' (Schmitt 1969: 71). The judge's decision is therefore neither a norm-governed nor a potentially arbitrary decision. It is normatively constitutive but makes a claim to contribute to an existing project that it could not make had it been arrived at by a throw of dice:

> [T]he system reproduces itself by way of the decisions of its judges. Judges are forced to make particular and singular judgments, yet they do not judge willfully or arbitrarily. They are not viewed as psychologically distinct, free agents, but as members of a community [*sensus communis*] of agents who claim a regulative universality for their particular judgments. In this way, the legal system 'bootstraps' its way into existence, much as the aesthetic sphere does, by virtue of exemplary decisions.
> (Rasch 2004b: 102)

Returning to the decision on the exception, one could argue that here, too, the decision contains an active impulse towards correctness that can only be understood as motivated by an existing context. This context does not govern or regulate the decision's content but determines the sovereign's orientation; that is, the decision's direction towards an existing order whose meaning or 'sense' (Schmitt 2005: 13) it (re-)establishes. The serious situation or *Ernstfall* arises when the contestation of meaning requires that one take a position, that one commit oneself to a 'definite' (Schmitt 2005: 9) point of view. This view is never arbitrary, but is a view of the possibilities that arise as part of an existing legal order.

Responsibility

Even if the sovereign's decision cannot be regarded as arbitrary, the absence of a normative framework to which it can be held means that its ultimate correctness must remain uncertain. It is this uncertainty that impacts the sovereign's ability to disburden himself of responsibility for the decision's consequences:

> We do decide that *this* war was fought for the right reasons, *that* one for the wrong ones, and that *this* ideal is worth fighting and dying for, while *that* one is not … but we do not really *know* whether we are correct or not. Barring revelation, which remains incommunicable, we have no ultimate or transcendental assurance that our decisions are valid for all times and all places. We make them without the assurance that their structure, that their 'form of validity,' absolves us from all responsibility of their having been made.
>
> (Rasch 2000: 1682)

In the political context, such responsibility is thematized by Max Weber, whose lecture *Politics as a Vocation* (Weber 2004) Schmitt attended in 1919, having already on number of occasions referred to Weber's writings in his own (Ulmen 1985: 5). As Schmitt would do later, Weber situates the politician outside of immanent order, in this case the bureaucratic hierarchy in which each action may be reviewed on the basis of rules, the compliance with which disburdens the actor from responsibility for the action's consequences. In this respect, Weber contrasts the role of the politician with that of an official amongst the ranks of civil servants:

> When an official receives an order, his honor lies in his ability to carry it out, on his superior's *responsibility*, conscientiously and exactly as if it corresponded to his own convictions. This remains the case even if the order seems wrong to him and if, despite his protests, his superior insists on his compliance … In contrast, the point of honor of the

political leader, that is, the leading statesman, is that he acts exclusively on his own responsibility, a responsibility that he may not and cannot refuse or shuffle off onto someone else.

(Weber 2004: 54)

At the same time, Weber distinguishes what he calls an 'ethics of responsibility' from an 'ethics of conviction' (Weber 2004: 83). The latter refers to a belief in truth as the guiding principle for action whereby the actor, as if under orders, acts not on his own, but on another's responsibility. Weber explains that when a Christian acts in accordance with his belief regardless of the concrete circumstances, he is able to do so without burdening his conscience, because he can refer the outcome of his actions either to the grace of God or the wickedness of the people. In either case, he does not need to assume responsibility himself. Not so for the politician, who must be aware that he himself 'holds in his hands a strand of some important historical process' (Weber 2004: 76) and that no one can answer in his place for the consequences of his actions. The politician, in other words, must adopt an ethics of responsibility.

For Weber, this responsibility arises in the absence of any guarantee of the decision's correctness. It is the assumption of one's own position in relation to a specific problem. The actor feels himself burdened, he 'takes on' or 'carries' this burden of the decision: 'What matters is the trained ability to scrutinize the realities of life ruthlessly, to withstand them and to measure up to them inwardly' (Weber 2004: 91). In contrast, those acting under an ethics of conviction lack this 'inner gravity'. They are 'windbags who do not genuinely feel what they are taking on themselves but who are making themselves drunk on romantic sensations' (Weber 2004: 92).

Schmitt describes a similar distinction in relation to the state, where religious and social associations pursue their own particular objectives without regard to the wider effects of their actions. In contrast, the sovereign has in mind the stability of the legal order as a whole, for which he takes responsibility (Schmitt 1938: 116–17). Both Weber and Schmitt also juxtapose political action in this sense (which may include the entering into war) with religious or just wars. For Weber, actors in religious wars justify what they do by the absolute value of the ends they intend to achieve in principle and are therefore able to exhibit a disregard for the concrete circumstances and likely consequences of their actions in the present. In phrases that Schmitt repeats almost identically (Schmitt 1996: 36), Weber writes: 'It is always the very *last* use of force that will then bring about a situation in which *all* violence will have been destroyed' (Weber 2004: 85).

This leaves one to consider as a final point whether the responsibility Schmitt has in mind may perhaps, as Heinrich Meier thinks, be the responsibility of the religious believer to do the right thing in the expectation of a final judgement. According to Meier, in the absence of knowledge of what such a decision would entail, '*probity* has to carry the whole burden' of making the right decision (Meier 1995: 80–1), while at the same time 'the certainty that the course of fate is always *in order* already and that *salvation* is the meaning of all world history' offers 'relief' (Meier 1995: 81). Although Meier's reading highlights the unilateral assumption of responsibility, the closure of meaning that the notion of a final judgement entails does not accord with Schmitt's own emphasis on continuing struggle that may never find an endpoint. Schmitt is not a thinker of the 'always-already' but of the 'not-yet'. For him, the task is not to respond and conform, but to struggle and create. Within this creative process, the decision's correctness cannot be known nor can it be anticipated. Therefore, the sovereign cannot but assume himself the burden of responsibility for its consequences.

Conclusion

In *Politics of Friendship*, Derrida writes that '[w]ithout the possibility of radical evil, of perjury, and of absolute crime, there is no responsibility, no freedom, no decision. And this possibility, as such, if there is one, must be neither living nor dead' (Derrida 1997: 218–19; on Derrida and Schmitt, see De Ville 2016, Chapter 9 in this volume). Schmitt's theory of the political with its notion of the free decision not subordinated to norms cannot rule out this possibility of radical evil. However, because of this possibility, the decision *can* be a decision and *can* be responsible.

This chapter has argued that the 'juristic' space between legal order and the state of nature (Schmitt 2005: 13) in which the decision is taken can be construed as a space between law, necessity and arbitrary freedom (on the 'in-between', see, however, Falk 2016, Chapter 12 in this volume). It began by explaining why necessity, whether in its guize as a situation of self-defence or as action determined by absolute values, is incompatible with the notion of the decision. The political, according to Schmitt, takes precedence over the moral because it represents the continuing and open struggle for meaning that makes life worth living. Necessity would negate the agency needed for this struggle, and would end its process.

This chapter has then shown that the sovereign, rather than deciding arbitrarily, ought to be imagined as oriented towards the legal order on which he decides. However, the decision nonetheless remains uncertain, and the sovereign therefore cannot avail himself of the burden of responsibility for its consequences. On the contrary, his is a responsibility for the order as a whole, and he actively assumes this burden in the struggle for a life that is more than mere existence.

This reading has been proposed to counteract the critical association of Schmitt with a practical tendency to present all political decisions in the light of existential necessity, enabling those in charge both to act outside of law *and* claim that their decisions were forced upon them by necessity (as if it went without saying that outside law, there existed only the state of nature). It has endeavoured to show that Schmitt ought not to be associated with this tendency, as necessity plays no part in his theory of the political. Furthermore, by restoring to Schmitt's decision its aspects of freedom and independence, one is able to highlight not only the implications of choice, but also establish a positive role for the political decision maker beyond the role of law-abiding subject, arbitrary dictator, or, helpless victim of higher forces.

Bibliography

Agamben, G. (2005) *State of Exception*. Trans. K. Attell. Chicago, IL: University of Chicago Press.

Brännström, L. (2016) 'Carl Schmitt's Definition of Sovereignty as Authorized Leadership', Chapter 1 in M. Arvidsson, L. Brännström and P. Minkkinen (eds), *The Contemporary Relevance of Carl Schmitt: Law, Politics, Theology*. Abingdon: Routledge.

De Ville, J. (2016) 'Rethinking the Concept of the Political: Derrida's reading of Schmitt's 'The Theory of the Partisan', Chapter 9 in M. Arvidsson, L. Brännström and P. Minkkinen (eds), *The Contemporary Relevance of Carl Schmitt: Law, Politics, Theology*. Abingdon: Routledge.

Derrida, J. (1997) *Politics of Friendship*. Trans. G. Collins. London: Verso.

Falk, H. (2016) '*Im Kampf um Rom*': Carl Schmitt's Critique of Rudolph Sohm and the Post-secular Turn', Chapter 12 in M. Arvidsson, L. Brännström and P. Minkkinen (eds), *The Contemporary Relevance of Carl Schmitt. Law, Politics, Theology*. Abingdon: Routledge.

Kahn, P.W. (2011) *Political Theology: Four New Chapters on the Concept of Sovereignty*. New York: Columbia University Press.

Löwith, K. (1995) *Martin Heidegger and European Nihilism* [1983]. Trans. G. Steiner. New York: Columbia University Press.

Meier, H. (1995) *Carl Schmitt and Leo Straus: The Hidden Dialogue*. Trans. J. H. Lomax. Chicago, IL: University of Chicago Press.

Rasch, W. (2000) 'A Just War? Or Just War? Schmitt, Habermas, and the Cosmopolitan Orthodoxy', *Cardozo Law Review*, Vol. 21, No. 5–6: 1665–84.

Rasch, W. (2004a) *Sovereignty and its Discontents*. London: Birkbeck Law.

Rasch, W. (2004b) 'Judgment: The Emergence of Legal Norms', *Cultural Critique*, Vol. 57: 93–103.

Schmitt, C. (1922) *Politische Theologie: Vier Kapitel zur Lehre von der Souveränität*. München: Duncker and Humblot.

Schmitt, C. (1938) *Der Leviathan in der Staatslehre des Thomas Hobbes: Sinn und Fehlschlag eines politischen Symbols*. Hamburg: Hanseatische Verlagsanstalt.

Schmitt, C. (1950) *Ex Captivitate Salus: Erfahrungen aus der Zeit 1945/47*. Köln: Greven Verlag.

Schmitt, C. (1963) *Der Begriff des Politischen* [1927]. *Text von 1932 mit einem Vorwort und drei Corollarien*. Berlin: Duncker and Humblot.

Schmitt, C. (1969) *Gesetz und Urteil: Eine Untersuchung zum Problem der Rechtspraxis* [1912]. München: C. H. Beck'sche Verlagsbuchhandlung.

Schmitt, C. (1978) *Die Diktatur: Von den Anfängen des modernen Souveränitätsgedankens bis zum proletarischen Klassenkampf* [1921]. Berlin: Duncker and Humblot.
Schmitt, C. (1986) *Political Romanticism* [1919]. Trans. G. Oakes. Cambridge, MA: MIT Press.
Schmitt, C. (1995) 'Die Raumrevolution' [1940], p. 388–91, in C. Schmitt, *Staat, Großraum, Nomos: Arbeiten aus den Jahren 1916–1969*. Berlin: Duncker and Humblot.
Schmitt, C. (1996a) *The Concept of the Political* [1927]. Trans. G. Schwab. Chicago, IL: University of Chicago Press.
Schmitt, C. (1996b) 'The Age of Neutralizations and Depoliticizations' [1929], p. 80–96, in C. Schmitt, *The Concept of the Political* [1927]. Trans. G. Schwab. Chicago, IL: University of Chicago Press.
Schmitt, C. (2004) *Legality and Legitimacy* [1932]. Trans. J. Seitzer. Durham, NC: Duke University Press.
Schmitt, C. (2005) *Political Theology: Four Chapters on the Concept of Sovereignty* [1922]. Trans. G. Schwab. Chicago, IL: University of Chicago Press.
Schmitt, C. (2008) *Constitutional Theory* [1928]. Trans. J. Seitzer. Durham, NC: Duke University Press.
Schmitt, C. (2014) *Dictatorship: From the Origin of the Modern Concept of Sovereignty to Proletarian Class Struggle* [1921]. Trans. M. Hoelzl and G. Ward. Cambridge: Polity.
Strauss, L. (1995) 'Notes on Carl Schmitt, The Concept of the Political' [1932], in H. Meier, *Carl Schmitt and Leo Straus: The Hidden Dialogue* [1988]. Trans. J. H. Lomax. Chicago, IL: University of Chicago Press.
Strong, T. B. (2005) Foreword, p. xvi–xxxv, to *Political Theology: Four Chapters on the Concept of Sovereignty* [1922], C. Schmitt. Trans. G. Schwab. Chicago, IL: University of Chicago Press.
Ulmen, G. L. (1985) 'The Sociology of the State: Carl Schmitt and Max Weber', *State, Culture, and Society*, Vol. 1, No. 2: 3–57.
Weber, M. (2004) 'Politics as a Vocation', in M. Weber, *The Vocation Lectures* [1919]. Trans. R. Livingstone. Indianapolis, IN: Hackett.
Williams, B. A. O. (1981) *Moral Luck: Philosophical Papers 1973–1980*. Cambridge: Cambridge University Press.
Žižek, S. (1999) 'Carl Schmitt in the Age of Post-Politics', in C. Mouffe (ed.) *The Challenge of Carl Schmitt*. London: Verso.

Chapter 8

Representation and the unrepresentable

Ernst Jünger, Carl Schmitt and the limits of politics

Mårten Björk

Ernst Jünger and Carl Schmitt: an estranged relationship

The relationship between Ernst Jünger and Carl Schmitt was in many ways one of estrangement.[1] This is evident both in the notes on Jünger that Schmitt made in his *Glossarium* (Schmitt 1991) and in their correspondence (Jünger and Schmitt 2012). Although their friendship lasted for fifty years, from when they met in Berlin to when Schmitt died in 1987, it was marked by tensions between them. These tensions did not only have to do with personal differences, but also with philosophical differences of outmost importance. They both belonged to what has been called the conservative revolution (Mohler 1972), but in the years after the First World War, Jünger, much more so than Schmitt, was a radical conservative or even fascist activist. Adolf Hitler had written to Jünger in 1926 that he had read all his books and Jünger gave the future dictator a dedicated copy of *Feur und Blut* (Trawny 2009: 49). But Jünger never followed Schmitt when his friend joined the National Socialist German Workers' Party and subsequently became 'the Crown Jurist of the Third Reich' (Frye 1966). This sealed the fate of the two friends. Schmitt was arrested after the Second World War and detained for interrogation, whereas Jünger embarked on a journey as a celebrated author (Balakrishnan 2000).

So what lead Jünger, who much more than Schmitt had championed an anti-democratic nationalism at least until the 1930s, and for many years, had an ambivalent rather than an openly hostile relation to Hitler (Kiesel 2007), to avoid National Socialism while Schmitt embraced it? Their conservative, but nonetheless, different views on the question of the

---

[1] Some of Ernst Jünger's numerous books and essays have been translated to English. Examples of these are: *The Forest Passage* (2013), *The Adventurous Heart* (2012) *Eumeswil* (1993), *The Peace* (1948). An introduction to Jünger can be found in *A Dubious Past: Ernst Jünger and the Politics of Literature after Nazism* (Neaman 1999).

political could be one way of answering this question. The political and philosophical differences between the two friends have been noted in the quite scarce literature on them (Hohendahl 2003; Horn 2004; Morat 2007; Steil 1984), but a proper discussion on how these differences evolved and crystallized is still lacking. In this chapter I highlight the philosophical difference between Jünger and Schmitt by discussing the relation between politics, representation and what we can call the unrepresentable. Although this leaves many problems unsolved, it may explain not only how the political views of the two friends differ but also why their politics, albeit in divergent ways, address key questions of our times – such as how an ethics and politics can be developed in a world characterized by the crisis of the nation state (Hohendahl 2003).

The world of the worker

In a diary note from 1951, Schmitt writes a resentful comment on Jünger: 'One can say many things of me. One can insult me and call me a Crown Jurist, but I have never fallen to the myth of the worker. I have never written a book like *Der Arbeiter*' (Schmitt 1991: 313). *Der Arbeiter* was Jünger's book. Schmitt not only mocks his friend for writing *Der Arbeiter: Herrschaft und Gestalt*, originally published in 1932 (Jünger 1981) but also for the novel *Heliopolis* (Jünger 1949), in which Jünger allegorically criticizes the anti-Semitism of the Third Reich. This comment should be kept in mind when Schmitt, four year later, contributes to *Freundschaftliche Begegnungen* (Mohler 1955), a Festschrift dedicated to Ernst Jünger on his sixtieth birthday. Schmitt's essay is a critique of Jünger's book *Der Gordische Knoten* (Jünger 1953) and especially his use of the symbols of ship and forest.

To Jünger, the ship is a symbol of the world of the worker, a world constantly threatened to shipwreck. The worker is an ontological form and cannot adequately be understood as an empirical phenomenon. Work 'knows ... no opposition outside itself, it is like a fire which consumes everything combustible' (Jünger 1981: 22).[2] The fact that civilization has been transformed into the burning fire of work, which potentially consumes everything as material for its growth, makes Jünger in his later work, for example *The Forest Passage* from 1951 (Jünger 2001a/2013), write about his time as a ship or more specifically as a Titanic, a civilization prone to sink into the dark void of catastrophe. Man as an individual, a singular exemplar of the species, lives in a society which floats on a sea that can be calm as the spring breeze or violent as rapturous lightning:

---

2   References to English editions have been made whenever possible. All translations from the German are, however, mine.

> The individual no longer stands in society like a tree in the forest, he is rather like a passenger on a fast moving vehicle, that both can be called Titanic or Leviathan. As long as the weather is good and the view pleasant is the state of less freedom that he lives in hardly perceivable.
>
> (Jünger 2001a: 30)

The world of the worker in *The Forest Passage* is symbolized by this oscillation between the sinking ship and the sea monster Leviathan, which Thomas Hobbes mythically conjured as a symbol of the state. Man is captured in a dialectic where the state secures its citizen's existence through the rule of conformity which can turn into the war against all that Hobbes had hoped his poor beast would save man from. Jünger points out this dangerous dialectic between the administration of things (Leviathan) and the potential destruction of the state of being which the sea monster promises to defend (Titanic), and uses the symbol of the ship for this oscillation between conformity and civil war. The ship has its counter concept in the forest, *der Wald*, which is the form of freedom that it is possible to develop while one still is living on the ship (Jünger 2001a: 19).

In 1941, ten years before *The Forest Passage* was published, and in the midst of war, Jünger wrote *The Peace* (Jünger 1948). He secretly circulated it amongst friends and colleagues in the army. The essay was a manifesto for peace, and it radically broke with Jünger's pre-war nationalism and glorification of war. *The Peace* ends with the question of how 'the individual [*der Einzelne*]' can contribute to peace (Jünger 1980a: 235). Jünger acknowledges the dangerous and almost impossible situation for actions against the war but describes the work for peace waged by individuals as a light in a vast darkness (Jünger 1980a: 236). The individual has the ability to react against the situation of which it is a part and, even though its actions may prove to be ineffective, they represent and signal the future possibility of something else, of something that is unrepresentable in the current state of things. The action of the individual opens in this way hidden gaps and lacunas in the world of the worker; it shows that the individual can act against the conformity and laws of effectiveness that characterize the life of Leviathan, even though the actions seldom have more than symbolical meaning.

The forest and the individual are representations of what Jünger in later texts would call anarchy (Jünger 1980b; 1993). The Titanic, the Leviathan and the ship symbolize an order that can turn into war, whereas the order of peace is placed near the concept of anarchy and freedom, as it defy the limits and politics of the nations (Jünger 1980b: 523). This is why Jünger's use of the symbols of the ship and the forest is problematic to Schmitt: it moves beyond the order of politics towards ethics, ontology and even myth. Jünger uses his symbols as ontological concepts which describe a certain state of being. This state of being constitutes the political as such, whereas the ship, for Schmitt, designates a historical and political distinction between two modes of sovereignty, namely *land and sea* (see Langford and Bryan 2016, Chapter 14 in this volume). Even though Schmitt underlines that 'mechanization [*Technisierung*] and industrialization is the fate of our world' (Schmitt 1955: 161) the ship is not an image for the world of the worker. The territorial existence is a *nomos of the earth*, a set of laws and norms, which ground a territorial state. The concept of the *nomos* is for Schmitt 'the first land-appropriation understood as the first partition and classification of space' (Schmitt 2003: 67). The *nomos* takes and names land; it grounds man on earth as a spatial and political being. *The nomos names and constitutes a polis*, so when Kam Shapiro in his book on Schmitt says that 'all legal systems stem from a territorial order' (Shapiro 2008: 69), we have to add that this also can be said of all political systems. Political existence is a territorial existence, but what then of the ship? What can be said of the politics of maritime existence?

The ship and the *nomos* of the sea

It is no coincidence that Schmitt points out that the industrial revolution was spearheaded in England, an island country, which in the late seventeenth century transformed to what Schmitt calls a 'pure marine based existence' (Schmitt 1955: 158). This made it possible for England to become a world power and to stretch its dominion to all parts of the earth. When England had ripped itself from the *nomos* of Europe, the order of the land became weakened by the mores, rules and laws that fitted the new habitat of man – the ocean and its politics of commerce and industry:

> The sea prevailed over land, while the island England had understood and accepted the great challenges that the World Ocean meant, and therefore it relocated its whole existence to the sea ... The island ceases to be a separated land and turns itself into a ship.
> (Schmitt 1955: 160)

According to Schmitt the symbol of the ship therefore implies a change in the political order: 'At the place of the old, pure territorial *nomos* of the earth is a new *nomos*, which includes the World Ocean in its order, emerging' (Schmitt 1955: 160). The ship is, for Schmitt, an adequate symbol for a world where the politics of the land is threatened by the economy of the sea (Kervégan 1999: 66). This is why Schmitt can argue that: 'The time of the Leviathan ... is therefore now at its end' (Schmitt 1995a: 398). The politics of the Leviathan, the norms and laws of the good monster that secures the livelihood of the citizens in a geographically determined state, was threatened by the new *nomos*, which defies the territorial order that is essential for Schmitt's definition of the political.

The notion of the political as a distinction between friends and enemies in *The Concept of the Political* (Schmitt 2007a) is impossible to understand independently from Schmitt's conceptualization of the political as a public and spatial representation (see Falk 2016, Chapter 12 in this volume). The grounding of a *nomos* makes an enemy possible, and this is done through public representation as it differentiates a public, spatial community – a nation state – against another one. This view of the political as a form of public representation is especially evident in Schmitt's *Constitutional Theory*: 'To represent means to make visible an invisible entity through an entity which is publicly present' (Schmitt 2008: 243). This form of public representation is 'not a normative event' but rather 'something existential ... that presupposes a special kind of being. Something dead, something inferior or valueless, something lowly cannot be represented. It lacks the enhanced type of being that is capable of an existence, of rising into the public being' (Schmitt 2008: 243). The political therefore represents the glory of the nation and the state as an existential fact, which for Schmitt has its truth in the existential difference between friend and enemy.

In his critique of Jünger, Schmitt uses the geographer Jean Gottman's theories of an *iconographie régionale* – a regional iconography – as an example of this kind of enhanced being that has the possibility to represent a political order (Schmitt 1955: 139). A representation makes the invisible visible by occupying space, by becoming an image or an icon of a certain region of the world. Every representation is therefore an occupation of a distinct spatiality, a *nomos*, and if representation is a '*sichtbar machen*', a 'making visible' of the invisible through a spatial iconography, then the invisible is something that, for Schmitt, is produced as a representation in the public domain. This visibility of the invisibility is the nation state, which, as we have seen, is weakened by the *nomos* of the sea. But the decline of the Leviathan also signals a crisis of the *nomos* of sea, as it leads to the world we are living in today, a planetary, post-industrial reign of capital which Schmitt in the 1940s described as the destruction of both land and sea: 'The sea has lost its power and our world has turned into an airport' (Schmitt 1995b: 479). It is the growing impossibility of representing man as a political animal bound to a territorial state that signals the death of that spatial creature called the Leviathan, according to Schmitt. This does not mean that the politics of land is over once and for all. Schmitt finds in his later works, for example, a terrestrial form of politics in the partisan and the guerrilla fighter tied to land: 'The partisan will present a specifically terrestrial type of the active fighter for at least as long as anticolonial wars are possible on our planet' (Schmitt 2007b: 14). But this fact signals that the politics of land is weakened, it is something that is waged by partisans against a *nomos* that has uprooted itself from the land. The politics of representation that Schmitt defends is therefore essentially a politics of the place, which is weakened by the *nomos* of the sea, symbolized by the ship.

This is something radically different from Jünger's attempt to describe the political representation denoted by the form of the worker.

The strategy of the partisan, and more generally, a politics of spatiality, is problematic for Jünger in later life, as the world of the worker signals an irreversible crisis of the *nomos* of land. Peter Trawny (2009) is certainly right that *Der Arbeiter* was originally conceived as a nationalist tractate, but later in his life, Jünger argued that the world of the worker implies a development that surpasses the nation state and even sets the individual against the logic of the worker. For Jünger, as much as for Schmitt, the aeroplane becomes a symbol that shows the antiquity of the nation, but Jünger affirms this development as what he describes in *Der Weltstaat* as 'the destiny of the centre' (Jünger 1980b: 500). Peter Hohendahl (2008) has argued that Schmitt wrote his essay on the partisan against this hope of a world state. And it is true that Jünger describes in *Der Weltstaat* how the world of the worker produces the potentiality of a planetary reign beyond nations and borders, which can surpass the enmity that Schmitt defends as the truth of the political. Instead of the friend and enemy dichotomy, Jünger argues for a politics of 'both as well [*Sowohl-Als-Auch*]' and, as in his earlier essays, this hope is posited in the solitary being of the concrete person. The individual exemplar of the species can affirm this coming destiny as a new political potentiality of *Homo sapiens* (Jünger 1980b: 500). But it is the workers themselves that produce this potential and the world of the worker includes both the *nomos* of land and sea, although the rise of industry for Jünger begins in the *nomos* of the land rather than in the *nomos* of the sea. The world of the ship, that is the worker, is impossible without that territorial existence that is the *nomos of the land*. Because 'the worker', writes Jünger, is a 'son of the earth' (Jünger 1981: 164).

Man in the belly of a dying beast

Why is the worker a son of the earth? We can find an answer in Jünger's book *An der Zeitmauer*: 'Our machine park is unthinkable without the hand that stuck a stone to a stick for the first time', Jünger writes, and he ties technology to the development of the species as *Homo sapiens* (Jünger 1959: 134). The world of the machine cannot be understood independently from the millennial development of technology itself, and therefore neither can it be separated from the development of the state as a spatial entity. The latter was, for Jünger, first and foremost a question of technology and war. In *Maxima – Minima*, the comment to *Der Arbeiter* that he wrote 1964, Jünger points out that wars are the promoters of science and technology and the destruction of the 'musical world' (Jünger 1981: 162). The world of the worker is impossible without the agricultural and political revolution which bound man to the earth as a territorial state, as a nation that waged war against other nations. But the logic of war cannot be repressed by rules and laws. War creates its own norms and development and this historical trajectory of war – both territorial and maritime – leads to the world of the worker. This is why Jünger in *An der Zeitmauer* turns to Hesiod's ages of man in his poem 'Work and Days' to point out that the history of war is essentially the history of cities and states, a history of the *nomos*. But this is not the whole history of man. Jünger uses Hesiod's story about the golden age to conjure a world before economy and politics, before states and war and, most importantly, before gods and names; that is, *before the possibility of a nomos*. It is essential to state that this is not the mythic world for Jünger. The world of the myth is filled with gods, wars and names. *Nomos* belong to the mythical world of the Leviathan and the worker. The world before the name and the *nomos* is the world of *das Märchen*, of 'the tale', which can be violent and primitive but that knows no states, wars or names:

> The tale knows no names, even the author is nameless ... The tale does not yet know the mythical heroes, let alone the historical personalities. It knows about bad people, the giant, the renegade Dwarf, the homicide, but it knows nothing about the war, which is the great, yes, the only, theme in the mythical world ... It has probably plenty, but no gods [*Es hat wohl Überfluß, doch keine Götterwelt*].
>
> (Jünger 1959: 149)

The world of 'plenty', of '*Überfluß*', is a world that Jünger calls 'eternal peace'. He describes it as a 'habitat ... without limits', much like his later world state, where the solitary beings of the species can roam in peace (Jünger 1959: 126). This peace is a wilderness that is not bound by the state or the city, or grounded by names or gods, even the world state is described by Jünger in *Der Weltstaat* as the historical end of the state (Jünger 1980b: 525). It is important to note that this tale of the golden age is not an ideal state so much as a description of what Jünger – borrowing a term from Friedrich Hölderlin's poem 'Chiron' – calls the 'unurban [*unstädtisch*]' in men; that is, without state and city. This is why the time without wars, states and names is not only a Utopian description of a coming order or an age that once was but an anthropological potentiality that makes man a being that cannot completely be reduced to a *political animal* (Jünger 1959: 155).

The 'unurban' lives on in all that cannot be grounded in a myth, a *nomos* or in a political narrative; it is the unrepresentable, the point in man that is not possible to represent politically or publically. This potential to a freedom, or even anarchy, which defies the norms of the state, and surpasses the representation of spatiality that Schmitt's concept of the political reproduces, does not disappears in the post-political world of the worker. It is rather generalized to the species as such. The reduction of politics to administration and war to technique creates the possibility of a hidden retreat inside the lives of the anonymous masses. The unurban is shared democratically in the world of the worker to everyone. The anonymous worker, but first and foremost, the Unknown Soldier, paradoxically defies the nationalist or political rhetoric of states, according to the older Jünger, as we do not know to which nation the Unknown Soldier belongs. His presence is a sign that man exists at the limits of politics, as something anonymous, mysterious, unknown and in the end unrepresentable: 'The Unknown Soldier is ... not a hero ... He has neither personality nor individuality, no epic or history is tied to his deeds. He has no names and fundamentally no fatherland' (Jünger 1959: 103). The Unknown Soldier has transcended the *nomos* of the earth, as he no longer belongs to a political order. He is an expression of the singular life that the state has to subsume as a citizen, a member of a political community and which therefore exists beyond the state as a positivity. Or he is a corpse that cannot be represented as something other than a ghost, a sort of living invisibility. In this sense, the Unknown Soldier is the debased creature which, according to Schmitt, can never act as a proper representation (Schmitt 2008: 243). Even though the state uses the Unknown Soldier as a patriotic symbol, the dead and, especially, the dead and unknown soldiers and other victims of war, do haunt politics with an apolitical potential, according to Jünger. The Unknown Soldier represents a potential to undermine the distinction between friend and enemy, a distinction on which the political is grounded. He is the symbol of the *both-as-well* that craves the world state that for Schmitt would lead to the death of politics, namely the annulation of the either or of friend and enemy.

The apolitical life of the masses

If Schmitt is right about the political being the difference between enemy and friend, it implies that a political movement has to mediate the relations between the people and the state. For Schmitt, the people has to become the subject of a state, the site of the political. The movement politicizes the people as a member of a state, which has a specific, if only potential, enemy. In *State, Movement, People* Schmitt therefore defines the movement (or the party) and the state as the dynamic, respectively static, sides of the political (Schmitt 2001: 12). Outside of them lies the third term – the people – which represents 'the apolitical side, growing under the protection, and in the shade of the political decision' (Schmitt 2001: 12). These masses of men who live in 'the apolitical private sphere' (Schmitt 2001: 25) come before politics, and exist as those who can only say yes or no to the political decision that the sovereign, represented in the movement, puts forth: 'The people can only respond yes or no. They cannot advise, deliberate, or discuss. They cannot govern or administer' (Schmitt 2004: 89). Schmitt's apolitical definition of the people as the shade of the public life of the state can be read through Jünger as an example of the growing anonymity of the masses, for which the worker and the Unknown Soldier stand. The people are caught in the political decision, especially as the limits between the political and apolitical side of life is a political decision in itself. But, as Jünger reminds us, 'the people' are made up of concrete subjects, singular exemplars of the species who can reject the political decision, and answer it with a form of brutal indifference to the movements that posits the people in relation to the state.

Schmitt's thesis is that the people are politicized by the political movements which transform them into citizens in and for a certain state and therefore into subjects with a potential enemy. But Jünger tries to understand the limit of this process by discussing the forms of life and phenomena, such as the Unknown Soldier, which cannot adequately be represented in the life of the state. Even though the soldier probably did his duty, and died for his country, his remnants show a limit of the political as such, namely the singular being of man; this is the corporeal creature that has the possibility to defy the binary opposition between friend and enemy which the political reproduce through the obedience and acclamations of the people. The anonymous and mysterious creatures which constitute the people show that there is a 'forest passage' for every man, or what Jünger in *Der Weltstaat* and his novel *Eumeswil* calls an anarchical way of life.

The singular being of the species and, of course, groups and classes of men, can defy the role of the apolitical force which grounds the political. Jünger does not deny that politics is a fundamental part of human life. The facts of life forces our species in to politics which, for Jünger, means that state building is part of animal existence as such (Jünger 1980b: 523). Politics, and the order of the state, are zoological phenomena; they do not define the *Homo sapiens* as human. The political rather binds our species to the animal and natural world:

> Spiritual freedom characterizes the human species. One only finds it in him. To be a political creature, or to build a state is not something that only characterizes humans. Humans have lived long without states and will maybe be able to do that again.
>
> (Jünger 1959: 277)

The potentiality of man as a species is to evolve beyond the sheer animality of the state and the economy. Not necessarily to criticize it or try to live outside it, but to understand that the potential of our species-being is to live at the limits of the politics, in a freedom that may be grounded by economy and politics but that certainly is not identical with it.

The anarchical life of the species

The essential limit of politics is, for Jünger, the singular exemplar of the species; more precisely, it is the potential of this creature to differentiate itself from the current destiny of *Homo sapiens*, as the life of the species has become the political and economical life of the worker. But the possibility of a sort of exodus from the world of the worker is, as we have seen, produced by this world as the possible advent of a political order beyond the nation state. This should not be read as some sort of Hegelian teleology: the only ethical truth that exists in history for Jünger in later life is the one that lies in the capacity of the singular exemplar of our species to act against the Titanic, but contingent, forces that mould the history of *Homo sapiens*. It is telling that Jünger, when he was ninety-four years old, comments on Schopenhauer in *Die Schere*: 'For Schopenhauer the world history is not more than a trajectory of contingent constellations – real, however, is the individual (der Einzelne)' (Jünger 2001b: 19). If Jünger accepts this Schopenhauerian metaphysics of the concrete then Schmitt is closer to the philosophy of Hegel. This is evident in one of Schmitt's most interesting early works, *Der Wert des Staates und die Bedeutung des Einzelnen* (Schmitt 1914). In this book, Schmitt develops what we can call a transcendentalism of the state: the state is not a sum of individual atoms and not constituted by its parts, it does not perceive the individuals it defends and protects as something outside of itself. The state rather produces individuals as citizens, as entities already subsumed in its life and offices. But this early work should not be read as an anti-individualist tractate, at least not according to Schmitt. He explicitly states that the book is an attempt to save the dignity of the individual by developing a theory of the state and criticizing the false individualism which has no possibility to safeguard the objective value of the individual: 'A time, that is sceptic and precise, cannot … call itself individualistic: neither scepticism nor the preciseness of the natural sciences can ground an individual' (Schmitt 1914: 4).

The modern, industrial world is not an individualistic society *per se* for Schmitt, but rather, a society of affects, forces and passions which undermine the offices, mores and values which, according to Schmitt, are characteristics of a good society. It is the goodness of the offices of the state which can ground or even produce an individual and 'more important than that there are men, is that there are good and righteous men' (Schmitt 1914: 99). But goodness and righteousness comes from *das Recht*, the right, which cannot be deduced from individuals as such: 'The right … comes … before the individual … it knows absolutely of no individuals [*es kennt überhaupt keinen Einzelnen*]' (Schmitt 1914: 98–9). The value of man lies in his possibility to be a '*Werkzeug*', a tool of the political order, or a '*Diener der Staates*', a servant of the state (Schmitt 1914: 94). This is especially true of the leader of the state. The leader is meaningless as a corporeal person but filled with value as a legal and political representation of the state: 'The dignity that he may require or that is attributed to him only applies to his office, not to the mortal man' (Schmitt 1914: 96).

Schmitt's transcendentalism of the state is almost an inverted version of Jünger's philosophy. Jünger sees, in later life, the singular exemplar of the species as the anarchical and unrepresentable life of humanity. With every single being there is not only a continuation of the life of *Homo sapiens* but also an expression of something more, an excess and an anarchy which breaks with the transcendental functions that the state and the economy imposes on humanity. The individual can deny the role of the citizen and the worker, as they are roles and functions which have to be performed and reproduced by the corporeal beings which the world of the worker subsumes as workers. Jünger is no anarchist. The point of his critique of the state in *Eumeswil*, *The Forest Passage* and *Der Weltstaat* is not to describe a life outside the political order. The normalcy of anarchy brought forth by the life of the species, with every singular being, is from Jünger's perspective almost a pessimistic acceptance of the law's and the *nomos*' unsuccessfulness in bringing about peace and order. The *nomos* of the land did not protect our species from the two World Wars but rather led us into the world of the worker whose tendency to war and chaos, according to Jünger, only can be stopped by an order that goes beyond the world of nations and states (Jünger 1980b). This cosmopolitical order is obviously not here yet, and in the wait for the development of a state of things that transcends the nation, the individual beings of the species must face the world of the worker as a ship on which they have to travel and therefore find the gaps and lacunas between their corporal beings and the transcendental functions that the state and the economy imposes on them. Jünger argues that the life of *Homo sapiens* is stuck in the bestial life of the state and the worker but against Schmitt, he affirms the possibility for the singular being and groups of men to avoid and therefore relativize the order that finds the dignity of *Homo sapiens* in its political being; that is, in the transcendentalism of the political.

Jünger never denies that the human ape is a political animal but its freedom, and therefore its survival as a human, depends not solely on politics but rather on its possibility to develop a life which cannot be fully represented in the public domain of man. Anarchy is the true being of our species, according to Jünger, and it is this anarchic form of life that the singular being of the species can represent as a freedom that transgresses the offices, values and norms which Schmitt sees as essential for human life. Jünger's notion of the anarchic is problematic for Schmitt, as the individual, according to Schmitt, has no real life outside the state. The state is not an organism constructed by men, but rather a machine that produces man as a political animal: 'the state is not a construction that the men have done, it is rather the state that makes a construction of every man' (Schmitt 1914: 93). It is important to emphasize that this does not necessarily lead to a totalitarian theory of the state and that the construction that the state makes of man could be the democratic citizen, the animal inside the *polis*, as much as anything else. When Schmitt therefore writes that 'no individual has autonomy inside the state' (Schmitt 1914: 101), this is because the transcendentalism of the state is, negatively, an endeavour to avoid the relativity of the corporeal individual and, positively, an attempt to ground law in an objectivity that avoids the contingency of the living and corporeal (Schmitt 1914: 102).

Man is not represented as a corporeal being in the state, but as a legal person, a citizen with rights. But the problem for Jünger is that the concept of the citizen, the man with rights, tends to become a trap in a world where more and more people live outside the life of rights and citizenry. The concept of the citizen is almost a prison as long it is not universal and developed for a world state that gives humanity a common political destiny. As a part of the Leviathan, that dying beast that is still rooted in the nation, the individual is caught in an oscillation between the Leviathan and Titanic, between civilization as a defender of order and a bringer of chaos. This is why, paradoxically, the unrepresentable ground of man (that is, the fact that the corporeal being of man can never be completely subsumed under politics or economy) is a representation of a future freedom that transcends the *nomos* of both earth and sea. What is needed, from Jünger's perspective, is a political form that fits the unrepresentable life of the species. In the interim period, the freedom of the singular *Homo sapiens* can conserve and represent man as a creature that belongs to more than economy and politics, namely the anarchical form of life itself.

Bibliography

Balakrishnan, G. (2000) 'Two on the Marble Cliffs', *New Left Review*, No. 1: 162–8.
Falk, H. (2016) '*Im Kampf um Rom*': Carl Schmitt's Critique of Rudolph Sohm and the Post-secular Turn', Chapter 12 in M. Arvidsson, L. Brännström and P. Minkkinen (eds), *The Contemporary Relevance of Carl Schmitt. Law, Politics, Theology.* Abingdon: Routledge.
Frye, C. E. (1966) 'Carl Schmitt's Concept of the Political', *Journal of Politics*, Vol. 28, No. 4: 818–30.
Hohendahl, P. (2008) 'Reflections on War and Peace after 1940: Ernst Jünger and Carl Schmitt', *Cultural Critique*, Vol. 69: 22–51.
Horn, E. (2004) '"Waldgänger", Traitor, Partisans', *New Centennial Review*, Vol. 4, No. 3: 125–43.
Jünger, E. (1948) *The Peace* [1945]. Trans. S. O. Hood. Hinsdale: Henry Regnery.
Jünger, E. (1949) *Heliopolis: Rückblick auf eine Stadt*. Tübingen: Heliopolis-Verlag.
Jünger, E. (1953) *Der Gordische Knoten*. Frankfurt am Main: Vittorio Klostermann.
Jünger, E. (1959) *An der Zeitmauer*. Stuttgart: Klett Cotta.

Jünger, E. (1980a) 'Der Friede: ein Wort an die Jugend Europas und an die Jugend der Welt' [1945], p. 195–236, in E. Jünger, *Sämtliche Werke. Band 7. Essays 1: Betrachtungen zur Zeit.* Stuttgart: Klett Cotta.

Jünger, E. (1980b) 'Der Weltstaat: Organismus und Organisation' [1960], p. 481–526, in E. Jünger, *Sämtliche Werke. Band 7. Essays 1: Betrachtungen zur Zeit.* Stuttgart: Klett Cotta.

Jünger, E. (1981) *Der Arbeiter: Herrschaft und Gestalt* [1932]. Stuttgart: Klett Cotta.

Jünger, E. (1993) *Eumeswil* [1977]. Trans. J. Neugroschel. New York: Marsilio.

Jünger, E. (2001a) *Der Waldgang* [1951]. Stuttgart: Klett Cotta.

Jünger, E. (2001b) *Die Schere* [1990]. Stuttgart: Klett Cotta.

Jünger, E. (2012) *The Adventurous Heart: figures and capriccios* [1938]. Trans. T. Friese. Candor, NY: Telos.

Jünger, E. and C. Schmitt (2012) *Briefe 1930–1983.* Stuttgart: Klett Cotta.

Jünger, E. (2013) *The Forest Passage* [1951]. Trans. T. Friese. Candor, NY: Telos.

Kervégan, J.F. (1999) 'Carl Schmitt and "World Unity"', p. 54–74, in C. Mouffe (ed.) *The Challenge of Carl Schmitt.* London: Verso.

Kiesel, H. (2007) *Ernst Jünger: Die Biographie.* Berlin: Siedler Verlag.

Langford, P. and I. Bryan (2016) 'Beyond the Jurist as a Theologian of Legal Science: The Question of Carl Schmitt and the International Legal Order', Chapter 14 in M. Arvidsson, L. Brännström and P. Minkkinen (eds), *The Contemporary Relevance of Carl Schmitt. Law, Politics, Theology.* Abingdon: Routledge.

Mohler, A. (ed.) (1955) *Freundschaftliche Begegnungen, Festschrift fur Ernst Junger zum 60. Geburtstag.* Frankfurt am Main: V. Klostermann.

Mohler, A. (1972) *Die konservative Revolution in Deutschland 1918–1932: ein Handbuch.* Darmstadt: Wissenschaftliche Buchgesellschaft.

Morat, D. (2007) *Von der Tat zur Gelassenheit: konservatives Denken bei Martin Heidegger, Ernst Jünger und Friedrich Georg Jünger, 1920–1960.* Göttingen: Wallstein.

Neaman, Y. E. (1999) *A Dubious Past: Ernst Jünger and the Politics of Literature after Nazism.* Berkeley, CA: University of California Press.

Schmitt, C. (1914) *Der Wert des Staates und die Bedeutung des Einzelnen.* Tübingen: J. C. B. Mohr.

Schmitt, C. (1955) 'Die geschichtliche Struktur des heutigen Welt-Gegensatzes von Ost und West', p. 135–67, in A. Mohler (ed.), *Freundschaftliche Begegnungen – Festschrift für Ernst Jünger zum 60. Geburtstag.* Frankfurt am Main: Vittorio Klostermann.

Schmitt, C. (1991) *Glossarium: Aufzeichnungen der Jahre 1947–1951.* Berlin: Duncker and Humblot.

Schmitt, C. (1995a) 'Das Meer gegen das Land' [1941], p. 395–400, in C. Schmitt, *Staat, Großraum, Nomos – Arbeiten aus den Jahren 1916–1969.* Berlin: Duncker and Humblot.

Schmitt, C. (1995b) 'Maritime Weltpolitik' [1949], p. 478–80, in C. Schmitt, *Staat, Großraum, Nomos – Arbeiten aus den Jahren 1916–1969.* Berlin: Duncker and Humblot.

Schmitt, C. (2001) *State, Movement, People: The Triadic Structure of the Political Unity; The Question of Legality* [1933]. Trans. S. Draghici. Corvallis: Plutarch.

Schmitt, C. (2003) *The Nomos of the Earth in the International Law of the Jus Publicum Europaeum* [1950]. Trans. G. L. Ulmen. Candor, NY: Telos.

Schmitt, C. (2004) *Legality and Legitimacy* [1932]. Trans. J. Seitzer. Durham, NC: Duke University Press, 2004.
Schmitt, C. (2007a) *The Concept of the Political* [1932]. Trans. G. Schwab. Chicago, IL: Chicago University Press.
Schmitt, C. (2007b) *Theory of the Partisan: Intermediate Commentary on the Concept of the Political* [1963]. Trans. A. C. Goodson. Candor, NY: Telos.
Schmitt, C. (2008) *Constitutional Theory* [1928]. Trans. J. Seitzer. Durham, NC: Duke University Press.
Shapiro, K. (2008) *Carl Schmitt and the Intensification of Politics*. Lanham: Rowman and Littlefield.
Steil, A. (1984) *Die imaginäre Revolte: Untersuchungen zur faschistischen Ideologie und ihrer theoretischen Vorbereitung bei Georges Sorel, Carl Schmitt und Ernst Jünger*. Marburg: Verlag Arbeiterbewegung und Gesellschaftswissenschaft.
Trawny, P. (2009) *Die Autorität des Zeugen: Ernst Jüngers politisches Werk*. Berlin: Matthes and Seitz.

Chapter 9

Rethinking the concept of the political
Derrida's reading of Schmitt's 'The Theory of the Partisan'

Jacques de Ville

Introduction

In 'The Theory of the Partisan' (Schmitt 2004),[1] Schmitt attempts to cover a field which on his own account he had neglected to treat fully in *The Concept of the Political* (Schmitt 2007a), where he sets out to define the political with reference to the drawing of a distinction between friend and enemy. In the new Preface to the 1963 German edition of *The Concept of the Political* (Schmitt 2002), he acknowledges that he had failed to distinguish clearly and precisely enough in the earlier editions between the different forms of hostility; that is, conventional, real and absolute (Schmitt 2002: 17). In addressing this neglected issue, 'The Theory of the Partisan' effectively rethinks the concept of the political thirty-six years after the first publication of *The Concept of the Political* (see also Horn 2004: 125–43). With this aim in mind, Schmitt in 'The Theory of the Partisan' identifies two forms of partisan: the telluric (characterized by real hostility) and the revolutionary (characterized by absolute hostility), in contrast to the conventional hostility and its degeneration (into the hostility towards the 'foe') at stake in *The Concept of the Political*. Derrida, in chapter six of *Politics of Friendship* (Derrida 1997), provides what can be termed a 'quasi-psychoanalytical' reading of Schmitt's 'The Theory of the Partisan', and in the process, further transforms Schmitt's concept of the political (see also de Ville 2015).

The aim of the discussion that follows is to bring to the fore the quasi-psychoanalytical dimension of Derrida's reading (see also de Ville 2011: 28–37) and in this way to explain how he arrives at a new concept of the political, insofar as it can still be called such. In the discussion that follows, we first enquire briefly into Schmitt's four criteria for recognising the true partisan and the consequent distinction between the two forms of partisan.

---

1 Reference will be made in this chapter to the arguably more reliable Goodson translation (Schmitt 2004) of Schmitt's *Theorie des Partisanen* rather than the translation of Ulmen (Schmitt 2007b).

Of importance for Derrida in this regard is the tension between the criteria of the 'telluric' and of 'mobility', as well as the difficulty of maintaining the distinction between the two forms of partisan. Schmitt's attempt to locate the moment of the opening of what Schmitt refers to as 'an abyss [*einem Abgrund*]' of absolute hostility leads to a discussion of the Geneva and Hague Conventions, as well as an invocation by Schmitt of the Acheron. On Derrida's reading, we find in this discussion an acknowledgement on the part of Schmitt of the fragility of the concept of the political as well as of the distinctions (between different forms of hostility) on which it relies. By invoking the 'abyss' and the 'Acheron', Schmitt also appears to be acknowledging the role played by 'unconscious' forces in the coming to the fore of absolute hostility. The latter acknowledgement means that it would be impossible to determine the precise moment when the rigid distinctions of the concept of the political and the bracketing of hostility that goes along with it start dissolving. On Derrida's reading, this dissolution is always already in progress in view of what can be referred to as the 'human structure'. In the next section a discussion takes place of Schmitt's designation of the brother as the absolute enemy, which Derrida reads alongside the figure of the double in Freud's 1919 essay 'The Uncanny' (Freud 2001b). In the latter text Freud relates the double to narcissism, the repetition compulsion, and our relation to death. On Derrida's reading, the brother as invoked in Schmitt's texts such as *The Concept of the Political* and 'The Theory of the Partisan' points to this mirroring as well as threat to the self. Schmitt's exclusive focus on the brother and exclusion of the sister leads to Derrida's suggestion that woman (*la femme*) may be the absolute partisan; that is, the 'other' or the 'beyond' of the political, which also functions as its condition of possibility. With this suggestion, where the figure of 'woman' alludes to an absolute unbinding or what Derrida elsewhere refers to as the 'perfect gift', we arrive at the deconstructed concept of the political, which is briefly analyzed in the final section. The implications for public law theory of this 'new' concept of the political, in so far as it can still be called such, will be explored elsewhere.

Criteria for identifying the partisan

Schmitt's 'The Theory of the Partisan' can in broad terms, be said to trace the origin and further development of the partisan, with the latter's 'status as a political actor ... [being] a symptom ... of larger structural transformations in international law and world order', as Müller (2006: 67) elegantly puts it. Schmitt finds the origin of the partisan in the Spanish resistance against Napoleon in the early nineteenth century and proceeds to lay down four criteria which distinguish the true partisan (as ideal type) from its degenerated historical counterpart (Hooker 2009: 163; see also Gunneflo 2016, Chapter 3 in this volume). These criteria are, firstly, irregularity, thereby distinguishing the partisan from the modern regular army; secondly, intense political engagement, thereby distinguishing the partisan from criminal gangs and pirates; thirdly, mobility, speed and the element of surprise;[2] and fourthly, a telluric dimension, thereby rooting the partisan in the soil and giving him a fundamentally defensive function (Schmitt 2004: 9–14). The telluric criterion is especially important for Schmitt in view of the 'metaphysical' approach he adopts in relation to space (see Bjork, Chapter 8, and Wittrock 2016, Chapter 13 in this volume) and he consequently views the autochthonous partisan, associated with real hostility and with the ability to make a concrete identification of the enemy in the absence of the ability of the state to do so, as the true partisan. This true partisan stands opposed to the revolutionary (communist) partisan, who fights a global revolutionary war, therefore failing to meet the telluric criterion, and who is associated with absolute hostility (*aboluten Feindschaft*) (Schmitt 2004: 33–43; see also Bargu 2010: 2; Dean 2006: 7). The philosophical recognition of the partisan takes place in Prussia in 1812–13 during the time of the French occupation but quickly disappears again from view. Whereas the (telluric) partisan remains a marginal figure until World War One, in the hands of Lenin, and later Mao and Stalin, he becomes a central figure of war in the twentieth century. Lenin's revolutionary partisan furthermore explodes the attempt at containing war and hostility which was imposed by European international law from the time of the peace of Westphalia (1648) until the end of World War One. Schmitt sees a close association between the telluric partisan, resurrected by Mao, and his own vision of great spaces (*Grossräumen*) as set out in *The Nomos of the Earth* (Schmitt 2004: 41).

The revolutionary partisan, as noted above, is condemned by Schmitt as a 'fall' from an essential purity. Mobility (that is, technology) plays a central role in Schmitt's account in the displacing of the telluric dimension and threatens to dissolve the concept of the political. However, as Derrida (1997: 142) points out, thereby overturning the perceived order of things, 'telluric autochthonism is already a reactive response to a de-localization and some tele-technology, regardless of its degree of development, power and speed'. Technology, in other words, dislocates, expropriates, delocalizes, deracinates, dis-idiomatizes, de-territorializes and dispossesses, thereby giving rise to a 'reaction' or 'response' towards the 'home' (Derrida 1998: 45; Derrida and Stiegler 2005: 79). This desire for rootedness or for presence follows more specifically from technology's announcement of our own death (Derrida and Stiegler 2005: 39, 115). What Schmitt points to in relation to the modern partisan (that is, that he

---

[2] In a discussion about partisans, Schmitt links mobility specifically to the incalculability of the partisan and his ability of disguise (see Schmitt and Schickel 1970: 15).

is losing his telluric character because of technological developments and is in danger of becoming completely displaced) could, in other words, already be said of the most classical combatant.

Philosophy and the Acheron

> The Acheron does not allow itself to be calculated, and does not obey every conjuration.
>
> (Schmitt 2004: 58, translation modified)

In his discussion of the Geneva Conventions of 1949, Schmitt is complementary, especially insofar as they give recognition to new forms of enemy fighters while still remaining tied to classical international law and its tradition. The basis of these Conventions remains the war between states as well as the containment of war with clear distinctions between war and peace, military and civilian, enemy and criminal, inter-state war and civil war. Schmitt, however, at the same time criticizes the Conventions for loosening or even challenging these essential distinctions with the consequence that the door is opened 'for a kind of war that would knowingly destroy such clear divisions' (Schmitt 2004: 22–3).[3] These Conventions were, like the Hague Convention of 1907, based on a compromise between larger and smaller states but with Russia this time on the side of the smaller states. Of particular interest to us here is Schmitt's comment that many of the norms of the Conventions appear only as 'the fragile bridges over an abyss [*die dünne Brücke über einem Abgrund*] concealing portentous metamorphoses in the concepts of war, peace, and the partisan' (Schmitt 2004: 23). Schmitt is, here, effectively acknowledging that the clear distinctions or 'conceptual shores' he tried to construct so carefully in *The Concept of the Political*, and even here, in 'The Theory of the Partisan' are being threatened by the abyss (Derrida 1997: 143).

Schmitt appears to believe that he can pinpoint with reference to places, events and dates, when this abyss opened up (Derrida 1997: 145). Yet, as Derrida points out, one can always give a counter example or an earlier example, in an infinite regression. The criticism levelled by Schmitt against the legal experts of European international law – that they have stubbornly repressed from consciousness (*hartnäckig aus ihrem Bewußtsein verdrängt*) the new reality which has emerged since 1900 (Schmitt 2004: 25) – can therefore also be raised against Schmitt (Derrida 1997: 145). Schmitt, in other words, locates a mutation in the nature of war and hostility in the twentieth

---

3   Schmitt, here, could be referring to the Cold War (see the Preface to Schmitt 2002: 19) or, more broadly, to the just war tradition, which has again been revived in the twentieth century (Schmitt 2004: 64–8). In both respects, at stake is a new theory of absolute war and absolute hostility (Schmitt 2004: 35).

century but he is constantly forced to go back, step by step, to take account of beginnings and the beginnings of those beginnings, without (really) taking account thereof (Derrida 1997: 145). Of interest to Derrida here is specifically Schmitt's invocation of the Acheron. This interest is undoubtedly triggered by Freud's understanding of the phrase *Acheronta movebo* ('*Flectere si nequeo Superos, Acheronta movebo*', from Virgil's *Aeneid*, 7.312)[4] as referring to 'the efforts of the repressed instinctual impulses' or more literally, of the 'drive movements [*das Streben der verdrängten Triebregungen*]' (Freud 1925: 169). The examples which Derrida gives of this backward movement in Schmitt are, first, the acherontic moment in the Prussian soldier state, that is, the Bismarckian invocation in 1866 of the *Acheronta movebo* (or *movere*, as Schmitt has it) against the Habsburg empire and France and, secondly, the acherontic moment in 1812/13 in Prussia (Schmitt 2004: 28). Noteworthy here is the Prussian king's edict (of April 1813) calling for partisan warfare against Napoleon, which was in turn based on the Spanish reglement of 1808 and the decree of 1809 (Schmitt 2004: 29). In the Prussian Edict, as Schmitt points out, there is a call (by a legitimate king) for using every means against the enemy and for the unleashing of total disorder (*totalen Unordnung*). Schmitt describes this document, in Derrida's words (Derrida 1997: 145, translation modified), with 'trembling fervour [*un tremblement de ferveur*]' as counting 'among the most astonishing documents of the whole history of partisanship' (Schmitt 2004: 29). It was, however, amended on 17 July 1813 and, in the words of Schmitt, 'purged of every partisan danger, of every acherontic dynamic' (Schmitt 2004: 30). The king's original edict, as Schmitt further points out, again stepping back in time, was influenced by the spirit of the French revolution. Schmitt, in addition, refers to Clausewitz's contribution in this regard, as well as to Fichte and von Kleist, all influenced by the French Enlightenment and revolution (Schmitt 2004: 30–32).

With the events in Prussia as described above, Schmitt contends that a certain alliance is formed between philosophy and the partisan. Yet this alliance did not lead to an insurrectional war against Napoleon in Prussia. Schmitt explains this with reference to the fact that Clausewitz was a reform-minded vocational officer of his time and that he was not able to germinate the seeds (*Keime*) that became visible here. This would only happen much later, and needed an 'active professional revolutionary [*eine activen Berufsrevolutionärs*]' (Schmitt 2004: 32). Philosophy here remained, as Derrida notes, following Schmitt, in 'a still-abstract "theoretical form" and, as such, a spark, a flash, a flame, a light awaiting its heir' (Derrida 1997: 147). The Acheron, which had been unleashed, Schmitt observes:

---

4   'If I cannot sway the gods, I'll stir the Acheron [the netherworld]' (trans. A. S. Kline).

receded immediately into the channels of state order. Following the wars of freedom, the philosophy of Hegel was dominant in Prussia. It attempted a systematic mediation of revolution and tradition. It could be considered conservative, and it was. But it also conserved the revolutionary sparks, and provided, via its philosophy of history, a dangerous ideological weapon for the forward driving revolution, more dangerous than Rousseau's philosophy in the hands of the Jacobins.

(Schmitt 2004: 33)

Its early heirs, Marx and Engels, were likewise too philosophical, and thus not philosophical enough. In Schmitt's view, they were 'thinkers more than activists of the revolutionary war' (Schmitt 2004: 33). For Schmitt, Lenin was the first authentic heir of the Prussian *Magna Carta*, which was in turn inherited by Mao, and further radicalized (Derrida 1997: 147).[5] Schmitt (2004: 34) notes in this respect that the concept of the political takes a subversive turn with events in Russia in the twentieth century.[6] The classical concept of the political, founded in the eighteenth and nineteenth centuries of European international law based on inter-state war with its containments (*Hegungen*), was now replaced by a revolutionary war of parties (*Parteien-Krieg*) (Schmitt 2004: 34). Hostility, Derrida notes, following Schmitt, is, with Lenin, taken to its absolute limit (Derrida 1997: 147).[7] Derrida then points to the coincidence here between the purest philosophy and 'the most intense concrete determination' (Derrida 1997: 148).[8] This alliance between philosophy and the partisan moreover releases

---

5   Meier criticises Derrida inter alia for referring to Lenin as positing a link between philosophy and the partisan (see Meier 2013: 178 n. 37) and yet Derrida is simply following Schmitt here, who explicitly refers to the alliance established by Lenin between philosophy and the partisan, and the unexpected new, explosive forces that it unleashed (see Schmitt 2004: 36).

6   The English translation (Derrida 1997: 147) incorrectly suggests that this development is to be attributed to Mao.

7   Lenin thereby overturns Schmitt's (explicit) analysis in *The Concept of the Political* where external war was viewed as true war vis-à-vis civil war, and goes beyond this opposition with the notion of absolute hostility, which, as Derrida (Derrida 1997: 149) notes, is worse than civil war.

8   A few pages earlier, Derrida (Derrida 1997: 146) had referred to philosophy as the institution which is the actual producer 'of the purely political, and hence of pure hostility'. Meier (Meier 2013: 178, n. 37) criticises Derrida for this invocation of pure hostility and pure politics, which he says Schmitt abandoned in 1930. Meier however appears to incorrectly assume that Derrida is speaking here about the (purely) political in contradistinction to the domains of the moral, the economic, etc. At stake here is instead an understanding of politics in its ontological sense, that is, an understanding of opposition itself, which can be said to have remained a concern for Schmitt, also in his authorship of 'The Theory of the Partisan'.

unexpected forces that, according to Schmitt, led to the explosion (*Sprengung*) of 'the whole Eurocentric world, which Napoleon had tried to save and the Congress of Vienna had hoped to restore' (Schmitt 2004: 36–7). Yet, in comparison with the concrete telluric reality of the Chinese partisans, there was 'something abstract and intellectual' in Lenin's determination of the enemy (Schmitt 2004: 43). It is thus, as we saw earlier, with Mao (and also Stalin) that this war is (again) provided with a telluric rooting (Schmitt 2004: 38–43) or, in Derrida's terminology, with a form of presence. This would be the absolute fulfilment, 'the philosophical and historic concretization of absolute hostility' (Derrida 1997: 148).[9] Schmitt notes:

> However, with Mao an additional concrete moment is added in relation to the partisan, whereby he comes closer than Lenin to the heart of the matter, and whereby he attains the possibility of extreme theoretical consummation [*wodurch er die Möglichkeit der äußersten gedanklichen Vollendung erhält*]. In short: Mao's revolution is more tellurically underpinned than that of Lenin.
>
> (Schmitt 2004: 40, translation modified)

What interests Derrida particularly is this alliance between philosophy, the partisan and absolute presence in its relation to technology, spectrality and the Acheron. He therefore shifts his focus to Schmitt's discrete mention of the brother in the analysis of the movement from Lenin to Mao; that is, in the context of a discussion of absolute hostility.

The brother as double

Derrida points out that for Schmitt the absolute war, the revolutionary war that drives the theory of the partisan to its most extreme point, the war which violates all the laws of war, 'can be a fratricidal war [*cela peut être une guerre fratricide*]' (Derrida 1997: 148). This theme of a brother enemy, as Derrida further comments, has an immense tradition, both Greek and Biblical. This comment takes us back to the question raised earlier about determining precisely when the abyss to which Schmitt appeals, opened up

---

9   Meier (2013: 178, n. 37) further criticises Derrida for not properly distinguishing between total or real hostility on the one hand and absolute hostility on the other. Derrida's 'failure' should however be understood in view of the 'inconsistency' to be found in Schmitt's text itself in this respect; see infra on 'The brother as double'. Horn (2004: 140–1) points out that the involvement of an interested third party inevitably means that the telluric partisan with his real hostility gets mixed up in global hostility and thus in absolute hostility (see also Pan 2013 on the inevitability of the breakdown of this distinction). It needs to be noted here that Derrida (1997: 162) also casts doubt on the viability of Schmitt's distinction between the annihilation of the enemy (in the case of absolute hostility) and his mere killing (in the case of conventional and real hostility).

as well as to Schmitt's invocation of the Acheron. Derrida's 'thesis' is that there is nothing strange about a brother being the subject matter (*sujet*) of absolute hostility. There is in fact, he provocatively contends, only absolute hostility for or against a brother. At stake here, as we see below, is more specifically the 'phantasm of the brother'. The equation by Schmitt of the brother and of (absolute) hostility accords with the whole history of friendship, which is simply the experience, in this respect, of what appears to be an unspeakable synonymy, a deadly tautology. Schmitt's mention of the brother happens furtively and is similar to a ghostly apparition (Derrida 1997: 148). What Derrida refers to as the 'double passage of a brother ([*d*]*ouble passage d'un frère*)' (ibid.), occurs in Schmitt's discussion under the heading 'from Lenin to Mao Tse-tung', of the wars in the erstwhile Yugoslavia between 1941–45, where communist and monarchical partisans fought against each other; and of the battle between Mao and the Kuomintang (the National People's Party) (Schmitt 2004: 38–41). Schmitt refers to the first instance as a war between brothers (*Bruderkampf*) and, to the second, as a war against the own national brother (*den eigenen, nationalen Bruder*). In the course of these wars, 'absolute hostility directs itself at the brother, and converts the internal war, this time into real war, into an absolute war, and thus into an absolute politics' (Derrida 1997: 149, translation modified).[10] Whereas, in *The Concept of the Political*, the friend/brother stood in opposition to the enemy, now the brother becomes the absolute enemy. One can consequently say that a vertiginous reversal is taking place here in the truth of the political and Derrida notes that it happens precisely 'at the moment that one touches the limit, of oneself or one's double (*son double*), the twin, this absolute friend that always comes in the guise of the brother' (ibid.).

The figure of the double makes a number of appearances in *Politics of Friendship*, inter alia with reference to descriptions of friendship in its ideal sense (Derrida 1997: viii, 4, 116, 149, 152, 172). In an analysis of Cicero's *On Friendship, or Laelius*, Derrida for example notes that 'one projects or recognizes in the true friend one's exemplar, one's ideal double (*son double*

---

10   At first sight, there seems to be a problem here with Derrida's reading because, as indicated above, Schmitt appears to distinguish between real and absolute hostility, and to associate only the first-mentioned with the telluric defence of the home soil (cf. Meier 2013: 178, n. 37). Mao (as well as Stalin) is praised by Schmitt for retaining the telluric element, yet he (Mao) is not consistently associated with real hostility. At the point where Derrida invokes the war against the brother, absolute hostility is indeed at stake: Schmitt (Schmitt 2004: 41) comments that '[v]arious kinds of enmity [racial, national and internecine] are joined in Mao's concrete situation, rising up to absolute enmity [*die sich zu einer absoluten Feindschaft steigern*]'. Elsewhere Schmitt speaks of fratricidal war as being 'particularly cruel/dreadful [*etwas besonders Grausames*]' (Schmitt 2010b: 56–8) as he does when he speaks about the battle between the 'brothers' Tito and General Mihailovitch (Schmitt 2004: 38).

ideal), one's other self, the same as the self, yet better' (Derrida 1997: 4, translation modified; see also p. 276). In commenting on Schmitt's insistence on the identification of the friend and the enemy in *The Concept of the Political*, Derrida somewhat similarly remarks that the logic of *philautía* (self-love) or narcissism, the fraternal double, are obscurely at work in this discourse. At stake in these texts as well as others where a rivalry between brother enemies plays itself out (for example, *The Purloined Letter* and the Biblical account of Cain and Abel)[11] appears to be the projection of a dangerous secret of the self on to the figure of the brother (the double thereby both mirroring and threatening the self), which seems to suggest that the friend as brother, the ideal double as reflection of the self, as constructed in the philosophical tradition, is ultimately so constructed to protect the self against the abyss, against the Acheron; that is, against the doubling of the double.[12] In reading Schmitt's *Concept of the Political* and 'The Theory of the Partisan' together, the ideal double of the self turns out to itself be double: the brother as friend in *The Concept of the Political*, and in 'The Theory of the Partisan' as (absolute) enemy.[13] This (philosophical) construction, or perhaps rather phantasm, of the double as brother, with its structural exclusion of the sister, points to its condition of possibility beyond the political: perhaps to woman as the absolute partisan, as we will see below. The self, here translated into the concept of the political, is in other words an effect of what will be termed below, the 'feminine operation'.

Woman as the absolute partisan

Schmitt never appears to speak of the sister, at least not in the texts that concern themselves with the political (Derrida 1997: 149). Derrida refers in this regard to 'a certain desert [*un certain desert*]', which refers back to his analysis in chapter five of *The Concept of the Political* at the point where

---

11 'Adam and Eve had two sons, Cain and Abel. Thus begins the history of mankind. Thus appears [*sieht aus*] the father of all things. This is the dialectical tension that keeps world history in motion, and world history is not at an end yet' (Schmitt 2010b: 89, translation mine).
12 Space does not allow for a discussion here of Derrida's analysis of the double in texts such as 'The Double Session' (Derrida 2004) and *The Post Card* (Derrida 1987), which enquire into Freud's *Das Unheimliche*, as well as Freud's *Beyond the Pleasure Principle*.
13 In the discussion of General Salan and the Algerian War of Independence, Schmitt (Schmitt 2004: 60–1) elusively raises the following questions which could be read to tie in with our discussion of the double: 'Every two-front war poses the question of who is the real enemy [*der wirkliche Feind*]. Is it not a sign of inner division [*innerer Gespaltenheit*] to have more than one single real enemy? The enemy is our own question as *Gestalt* [figure]. If we have determined our own *Gestalt* unambiguously, where does this double enemy come from?' As Deuber-Mankowsky (2008: 148) points out, having only one real enemy would, in terms of this logic, be a sign of inner unity (see, however, Derrida 2003: 112).

Schmitt speaks of depoliticization and which Derrida likens to a dehumanized desert (*un desert déshumanisé*) (Derrida 1997: 130). The desert at stake in chapter six is however one teeming with people, or rather with men. In Schmitt's 'The Theory of the Partisan' as well as in *The Concept of the Political*, only men are mentioned. All the partisans, generals, politicians, professors, and so on, being referred to, are men. There is not even a mirage of woman in this desert (Derrida 1997: 155–6).[14] And there is furthermore no mention by Schmitt of the role women have played throughout history in partisan warfare in the two world wars (or resistance movements during the war; for example, in France) and in wars of national liberation after these wars or, Derrida seems to suggest, of the war for their own liberation from patriarchy. The fact that woman herself does not appear in 'The Theory of the Partisan' (that is, in the theory of the absolute enemy), the fact that she never exits from this enforced clandestinity, from such invisibility, makes one wonder: 'What if woman [*la femme*] were the absolute partisan? What if woman were the other absolute enemy of Schmitt's theory of the absolute enemy, the spectre of hostility, conjured for the sake of sworn brothers ... ?' (Derrida 1997: 157, translation modified).

By raising the question of woman as the absolute partisan, Derrida seeks to 'transform' the structure of the concept of the political, in line with his attempts elsewhere to think a beyond to the metaphysics of presence. The figure of woman plays an important role in a number of his texts in thinking this beyond. In *Spurs: Nietzsche's Styles*, for example, at stake in the displacement of truth by woman (to be understood here not as female sexuality but as non-identity, non-figure and as simulacrum, as gift without exchange), is what Derrida refers to as the feminine 'operation' (Derrida 1979: 49, 57). Read in view of Freud's 'Beyond the Pleasure Principle' (Freud 2001a), we can detect in Schmitt's text the force of an unbinding, the threat therefore of the (feminine) absolute enemy, always already restricting (that is, concealing) herself, dissimulating herself, somewhat analogous to a partisan operation. The spectre, the one who bears witness to the (return of the) absolute unbinding, is, however, immediately ontologized by the one who conjures it (Derrida 2006: 240, n. 14). The spectre is, in other words, constructed as the double of something real – that is, in the present context, the brother of flesh and blood – whereas s/he actually comes from elsewhere. Woman's exclusion from the concept of the political is in other words a 'necessary' or structural exclusion, an exclusion which ultimately reveals the law or the differential topology that is at stake here.

---

14 To be fair to Schmitt, he does mention Joan of Arc, although she was not a partisan, to explain the necessary link with territory (Schmitt 2004: 66).

The restructured concept of the political

The concept of the political is central to public law theory, and determines, in turn, the understanding of concepts such as sovereignty, the state, constituent power, democracy, equality and freedom, as well as the nature of the world order. We saw in the above analysis how Derrida succeeds in bringing to the fore a concept of the political which incorporates Freud's thinking on the death drive, as deconstructed in *The Post Card* (Derrida 1987). The drawing of a distinction between friend and enemy is, in other words, preceded by and made possible by a 'desire' for self-destruction. It is especially in the autoimmune terror of the early twenty-first century that this structure of the political shows itself (Derrida 2003), although it already appears from Schmitt's analysis of classical, civil and partisan warfare. We saw this specifically in Schmitt's invocation of the Acheron but also in his attempts to fend off the dissolution of the concept of the political because of technological developments, the link which he makes between the brother and absolute hostility, as well as his exclusion of woman from the concept of the political. The rethinking of the founding concepts of public law theory is an urgent task, as Schmitt reminds us:

> In the political battle, concepts and conceptualized words are anything but empty sound. They are the expression of sharp and precisely elaborated oppositions and friend-enemy constellations. Understood thus, the content of world history which is accessible to our consciousness has at all times been a battle for words and concepts. These are of course not empty, but energy-laden words and concepts, and often very sharp weapons.
> (Schmitt 1994: 218, translation mine)

Bibliography

Bargu, B. (2010) 'Unleashing the Acheron: Sacrificial Partisanship, Sovereignty, and History', *Theory and Event* 13: doi: 10.1353/tae.0.0111.

Bjork, M. (2016) 'Representation and the Unrepresentable: Ernst Jünger, Carl Schmitt and the Limits of Politics', Chapter 8 in M. Arvidsson, L. Brännström and P. Minkkinen (eds), *The Contemporary Relevance of Carl Schmitt: Law, Politics, Theology*. Abingdon: Routledge.

de Ville, J. (2011) *Jacques Derrida: Law as Absolute Hospitality*. Abingdon: Routledge.

de Ville, J. (2015) 'The Foreign Body within the Body Politic: Derrida, Schmitt and the Concept of the Political', *Law and Critique*, Vol. 26, No. 1: 45–63.

Dean, M. (2006) 'A Political Mythology of World Order Carl Schmitt's *Nomos*', *Theory Culture Society*, Vol. 23, No. 5: 1–22.

Derrida, J. (1979) *Spurs: Nietzsche's Styles/Éperons: Les Styles de Nietzsche*. Trans. B. Harlow. Chicago, IL: University of Chicago Press.

Derrida, J. (1987) *The Post Card: from Socrates to Freud and Beyond*. Trans. A. Bass. Chicago, IL: University of Chicago Press.
Derrida, J. (1997) *The Politics of Friendship*. Trans. G. Collins. London: Verso.
Derrida, J. (1998) 'Faith and Knowledge: The Two Sources of "Religion" at the Limit of Reason Alone', p. 1–78, in J. Derrida and G. Vattimo (eds), *Religion*. Translated by D. Webb *et al.* Redwood City, CA: Stanford University Press.
Derrida, J. (2003) 'Autoimmunity: Real and Symbolic Suicides: A Dialogue with Jacques Derrida', p. 85–136, in G. Borradori, *Philosophy in a Time of Terror: Dialogues with Jürgen Habermas and Jacques Derrida*. Chicago, IL: University of Chicago Press.
Derrida, J. (2004) *Dissemination*. Trans. B. Johnson. London: Continuum.
Derrida, J. (2006) *Specters of Marx: The State of Debt, The Work of Mourning, and the New International*. Trans. P. Kamuf. New York: Routledge.
Derrida, J. and B. Stiegler (2005) *Echographies of Television*. Cambridge: Polity.
Deuber-Mankowsky, A. (2008) 'Nothing is Political, Everything can be Politicized: On the Concept of the Political in Michel Foucault and Carl Schmitt', *Telos*, No. 142: 135–61.
Freud, S. (1925) 'Ergänzungen und Zusatzkapitel zur Traumlehre' [1900], p. 1–185, in S. Freud, *Gesammelte Schriften. Dritter Band*. Leipzig: Internationaler Psychoanalytischer Verlag.
Freud, S. (2001a) 'Beyond the Pleasure Principle' [1920], p. 7–64, *The Standard Edition of the Complete Psychological Works of Sigmund Freud. Vol. XVIII: Beyond the Pleasure Principle, Group Psychology, and Other Works*. London: Vintage.
Freud, S. (2001b) 'The Uncanny' [1919], p. 217–56, in S. Freud, *The Standard Edition of the Complete Psychological Works of Sigmund Freud. Vol. XVII: An Infantile Neurosis and Other Works*. London: Vintage.
Gunneflo, M. (2016) 'Political Community in Carl Schmitt's International Legal Thinking', Chapter 3 in M. Arvidsson, L. Brännström and P. Minkkinen (eds), *The Contemporary Relevance of Carl Schmitt. Law, Politics, Theology*. Abingdon: Routledge.
Hooker, W. (2009) *Carl Schmitt's International Thought: Order and Orientation*. Cambridge: Cambridge University Press.
Horn, E. (2004) '"Waldgänger," Traitor, Partisan: Figures of Political Irregularity in West German Postwar Thought', *New Centennial Review*, Vol. 4, No. 3: 125–43.
Meier, H. (2013) *Carl Schmitt, Leo Strauss und 'Der Begriff des Politischen'*, 3 Aufl. Stuttgart: Verlag J.B. Metzler.
Müller, J-W. (2006) '"An Irregularity that cannot be regulated": Carl Schmitt and the "War on Terror"', *Notizie di Politeia: Rivista di Etica e Scelte Pubbliche*, Vol. 22, No. 84: 65–78.
Pan, D. (2013) 'Carl Schmitt's *Theory of the Partisan* and the Stability of the Nation-State', *TELOSscope*, 2 January 2013. Available at www.telospress.com/carl-schmitts-theory-of-the-partisan-and-the-stability-of-the-nation-state (accessed on 15 April 2015).
Schmitt, C. (1994) 'Reich – Staat – Bund' [1933], p. 217–26, in C. Schmitt, *Positionen und Begriffe im Kampf mit Weimar – Genf – Versailles 1923–1939*, 3. Aufl. Berlin: Duncker and Humblot.
Schmitt, C. (2002) *Der Begriff des Politischen. Text von 1932 mit einem Vorwort und drei Collarien* [1927]. 7. Aufl., 5. Nachdruck der Ausgabe von 1963. Berlin: Duncker and Humblot.

Schmitt, C. (2004) 'The Theory of the Partisan: A Commentary/Remark on the Concept of the Political' [1963], *New Centennial Review*, Vol. 4, No. 3: 1–78.

Schmitt, C. (2006) *The Nomos of the Earth in the International Law of the Jus Publicum Europaeum* [1950]. Trans. G. L. Ulmen. New York: Telos.

Schmitt, C. (2007a) *The Concept of the Political* [1927]. Expanded edn. Trans. G. Schwab. Chicago, IL: University of Chicago Press.

Schmitt, C. (2007b) *Theory of the Partisan: Intermediate Commentary on the Concept of the Political* [1963]. Trans. G. L. Ulmen. New York: Telos.

Schmitt, C. (2010a) *Theorie des Partisanen: Zwischenbemerkung zum Begriff des Politischen* [1963]. 7. Aufl. Berlin: Duncker and Humblot.

Schmitt, C. (2010b) *Ex Captivitate Salus* [1950] 3. Aufl. Berlin: Duncker and Humblot.

Schmitt, C. and J. Schickel (1970) 'Gespräch über den Partisanen', p. 9–29, in J. Schickel (ed.) *Guerrilleros, Partisanen: Theorie und Praxis*. München: Carl Hanser Verlag.

Wittrock, J. (2016) 'Processes of Order and the Concreteness of the Sacred: On the Contemporary Relevance of Carl Schmitt's Critique of Nihilism', Chapter 13 in M. Arvidsson, L. Brännström and P. Minkkinen (eds), *The Contemporary Relevance of Carl Schmitt: Law, Politics, Theology*. Abingdon: Routledge.

Chapter 10

Eschatology and existentialism
Carl Schmitt's historical understanding of international law and politics

Walter Rech

Introduction

As China is turning into a global superpower, debate is raging as to whether it will keep pursuing a 'peaceful rise' or confront the United States to the point of creating a new Cold War scenario (Mearsheimer 2006; Posner and Yoo 2006; Buzan 2010; Kissinger 2012; Rudd 2013; Suri 2013). A number of western observers are crying havoc and mourning the good old days, while Chinese policy makers and international lawyers are putting in all the effort in persuading foreign observers to trust China. While this divergence might be expected, what is surprising is the rhetorical strategy to which some Chinese advocates are resorting. They are arguing that China is not only currently working for promoting peace, international trade and cooperation, but also that it will continue doing so 'in 100 years or even 1000 years' and thus will contribute to the progress of mankind, as top foreign policy official Dai Bingguo puts it (Dai 2012: 2). *Prima facie*, these arguments might be construed as merely reassuring western foreign policy experts about China's peaceful intentions in the long term, but there might be more to it. By championing 'co-progressiveness', Chinese authors are purposefully appropriating and remodelling the western narrative of progress, a narrative that peaked in international legal discourse in the mid-eighteenth century, precisely when China was forced to enter the 'international community' by the military intervention of the western powers'.[1] Upon adjustment based on 'Asian values', the Chinese concept of progress might become a tool for critiquing those who once applied it to delegitimize and crush the Middle Kingdom. According to Sienho Yee, the editor of the *Chinese Journal of International Law*, 'co-progressiveness', from a Chinese perspective, involves a specific sensibility for cultural difference, which, if disregarded, may preclude the true progress of humanity (and presumably Chinese cooperation on 'global challenges' too) (Sienho 2013:

---

1 The international legal mainstream around 1850 was fully progressivist (see, for example, Manning 1839; Mamiani 1861; Vergé 1864; Bluntschli 1868).

12). Like its western counterpart in the past, the Chinese notion of progress at present seems broad enough to underpin any kind of policies.

Interestingly, progressivist narratives have formerly been used not only by the great powers asserting their influence in China but also, as German jurist Carl Schmitt noted, by the superpowers in the Cold War period. If Schmitt were still alive and quarrelsome, he would probably warn that the ideology of progress now proclaimed by China, not unlike the one earlier predicated by the United States and the Soviet Union, will inevitably lead to hegemonic policies. In a series of articles published in the 1950s, Schmitt contended that the superpowers' faith in historical progress had driven them to chase a Utopian and naïve dream of global hegemony, a dream impeding the re-establishment of any 'concrete' world order in the post-war period (Schmitt 2009; Schmitt 1952; Schmitt 1955).

To counter progressivism, Schmitt defended British historian Arnold Toynbee's thesis that human history consists of a succession of independent paradigms within which all civilizations strive to address specific epochal challenges, thereby instituting (or failing to institute) a particular kind of international order (Toynbee 1951: 271). As he embraced this view, Schmitt postulated that neither superpower dualism nor the predominance of a single superpower could meet the challenges of the post-war era and secure an enduring world order. The latter, he argued, would rather result from a multipolar constellation of 'large spaces'.

At least two fundamental questions, however, can be raised with respect to Schmitt's position: was his theory of history tenable and persuasive? And could it still be used, as a whole or in part, to read the state of affairs in international law and politics today? It is the aim of this chapter to engage with these questions.

Superpower hegemony and the philosophy of progress

From the 1940s onwards, Carl Schmitt began to approach the classical problem of legal and political order from the specific viewpoint of the philosophy of history (Hofmann 2002; Nicoletti 1990). This came largely as a result of his increasing engagement with international law, which led him to delve into 'world history' (*Weltgeschichte*) and to elaborate an 'epochal' conception of the law of nations.[2] Schmitt's historico-philosophical turn became visible in *Land and Sea* (Schmitt 1997), where he postulated that world order is essentially epoch-related and hinges, in particular, on the struggle between continental and maritime powers. In the later *The Nomos of the Earth* (Schmitt 2003), he built on these intuitions to narrate a history

---

2 This concept was not novel but Schmitt popularized it and make it appealing to other international legal historians (most importantly, Grewe 2000).

of the law of nations and evoke a new global *nomos* replacing the old *jus publicum Europaeum*. Schmitt would expand on these historico-philosophical views in his 1950s papers.

Schmitt's articles from the 1950s can be read as a crusade against the foreign policies of the United States and the Soviet Union. Therein he formulated a sweeping critique of the way in which the superpowers had altered the old world order just to replace it with what he regarded as a global civil war. He branded the American–Soviet dualism as the main factor preventing the establishment of a new *nomos* for the postwar era, a *nomos* which should have been grounded, instead, on a new division of the earth and a new drawing of boundaries (including, implicitly, German boundaries). Schmitt's main argument against the current state of affairs was that 'concrete' international order could only arise from the multipolar balance of power of equally strong political entities, be they national states or 'large spaces' (Schmitt 1952: 5). In his 1952 article 'The Unity of the World' (Schmitt 1952: 4), Schmitt argued that far from generating a sustainable international equilibrium, the current global dualism had brought about 'unbearable tension' preventing the international community from exiting the phase of 'transition' into which it had plunged since the decay of the *jus publicum Europaeum*.

Schmitt described the time of the Cold War as an eminently historico-philosophical era in which all major political, moral and legal claims, especially the superpowers' hegemonic pretences, were articulated through a vocabulary of historical progressivism (Schmitt 2009: 167; Schmitt 1952: 6–7). Older European powers were accustomed to enlisting allies by portraying themselves as defenders of international law, morality or true religion, but such arguments no longer sufficed to back superpower demands for allegiance with the prospect of a nuclear struggle. To offset this threat, the superpowers needed to mobilize support by proclaiming their vision of the future of mankind as a progressive march towards utmost prosperity and freedom.

Schmitt postulated that the United States' and the Soviet Union's belief in progress, in particular their faith in modern rationality, technology, and industrial development, was not only naïve but also, and more essentially, detrimental to international order (Schmitt 1952: 9; Schmitt 1955: 140). This very belief was pushing the superpowers to seek universal hegemony. Driven by their faith in progress, each superpower claimed global leadership in the historical progression towards fulfilling the dream of the political–technological unity of the world, the highest aspiration of human kind (Kervégan 1999: 69). As a result, there was no essential difference between American and Soviet attitudes towards progress. Sure, the United States relied on the progressivist philosophy of eighteenth-century Enlightenment, whereas the Soviet Union proclaimed a Marxist idea of progress as leading to a perfect socialist community (Petito 2007: 178). And yet, both sides believed in the endless possibilities of rationality and technology, in the power of modern industry and economy, in technocratic government and in humanity's advancement towards larger freedom and equality. As Schmitt had put it in *Roman Catholicism and Political Form* a few years earlier:

> The world-view of the modern capitalist is the same as that of the industrial proletarian, as if the one were the twin brother of the other ... The big industrialist has no other ideal than that of Lenin – an 'electrified earth'. They disagree essentially only on the correct method of electrification. American financiers and Russian Bolsheviks find themselves in a common struggle for economic thinking, that is, the struggle against politicians and jurists.
>
> (Schmitt 1996: 13)

The main crux of Schmitt's argument lay in his establishing a direct correlation between progressivism and hegemony. While intuitive, the interdependence between these two concepts is probably not as self-evident as he presented it. As Martti Koskenniemi has claimed, progressive, teleological and Utopian notions have often proved a fundamental tool for international lawyers to engage with imperialism and power politics, and to assert the need of normativity in opposition to policy-centred approaches to international affairs (Koskenniemi 2012: 9). Further, the progressivism/hegemony association theorized by Schmitt sounds objectionable for the obvious reason that great powers have constantly pursued hegemonic policies, mostly without availing themselves of any progressivist ideology. For instance, the Axis powers during World War Two aspired to hegemony in just the same way as progressivist France under Napoleon or the United States and the Soviet Union in the age of the Cold War. Although the former, authoritarian states (with which, incidentally, Schmitt was sympathetic) were prone to backing their conduct by communitarian rhetoric or sheer political realism instead of cosmopolitan progressivism, they still acted hegemonically.

It might also be questioned whether the progressivism of the superpowers truly changed political and legal discourse, and for the worse, as Schmitt assumed. Their progressivist philosophy actually contained a traditional, prescriptive core, which hardly differed from earlier justification narratives. In the age of the *jus publicum Europaeum*, mostly idealized by Schmitt in *The Nomos of the Earth* (Schmitt 2003: 140), it was common to rationalize domestic state power in paternalistic terms and to legitimize war by just war rhetoric and public manifestos, no matter if in good faith. The United States and the Soviet Union behaved likewise, vindicating well-known values such as justice, prosperity and freedom, sometimes as mere façade. The superpowers did not envisage historical change and revolution as such, as Schmitt cried out. Their idea of progress was simply a catalyst, a new, fashionable receptacle for presenting familiar values in an appealing way. Just like the powers of old, the United States and the Soviet Union combined ethics with political realism, something that Schmitt entirely overlooked as he sought to depict Americans and Soviets as naïve believers in a progressive utopia. Incidentally, Schmitt himself had been instrumental in making realism the global mainstream in political thinking, notably via Hans Morgenthau, and could barely fail to see its considerable impact on American and Soviet 'hegemonic' policies by the 1950s (on Schmitt and Morgenthau, see Koskenniemi 2001: 436).

Schmitt also deserves criticism for failing to mention the theological roots of the philosophies of history he attacked, especially those of the United States. While insisting on Enlightenment utilitarian and progressivist notions such as freedom and opportunity, American political discourse has constantly appealed to the sacred. It has portrayed the United States as a nation chosen to spread peace and democracy and lead humanity on the path traced by divine providence (Merk 1963: 24). Yet, being an advocate of Christian eschatology himself, Schmitt glossed over the religious aspects of American political narratives and launched his attack on the philosophy of progress instead (on Schmitt's political theology as the background of his international law theory, see Koskenniemi 2004). By doing so he concealed the very 'structural' analogies between the political and the theological that he had made his task to unveil since his early works on Catholicism and political theology (Schmitt 2005: 36; Schmitt 2008: 107).

Schmitt's biases do not entirely undermine his critique of progressivism. For today's readers, his critique of technology, technocratic rule and economic rationalism remains extremely topical (Schmitt 1950: 83; Schmitt 1955; Schmitt 1996: 13). Many have carried on this critique of modernity to problematize the frenzy of industrialization, environmental degradation or the occurrence of nuclear disasters, and have branded modern technology as a self-referential entity that cannot be mastered, or can be mastered only by experts. In both cases technology, including economic and financial technology, escapes political control and the democratic space, be it conceived in a liberal or Schmittian way.

Existentialist history and Christian eschatology

Schmitt did not restrain himself to the *pars destruens* censuring progressivism. He sketched his own philosophy of history in the essay 'The Historical Structure of the Present Global Opposition of East and West', published in a *Festschrift* composed on occasion of the sixtieth anniversary of Ernst Jünger, in 1955 (Schmitt 1955; see also Bjork 2016, Chapter 8 in this volume). In this piece, Schmitt submitted that historical events should be read in their contextual significance, not in light of their supposed function within grand utopian narratives. For him, any recourse to metanarratives would distort the significance of historical phenomena. He advocated for an existentialist account of history in which every historical age instantiated a unique complex of meaningful events and experiences, as well as a specific *nomos* of the earth. To make this point, Schmitt relied on British historian Arnold Toynbee's 'challenge and response' theory, which provided him with a powerful framework to interpret international history. Just as in the 1920s, Schmitt had drawn on Kierkegaard's existentialism to develop a theory of political decisionism, now he took inspiration from Toynbee to elaborate a form of historical existentialism.

Toynbee voiced his existentialist theory in the first volume of *A Study of History*, where he characterized human history as a succession of epochal 'challenges' and 'responses', each major civilization embodying a successful response to the main challenges of the time (Toynbee 1951: 271). In 'The Historical Structure', Schmitt fully sustained this conception and went on providing a few examples of its validity. He explained how Britain had managed to deliver a successful historical response to the challenge of modern times by choosing a 'maritime existence', developing global trade and industrial capabilities, an instance he had already narrated in *Land and Sea* (Schmitt 1955: 160; Schmitt 1997: 54). Importantly, Schmitt insisted that both the modern geopolitical challenge and the British response had been unrepeatable junctures. They could not ground a *nomos* of the earth for the post-war era.

Besides existentialist history à la Toynbee, the other major source of inspiration for Schmitt's historical reflections was Christian eschatology. This was especially visible in a piece that Schmitt wrote for the journal *Universitas* in 1950, 'Three Possibilities of a Christian Interpretation of History', a book review of Karl Löwith's *Meaning in History* (Löwith 1949). Löwith, who under the Nazi regime, left Germany to escape anti-Jewish persecution, published this work in the United States a few years before returning to Germany to teach at the University of Heidelberg. With World War Two and the Holocaust in mind, Löwith intended *Meaning in History* to contribute to a reassessment of the tradition of the philosophy of history in an age of deep political and cultural crisis. The book, widely quoted, would prove one of the seminal outputs in the historico-philosophical debate of those years.

Schmitt depicted Löwith's book as a major intellectual achievement. He especially commended Löwith's implication that the modern theories of progress articulated since the age of Enlightenment had merely secularized but never truly superseded, Christian eschatology. In addition, Schmitt appreciated the unconventional structure of Löwith's book, which commenced with an analysis of modern texts, went back to the Middle Ages and finally peaked with Christian antiquity. Schmitt thus described Löwith's book as a 'path of initiation' leading the reader away from modern scholarship back to the illuminating doctrines contained in the works of Saint Augustine, Orosius and the Bible (Schmitt 2009: 167).

Schmitt explicitly wrote his comments on Löwith's book as a Christian. Accordingly, he took care of stressing that Christians also, not unlike Löwith and other critical historians, may possess a profound 'historical consciousness [*Geschichtsbewußtsein*]' (Schmitt 2009: 169). He contended that eschatological faith and historical consciousness can coexist, and one example of this coexistence, he argued, was the doctrine of the *katechon* as expressed in the Second Epistle to the Thessalonians. Therein, Saint Paul described the *katechon* as a person or entity tasked with delaying the premature arrival of the Antichrist by preserving peace and order on earth. Saint Paul remained mysterious as to the identity of this providential figure, only adding that he did not need to spell it out because the Thessalonians already knew 'who is holding [the Antichrist] back' (2 Thess. 2:6). According to the prevalent reading, Saint Paul was here hinting at the Roman Empire (Cacciari 2013: 31; see also Arvidsson 2016, Chapter 15 in this volume).

Schmitt recurrently mentioned Saint Paul's eschatological doctrine in his works, but his account of the identity of the *katechon* varied according to the circumstances and the genre of writing (Nicoletti 1988). In a historical book like *The Nomos of the Earth*, for instance, Schmitt equated the *katechon* with the Roman Empire, and even asserted that the Roman Empire had embodied the sole, true *katechon* ever seen on earth. As later Medieval rulers claimed, *katechon* status, he argued, they were in fact manipulating and degrading Saint Paul's original doctrine (Schmitt 2003: 60). But Schmitt's identification of the Roman Empire with the true *katechon* sounded like an unorthodox statement. For Saint Paul had made clear that the removal of the *katechon* would open the door for the Antichrist to enter the scene and inaugurate the end time, which, apparently, was still out of sight by the time Schmitt wrote *The Nomos of the Earth*.

In other writings Schmitt contemplated the possibility of later and even contemporary *katechons* (Meier 1998: 160). In a statement collected in *Glossarium* he pondered whether Winston Churchill or John Foster Dulles might presently be eligible to *katechon* status, only to conclude, however, that neither fits the bill (Schmitt 1981: 63). In any case, such conjectures were premised, again, on a theological blunder. Schmitt here indicated that *katechons* might crop out, die and be replaced throughout human history just like any other political figure. Conversely, Saint Paul had characterized the *katechon* as a unique person or institution with a specific eschatological function, anticipating the struggle between the Antichrist and the Lord. In his exegesis, Schmitt dropped any eschatological concern to turn the *katechon* into a merely secular concept and possibly make it palatable to non-Christian scholars, thereby trivializing it. This would be a legitimate intellectual operation, if it were not incongruous with Schmitt's own posing as a Christian thinker endeavouring to revive the spiritual meaning of human history.

Schmitt might even have disappointed his lay audience as he failed to clarify why they should regard the *katechon* doctrine as relevant to their work and to a modern understanding of history more generally. While Schmitt presented the *katechon* as a 'stunning example' of how eschatology and 'historical consciousness' might be bridged, he did not follow through on that promise. He simply surmized that the *katechon* doctrine is eminently political. In Schmitt's view, Saint Paul, by the very act of invoking the *katechon*, called attention to the concrete problem of political order. His invocation meant that human history is worth being prolonged and that human existence is meaningful here and now, not only in light of the final coming of Christ. Thus, in Schmitt's reading, Saint Paul appears as the early representative of a healthy political realism and 'historical consciousness' within the Christian tradition, in opposition to apocalyptical and apolitical fanatics preaching a withdrawal from the world (Schmitt 2009: 169; Nicoletti 1988: 122). But none of this throws any more light on the relevance of the *katechon* doctrine for non-Christian and realist scholars. While they might recognize Saint Paul as a 'historically conscious' writer, they clearly do not need his doctrine to articulate their claims, and they might actually view any reliance on it as simply obstructing sound political argument and historical research.

Schmitt made a subsidiary point to bring Christian 'historical consciousness' to the fore and reconcile it with non-Christian scholarship. Christianity, he argued, was a deeply 'historical' belief (Schmitt 2009: 169). It was the faith in a single, historical event, the incarnation of God, and in the story of salvation narrated in the Bible. Yet Schmitt does not sound entirely persuasive in this description of Christianity as a historical religion. It is not clear to what extent Christianity differs from other beliefs, especially from monotheistic beliefs, equally relying on historical narratives. Further, it is hard for the reader to agree with Schmitt that the reason why Christians possess historical consciousness is that they place emphasis on the uniqueness of biblical events, in particular the incarnation. Being aware of the uniqueness of the episodes of sacred history does not necessitate any historical consciousness, quite the contrary. Christians rather believe that Biblical events, although historically unique, possess eternal value and normative force. As sacraments, the most fundamental of these events are ritualized and must invariably be re-enacted through a fixed liturgy until the end of times. This approach is precisely denied by modern 'historical consciousness', which regards any events as contingent and situates them within their historical contexts (Bultmann 1957: 141). For the modern historian, the uniqueness of historical events goes hand in hand with their sheer relativity, whereas Christian theologians assume that a unique yet sacred occurrence such as the incarnation embodies the eternal mediation of the relative and the universal. Christians might be historical relativists as regards human history, not, however, when it comes down to sacred history.

Arguably, the strengths of Schmitt's philosophy of history lay in its broadly existentialist motives, not in its Christian core. Existentialism allowed Schmitt to move beyond simplistic nineteenth-century descriptions of international history as a naked struggle for power (or, in a more sophisticated way, as a struggle sublimated by the unfolding of universal Reason) to a more tangible 'problem history [*Problemgeschichte*]'. Force and violence continued playing a central role in his understanding of the *nomos* but were read in light of the creation of a concrete and existentially meaningful order in history. While Schmitt's idea of concrete order and its application to international law remain highly problematic, his sensibility for the existential character of law and politics might still offer an insightful alternative to realist accounts of international affairs.

Schmitt's prophecies on the future of international law

Schmitt's reflections on the philosophy of history were deeply intertwined with his theory of international law. It was largely to advocate a new *nomos* and to rebuke American and Soviet hegemonic aspirations that he elaborated his Christian and existentialist conception of history.

But how would the new *nomos* look like? In 'The Unity of the World' Schmitt conjectured two possible answers to this question. First he suggested that the bipolar Cold War system might end with unipolarity; that is, with the defeat of either side and the rise of the victor power to the status of global, uncontested hegemon (Schmitt 1952: 4; Mouffe 2007: 150). Yet this scenario counted as the least probable, and as detrimental to any international actor other than the hegemon. More likely, Schmitt said, the two superpowers would maintain their relative strength in the long term and be flanked by emerging powers gradually bringing about a multipolar constellation (Schmitt 1952: 5). This process was already under way, he claimed, as both superpowers were furnishing military and financial assistance to minor powers which they wished to enlist for their cause (Schmitt 2007: 74). This would result in some of the minor powers emancipating themselves and establishing a pluralist international equilibrium. Schmitt here championed the creation of regional 'large spaces', such as America, Europe, China and India, each with its peculiar form of international order enforced by a hegemonic power – an idea he had already promoted in the past, as an advocate of the German *Reich* (Schmitt 1991: 46–8). In his articles of the 1950s, Schmitt cautiously refrained from stating that 'large spaces' must come with a hegemonic power. Implicitly, though, he still upheld that claim. He hinted that the powers of the future, grown powerful thanks to American and Soviet support, will give rise to a multipolar *nomos* by extending their own 'spheres of influence', thereby turning into regional *hegemons de facto* (Schmitt 1952: 5). Arguably, in the constellation described by Schmitt, Europe might feature as the only 'large space' not dominated by a hegemonic power.

Schmitt himself cautioned that far from being entirely novel, his large spaces theory maintained 'some analogies with the European international law of the eighteenth and nineteenth centuries, which equally rested on the equilibrium of several powers' (ibid.). His only creative addition here lay in the global character of the new large spaces, and in the balance of power being situated 'on a new plane and with new dimensions', making room for non-European hegemonic actors (ibid.). At any rate, this analogy between the new *nomos* and the *jus publicum Europaeum* disproved Schmitt's own existentialist idea that all effective responses to historical challenges are unique and cannot be derived from events and situations occurred in previous epochs.

More importantly, Schmitt failed to provide any substantial political and legal argument in favour of the large spaces doctrine and against the Cold War system. Based on dubious theological and metaphysical assumptions, Schmitt simply posited that all duality is 'evil and dangerous as such' (Schmitt 1952: 4). He further postulated that the current opposition between East and West qualified as an especially 'ominous duality' causing an 'unsustainable state of transition' in international affairs (Schmitt 1952: 3–4). But he furnished no clarification as to what exactly were the downsides of a dual world order compared with unipolarity or multipolarity.

Any elucidation in this respect must be reconstructed in light of Schmitt's broader oeuvre, principally his concept of concrete order and the notion of absolute enmity. For example, the superpowers might not create any 'concrete' order because, in Schmitt's eyes, they failed to enforce 'real' peace and wage 'real' war. They thus perpetuated international instability and contributed to the 'unclear' conceptualities of contemporary international law after the demise of the *jus publicum Europaeum*. From another Schmittian angle, the superpowers surely erred by stoking 'absolute' and ideological hostility, thus blurring the fundamental legal distinction of enemy and criminal (Schmitt 2007: 93). In his 1962 paper 'The Order of the World', Schmitt emphatically defined the enemy/criminal distinction as the foundation of all classical differentiations in classical international law, such as war/peace, combatant/non-combatant and neutral/belligerent. He declared that every humanitarian achievement in the history of international law was grounded on the neat demarcation of criminality and belligerency, which had allowed the creation of belligerent and neutral rights and sanctioned the moderation of warfare (Schmitt 1995: 598).

But Schmitt's emphasis on dichotomies such as friend/enemy and peace/war raises some difficulties. In the eighteenth century, the age that

Schmitt idealized as the one which formalized a neat distinction between allies and enemies or war and peace, all European powers actually devoted peacetime to fortifying their borders, strengthening their armies and shifting alliances through secret diplomacy to prepare for the upcoming clash (McKay and Scott 1983). That sounds like 'cold war', not 'true peace', and indeed it may be doubted whether international relations have ever experienced what Schmitt calls a 'true peace'. Certainly, the Cold War situations typical of the age of the *jus publicum Europaeum* might still be favoured over twentieth-century superpower rivalry, but Schmitt's aprioristic arguments about 'true peace' and 'concrete order' would be of little use to prove this point beyond mere intuition.

Likewise unconvincing was Schmitt's thrust that the institution of a multipolar *nomos* would eradicate absolute ideological hostility (Schmitt 1952: 6). *Pace* Schmitt, it does not seem that the institution of a plurality of 'large spaces' would necessarily diminish the likelihood of total war. Any regional hegemon in a 'large space' would predictably attempt to secure its own existence and interests by seeking alliances with other regional hegemons, as all western powers have done in the whole of modern history. Out of these alliances some balance of power might emerge, yet it would in turn increase reciprocal fear, leading to arms races and possibly to a general war, as happened in the run up to World War One. Schmitt was, of course, fully aware that the nineteenth-century balance of power had plunged European powers into total warfare. But he left the matter off the table under the assumption that international equilibrium is always desirable and universalism deleterious. His goal was to celebrate the principle of the balance of power as a fundamental instrument to regulate international relations in the epoch of the *jus publicum Europaeum*, an epoch that he nostalgically and uncritically romanticized (Koskenniemi 2001: 421; Koskenniemi 2004: 495).

Plausibly, the effectiveness and desirability of international order does not hinge simply on the number of players involved and their relative strength, as Schmitt asserted, but on the wider and complex historical context in which they interact. In opposition to a contextual theory, he characterized unipolarity as an absolute evil, and deemed bipolarity a slightly better but still inherently flawed situation compared with multipolarity. Schmitt sketched these ideas in a short article of 1955, 'The New *Nomos* of the Earth', presenting unipolarity, bipolarity and multipolarity as three possible scenarios of future international relations. He decried the currency of the unipolarity concept in public debates and tried to bring the alternatives of bipolarity and multipolarity to the fore (Schmitt 2003: 354).

Schmitt's most curious hint in this 1955 paper, compared with 'The Unity of the World' from 1952, was that the Cold War system might survive in the long term. He suggested that the system would endure as long as it rested on a traditional and established form of political equilibrium, that between land and sea, represented by a 'terrestrial' power like the Soviet Union and a 'maritime' power like the United States. On the other hand, Schmitt maintained that a multipolar system of large spaces would remain the most 'rational' option, assuming that they are 'reasonably demarcated and internally homogeneous', as was Christian Europe (ibid.).

Schmitt's reflections on history and the present international scenario

What seems to have happened from the close of the Cold War up until now is a rapid succession of all alternatives mentioned by Schmitt: unipolar, multipolar and bipolar. As he feared, the war did end with the supremacy of a single superpower, the United States, though the latter's ascendancy ensued from the implosion of the Soviet Union, not from a lethal military confrontation. Then, at the turn of the twentieth century, a multipolar constellation seemed to come into existence, given the declining hegemony of the United States, the increasing weight of new powers such as China, India and Brazil, and the comeback of Russia as an active international actor. However, the latter countries have not displayed the same economic and military potential or capability of autonomously shaping their foreign policies. The recent financial and economic crisis has unveiled the weaknesses of India and Brazil (as well as the fragility and internal divides of another would-be global actor, the European Union). As to Russia, the strong dependence of the country's economy on the export of natural resources represents a significant liability for Moscow,[3] so that Vladimir Putin's aggressive foreign policy appears as a risky bet. In this constellation, China alone is rising to superpower status to defy the United States, and to claim predominance over American-backed regional players like Japan and South Korea. In the near future, international relations might again take the shape of a dual superpower balance, a balance that Schmitt regarded as fundamentally unstable.

Some Western scholars, unsettled by the loss of power of the United States, have contended that the American–Chinese rivalry might soon turn into a new Cold War. They have questioned China's peacefulness and condescending attitude toward international law and institutions, and have suggested that economic interdependence will not suffice to prevent conflict between the Asian superpower and the United States (Posner and Yoo 2006). This stance is best condensed in the lapidary opening line of a paper on China by realist international relations scholar John Mearsheimer: 'Can China rise peacefully? My answer is no' (Mearsheimer

---

3   Despite growing Russian international activism under Vladimir Putin, Sir Tony Brenton has candidly defined the relationship between China and Russia as one between an emerging and a declining power (Brenton 2014).

2006). Such 'China threat' narratives have exercised a considerable effect on American public opinion and foreign policy in the last few years, and have likely contributed to prompting the United States' 'pivoting' towards Asia, predicated by Hilary Clinton in 2011 (Clinton 2011). In the meantime, western realist observers have seen their worries justified by events such as the Senkaku Islands dispute or the substantial increase of China's military budget (see, for example, The Economist 2014), while Chinese realists might have been just as troubled by the growing military presence of the United States in South-East Asia (Tanter 2013).

Yet another prong of scholarship takes a constructivist viewpoint to argue that realists, highly influential in both the American and Chinese camps, are part of the problem, as they aprioristically define the competitor as an enemy and expect that, at some point, the worst will inevitably happen (Buzan 2010: 23). In fact, it seems to be a long shot for the realists to argue, as they sometimes do, that because the growth of some old power, say, Germany or Russia, was accompanied by aggressive imperialism, China will behave in the same way. Despite their disagreement on a number of issues, the Chinese and American leaderships still have major economic and strategic interests in common and are not yet divided by an ideological hostility comparable with that which affected Soviet–American relations (Kissinger 2012). According to former Australian Prime Minister and Minister of Foreign Affairs Kevin Rudd, a reputed China expert, the process of Chinese growth should be acknowledged, not opposed, by the United States. It ought to be accompanied by regular summitry and leader-to-leader engagement seriously to tackle selected key issues, such as the Doha Round or climate-change negotiations, to build mutual trust for future cooperation (Rudd 2013).

To some extent, the warlike position of realist scholars today can be compared with Schmitt's. He also was convinced that as soon as a polity attains a certain degree of economic and military power – such as China today – it will use it, and that the power built on modern military technology, once available, will likely be put to work. The latter had been the case, he claimed, with submarine warfare and aerial bombing, which had been deployed since World War One in blatant violation of the classical *ius in bello* (Schmitt 2003: 313; Schmitt 2011; Rech 2012). Indeed, if politics are grounded on the friend/enemy distinction as Schmitt assumes, it would be foolish not to apply any means available to protect one's core interests and weaken the adversary, notwithstanding strategic alliances with like-minded states. From this angle, Schmitt would today agree with Mearsheimer that China is likely to seek military superiority and political hegemony just as any great power has done at some point in the past (Mearsheimer 2006).

Aware as he was of the link between hegemony and ideology, Schmitt would no doubt stress that the likelihood of a new Cold War might augment as a result of China's ideological orientations. Although western observers have recurrently pointed to the Chinese leadership's shying away from articulating any coherent foreign policy doctrine that would eventually curb its leeway, Chinese politicians and scholars seem to be endorsing at least flexible ideologies that might back a broad range of policies.[4] The most familiar of these doctrines is that of a 'harmonious' universal society based on Confucian principles, an idea articulated by political philosopher Zhao Tingyang in his 'All-under-heaven' theory (Zhao 2009). While hypothetically cosmopolitan, this approach may raise doubts among the non-Chinese as it deliberately leaves the notion of universal 'harmony' indeterminate and reserves a privileged role for China in the shaping of the new, 'harmonious' world order (for a critical review of the 'all-under-heaven' theory, see The Economist 2011).

Compared with this Sinocentric political doctrine, the philosophy of progress recently promoted by State Councillor Dai Bingguo sounds much gentler and acceptable to the non-Chinese (Dai 2012). Dai has been a vocal supporter of China's peaceful rise and was cited as a valuable and cooperative partner by Hilary Clinton, even in her notorious paper 'America's Pacific Century', in which she announced the rebalancing of the United States' foreign policy towards Asia (Clinton 2011). In Dai's discourse, 'progress' is a positively connoted term, associated with international cooperation and peace. On the other hand, as the western experience amply demonstrates, the concept of progress can be deployed in confrontational ways, too. Lately, in a moderate yet slightly polemic paper, Chinese international lawyer Sienho Yee has made clear that because of cultural specificities, nations define what counts as 'progress' and 'progressive' international law in different ways and should not be forced to accept others' views on the matter (Sienho 2013). It is hard to tell whether in Sienho Yee's account there is anything 'progressive' apart from the wording.

According to a Schmittian reading, Dai Bingguo's and Sienho Yee's progressivism, as well as Zhao Tingyang's doctrine of universal 'harmony', would all belong to the same ambivalent, cosmopolitan discourse, incapable of producing 'concrete' order. Whether this progressivism will turn into an instrument of political hegemony, as a Schmittian perspective would imply, it remains to be seen. In versions such as Dai's, progressivism surely appears as non-belligerent but it remains a one-size-fits-all doctrine suitable for legitimizing any international conduct when needed. In the past, as Schmitt noted, progressivism has been as a rhetorical weapon in the hands of the United States and next it might be wielded by China.

Critics of the current world order might join Schmitt in his critique of the ideology of progress and take his line of reasoning further. They might

---

4 Barry Buzan has especially noted that China lacks a universalist foreign policy ideology comparable to the United States' and this lack might turn into a considerable liability (Buzan 2010: 22).

claim that progressivism today is being put to use by the world's major international financial and trade institutions, in whose rhetoric the traditional idea of progress pops up in the fashionable form of economic 'growth', 'development' and the 'removal of obstacles' to free trade. Not unlike great powers, these institutions are fostering an eclectic ideology of progress ambiguously merging the language of economy and technical expertise with legal and ethical concepts that can be easily instrumentalized, such as human rights, self-determination and the rule of law. Within this and other justification narratives of the present day, 'progress' looms large as the common denominator of legal and political modernity, an expedient rhetorical umbrella under which to create the appearance of international consent.

Some contemporary readers might actually feel uncomfortable with some aspects of Schmitt's approach, in particular his attempt to situate the meaning of human history within an eschatological horizon. Yet they might appreciate his broader existentialist emphasis on the meaningfulness of historical existence and his insistence on context as opposed to progressive metanarrative. By building on Toynbee's 'challenge and response' theory, Schmitt certainly provides a captivating alternative to progressivism and other non-situational, speculative theories of history and international relations.

Present scholars might still wonder whether it is necessary to take an existentialist approach to debunk the myth of progress and produce a concrete, disillusioned understanding of history. Standard political realism as well as critical history à la Foucault, for example, have achieved the same goals without any need of existentialist and theological adornments. And yet, neither political realism nor critical theory provides the intriguing and imaginative view of history that Schmittian existentialism conveys. Both realists and Foucaultians deprive history of any deeper meaning as they either subordinate historical events to narrow scientific methodologies, or nihilistically reduce history as a bunch of discipline-enforcing and eventually senseless discourses. Conversely, existentialists conceive of historical events as exceptional occurrences that awake a drowsy mankind and make true active life possible. To be sure, this is a theoretically burdensome view, relying on intuition and personal experience rather than demonstration. It would be up to Schmitt readers to regard the intuitive character of his existentialist position as a weakness or a strength.

Existentialism definitely remains vulnerable to the further criticism that it does not supply any guidelines for action. From an existentialist standpoint the experience of the event, including the event of the *nomos* in Schmitt's work, comes out as unpredictable, unique and only enigmatically 'truthful'. Within this framework, such disparate political phenomena as Fascism, Nazism, Stalinism, May 1968 or 9/11 might all count as highly significant events calling for commitment and authenticity. Yet, despite its normative emptiness, the existentialist standpoint today looks like the closest one can get to making sense of historical existence and moral intuitions, and as an inspiring alternative to the progressivist and technocratic beliefs still prevailing in public discourse. As long as mainstream scholarship and political leaderships reproduce a blind faith in economic progress and technocratic rule, Schmitt's theory of history might act as a springboard for raising the forgotten question of historical and existential meaning in law and politics.

Bibliography

Arvidsson, M. (2016) 'From Teleology to Eschatology: The *Katechon* and the Political Theology of the International Law of Belligerent Occupation', Chapter 15 in M. Arvidsson, L. Brännström and P. Minkkinen (eds), *The Contemporary Relevance of Carl Schmitt: Law, Politics, Theology*. Abingdon: Routledge.
Björk, M. (2016) 'Representation and the Unrepresentable: Ernst Jünger, Carl Schmitt and the Limits of Politics', Chapter 8 in M. Arvidsson, L. Brännström and P. Minkkinen (eds), *The Contemporary Relevance of Carl Schmitt: Law, Politics, Theology*. Abingdon: Routledge.
Bluntschli, J.C. (1868) *Das moderne Völkerrecht der civilisirten Staaten als Rechtsbuch dargestellt*. Nördlingen: Beck.
Brenton, T. (2014) 'Russia and China: An Axis of Insecurity', *Asian Affairs*, Vol. 44, No. 2: 231–49.
Bultmann, R. (1957) *The Presence of Eternity: History and Eschatology*. Westport, CT: Greenwood.
Buzan, B. (2010) 'China in International Society: Is 'Peaceful Rise' possible?', *Chinese Journal of International Politics*, Vol. 3, No. 1: 5–36.
Cacciari, M. (2013) *Il potere che frena*. Milano: Adelphi.
Clinton, H. (2011) 'America's Pacific Century', *Foreign Policy*, Vol. 189, No. 1: 56–63.
Dai, B. (2012) 'Asia, China and International Law', *Chinese Journal of International Law*, Vol. 11, No. 1: 1–3.
The Economist (2011) 'Nothing New Under Heaven', *The Economist*, 16 June 2011. Available at www.economist.com/node/18836024 (accessed 2 June 2015).
The Economist (2014) 'At the Double', *The Economist*, 13 March 2014. Available at www.economist.com/news/china/21599046-chinas-fast-growing-defence-budget-worries-its-neighbours-not-every-trend-its-favour (accessed 2 June 2015).
Grewe, W. G. (2000) *The Epochs of International Law*. Berlin: De Gruyter.
Hofmann, H. (2002) *Legitimität gegen Legalität. Der Weg der politischen Philosophie Carl Schmitts*. Berlin: Duncker and Humblot.
Kervégan, J.-F. (1999) 'Carl Schmitt and World Unity', p. 54–74, in C. Mouffe (ed.), *The Challenge of Carl Schmitt*. London: Verso.
Kissinger, H. (2012) 'The Future of U.S.-Chinese Relations: Conflict is a Choice, not a Necessity', *Foreign Affairs*, Vol. 91, No. 2: 44–55.
Koskenniemi, M. (2001) *The Gentle Civilizer of Nations: The Rise and Fall of International Law 1870–1960*. Cambridge: Cambridge University Press.
Koskenniemi, M. (2004) 'International Law as Political Theology: How to Read *Nomos der Erde*?', *Constellations*, Vol. 11, No. 4: 492–510.

Koskenniemi, M. (2012) 'Law, Teleology and International Relations: An Essay in Counterdisciplinarity', *International Relations*, Vol. 26, No. 3: 3–34.
Löwith, K. (1949) *Meaning in History*. Chicago, IL: University of Chicago Press.
Mamiani, T. (1861) *D'un nuovo diritto europeo*. Torino: Tipografica Scolastica.
Manning, W. O. (1839) *Commentaries on the Law of Nations*. London: Sweet.
McKay, D. and H. M. Scott (1983) *The Rise of the Great Powers 1648–1815*. London: Longman.
Mearsheimer, J. (2006) 'China's Unpeaceful Rise', *Current History*, Vol. 105, No. 690: 160–2.
Meier, H. (1998) *The Lesson of Carl Schmitt: Four Chapters on the Distinction between Political Theology and Political Philosophy*. Trans. M. Brainard. Chicago, IL: University of Chicago Press.
Merk, F. (1963) *Manifest Destiny and Mission in American History: A Reinterpretation*. New York: Knopf.
Mouffe, C. (2007) 'Carl Schmitt's Warnings on the Dangers of a Unipolar World', p. 147–53, in L. Odysseos and F. Petito (eds), *The International Political Thought of Carl Schmitt: Terror, Liberal War and the Crisis of Global Order*. Abingdon: Routledge.
Nicoletti, M. (1988) 'Die Ursprünge von Carl Schmitts "Politische Theologie"', p. 109–28, in H. Quaritsch (ed.), *Complexio Oppositorum: über Carl Schmitt*. Berlin: Duncker and Humblot.
Nicoletti, M. (1990) *Trascendenza e potere: la teologia politica di Carl Schmitt*. Brescia: Morcelliana.
Petito, F. (2007) 'Against World Unity: Carl Schmitt and the Western-centric and Liberal Global Order', p. 166–84, in L. Odysseos and F. Petito (eds), *The International Political Thought of Carl Schmitt: Terror, Liberal War and the Crisis of Global Order*. London: Routledge.
Posner, E. and J. Yoo (2006) 'International Law and the Rise of China', *Chicago Journal of International Law*, Vol. 7, No. 1: 1–15.
Rech, W. (2012) 'Rightless Enemies: Schmitt and Lauterpacht on Political Piracy', *Oxford Journal of Legal Studies*, Vol. 32, No. 2: 235–63.
Rudd, K. (2013) 'Beyond the Pivot: A New Road Map for U.S.-Chinese Relations', *Foreign Affairs*, Vol. 92, No. 2: 9–15.
Schmitt, C. (1950) *Ex captivitate salus. Erfahrungen der Zeit 1945/47*. Köln: Greven.
Schmitt, C. (1952) 'Die Einheit der Welt', *Merkur*, Vol. 6, No. 1: 1–11.
Schmitt, C. (1955) 'Die geschichtliche Struktur des heutigen Welt-Gegensatzes von Ost und West', p. 135–67, in A. Mohler (ed.) *Freundschaftliche Begegnungen: Festschrift für Ernst Jünger zum 60. Geburtstag*. Frankfurt am Main: Klostermann.
Schmitt, C. (1981) *Glossarium: Aufzeichnungen der Jahre 1947–1951*. Berlin: Duncker and Humblot.
Schmitt, C. (1991) *Völkerrechtliche Großraumordnung mit Interventionsverbot für Raumfremde Mächte: ein Beitrag zum Reichsbegriff im Völkerrecht* [1939]. Berlin: Duncker and Humblot.
Schmitt, C. (1995) 'Die Ordnung der Welt nach dem Zweiten Weltkrieg' [1962], p. 592–618, in C. Schmitt, *Staat, Großraum, Nomos: Arbeiten aus den Jahren 1916–1969*. Berlin: Duncker and Humblot.
Schmitt, C. (1996) *Roman Catholicism and Political Form* [1923]. Trans. G. L. Ulmen. Westport, CT: Greenwood.

Schmitt, C. (1997) *Land and Sea* [1942]. Trans. S. Draghici. Washington, DC: Plutarch.
Schmitt, C. (2003) *The Nomos of the Earth in the International Law of the Jus Publicum Europaeum* [1950]. Trans. G. L. Ulmen. New York: Telos.
Schmitt, C. (2005) *Political Theology: Four Chapters on the Concept of Sovereignty* [1922]. Trans. G. Schwab. Chicago, IL: University of Chicago Press.
Schmitt, C. (2007) *Theory of the Partisan: Intermediate Commentary on the Concept of the Political* [1963]. Trans. G. L. Ulmen. New York: Telos.
Schmitt, C. (2008) *Political Theology II: The Myth of the Closure of Any Political Theology* [1970]. Trans. M. Hoelzl and G. Ward. Cambridge: Polity.
Schmitt, C. (2009) 'Three Possibilities of a Christian Interpretation of History' [1950]. Trans. M. Venning. *Telos*, No. 147: 167–70.
Schmitt, C. (2011) 'The Concept of Piracy' [1937]. Trans. D. Heller-Roazen. *Humanity*, Vol. 2, No. 1: 27–9.
Sienho, Y. (2013) 'The International Law of Co-progressiveness and the Co-progressiveness of Civilizations', *Chinese Journal of International Law*, Vol. 12, No. 1: 9–17.
Suri, M.V. (2013) 'Conceptualizing China within the Kantian Peace', *Harvard Journal of International Law*, Vol. 54, No. 1: 219–58.
Tanter, R. (2013) 'The US Military Presence in Australia: Asymmetrical Alliance Cooperation and its Alternatives', *Asia-Pacific Journal*, Vol. 11, No. 45. Available at www.globalresearch.ca/the-us-military-presence-in-australia-the-asia-pacific-pivot-and-global-nato/5357653 (accessed 17 April 2015).
Toynbee, A. (1951) *A Study of History*, Vol. 1. Oxford: Oxford University Press.
Vergé, C. H. (1864) 'Le droit des Gens avant et depuis 1789', p. i–lv, in G. F. de Martens, *Précis du droit des gens moderne de l'Europe*. 2nd edn, Vol. 1. Paris: Guillaumin.
Zhao, T. (2009) 'A Political World Philosophy in Terms of All-under-Heaven (Tianxia)', *Diogenes*, Vol. 56, No. 1: 5–18.

Chapter 11

Carl Schmitt and the new world order

A view from Europe

Massimo Fichera

> 'Morality is the last refuge of Eurocentrism.'
>
> H. M. Enzensberger (1994: 61)

Introduction: security and identity in the EU

The European Union (EU) constitutional project of integration is, at its heart, an ambitious project of expansion through the promotion of human rights and the rule of law. My claim is that imperialistic features transpire from the EU's official discourse and that its role can be best defined as that of a 'transnational security entrepreneur' (as explained later in this chapter). Security is thus a key element of EU identity and the reason for this is simple. The spirit of European integration is represented not merely by market values, but also by a commitment to the creation of a 'security zone' in which war between states is to be 'bracketed' (to use a Schmittian expression). The question of how large and how integrated this 'security zone' should be, and which lines of inclusion and exclusion should be drawn, is still open.

Security is a broad, ever-expanding notion, which is capable of embracing a variety of fields, including the economy or the environment. It is in light of this conceptual framework that EU identity ought to be reassessed. EU identity ought to be viewed *through* security lenses, in the sense that the project of EU integration is presented time and again as something that needs to be preserved at all costs to ensure peace and a prosperous development of the internal market.

The close link between security and identity is confirmed by the fact that, after the Cold War, the questions of the enlargement of the EU and of its stability have become increasingly important (Zielonka 2006: 164). Enlarging the EU has also traditionally meant stretching the borders of Europe towards two geopolitical areas: one formerly under the influence of the Soviet Union/the Russian Federation and the other one neighbouring the Middle East. This inevitably leads to tensions and conflicts.

The construction of the idea of Europe can thus be defined in security terms, in the sense that over the years a security discourse has been powerfully developed along the lines fragmentation/integration (Waever 1996: 121). The European project acquires not only a dynamic, fluid nature but also an *existential* connotation (Waever 1996: 124). In other words, the EU is situated at the centre of a security–identity *continuum* because most, if not all, its areas of competence, both internal and external, *including those related to economy and trade*, may be conceptualized as security issues; that is, they become questions of survival of the European project itself.

However, the EU constitutional project of integration must be viewed from a critical angle. From this particular angle, one may observe that two recent areas of development of the EU; that is, the area of freedom, security and justice (AFSJ), especially its external dimension, as well as the Common Foreign and Security Policy (CFSP) and European Security Defence Policy (ESDP), are much more significant than it would appear at first sight. AFSJ and CFSP/ESDP represent the former intergovernmental pillars of the EU (respectively, third and second), which were abolished by the Treaty of Lisbon. They now form part of a single institutional framework but still retain some intergovernmental traits. While AFSJ covers immigration, asylum, judicial cooperation in civil and criminal matters and family law, CFSP and ESDP typically embrace foreign affairs and defence policies. Although embryonic versions of them emerged in the 1970s and 1980s, their parallel development officially began in the 1990s with the Treaty of Maastricht (Denza 2002; Eeckhout 2011).

These areas, in fact, ought to be considered as essential components of a security–identity *continuum* as a constitutive feature of the EU. The idea is that not only does the EU need to project an image of internal and external security to advance its constitutional and foundational claims (Bigo 2000: 174), but this interconnection is also especially relevant for the construction of European identity.

For example, the Rhodes Declaration on the International Role of the European Community (European Parliament 1988) already emphasized that coordination on the political and economic aspects of security had to be ensured for the protection of human rights, free movement of people, 'the establishment of a secure and stable balance of conventional forces in Europe' and 'the strengthening of mutual confidence'. In this light, the European Council invited all countries 'to embark with the European Community as a world partner on an historic effort to leave to the next generation a Continent and a world more secure, more just and more free' (European Parliament 1988). This statement expresses a *trait d'union* between the internal and external dimensions of security. When the Cold War ended and the Soviet Union collapsed, the relationship between Europe and its neighbours changed radically. Partly in response to this, on the one hand, security no longer needed to be restricted to military strategies and, on the other, the European project could expand towards the East and commit itself to a deeper level of integration. This bidirectional move, towards the outside and towards the inside, was fundamental for the emergence and development of the binomial security–identity.

In order to support these claims, this chapter employs Carl Schmitt's writings in the area of international law and shows that, if reinterpreted in a new light, they can prove useful for a broader understanding of what type of identity is projected internationally by the EU. In particular, the idea behind this work is that the EU security–identity *continuum* does not merely embrace AFSJ, CFSP and ESDP but spills over into other fields and reaches into the core of the EU project – to the extent that it poses questions of normativity and inclusion.

Moreover, AFSJ, CFSP and ESDP possess an inherently existential life force, which was present at an embryonic stage at the beginning of the process of European integration and which gradually developed across the decades.[1] In this regard, looking at the historical development of European integration is instructive. In international relations and political theory, the issue of the nature of the EU as an international organization, as an autonomous polity or as some other entity standing between EU law and international law has been debated for a long time. The EU has also been depicted as a civilian power, as a normative power or even as an empire (Manners 2002, 2006; Nicolaïdis and Howse 2002; Zielonka 2006). These approaches emphasize the capacity of the EU to expand its normative influence to other regions in the world, both in the neighbouring areas and in other continents.

Perhaps the image of Post-Westphalian empire conveys these characteristics more effectively than that of normative power. This would be confirmed, it has been maintained, by elements such as the multiplicity of overlapping military and police institutions, the lack of fixed borders and the very fact that the EU cares more about exporting goods and norms than imposing its rules externally (Zielonka 2006: 143–50). Because an empire has no fixed borders, security problems are dealt with through external expansion (Beck and Grande 2011: 25–6). This expansion does not take place militarily but by exporting a model of regional integration based on the rule of law. Nevertheless, the idea of empire should be enriched by re-qualifying the EU region not as territory but as autonomous *space*. Whereas a territory is very much linked to the Westphalian ideas of sovereignty, nation, fixed borders, a *space* is more fluid, open and ready to be expanded (for a partly similar application of the concept of space to

---

1 See, for example, Traité instituant la Communauté Européenne de Défense, Paris, 27 Mai 1952; Treaty on Economic, Social and Cultural Collaboration and Collective Self-Defence, Brussels, 17 March 1948 and the Protocol Modifying and Completing the Brussels Treaty, Paris, 23 October 1954 (Paris Agreements).

Europe, see Kaiser and Starie 2005). In my interpretation, a space is characterized, in particular, by the act of appropriation of values and by the delimitation of fluid borders beyond State sovereignty.

Decisions on the delimitation of borders and on the appropriation of values are thus security decisions. In fact, internal and external security are two sides of the same coin: they point to the ability of a polity to draw borders, to decide who is in and who is out. From a broad, existential perspective, they express the foundational, constitutional nature of borders.

In this regard, this chapter employs the Schmittian idea of *large space* but it also recognizes its limits. First, Schmitt's notion of *large space* relies on a simplistic distinction between friend and enemy and, second, it focuses on land appropriation, rather than value appropriation.

Ultimately, however, Schmitt's critique of the liberal language of morality turns into a critique of the EU's self-representation as a universal project, which is in fact driven by expansionistic ambitions.

Schmitt and the new world order

Schmitt is one of the first theorists of globalization and his post-World War analysis anticipates many contemporary themes. However, it is important to flesh out what can be really interesting for our contemporary eyes.

His writings often focus on the idea of *nomos*. For him the Greek word *nomos* should not be translated as law, but rather, as the measure by which the land is divided, and the form of order that results from this operation. Its dimension is essentially spatial and concrete, and its constitutive act is represented by land appropriation (Schmitt 2003a: 70–1). The history of the world is characterized by a succession of *nomoi* and the beginning of each *nomos* corresponds to a major event; that is, occupation or discovery. The first *nomos* was replaced by the second *nomos* around the sixteenth century, after America was discovered and the oceans circumnavigated; the second *nomos* was destroyed after World War I and a new *nomos* shall come, which shall no longer be Eurocentric but, for the first time, truly global (Schmitt 2003b: 353). Under the first *nomos*, the notion of just war was determined by the authority of the Church and was therefore just in so far as it possessed a *justa causa*: those against whom war was waged, being without a just cause, were to be punished as outlaws and could therefore be annihilated (Schmitt 2003a: 120). Sovereignty was in this sense a moral theological attribute. The medieval spatial order was supported by empire and papacy: the empire was legitimate because it was Christian and its historical task was to act as a restrainer of the Antichrist (the so-called '*Katechon*') (Schmitt 2003a: 59–66). The second *nomos* succeeded in removing the Church's *potestas spiritualis*. Its purpose was to eliminate religious and civil conflicts by setting up a framework of states capable of monopolizing the recourse to violence and mobilizing the economic resources necessary to maintain peace and stability. For this to occur, war was to be secularized and legitimate: no state could claim a condition of moral superiority. *Jus publicum europaeum* was thus grounded on a formalization and rationalization of the relationship between sovereign states: in case of war, the belligerents recognized each other as *justi hostes* as long as they behaved according to the procedural rules in force within a Eurocentric enclosed space populated by territorially defined states (Schmitt 2003a: 120–1, 140–8). Of course, beyond the European world these rules no longer applied and literally everything was allowed (see Gunneflo, Chapter 3, Langford and Bryan, Chapter 14, and Arvidsson 2016, Chapter 15 in this volume).

With the rise of the United States as a superpower (officially marked by the 1941 declaration of its entry into the Second World War) and the development of a moralistic and universalistic form of interventionism, the old *jus publicum Europaeum* would dissolve (Schmitt 2003a: 259–80). But what kind of *nomos* would emerge? Schmitt believed that the concept of *justa causa* would make a comeback, deprived of its theological undertone. Opponents of the established hegemony would be branded *ipso facto* as 'enemies of humanity'. He imagined three possible alternatives (Schmitt 2003a: 354). A first possibility was that one of the two superpowers struggling for hegemony on land, sea and air (in his time, the United States and Soviet Union) would prevail, thus leading to a unipolar world divided according to the victor's criteria. It is well known that Schmitt considered this not only unlikely but also undesirable (Schmitt 1987: 80). In a second hypothetical scenario, the already existing balance of powers would be preserved and managed by the United States. The third option (which Schmitt cherished) was the most interesting for the current political climate: there would be a balance among internally homogeneous spaces or blocks of powers (*Großräume* or *large spaces*). In other words, a pluralistic system in which no single power would rise above the others. In Schmitt's view, the first model, leading to the creation of the United Nations, emerged in the aftermath of the Cold War (1942–1947), before giving way to the second model, which itself would eventually pave the way for the third model (Schmitt 1990). Who would be the actors of this new *nomos*? Schmitt referred at times to China, India, Europe, the Commonwealth, the Hispanic area, the Arab block or some other groups of states (Schmitt 1986: 123) and at other times to the United States, the Soviet Union, China and a group of non-aligned States, which would be under the influence of one of the three *large spaces* (Schmitt 1987: 80–1).

The theory of *large space* is central to the understanding of *nomos* (Salter 2012; Gattini 2002; Carty 2001). A *large space* by definition relies on the demarcation of a zone of security (in the sense of self-defence) and a related claim of spatial sovereignty that exceeds state borders. The proclamation by the United States of the Monroe Doctrine over the so-called 'Western hemisphere' (1823) was, for Schmitt, emblematic of the new world order, politically opposed to the Eurocentric order that disappeared between the nineteenth and the twentieth centuries (Schmitt 2003a: 281). Here is the true paradox of modern times: 'America' as a concept, as the new centre of civilization, emerged as antithetic to 'Europe', old and tarnished by corruption and absolutism. However, at the same time, *precisely because of its moral and cultural claim of superiority*, 'America' could aspire to become the true 'Europe' (Schmitt 2003a: 286–91).

Schmitt's view of international law – and, in general, his theory of law – can be undoubtedly criticized from many perspectives. It is not just his problematic conception of statehood and political community as grounded in the simplistic dichotomy friend–enemy (Schmitt 2007a: 19). Nor does the problem lie only in his opposition between a shiny past and a dark present, or the fact that his attack on liberal universalism (which in his view is nihilistic because it aims at neutralizing and depoliticizing conflict) hides his own idea of universalism (Koskenniemi 2004: 495). What can be deeply questioned is his existential understanding of a political community. For Schmitt, only issues that concern the very survival of a community qualify as political (however, see Brännström, Chapter 1 of this volume, who believes that the Schmittian notion of 'political' includes the state's role in upholding a community's prevalent way of life; see also Vinx 2016, Chapter 2 in this volume). When it comes to international law, existential questions become questions of political self-determination. Hence, 'a people which exists in the sphere of the political cannot in case of need renounce the right to determine by itself the friend-and-enemy distinction' (Schmitt 2007a: 50). Since a homogeneous people's will is reflected in the state's executive power, it is only the state that can decide whether or not to wage war without being bound by international law (Schmitt 2007a: 45–58).

This argument entails a few unacceptable normative consequences. First, a community claiming to be an essentially political entity could never be subject to international rules, including those of *jus cogens*; this would apply, for example, to the law on the use of force. Second, all those individuals who are perceived for any reason as a threat to a community's substantive identity (or homogeneity) would not be entitled to legal protection and would therefore be excluded from the demos. Homogeneity is to be intended as both identitarian (that is, a set of values shared by the members of a society, so that equals are treated equally and unequals unequally) and institutional (Croce and Salvatore 2013: 169). This appears unrealistic in the contemporary world and threatens the very stability it purports to preserve by building up artificial walls between political entities. Third, virtually anything declared as a threat to a political community would automatically rise to the category of the exceptional and fall under the domain of the sovereign State, because 'Sovereign is he who decides on the exception' (Schmitt 1985: 5).

Schmitt's political existentialism thus identifies the decision as an event that transcends the norm, yet is the presupposition of every norm. In other words, the normal, and even the human condition, is defined by the exceptional and war is the exception *par excellence*.[2] As is well known, this approach influenced considerably the realist school in the twentieth century and this is one of the reasons why it has been attacked (Morgenthau 1978; Koskenniemi 2001: 413–509). It has become almost commonplace to blame Schmitt for articulating sheer existence as the highest value in life (Wolin 1990). I would like to add that Schmittian political existentialism leaves no space for questions that are political precisely because they are subject to nuanced judgments, multifaceted opinions, and endless debate.

Yet it is possible to rescue some jewels from Schmitt's complex and at times contradictory grid of works or – as has been maintained – to use him against himself (Mouffe 2005: 14). This is especially true of his conceptualization of international law. He unmasked the empty formalism of the rhetoric of universalization that characterized the twentieth century international legal discourse and is still very much fashionable in academic and diplomatic circles. For him, this rhetoric is linked to the essential feature of liberalism, which is that of depoliticizing and neutralizing conflict. There is no need to follow his critique to the extreme consequences of judging liberalism as an aesthetic view that is ultimately inactive and incapable of ethical and legal valuation, owing to its inability 'to deliberately take sides and make a decision' (Schmitt 1986: 124). However, it should be recognized that dangers lurk behind abstract normativity. Today, more than ever, liberalism's claim to achieve a neutral, impartial and objective standpoint sounds hollow. We should be aware of liberalism's tendency to reduce problems to economic and technological issues. As Schmitt observed:

> Great masses of industrialized people today still cling to a torpid religion of technicity because they, like all masses, seek radical results and believe subconsciously that the absolute depoliticization sought after four centuries can be found here and that universal peace begins here. Yet technology can do nothing more than intensify peace or war; it is equally available to both.
>
> (Schmitt 2007b: 95)

---

2 'The exception is more interesting than the rule. The rule proves nothing, the exception proves everything: it confirms not only the rule, but also its existence, which derives only from the exception' (Schmitt 1985: 15).

Schmitt and the EU internal and external dimension of security

In light of the conceptual framework outlined above, the question is therefore whether the external and internal projections of security in a broad sense contribute to qualifying the EU as a contemporary large space in the Schmittian sense; that is, as an internally homogeneous space.

Nowadays, there are many elements that may point towards a constellation of *large spaces* that is gradually replacing the monopolistic hegemony of the United States. I would like to argue that the EU in particular emerges as a '*transnational security entrepreneur*' that trades security for influence, especially in the developing and candidate countries. In other words, the EU is trying to assert itself on the global scene through a non-military type of hegemony, by emerging as a normative and imperial space promoting liberal/western values. *Security entrepreneurship* implies the ability to sell the image of a human rights sponsor to integrated and neighbouring areas, which, once received the relevant 'trademark', have an incentive to enter in the EU zone of influence.

Inevitably, moralism is a strong feature of EU entrepreneurship. Moreover, the new *jus publicum Europaeum* is not only about rationalizing and limiting war but also about setting up a transnational space in which sovereignties overlap. From a constitutional pluralist perspective, it is not only the war that is suspended but also the decision on which is the ultimate authority (Kumm 1999). Of course, although war is 'bracketed' within the European space, borders may constantly be reshaped.

As a matter of fact, in Europe the joint development of a project for an AFSJ/CFSP/ESDP *and* an internal market have transformed the concept of border, while at the same time reconfiguring the constitutional tensions between the national and the supranational sphere. Borders among member states are more porous and, in addition, there is one border common to all of them.

In this context, security plays a fundamental role. Leading the security discourse, in the sense of developing an official rhetoric, as is done especially by the EU institutions, means deciding its (more or less broad) content, the nature of the threats and the powers necessary to deal with them. One could even say that:

> With regard to these political concepts, it depends on who interprets, defines and uses them; who concretely decides what peace is, what disarmament, what intervention, what public order and security are. One of the most important expressions of humanity's legal and spiritual life is the fact that whoever has true power can determine the content of concepts and words. *Caesar dominus et supra grammaticam.* Caesar is emperor over the grammar as well.
>
> (Schmitt 1988: 202)

Whoever leads the security discourse is also the master of a vocabulary of immediacy, urgency, threat, which leaves little space for reflection and renegotiation. The very same 'security' rhetoric has been effectively employed by the EU institutions to justify the adoption of exceptional measures during the recent financial crisis of the EU (European Council 2012; European Parliament 2013). If you claim that you can provide security, on the one hand you possess a legitimizing ground for your actions and, on the other, you gain authority towards those who in your view might benefit from your role of security provider. Moreover, by demilitarizing the security discourse, you also own a logo of promoter of progress and stability that is harder to contest. In a sense, the external security strategies of the EU represent a new 'Monroe doctrine' and the EU is now trying to claim back its old title of 'Europe' that had been usurped by the United States (to use Schmitt's metaphor). Or, perhaps in an inverted relationship, the EU now aspires to be the new United States. Whether this aspiration corresponds to reality is, of course, another matter.

The use of security rhetoric by the EU institutions shows that Schmitt's political existentialism is somehow reflected in the EU's external and internal dimensions of security. However, this analysis should be performed with some caution. To begin with, the Schmittian *large* space presupposes homogeneity, which can be observed only to a limited extent in the European region. In Schmitt's work, pluralism is inconceivable within a political community, but only outside it. Competing forces are admitted, even advocated, but only in the domain of international relations. Obviously, the connection between internal and external security in the EU emerges in a rather different environment, which is essentially pluralistic. Second, the constitutive act of the *nomos* of the earth was, according to Schmitt, an act of land appropriation, whereas the external security of the EU relies also on a form of *value* appropriation (as seen in the official documents indicated in this work). The values of peace, prosperity, stability, wellbeing, announced as a great achievement of European integration, are promised to the EU's partners as a good to be bought or as a model to be followed.

In many ways, the external dimension of security betrays the EU's universalistic interventionism. For example, the European Council (1999) in Cologne emphasized the EU's role in promoting stability, peace and security in Central and Eastern Europe.

In this light, how should we look at the decision of the Court of Justice of the EU in the famous *Kadi* case (Court of Justice of the European Union 2008)? From a purely functional/monist perspective, the United Nations (UN) Security Council can claim to be more effective than the EU in the maintenance of international peace and security. This seems to be the argument of the Court of First Instance. However, from a dualist perspective, the *Kadi* ruling can be read in the sense of the EU's self-assertion that it is an autonomous legal order, which vindicates the authority to protect its own fundamental values. This is a strong statement of identity, which has been criticized by many international lawyers. However, a constitutional pluralist interpretation is also possible. According to this view, the CJEU still recognizes the primary responsibility of the UN Security Council in the field of security, with the proviso that it may review the legality of non-EU rules when they seriously affect the EU fundamental values (Kumm 2011: 133–4). EU fundamental values are meant to be universal.

Criticising the universalist attitude of certain liberals, as this chapter does, means emphasizing the weaknesses of a human rights-focused approach that strives for coherence in international law. In other words, the EU as a transnational security entrepreneur should aim to forge its own expansive security discourse but without the pretentiousness of a unilateral hegemon.

To be sure, despite the proviso mentioned earlier, constructing Europe as a transnational *large* space entails a few paradoxes. A few implications derive from asserting that the EU is a polity that tends to expand, partly due to the expansionistic nature of security. For how can a normative project preserve its own original claims and *at the same time* promote enlargement? What are (if any) the borders of Europe's normativity? In other words, where does Europe end, not merely in a geographical sense? As the EU enlargement programme is scrupulously implemented, the territory of the EU includes an ever greater variety of political and cultural communities. In addition, new agreements are struck and new interactions forged.[3] This simultaneously goes against the Schmittian value of homogeneity and exposes some of the contradictions that lie at the heart of European liberalism. As the EU liberal agenda proclaims its values of pluralism and discursivity, it constantly risks turning into sheer, faceless functionality. Admittedly, as Schmitt would have it, liberalism's attempt to deny conflict is itself a political move that is not able to eliminate conflictuality. However, what is really problematic in Schmitt – and what the European constitutional project has not yet come to terms with – is that, in general, the idea of enmity is much more nuanced than he believed.

Enmity and enclosure have a reflexive nature that was overlooked by Schmitt. Indeed, adhering to an exclusively existential understanding of a political community amounts to arguing that the existential element of constitutions is superior to the normative element (Schmitt 2008: for example, 150–8). This assertion is problematic. True, enclosure is an essential element in the foundation of a political community. However, it is one thing to argue that the validity of a constitutional framework derives from a prior fundamental political decision by those who hold constituent

---

3   See, for example, European Commission (2014) Press Release, 'EU trade chief following EU-US trade deal stock taking: good progress, time to go the extra mile'.

power. There exist many versions of decisionism and some of them have made their way to various constitutional theories that are still popular in some European countries. It is quite another to maintain that discursivity ends where the right to self-preservation of a political community is asserted.

Conclusions

This chapter claims that the EU can be configured as a space and its global role is that of a transnational security entrepreneur.

In this light, security is very well suited to describe the expansionistic nature of the EU. In particular, the joint development of the AFSJ (both its internal and external dimension) and CFSP/EDSP elucidates how security can be both crosscutting and crucial in projecting the international identity of the EU. As many official documents of the EU institutions, agreements with third countries and provisions of the Treaty of Lisbon show, the key notion in this ambit is that of threat from outside. Highlighting the need to cope with existential threats justifies, first of all, the adoption of a number of measures by reason of a declared state of emergency. Secondly, it contributes to building up an image of security provider that legitimizes the increased role of the EU in its relationship with the outside world. In fact, this chapter argues that the EU emerges as a 'transnational security entrepreneur', offering security in exchange for geo-political influence.

In a sense, this is the re-elaboration of the existing studies on the imperialistic attitude of the EU. However, the distinctive feature of the expansion of the AFSJ and CFSP/EDSP is that they are key to understanding the EU as a transnational space, which, as part of the old reassuring scheme of western liberal values, is projected as a virtuous model to be followed. Some aspects of Schmittian constitutional and political theory can provide us with useful tools of interpretation.

However, reducing 'otherness' to the dualism enmity–friendship, as Schmitt does, is a mistake both epistemologically and normatively. A political community is not defined merely by what it is able to include but also by what it decides to exclude and how. And yet, patterns of inclusion and exclusion are never settled. This does not only mean that identity (even *collective* identity) should be conceived of as narrative identity in the dialectic between sameness and selfhood, *idem*-identity and *ipse*-identity, numerical and qualitative identity (Ricoeur 1992: for example, 116). Nor does it merely suggest that oneself is also always *strange* and 'legal boundaries include by excluding and exclude by including' (Lindahl 2013: 181). It also means that there is no single moment which authorizes a final word on who is our friend and who is our enemy. The constellation of practical possibilities which allows a political community to draw a distinction between inside and outside is so vast and in constant flow, subject to cultural and social factors, that there is little point in employing the neat conceptual categories of friend and enemy.

Acknowledgements

I would like to thank the editors and the anonymous reviewer for their valuable comments on earlier drafts. Responsibility for errors or omissions is mine.

Bibliography

Arvidsson, M. (2016) 'From Teleology to Eschatology: The *Katechon* and the Political Theology of the International Law of Belligerent Occupation', Chapter 15 in M. Arvidsson, L. Brännström and P. Minkkinen (eds), *The Contemporary Relevance of Carl Schmitt: Law, Politics, Theology*. Abingdon: Routledge.

Beck, U. and E. Grande (2011) 'Empire Europe: Statehood and Political Authority in the Process of Regional Integration', p. 21–46, in J. Neyer and A. Wiener (eds) *Political Theory of the European Union*. Oxford: Oxford University Press.

Bigo, D. (2000) 'When Two Become One: Internal and External Securitisations in Europe', p. 171–204, in M. Kelstrup and M. C. Williams (eds) *International Relations Theory and The Politics of European Integration. Power, Security and Community*. London: Routledge.

Brännström, L. (2016) 'Carl Schmitt's Definition of Sovereignty as Authorized Leadership', Chapter 1 in M. Arvidsson, L. Brännström and P. Minkkinen (eds), *The Contemporary Relevance of Carl Schmitt: Law, Politics, Theology*. Abingdon: Routledge.

Carty, A. (2001) 'Carl Schmitt's Critique of Liberal International Legal Order Between 1933 and 1945', *Leiden Journal of International Law*, Vol. 14, No. 1: 25–76.

Court of Justice of the European Union (2008) Joined Cases C-402/05 P and C-415/05, *Yassin Abdullah Kadi and Al Barakaat International Foundation v Council of the European Union and Commission of the European Communities* [2008] ECR I-6351.

Court of Justice of the European Union, Joined Cases C-402/05 P and C-415/05, *Yassin Abdullah Kadi and Al Barakaat International Foundation v Council of the European Union and Commission of the European Communities* [2008] ECR I-6351.

Cremona, M. (2004) 'The Union As A Global Actor: Roles, Models and Identity', *Common Market Law Review*, Vol. 41, No. 2: 553–73.

Croce, M. and A. Salvatore (2013) *The Legal Theory of Carl Schmitt*. New York: Routledge.

Denza, E. (2002) *The Intergovernmental Pillars of the European Union*. Oxford: Oxford University Press.

Eeckhout P. (2011) *EU External Relations Law*. Oxford: Oxford University Press.

Enzensberger, H. M. (1994) *Civil War*. London: Granta Books.

European Commission (2014) 'EU trade chief following EU-US trade deal stock taking: good progress, time to go the extra mile' [Press release] 18 February. Available at http://trade.ec.europa.eu/doclib/press/index.cfm?id=1028 (accessed 17 April 2015).

European Council (2012) Conclusions 28/29 June 2012. document no. ST 76 2012 INIT. Brussels: General Secretariat of the Council. Available at www.consilium.europa.eu/register/en/content/out/?&typ=ENTRY&i=ADV&DOC_ID=ST-76-2012-INIT (accessed 17 April 2015).

European Council (1999) Presidency Conclusions, Cologne European Council, 3 and 4 June 1999. Available at www.consilium.europa.eu/ueDocs/cms_Data/docs/pressData/en/ec/kolnen.htm (accessed 17 April 2015).

European Parliament (2013) *Resolution of 18 April 2013 on the Impact of the Financial and Economic Crisis on Human Rights 2012/2136*. P7_TA-PROV(2013)0179. Available at www.europarl.europa.eu/document/activities/cont/201304/20130429ATT65432/20130429ATT65432EN.pdf (accessed 17 April 2015).

European Parliament (1998) Rhodes Declaration on the International Role of the European Community, Conclusions of the Presidency, European Council 2 and 3 December 1988 in Rhodes. *European Parliament Activities*, Special Edition. Available at www.europarl.europa.eu/summits/rhodes/default_en.htm (accessed 17 April 2015).

Gattini, A. (2002) 'Sense and Quasisense of Schmitt's *Grossraum* Theory in International Law – A Rejoinder to Carty's "Carl Schmitt's Critique of Liberal International Legal Order"', *Leiden Journal of International Law*, Vol. 15, No. 1: 53–68.

Gunneflo, M. (2016) 'Political Community in Carl Schmitt's International Legal Thinking', Chapter 3 in M. Arvidsson, L. Brännström and P. Minkkinen (eds), *The Contemporary Relevance of Carl Schmitt. Law, Politics, Theology*. Abingdon: Routledge.

Kaiser, W. and P. Starie (2005) *Transnational European Union – Towards a common political space*. London: Routledge.

Koskenniemi, M. (2004) 'International Law as Political Theology: How to Read *Nomos der Erde?*', *Constellations*, Vol. 11, No. 4: 492–511.

Koskenniemi, M. (2001) *The Gentle Civilizer of Nations: The Rise and Fall of International Law 1870–1960*. Cambridge: Cambridge University Press.

Kumm, M. (2011) 'How Does European Union Law Fit into the World of Public Law? *Costa, Kadi*, and Three Conceptions of Public Law', p. 111–38, in J. Neyer and A. Wiener (eds), *Political Theory of the European Union*. Oxford: Oxford University Press.

Kumm, M. (1999) 'Who is the Final Arbiter of Constitutionality in Europe?: Three Conceptions of the Relationship Between the German Federal Constitutional Court and the European Court of Justice?' *Common Market Law Review*, Vol. 36, No. 9: 351–86.

Langford, P. and Bryan, I. (2016) 'Beyond the Jurist as a Theologian of Legal Science: The Question of Carl Schmitt and the International Legal Order', Chapter 14 in M. Arvidsson, L. Brännström and P. Minkkinen (eds), *The Contemporary Relevance of Carl Schmitt. Law, Politics, Theology*. Abingdon: Routledge.

Lindahl, H. (2013) *Fault Lines of Globalization. Legal Order and the Politics of A-Legality*. Oxford: Oxford University Press.

Manners, I. (2006) 'Normative power Europe reconsidered: beyond the crossroads', *Journal of European Public Policy*, Vol. 13, No. 2: 182–99.

Manners, I. (2002) 'Normative Power Europe: A Contradiction in Terms?', *Journal of Common Market Studies*, Vol. 40, No. 2: 235–58.

Morgenthau, H. (1978) *Politics Among Nations: The Struggle for Power and Peace* [1948]. New York: Alfred A. Knopf.
Mouffe, C. (2005) *On the Political*. London: Routledge.
Neyer, J. and A. Wiener (eds) (2011) *Political Theory of the European Union*. Oxford: Oxford University Press.
Nicolaïdis, K. and R. Howse (2002) 'This is my EUtopia: Narrative as Power', *Journal of Common Market Studies*, Vol. 40, No. 4: 767–92.
Ricoeur, P. (1992) *Oneself as Another*. Chicago, IL: University of Chicago Press.
Salter, M. (2012) 'Law, Power and International Politics with Special Reference to East Asia: Carl Schmitt's *Grossraum* Analysis', *Chinese Journal of International Law*, Vol. 11 No. 3: 393–427.
Schmitt, C. (2008) *Constitutional Theory* [1928]. Trans. J. Seitzer. Durham, NC: Duke University Press.
Schmitt, C. (2007a) *The Concept of the Political* [1932]. Trans. G. Schwab. Chicago, IL: University of Chicago Press.
Schmitt, C. (2007b) 'The Age of Neutralization and Depoliticization' [1929], p. 80–96, in C. Schmitt, *The Concept of the Political* [1932]. Trans. G. Schwab. Chicago, IL: University of Chicago Press.
Schmitt, C. (2003a) *The Nomos of the Earth in the International Law of the Jus Publicum Europaeum* [1950]. Trans. G. L. Ulmen. New York: Telos.
Schmitt, C. (2003b) 'The New Nomos of the Earth', p. 351–5, in C. Schmitt, *The Nomos of the Earth in the International Law of the Jus Publicum Europaeum* [1950]. Trans. G. L. Ulmen. New York: Telos.
Schmitt, C. (1990) 'Die Ordnung der Welt nach dem zweiten Weltkrieg: Vortrag von 1962' [1962], p. 11–30, in P. Tommissen (ed.) *Schmittiana II*. Brussels: Economische Hogeschool Sint-Aloysius.
Schmitt, C. (1988) 'Völkerrechtliche Formen des modernen Imperialismus' [1932], p. 162–80, in C. Schmitt, *Positionen und Begriffe in Kampf mit Weimar-Genf-Versailles 1923–1939*. Berlin: Duncker and Humblot.
Schmitt, C. (1987) 'The legal world revolution', *Telos*, No. 72: 73–89.
Schmitt, C. (1986) *Political Romanticism* [1919]. Trans. G. Oakes. Cambridge, MA: MIT Press.
Schmitt, C. (1985), *Political Theology. Four Chapters on the Concept of Sovereignty* [1922]. Trans. G. Schwab. Cambridge, MA: MIT Press.
Vinx, L. (2016) 'Carl Schmitt and the Problem of Constitutional Guardianship', Chapter 2 in M. Arvidsson, L. Brännström and P. Minkkinen (eds), *The Contemporary Relevance of Carl Schmitt. Law, Politics, Theology*. Abingdon: Routledge.
Waever, O. (1996), 'European Security Identities', *Journal of Common Market Studies*, Vol. 34, No. 1: 103–32.
Weiler J. and U. Haltern (1998) 'Constitutional or International? The Foundations of the Community Legal Order and the Question of Judicial Kompetenz-Kompetenz', p. 331–64, in A. M. Slaughter, A. Stone Sweet and J. Weiler (eds) *The European Courts and National Courts – Doctrine and Jurisprudence*. Oxford: Hart.
Wolin, R. (1990) 'Carl Schmitt, Political Existentialism, and the Total State', *Theory and Society*, Vol. 19: 389–416.
Zielonka, J. (2006), *Europe as Empire: The Nature of the Enlarged European Union*. Oxford: Oxford University Press.

Part III
Theology

Chapter 12

'Im Kampf um Rom'
Carl Schmitt's critique of Rudolph Sohm and the post-secular turn

Hjalmar Falk

Carl Schmitt and the post-secular turn

The rise of a discourse on increased visibility of religion, sometimes put in terms of a 'post-secular turn', has coincided with an ever-increasing interest in the ideas of Carl Schmitt. While large parts of the international reception of Schmitt's work have centred on his thought on sovereignty and international law, there is growing recognition of its theological aspects. According to John P. McCormick, by the 1990s the European reception of Schmitt's work was dominated by a practically hegemonic view of the author as motivated by a sometimes open, sometimes hidden Catholic political theology (McCormick 1998: 831). The fact that Schmitt is generally regarded as a defining point of reference for discussions of political theology, even if only as an abject authoritarian expression of it, attests to his relevance for this field. The role of Schmitt's work for the writings of acknowledged post-secular theorists like Giorgio Agamben and Eric L. Santner is also worthy of note. One can therefore conclude that there are clear connections between Schmitt and the so-called post-secular turn in theoretical discourse but that Schmitt's status within this discourse is unclear.

One leading proponent of what might be called a 'post-secularization thesis', the radical orthodox theologian John Milbank, regards Schmitt as the crowning result of a long line of secular reasoning from Kant to Weber (Milbank 2006: 100). So, while Schmitt is viewed as a political theologian by some, he is simultaneously cast as an endpoint of secular metaphysics. In what follows, I show how serious attention to Schmitt's intellectual contexts may contribute not only to the understanding of his work but also to a greater understanding of its contemporary relevance. I also show how this entails an attention to theological themes.

In a recent reflection on Schmitt's political theology, Paul W. Kahn draws a sharp distinction between the work of the political philosopher and the intellectual historian. He claims that 'there is little point in elaborating the views of those long-gone European theorists who occupied Schmitt's attention' (Kahn 2011: 4). But central to Schmitt's politico-theological project is its attention to the intellectual history of law and political theory. It is this project that this chapter aims to investigate. It also makes an argument for a contextual understanding of Schmitt's professed Catholicism, an argument which can be read through a quip about 'a struggle for Rome', '*Kampf um Rom*'. This struggle, ultimately with the thoughts of German legal scholar Rudolph Sohm, supplies a largely ignored context for Schmitt's work. This has applications not only for how we are to understand some aspects of Schmitt's relation to Weber but also for how one might consider the contemporary relevance of Carl Schmitt.

The (Catholic) political theology of Carl Schmitt

Schmitt's Catholicism has played a surprisingly small role in the reception of his political theology. With the exception of a few works (see Faber 2001; Koenen 1995; Dahlheimer 1996), the topic of Catholicism is rarely made into a central part of inquiry. Heinrich Meier claims that it would be wrong to view Schmitt as a 'Catholic doctrinaire' (Meier 1998: vii), while Gopal Balakrishnan emphasizes the idiosyncratic character of his thought in general as well as on Catholicism (Balakrishnan 1999: 43, 50, 203). There seems to be a general agreement that Schmitt's Catholic upbringing had little impact on his work, even though he called himself a Catholic by 'inheritance' and even 'race', contending as he did so that 'the secret keyword' behind his intellectual (*Geistigen*) and authorial existence was the struggle with an 'originally Catholic intensity' (Schmitt 1991: 131). This emphasis on both inherited tradition and an intellectual engagement with this tradition would seem to belie dominant strands of reception, in which it is as if the meaning and intention of the theological can only be related to its grounding personal faith and confession, not theoretical work.[1]

The question of what a concept of political theology might mean as a theoretical tool becomes even more pressing in the double illumination of post-secularism and a hermeneutical engagement with Schmitt's own proclamations on not only political theology, but also the political itself. To Schmitt, the political is never private (Schmitt 2007a: 28) and the project of conceptual sociology sketched in *Political Theology* is oriented towards describing the relationship between metaphysical conceptions of the world and political conceptions of social organization (Schmitt 2005: 46). Also, if

---

1   I would claim that this even goes for the German anthology dedicated to the meaning of the quote about 'catholic intensity'. It barely mentions Sohm or Schmitt's engagement with Weber and charisma, and it downplays Sohm's importance for Schmitt (see Wacker 1994). The same goes for Catherine Colliot-Thélène's essay on Schmitt and Weber, which calls Schmitt's relation to Sohm 'complex' and suggests that it might be explained through recourse to intellectual biography but does not investigate further (Colliot-Thélène 1999: 154, n. 33, 152).

all the differing varieties of post-secularism can be said to agree on one thing, it is that the secularist notion of religion being relegated to a purely personal role limits the modern understanding of both beliefs and social practices, including theory. In neither Schmitt's own work, nor dominant strands of post-secular thought, the historically determined distinction between theology and political theory is taken for granted.

It is also clear that there are obvious connections between the position Schmitt takes in *Political Theology* and the one he states in *On the Three Types of Juristic Thought* (Schmitt 2004a) twelve years later. Schmitt's central issue is with juridico-political order in both the latter and the first, as well as in for example the 1912 *Law and Judgement* (Schmitt 2009) which deals with the office of the judge as the proper bearer of juridical decision. While it may be true that Schmitt argues for decisionism in *Political Theology*, this should be seen as an exception to a Schmittian norm of primary concern with order in the form of what he would later call 'order thinking'. What is at issue, in 1912, 1922, as well as in 1934 and later, is the question of how to relate the groundlessness of decision to the concreteness of order.[2]

That Schmitt finds a model for an operation combining order and an ultimately groundless decision in Christian theology is hardly unique. In fact, Hans Kelsen did the same thing in the same year, albeit in an attempt to disqualify the theological form for political thought (Kelsen 1973). To Kelsen, the source for the politico-theological fiction of the state was the attribution of extra-legal capacities to the sovereign. Like the God of the theologians, the sovereign of traditional theories of state was seen as both the creator and part of created order. Kelsen's project consisted of removing such capacities from legal theory and political praxis, making the state fully synonymous with and subordinate to law. To him, there could be no extra-legal political substance of state, only functions of law, in line with the modern physical sciences which had abandoned concepts of substance for concepts of function (Kelsen 1973: 82). Every reader of Schmitt's *Political Theology* will recognize the problem of the sovereign's metajuridical or extra-legal status in relation to the state of exception, down to Kelsen's critique of the belief in state sovereignty as a form of 'legal miracle' (Kelsen 1973: 78).

Schmitt responds to Kelsen by turning the tables and affirming the theological form of thought as fully adequate for conceptualizing the sovereign's relation to law. He criticizes the positivist Kelsen for being misled by a mathematical scientistic metaphysical worldview of pure immanence, incapable of grasping the fundamentals of state theory (Schmitt 2005: 42). And here the original feature of Schmitt's discussion of political theology emerges: its

---

2   I here concur with Leila Brännström's reading (Chapter 1 of this volume) of Schmitt's work as first and foremost an example of concrete order thinking rather than decisionism (see also Günther 2011).

character of what he calls conceptual sociology, that is the analysis of how politico-juridical concepts and certain metaphysical assumptions correspond to each other. This is how Schmitt comes to associate positivism with the de-politicizing metaphysics of 'technicity', analysed in 'The Age of Neutralizations and Depoliticizations' (Schmitt 2007b), and this is how one should approach the theoretical aspect of Schmitt's own professed Catholicism. To him, the metaphysics of Catholicism implies a certain conception of not only a metaphysical, but also of a political structure.

To further investigate this conception of Catholicism, I look closer at an almost unrecognized and definitely under-investigated context of Schmitt's work, which shows how it already contains hints of a greater project.[3] I focus on a context to the Schmittian discourse on the concept of representation and the visibility of the church. Very little has been done with the fact that Schmitt so obviously raises the question of representation through a discussion of the importance of Roman Catholicism for political form. Even if Schmitt's positioning vis-à-vis Weber regarding Protestantism and Catholicism is well acknowledged in general terms, the theological context surrounding Weber's thoughts on legitimacy is not. It not only serves to explain the intellectual environment for Schmitt's political theology, it is also an example of how Schmitt's work shows its potential as a resource for critical thought.

The politico-theological concept of charisma

Schmitt's interest in Weber should be read against his interest in the work on church law by the scholar Rudolph Sohm (1841–1917). Relatively unknown today, Sohm was a hot topic not only in Germany at the turn of the century but in theology during a great part of the twentieth century as well. To Schmitt, Sohm is a towering figure of inspiration as well as an important adversary. Only through the recognition of Sohm's importance for Schmitt's work does the praise lauded on Hans Barion in the introduction to *Political Theology II* as 'a jurist in the same league of Rudolph Sohm, one of the great encyclopaedic researchers and teachers of jurisprudence' make sense (Schmitt 2010: 32).

What Schmitt sees in Sohm is the metaphysics and politics of the hegemony in which he was raised: the cultural hegemony of Wilhelmine Germany. This cultural hegemony shaped the thought of Weber and his generation, a cultural hegemony of which Weber himself was a foremost exponent. That Protestantism is a determining factor in Weber's thought

---

3 There are several other theological contexts that could be of interest for the reading of Schmitt. First and foremost, one could compare Schmitt's view of the church with that of his friend and critic Erik Peterson. An important context is also to be found in Friedrich Gogarten and dialectical theology. Here, much historical work remains to be done.

may not surprise. After all, one of his most famous theses is that 'the spirit of capitalism' is the descendant of a radical Protestant ethic. But the very word 'spirit [*Geist*]' can be said to carry a rather protestant meaning in the work of Weber, at least according to the critique here and there levied by Schmitt. Central to this critique is the statement that Weber's conception of *charisma* can only be entangled through Rudolph Sohm (Schmitt 1966: 306). Or, as Schmitt puts it in *Glossarium*: 'Sohm is the father of the theory of the charismatic leader; it is not about Max Weber, it is about Rudolf Sohm' (Schmitt 1991: 199). While some scholarship is available on Schmitt's relationship to Weber, very few have really followed up on this particular connection to Sohm.[4] In an investigation into Schmitt's important contribution to the understanding of Weber, religion and modernity, Robert Yelle notes Sohm's importance for Schmitt's designation of Weber as an exponent of political theology (Yelle 2010: 200). However, a closer attention to detail might have helped to illustrate just how Schmitt's reading of Sohm is important for his critique of modern thought.

The intersection between Schmitt, Sohm and Weber comes to the fore in the latter's definition of legitimacy. Weber's three ideal types of legitimacy – traditional, legal rational and charismatic – are widely known. 'Charisma' has become an important classical concept within sociology, as well as a widely used expression within modern western culture. As an ideal type it refers to the norm-breaking legitimacy attributed to extraordinary persons, a legitimacy beyond rules established by law and/or tradition (Weber 1978: 241–5). Genuine charisma breaks forth with a novelty, its legitimacy centred upon a leader on to whom followers project certain assumed extraordinary competences. On several occasions, Weber names Christ as an example of a charismatic leader but he also emphasizes that this is just one among many of an inherently universal phenomenon. The same quality has since been attributed to, for example, Hitler, something which does not really constitute an abuse of Weber's intentions. What is seldom noted, however, is Weber's crediting of Sohm's work in *Economy and Society* (Weber 1978: 1112).

Sohm's work on the organization of the early church took Paulinian formulations and used them to describe charisma as a certain form of authority. In St. Paul's letters, *charismata* are described as gifts of grace, distributed unequally within the congregation.[5] Among these gifts are speaking in tongues, healing by laying on hands, prophesying and inspirational teaching. Weber's appropriation of the concept for his sociology has been called a 'disenchantment' and 'psychologization', basically even a *democratization* of charismatic authority, since it shifts charisma from being a gift of

---

4 G. L. Ulmen mentions Sohm in passing in what must be seen as the central work on Weber and Schmitt (Ulmen 1991: 114–15, 159, 187; see also Fietkau 1986: 176–7; Rust 2012: 109–10, 115–16).
5 See, for example, I Corinthians, especially Chapter 12.

God into a quality invested in the leader by his or her followers, making the congregation an active agent in institutionalizing charisma (Smith 1998: 51; Haley 1980: 196). It effectively constitutes a generalization of an inherently Christian conceptualization of a transcendent presence within immanent creation. In Schmittian terms, Weberian charisma is therefore a *secularized theological concept* of certain significance for the modern theory of the state. It reproduces the structure of Sohm's theological reasoning.

Sohm's argument was aimed at a debate within German Protestantism during the late nineteenth century, a debate regarding the relation between law and gospel. His general claim was that the original Christian congregation, the *Urgemeinde*, knew no law and that its organization was of an otherworldly order. It was in his words a *charismatic organization*. This meant for Sohm that it was literally governed by God's grace, *directly*. Through the *charismata*, God made his continuous presence known. Sohm was a strict adherent of Luther's two-kingdom theory and strongly against any confusion between the kingdom of Christ and the kingdom of the world. In connection to this, it is therefore important to note that Sohm, a jurist and legal historian by profession, believed that secular law was a great benefactor of mankind, 'a primary means of social control and human fulfillment' (Adams 1959: 223). But Christianity's charismatic theocracy, the 'pneumocracy', knows no legal form (Sohm 1912: VIII). Following the continuous presence of God's spirit within the congregations, there are no 'elections' or 'decisions' in any particular congregation that can bind godly presence and contemporaneity, God's *Gegenwart*.

This charismatic organization was not to last, however. Sohm claims that the Christian Church's way towards the formation as a legal entity began already at the end of the first century of the Common Era (Sohm 1912: XXXII). The organization of the *Urgemeinde* was transformed through the binding of Christ's church to 'something exterior [*etwas Äußeres*]', 'something visible [*etwas Sichtbares*]'. The development into the exteriority of religion is what led to the establishment of a juridical framework, the 'bureaucracy of salvation' that is Catholic hierarchy emerged. The emergence of Catholicism followed from the rise of a regulated order of offices, the priesthood and the decline of charismatics (Sohm 1912: 34, 37–8).

Weber was undeniably very close to this dualistic line of thought when he defined his concept of charisma as standing against both legal rationality and tradition. As Norbert Bolz has pointed out, Weberian charisma is stirring and inspiring rather than authoritarian. In Weber's interpretation, charisma in politics is found in parties rather than in the state and in religion in the sects rather than in the institutions of the Catholic Church (Bolz 1985: 252). Weberian charisma thus emphasizes the exceptional and informality, not the formality of established legitimacy, like the *charisma veritatis*, the 'gift of truth' accorded to the holy offices of the Catholic

Church. In this, Weber follows Sohm's structure of charismatic organization perfectly, in contrast to Schmitt's conception of Catholicism.

Carl Schmitt's Catholicism: visibility against neutrality

In the light of the development during the Second Vatican Council during the 1960s, Schmitt is said to have formulated a humorous epigram to express his feelings towards its outcome: '*Im Kampf um Rom/Siegt Rudolph Sohm*' – 'In the struggle for Rome/Rudolph Sohm wins' (quoted in Spindler 2011: 158). While this epigram regards a specific topic, it also can be attributed to other matters concerning Schmitt and Sohm. Which view of Schmitt's political theology has come to dominate the reception of his work? Is it really Schmitt's concern with legal order or is it something more akin to Sohm's thoughts on exceptional grace?

In a strict sense, Schmitt wrote only one outwardly pure theological text, which is 'The Visibility of the Church', subtitled 'A Scholastic Consideration' and published in the Catholic journal *Summa* in 1917. 'The visible church' is 'the official church', according to Schmitt. Its essential characteristic is 'the transformation of spiritual tasks and functions into [public] offices, the separation of the office from whomever happens to occupy it' (Schmitt 1996a: 53). The Church is not identical with the singular person that in any given moment has the power to represent the Church, because 'then might, bare facticity, would become right again' (ibid.). Schmitt describes the Church as a 'hierarchy of mediation' (Schmitt 1996a: 56). In Schmitt's words, the elevation of human relations to relations of right – as the reforming of spiritual gifts and functions into offices – follow 'the rhythm of the emanation of the visible out of the invisible God', a 'rhythm' through which religion passes over into the church, love passes into marriage and, not of least interest here, the limitation of the *pneumatical* to the *juridical* (ibid.).

If we take Schmitt's analysis from *Political Theology* seriously, we should not view these words as peripheral to Schmitt's greater politico-juridical project. As shown in the discussion of Sohm, the *pneumatic*, spiritual power or the presence of the Holy Spirit itself, is of central importance for the debate on the visibility of the Church to which Schmitt meant to contribute with his 'scholastic consideration' in 1917. In *Roman Catholicism and Political Form* from 1923, he returns to the subject and develops his thoughts in terms more familiar to modern political theory. It is difficult to deny the striking structural similarities between the words on God's emanation out of the visible Church, on how the pneumatical subsumes itself into the juridical and, for example, how 'a higher type of being' is said to be made present through 'true' democratic representation and acclamation in *Constitutional Theory* (Schmitt 2008: 210). Representation in Schmitt's formulation means to make something invisible visible through a publicly present being – and this is how the people democratically both identifies itself and acknowledges its representation to itself according to him (ibid.). The enthusiasm of the acclamating crowd from *Constitutional Theory* shares the structure of transcendence with the role of representation in *Roman Catholicism and Political Form*. At the heart of Schmitt's theory of institution and constitution, there is an ecclesiology of mediation.

While Sohm is not mentioned, but obviously implied, in 'The Visibility of the Church', he is named twice in *Roman Catholicism and Political Form* and is clearly an exponent of the 'anti-Roman affect' that Schmitt opens the book by describing. But it is not a question of a simple demolition job. Rather, it is a reconstruction, or a reconstructive appropriation of central themes in Sohm. As Manfred Dahlheimer puts it, what the Protestant rejects, the Catholic embraces: 'Like Rudolph Sohm, Schmitt sees the essence (*Wesen*) of Catholicism in the identity between church in terms of law and church in terms of religion' (Dahlheimer 1998: 112). To Schmitt, the creation of the juridical out of the pneumatical is not a 'fall', but the origin of what he calls occidental, rationalist jurisprudence. It is, in short, what makes justice more than bare facticity, the separation of right from might, or perhaps the *qualification* of a certain might *as* right.

To Schmitt, the Roman Catholic Church is distinguished by its foundation on a public character, as opposed to 'private' liberalism (Schmitt 1996b: 29). As he puts it in *Glossarium*: 'Church law (and its history) proves itself ... to be a richer force as productive and as paradigmatic form than the whole privatized science of the traditional Roman law' (Schmitt 1991: 134). What signifies Church law from Roman law is its paradigmatic orientation towards a *public* form. This thought can also be recognized at the heart of *Roman Catholicism and Political Form*, wherein the political character of the Church is said to reside in its specifically representational form (Schmitt 1996b: 8). In short, the Church is public, it establishes a clear representation which makes something invisible institutionally visible and, not least, it creates a legal rational discourse of living tradition to regulate this order with a principle of *charisma veritatis* through offices. In this structure, charisma does not constitute the office. Instead, the office confers charisma, something Schmitt calls 'juristic in the highest sense' (Schmitt 2004b: 102).

Another detail is perhaps more peripheral but weighs in when the theological aspects of Schmitt's thought are to be examined. It is not uncommon to regard Schmitt as more akin to a Protestant than a Catholic (Meier 1998: 146) and some readers also claim to have found traces of Gnosticism in his thought (Faber 2007; Groh 1998). Schmitt's distancing from Sohm is never taken into account here. Of course, Schmitt was not a 'proper' Catholic in a pious, established sense. His was also a highly idiosyncratic Christianity. But he was an avowed Catholic in a sense that could have been formed *via Sohm* and he made clear that his appropriation of Catholic juristic rationalism kept its distance from what he called 'the Marcionite' Sohm, effectively labelling Sohm's thought – and hence by default significant parts of Protestant modernity – as Gnostic (Schmitt 1991: 118).

Put together, this would indicate a different theological (and hence political) stance in Schmitt's work than the decisionist-subjectivist-occasionalist-Gnostic he is sometimes made out to be. Instead, Schmitt's stance suggests a continuity from the early theory of right up unto the conceptions of concrete order thinking and *nomos*. Sohm's dualistic conception of spirit and law finds an echo in Schmitt, but it is not passively reproduced there. In fact, this dualism is a central point of problematization in Schmitt's work. Schmitt does realize the modern conflict between legitimacy and legality, spirit and law. The Church forms 'a hierarchy of mediation', which is probably what Schmitt envisaged the modern state (or the political entity following it) would be able to constitute as well. While quite aware of the inherently antinomian aspects of legal order, legal order's constant relationship to its own outside and need for a proper conception of transcendence, Schmitt does not follow Sohm's strict dichotomy between law and charismatic grace, a dichotomy inherited by Weber. For Schmitt, there is no necessary opposition between office and charisma.

One could claim, like David Norman Smith, that Catholics and Protestants 'may dispute the efficacy of official sacraments' but 'share the charismatic principle' and that their 'only real dispute is whether miracles flower freely, in every nook and cranny, or in ritual and the cathedral alone' (Smith 1998: 51). Smith would have the distinction between Catholics and Protestants signifying less than the one between Sohm's theological and Weber's disenchanted perspective on charisma. This could be questioned even along Weberian lines, but it is all the more questionable along Schmittian lines. Clearly, Weberian disenchantment is a central feature of *Protestant* modernity for Schmitt. Schmitt writes that the whole of the German university is of a 'protestant lineage [*protestantischer Herkunft*]' and what that means '*in concreto*' can be seen through the 'key figure of the nineteenth century's history of ideas, the great legal scholar Rudolf Sohm and his immeasurable influence on historians (like Georg von Below), sociologists (like Max Weber) and so on' (Schmitt 1991: 132). The secularization process as described in Weber's theory of modernity as rationalization is mirrored in Schmitt's description of modernity as an age of de-politicization and neutralization. Schmitt's narrative of a modern European neutralizing drive from theology to technology (via the spheres of metaphysics, morality and economy) as a continuous attempt to escape politicization even mentions it as a 'secularization' (Schmitt 2007b: 82).

A Schmittian contribution to a post-secular age

When investigating Schmitt's critique of Weber and Sohm, one might be reminded of the claims of Milbank. In the first chapter of *Theology and Social*

Theory Milbank emphasizes that the secular is a creation of history, and not one of necessity. The secular was not something latent within humanity, waiting to be released 'when the pressure of the sacred was relaxed'. Rather, 'the secular as a domain had to be instituted or imagined' (Milbank 2006: 9). This has become a leading thought in the post-secular theological movement of radical orthodoxy, which proposes a return to a neo-Platonic, Christian metaphysics as the central intellectual principle. It is in line with this thought that Milbank discredits Schmitt as a Weberian positivist sociologist. Why? The answer is Schmitt's assertion of a relative secular autonomy and his historicization of the emergence of the modern state.

In the introduction to a volume on political theology, Hent de Vries writes that Schmittian thought on the subject oscillates between two poles: that of claiming a foundation for modern politics in the theological and that of simply claiming a structural similarity between two fields (de Vries 2006: 47); de Vries describes Schmitt's oscillation as the result of a theoretical decision to avoid both transcribing the theological into the political as well as to 're-theologize' the political (ibid.). There is of course a tension between these poles, but the reason for upholding the polarity is not only a result of theoretical deliberation. Actually, it stems from Schmitt's view of the history of European public law and the theory of state. To Schmitt, the secular is located within this tension itself. It is constituted and upheld by this very polarity. This is important, because in contrast to several proponents of post-secular thought, Schmitt accords a positive, relatively autonomous existence to 'the secular'. The rationality of worldly jurisprudence is not *identical* with theological reason. It is *analogous* to it.

In an important essay written during his time in an American internment camp after the war, Schmitt names Jean Bodin and Thomas Hobbes as the precursors to a juridical tradition of which he regards himself to be the last conscious proponent. Bodin and Hobbes created a science of law which managed to establish a position, a *Zwischenlage*, for itself 'in-between' theology and technology. Schmitt writes that 'their authority was secularized, yet not profaned' (Schmitt 2002: 72). Bodin and Hobbes secured the continuity of a tradition and guarded its authority. Schmitt calls this tradition 'occidental rationalism', signifying the unification of Roman law with the Catholic Church and the analysis of decisive authority implied in 'Hobbes' all deciding' question of '*quis judicabit?*', 'who decides?' (Schmitt 2010: 51). As it left the Church, he writes, this juridical question regarding official competence found a new home in the state.

The same structure of ideas appears in Schmitt's theology as in his political theory. There is no qualitative difference between the 'fields' as they are modelled on each other, seamlessly. What makes this different from some post-secular thought, as in the guise of Milbank's political theology, is that Schmitt accords a theological structure to a secular field, specifically law, to which he also accords a concretely theological capacity. In Schmitt's work, theological structures are relevant outside the disciplinary boundaries of theology itself. What was once strictly theological has been opened to jurists while closed to the theologians. The structure of a politico-theological complex remains, but the robes have changed.

The position of a theoretical 'in-between', as being poised between theology and technology in a certain stage of modernity's move towards neutralization, is something that offers us a uniquely critical perspective in Schmitt's work. It is this perspective that I would like to emphasize as constituting an argument for the contemporary relevance of Carl Schmitt. The 'in-between', the *Zwischenlage*, of a secular space for thought between theology and technology should not only be read as conserving Christian doctrine in a reactionary way. It also raises our awareness as to what problems may arise for a thought that believes itself to have achieved a post-historical neutrality of universal applicability.

The Schmittian question regarding the location of ultimate decisive authority has been suggested as offering a critique of the way Jürgen Habermas envisions a 'post-secular society', where religious voices are thought to be able to contribute to democratic dialogue (Cerella 2012). But of even greater interest is the way Schmitt offers a critical perspective on the epistemological backdrop to modern social theory. Schmitt's critique of the belief in technology, the 'spirit of technicity', shows its further use than as a simple critical stance towards technological progress or social engineering. Whether or not the insistence on keeping state law in close contact with its Christian lineage is a project that interests us, the structural-analogical model it actualizes should. Developing a line of thought from Matthias Lievens, one could argue that Schmitt's political theology should in part be viewed as a tool for ideology critique (Lievens 2012).

We may, through insistent hermeneutical work on the historicity of our concepts, become more aware of where and how we impose modern western particularity under the guise of universality. I am not suggesting that theology is our fate and that politics needs to be measured towards some sort of fixed conceptual system of an inherently religious character. What Schmitt makes us aware of is that the modern drive towards neutralization, and the rise of a mentality of technicity, tends to universalize particularity. That particularity is still in crucial parts graspable through an understanding of the theological, something which makes the theological tradition a resource for critical perspectives on contemporary theory. This, I believe, attests to the contemporary relevance of Carl Schmitt: his insistence on the need for a structural analogically aware, historically grounded understanding of thought.[6] At the centre of his work is a critical engagement with intellectual history which we ignore at our own expense.

6 Peter Langford's and Ian Bryan's and Matilda Arvidsson's respective contributions to this volume (Chapters 14 and 15, respectively) could be read as concrete applications of this general sort of approach to legal studies, both with and against Schmitt, so to speak.

Bibliography

Adams, J. L. (1959) 'Rudolf Sohm's theology of law and the spirit', p. 219–35, in W. Leibrecht (ed.), *Religion and Culture: Essays in Honor of Paul Tillich*. New York: Harper.

Arvidsson, M. (2016) 'From Teleology to Eschatology: The *Katechon* and the Political Theology of the International Law of Belligerent Occupation', Chapter 15 in M. Arvidsson, L. Brännström and P. Minkkinen (eds), *The Contemporary Relevance of Carl Schmitt: Law, Politics, Theology*. Abingdon: Routledge.

Balakrishnan, G. (2000) *The Enemy: An Intellectual Portrait of Carl Schmitt*. London: Verso.

Bolz, N. (1985) 'Charisma und Souveränität', p. 249–62, in J. Taubes (ed.), *Religionstheorie und Politische Theologie. Band 1: Der Fürst dieser Welt. Carl Schmitt und die Folgen*. Paderborn: Wilhelm Fink Verlag/Verlag Ferdinand Schöningh.

Brännström, L. (2016) 'Carl Schmitt's Definition of Sovereignty as Authorized Leadership', Chapter 1 in M. Arvidsson, L. Brännström and P. Minkkinen (eds), *The Contemporary Relevance of Carl Schmitt: Law, Politics, Theology*. Abingdon: Routledge.

Cerella, A. (2012) 'Religion and political form: Carl Schmitt's genealogy of politics as critique of Jürgen Habermas's post-secular discourse', *Review of International Studies*, Vol. 38, No. 5: 975–94.

Colliot-Thélène, C. (1999) 'Carl Schmitt vs. Max Weber: juridical rationality and economic rationality', p. 138–54, in C. Mouffe (ed.), *The Challenge of Carl Schmitt*. New York: Verso.

Dahlheimer, M. (1998) *Carl Schmitt und der deutsche Katholizismus 1888–1936*, Paderborn: Ferdinand Schöningh.

de Vries, H. (2006) 'Before, around, and beyond the theologico–political', p. 1–88, in H. de Vries and L. E. Sullivan (eds), *Political Theologies: Public Religions in a Post-Secular World*. New York: Fordham University Press.

Faber, R. (2001) *Lateinischer Faschismus. Über Carl Schmitt der Römer und Katholiken*. Berlin: Philo Verlag.

Faber, R. (2007) *Politische Dämonologie: über modernen Marcionismus*, Würzburg: Königshausen and Neumann.

Fietkau, W. (1986) 'Loss of experience and experience of loss: remarks on the problem of the lost revolution in the work of Benjamin and his fellow combatants', *New German Critique*, Vol. 39: 169–78.

Groh, R. (1998) *Arbeit an der Heillosigkeit der Welt. Zur politisch-theologischen Mythologie und Anthropologie Carl Schmitts*. Frankfurt am Main: Suhrkamp.

Günther, F. (2011) 'Ordnen, gestalten, bewahren. Radikales Ordnungsdenken von deutschen Rechtsintellektuellen der Rechtswissenschaft 1920 bis 1960', *Viertaljahrshefte für Zeitgeschichte*, Vol. 59, No. 3: 353–84.

Haley, P. (1980) 'Rudolph Sohm on charisma', *Journal of Religion*, Vol. 60, No. 2: 185–97.

Kahn, P. W. (2011) *Political Theology: Four New Chapters on the Concept of Sovereignty*. New York: Columbia University Press.

Kelsen, H. (1973) 'God and the state' [1922/1923], p. 61–82, in H Kelsen, *Essays in legal and moral philosophy*. Trans. Peter Heath. Dordrecht and Boston: D. Reidel.

Koenen, A. (1995) *Der Fall Carl Schmitt: sein Aufstieg zum 'Kronjuristen des Dritten Reiches'*. Darmstadt: Wissenschaftliche Buchgesellschaft.

Langford, P. and Bryan, I. (2016) 'Beyond the Jurist as a Theologian of Legal Science: The Question of Carl Schmitt and the International Legal Order', Chapter 14 in M. Arvidsson, L. Brännström and P. Minkkinen (eds), *The Contemporary Relevance of Carl Schmitt. Law, Politics, Theology*. Abingdon: Routledge.

Lievens, M. (2012) 'Ideology critique and the political: Towards a Schmittian perspective on ideology', *Contemporary Political Theory*, Vol. 11, No. 4: 381–96.

McCormick, J. P. (1998) 'Political theory and political theology: the second wave of Carl Schmitt in English', *Political Theory*, Vol. 26, No. 6: 830–54.

Meier, H. (1998) *The Lesson of Carl Schmitt: Four Chapters on the Distinction between Political Theology and Political Philosophy*. Trans. Marcus Brainard. Chicago, IL: University of Chicago Press.

Milbank, J. (2006) *Theology and Social Theory: Beyond Secular Reason*. 2nd edn. Oxford: Blackwell.

Rust, J. (2012) 'Political theologies of the *corpus mysticum*: Schmitt, Kantorowicz, and de Lubac', p. 102–23, in G. Hammill and J. Reinhard Lupton (eds), *Political Theology And Early Modernity*. Chicago, IL: University of Chicago Press.

Schmitt, C. (1966) 'Andreas Bühler: *Kirche und Staat bei Rudolph Sohm*', *Das historisch–politische Buch*, Vol. 14: 306.

Schmitt, C. (1991) *Glossarium. Aufzeichnungen der Jahre 1947–1952*. Berlin: Duncker and Humblot.

Schmitt, C. (1996a) 'The visibility of the church: A scholastic consideration' [1917], p. 46–59, in C. Schmitt, *Roman Catholicism and Political Form*. Trans. G. L. Ulmen. Westport, CT: Greenwood.

Schmitt, C. (1996b) *Roman Catholicism and Political Form* [1923]. Trans. G. L. Ulmen. Westport, CT: Greenwood.

Schmitt, C. (2002) *Ex Captivitate Salus. Erfahrungen der Zeit 1945/47* [1950]. Berlin: Duncker and Humblot.

Schmitt, C. (2004a) *On the Three Types of Juristic Thought* [1934]. Trans. Joseph W. Bendersky. Santa Barbara: Praeger.

Schmitt, C. (2004b) *Der Wert des Staates und die Bedeutung des Einzelnen* [1914]. Berlin: Duncker and Humblot.

Schmitt, C. (2005) *Political Theology. Four Chapters on the Concept of Sovereignty* [1922]. Trans. G. Schwab. Cambridge, MA: MIT Press.

Schmitt, C. (2007a) *The Concept of the Political* [1927]. Expanded edn. Trans. G. Schwab. Chicago, IL: University of Chicago Press.

Schmitt, C. (2007b) 'The age of neutralizations and depoliticizations' [1929], p. 80–96, in C. Schmitt, *The Concept of the Political*. Trans. M. Konzett and J. P. McCormick. Chicago, IL: University of Chicago Press.

Schmitt, C. (2008) *Constitutional Theory* [1928]. Trans. J. Seitzer. Durham, NC: Duke University Press.

Schmitt, C. (2009) *Gesetz und Urteil* [1912]. München: C. H. Beck.

Schmitt, C. (2010) *Political Theology II. The Myth of the Closure of all Political Theology* [1970]. Trans. M. Hoelzl and G. Ward. Cambridge: Polity.

Smith, D. N. (1998) 'Faith, Reason, and Charisma: Rudolf Sohm, Max Weber, and the Theology of Grace', *Sociological Inquiry*, Vol. 68, No. 1: 32–60.

Sohm, R. (1912) *Wesen und Ursprung des Katholizismus*. Berlin: Teubner.

Spindler, W. (2011) *'Humanistisches Appeasement'?: Hans Barions Kritik an der Staats– und Sozialehre des Zweiten Vatikanischen Konzils*. Berlin: Duncker and Humblot.

Ulmen, G. L. (1991) *Politischer Mehrwert. Eine Studie über Max Weber und Carl Schmitt.* Weinheim: VCH.

Wacker, B. (1994) *Die eigentlich katholische Verschärfung ... Konfession, Theologie und Politik im Werk Carl Schmitts.* München: Wilhelm Fink.

Weber, M. (1978) *Economy and Society. An Outline of Interpretive Sociology* [1922]. Trans. G. Roth and C. Wittich. Berkeley, CA: University of California Press.

Yelle, R. (2010) 'The trouble with transcendence: Carl Schmitt's "exception" as a challenge for religious studies', *Method and Theory in the Study of Religion*, Vol. 22, No. 2–3: 189–206.

Chapter 13

Processes of order and the concreteness of the sacred

On the contemporary relevance of Carl Schmitt's critique of nihilism

Jon Wittrock

Space in the world

> 'It is not the world that is in space, but rather it is space that is in the world.'
>
> (Schmitt 1997: 59)

Schmitt's point is far from a trivial one. By stressing the foundations of how we conceptualize and measure space in relations of power and antagonism, he highlights that there is no neutral, simply given space. Rather, there are distinct ways of experiencing and thinking of space which carry different consequences. Hence, we could distinguish between contests *in* space, on the one hand, and spatiality, or the discursive and phenomenological domain for contests *of* space, on the other.

In the former case, Schmitt speculates about a possible shift from the state to the large space. This is a change pertaining to the dominant type of political entity, globally: the state came to be dominant, Schmitt says, during the era of European domination from the fifteenth to the nineteenth centuries, whereas the twentieth and twenty-first centuries may entail the emergence of a new entity, the large space, which might inherit the state as the dominant unit of global political power struggles. In the latter case, however, Schmitt emphasizes the gradual and continuous growth of one type of spatiality, establishing an 'abstract ... empty and overwhelming, mathematically and geographically determined spatial dimension' (Schmitt 2003: 283). In relation to this development, however, he does not really portray an alternative.

In other words, whereas there is at least a possible discontinuity pertaining to the global contest *in* space, there seems to be a continuity, conversely, pertaining to the global diffusion *of* a specific spatiality. To put it metaphorically, in the former case it is a question of the struggle between pieces on the chessboard; in the latter case, it is a matter of formulating an understanding of the board itself. So while there is discontinuity in the former case – that is, the pieces could possibly change – as the era of nation states gives way to an age of large spaces (or other entities), the board itself appears to be continuously developing in one direction only: it becomes more and more a matter of the spread of a conceptualization of space as abstract and calculable on a global scale. If we wish to extend the metaphor, the rules of the game could be seen as the formal and informal norms of global politics.

This chapter describes both dimensions in Schmitt's international thought and examines the way in which he describes the connection, and destructive disconnection, of a spatial order from its sacred orientation. Thereafter, the contemporary relevance of this Schmittian critique is considered. Specifically, I argue that Schmitt's analysis points to three areas for further reflection, pertaining to the continuing importance of symbols and rituals even in liberal democracies, the fragmentation of practices of a collective oscillation between the separation of labour and the coming together in a field beyond it and in the treatment of the sacred as a relation, rather than an inherent property of certain persons, sites, objects, or temporal intervals.

The struggle in space: from states to large spaces?

While politics incorporates various agents, institutions and practices, the political, according to Schmitt (Schmitt 2007a: 26–7), centres on the friend–enemy polarity, a polarity of differing intensity rather than a simple dichotomy. This polarity involves groups of people confronting each other as public enemies (Schmitt 2007a: 28). The political entity is an organized unit that seeks to control large-scale armed violence within and defend itself against attacks from the outside (Schmitt 2007a: 32). Political entities come in different forms, such as city states or empires; from the early modern era and onwards, interrelations between political entities in Europe increasingly concerned interrelations between states (Schmitt 2007a: 6).

In *The Nomos of the Earth*, Schmitt sketches a sweeping narrative of the growth of the first truly global order, which was made possible by the European voyages of discovery from the fifteenth century onwards and came to be embodied in an order of international law centred on the European states, collapsing in conjunction with World War I. The greatest achievement of this global order, to Schmitt (Schmitt 2003: 149), was its 'bracketing' of war; that is, its transforming wars from total to limited, from sacred to secular and hence transforming the enemy from someone to be annihilated by all means to someone to be respected and treated according to certain civilized rules of conduct. The brutal reality behind this amiable development, however, consisted in what Schmitt calls its *amity lines*, dividing the land areas of the globe fundamentally into two basic categories: the soil of Europe, the domain of bracketed, civilized and humane wars, and the rest, the non-European lands and the open seas, open to European appropriation and unlimited warfare (cf. Schmitt 2003: 184). Gradually, however, European powers became 'relativized' (Schmitt 2003: 217). Europe was reduced to an equal partner in world affairs, rather than being the sole and self-evident centre of the world. With the outbreak of World War I, this Eurocentric order started to collapse. The world was plunged into the pursuit of a new global order.

This is the scene that Schmitt is portraying in the late 1940s and early 1950s. However, his search for a novel entity to possibly inherit the state as the dominant one of global politics reaches back earlier than that, and the concept of 'large space' was already being used by Schmitt in the context of National Socialist foreign policy in the 1930s. In the 1939 essay 'Völkerrechtliche Großraumordnung mit Interventionsverbot für raumfremde Mächte', Schmitt seeks to sketch the contours of a new political entity, the German European large space, consisting of a *Reich*, a dominant power, and lesser peripheral ones. In a cunning rhetorical manoeuvre, Schmitt (1995: 281) evokes the US Monroe Doctrine of 1823, rejecting further colonization of the Americas by European powers. Whether Schmitt's interpretation of this doctrine is correct or not remains disputable, but the polemical point is as clear as it is clever. As Germany was radically reconsidering its own foreign policy in 1939, praising a cornerstone of the formulation of American foreign politics, the drastic comparison with its non-interventionism made it possible for the legal theorist of the German Reich to defend the latter's European aspirations. As Hooker (2009: 134) observes, both von Ribbentrop and Hitler used the analogy with the Monroe Doctrine in 1939, and 'Schmitt was apparently warned not to claim authorship of the idea so as to avoid offending the Führer's dignity'. But there is also a deeper significance to Schmitt's attempts, beyond mere political opportunism, for he is simultaneously considering the possibility, or at least claiming to do so, of describing a novel political entity which is neither a state, nor an empire, but something else. Having praised the Monroe Doctrine, Schmitt turns polemically to the British Empire, a patchwork system binding together various units into a greater whole. The major difference between the United States large space and the British Empire is that while the latter maintained, for the most part, a monopoly on power in occupied territories, the former came to rely on the extension of a zone of intervention/non-intervention, eventually rendering state sovereignty ambiguous, while not abolishing it entirely (Schmitt 2003: 252). Thus, the distinction comes to concern different *techniques of domination*: the occupation of a territory as opposed to the proclamation of a zone of non-intervention and, further on, a right of intervention.

Internally, Schmitt (1995) asserts, in the same 1939 essay, that the large space is supposedly held together and its political manoeuvres justified by what he calls its *political idea* and the latter's radiation. What this is supposed to entail more specifically, however, is a matter open to speculation, although other works by Schmitt, as well as the context of the composition of the essay, provide strong hints. A political idea should consist of a set of doctrines focused on a friend–enemy polarity and with a gravitational core in an underlying, unifying symbol. Its radiation could thus consist of speeches, rituals and celebrations tied to core symbols. Concerning the Third Reich, this political idea would have to be a version of National Socialist ideology, but it could also take on other forms, if we take seriously Schmitt's (1995: 278) ambition to suggest a thinking of large spaces, which would be applicable to different contexts. However, it should be noted that Schmitt (1995: 297) contrasts the notion of a *Reich* or core (German: 'realm') of a European large space, with the ethnic diversity of the late Roman Empire, as well as to that of the empires of the western democracies. Thus, attempts to appropriate Schmitt's notion of large spaces as a descriptive tool for the contemporary world may be fruitful but must also exercise a degree of caution (cf. Fichera 2016, Chapter 11 in this volume).

The large space reappears in *The Nomos of the Earth* but nothing new is added to it as an analytical concept. Even later, in 1954, Schmitt adds what seems like a strikingly prescient, if compact, analysis of a possible future global development, foreseeing the end of the Cold War and speculating on the order to come. Schmitt briefly outlines three alternatives, which one is tempted to read, not necessarily as distinct options, but perhaps just as well as successive stages in one, single, sequential development: the Cold War may end, Schmitt (2003: 354–5) concludes, in the victory of one of its antagonistic sides. Or the United States may appropriate the role formerly fulfilled by Britain, of balancing the rest of the world, through domination of the seas as well as through air power. Finally, the world may be divided into a balance between large spaces, none of which alone may dominate the others (see Rech 2016, Chapter 10 in this volume, for a deeper exploration of this issue, in conjunction with Schmitt's critique of progressivism and universalism).

The struggle of space: technicity and the site

Schmitt's historical narrative is of course sweeping and generalising, and he himself admits as much (cf. Schmitt 2007b: 9). At the most fundamental level, however, the analysis of *The Nomos of the Earth* is tied together by the concepts of order and orientation. If this is the most fundamental linkage around which this narrative revolves, the dangers of its possible dissolution constitutes the core of Schmitt's (2003: 66) critique of 'nihilism'. So what disconnects order from orientation? To understand this, I suggest that we turn to earlier works by Schmitt, which explore more openly a theme which is present but largely submerged and only appears in scattered remarks here and there within *The Nomos of the Earth* – the theme of technology and technicity.

As Schmitt (2007a: 81, 94) makes clear in his 1929 *The Age of Neutralizations and Depoliticizations*, technicity is the 'spirit' or 'anti-religion' that accompanies technology in the sense of technological devices, instruments. On the one hand, 'technology' is indeed neutral in the sense that it may be used by anyone equally and no particular normative implications appear to follow from it. On the other hand, however, its associated 'spirit of technicity' may be characterized, Schmitt suggests, as being 'evil and demonic', even 'satanic', since it is 'the belief in unlimited power and the domination of man over nature, even over human nature ... in the unlimited 'receding of natural boundaries,' and 'the unlimited possibilities for change and prosperity.' (Schmitt 2007a: 94). Schmitt, however, is hardly a thinker opposed to domination as such. His opposition to the specific type of domination exerted by the sway of the 'spirit of technicity', then, needs to be explained. Schmitt's works as well as his life incorporate difficult and sometimes mystifying tensions. One such characteristic key tension concerns Schmitt's defence of *occidental rationalism*, on the one hand, and his polemic against *technicity*, on the other. What must be explained in the following is Schmitt's opposition to the 'spirit of technicity' and the disjunction of the latter from the laudable aspects of occidental rationalism.

Perhaps the clearest exposition, as well as polemic, can be found in one of Schmitt's earlier, and most famous works, the 1922 *Political Theology*. This work, as its title indeed indicates, is concerned with sovereignty, but not at all exclusively so. One of Schmitt's concerns is to counterpose, to a certain kind of limited rationality, his own preferred type of reason, which he describes by the label of occidental rationalism. If this type of rationalism, as Schmitt insists, characterizes both the medieval, Catholic order as well as the secular, post-Reformation order of sovereign states, there must be some element that unites them. The theological and the legal form of rationality which Schmitt espouses as occidental rationalism, must be closely tied together, or structurally very similar. And that is indeed the case: 'Both have a double principle, reason ... and scripture ...' (Schmitt 2005: 37–8). What is depicted here are not simply the distinct spheres called 'theology' and 'jurisprudence', but rather an opposition between different forms of reason, which may manifest differently within theology, jurisprudence and the sciences. Schmitt describes forms of thinking, manifesting linguistically, which to a different degree may pervade different disciplines.

The kind of rationality which Schmitt opposes, which he sometimes calls 'technicity', is characterized by the *repression of the exception*. It is a form of rationality which aims to construct closed, coherent systems of 'uninterrupted unity and order', systems without exceptions: 'everything that contradicts the system is excluded as impure' (Schmitt 2005: 20–1). Thus, the different modes of reason are constituted by the way they relate to the exception: technicity represses the exception, occidental rationalism acknowledges it. Now, Schmitt, true to form, is not consistent in always using the same terms, but the opposition between two contrasting, overarching types of rationality pervades his works from the earlier to the later ones. And this, I believe, provides the key to unlocking Schmitt's thinking on *the site* in relation to the global space of technicity. If technicity thinks space as homogeneous ('empty and overwhelming'), Schmitt must counter by thinking a *spatial exception*. He cannot approach space as 'closed and coherent', but must allow for spatial exceptions, just as he allows for constitutive exceptions in other domains. And this is indeed the case: 'On the open sea,' Schmitt (2003: 43) observes in *The Nomos of the Earth*, 'there were no limits, no boundaries, no consecrated sites, no sacred orientations', as opposed to 'something walled or enclosed, or a sacred place, all of which are contained in the word *nomos*' (Schmitt 2003: 78).

The German original speaks of '*geweihten Stätten*' and '*sakrale Ortung*' (cf. Schmitt 1988: 14). Given how very nicely it would fit with the conceptual pair of *Ordnung* and *Ortung*, it is almost puzzling that Schmitt did not consistently use the German word '*Ort*' instead. Is there some esoteric reason for this, or is it the case that Schmitt came upon this thematic gradually or intuitively and hesitated to enforce a conceptual consistency here? Be that as it may; there is, then, to conclude, yet another key concept, besides order and orientation, and that is the sacred *site*, the concrete manifestation of a constitutive exception.

Techniques of domination, contested worship and fragmented festivals

If *The Nomos of the Earth* presents a narrative concerning the growth of a Eurocentric global order or *nomos*, what does this latter term mean, for Schmitt? Not simply a legal order (a common translation of the Greek *nomos* is exactly 'law'). Rather, Schmitt states, 'The Greek noun *nomos* comes from the Greek verb *nemein*', which allegedly has three related meanings: 'appropriate', 'divide/distribute', and 'pasturage'. These, Schmitt claims, signify 'three processes – appropriation, distribution, and production ... In every stage of social life, in every economic order, in every period of legal history until now, things have been appropriated, distributed, and produced' (Schmitt 2003: 326–7). Any *nomos* of the earth, then, constitutes a comprehensive weave of narratives and practices shaping human, communal existence.

Ultimately, the foundation of the Eurocentric global order, Schmitt claims, lay in the appropriation of the New World, of the Americas, by European powers. This was the original *Landnahme* or land appropriation, which constituted its 'original act', just like every basic order has its own original, constitutive act, its appropriation of some portion of the earth (Schmitt 2003: 78). And this 'original act', in turn, is informed by a religious orientation: 'The last great, heroic act of the European peoples – the land-appropriation of a new world and of an unknown continent', Schmitt declares, 'was not accomplished by the heroes of the *conquista* as a mission of the *jus commercii*, but in the name of their Christian redeemer and his holy mother Mary' (Schmitt 2003: 349).

It is when these two basic elements are disconnected that *nihilism* arises: when there is no longer any sacred orientation tied to the appropriation, distribution and production of resources. Sacred sites and orientations represent the ultimately ungraspable, transcendent, metaphysical exception, within the immanent world of human, everyday life and activities.

What, then, can Schmitt's hopes and fears concerning nihilism and power politics tell us today? It is clear that nation states have neither been consistently replaced by or subsumed under 'large spaces', but nonetheless, what I called a distinction between *techniques of domination* pointed out by Schmitt remains descriptively relevant. While the imperialism of the great powers of the Eurocentric order entailed the *consistent occupation and pacification* of territories which were often considered as 'colonies', the *rendering sovereignty ambivalent* by means of declaring a right of intervention and support is a key feature for example of the super power politics of the United States and is also arguably present, in some ways, in the project of European integration. Furthermore, it is true that a conceptualization of space as calculable has spread rapidly with the diffusion of modern technology, and human rights are allegedly independent of any specific religious revelation. Also, debates on the cultural horizon of both the United States and the European Union – are they, and if so to what extent, Christian or not? – do show that there is a longing, at least in some quarters, for a cultural and religious significance to political spaces transcending a merely civic and territorial understanding of political entities.

It would be easy, too easy, to dismiss Schmitt's thoughts on the ties between sacred orientations and the constitution of an order, as well as the risks of disconnecting the two, as the musing of a political theologian coming from an obscure and particularistic perspective. Regardless of the specificities of Schmitt's own conceptual apparatus in dealing with these matters – which I have attempted to outline above – he is certainly on to something important, which could be put, however, differently, and with the aid of conceptual tools and empirical studies to which he did not and in some cases could not refer. In the following, rather than dismiss Schmitt as an outdated political theologian, or, direct polemics against the details of his conceptual architecture (as I have interpreted it) I attempt to use it instead as a point of departure, delving into the key problem explored in this chapter; that is, the ties, or lack of them, between order, as understood by Schmitt, and sacred orientation.

To recapitulate somewhat, an order or *nomos* consists at the most basic level in the appropriation, distribution and production of resources and it is these processes, then, that are supposed to be tied, in a non-nihilistic order, to a sacred orientation, concretely manifested in sacred sites. Schmitt's focus on the ties between order and sacred orientation does pertain to more general functions and problems which, if not necessarily omnipresent in any order, can at least be observed empirically in human communities throughout history. Those are the functions of on the one hand *sacred* or *pseudo-sacred symbols,* and on the other, of what I propose to call *collective oscillation,* and their associated risks and possibilities.

Despite talk about political secularization, in European liberal democracies, the rites and symbols of the nation have largely replaced, but also in many cases, complemented, those of the churches. Schmitt states in his last published book during his lifetime, *Political Theology II,* that Hobbes '*brought the Reformation to a conclusion* by recognising the state as a clear alternative to the Roman Catholic church's monopoly on decision-making' (Schmitt 2008: 125–6). In actual fact, the state was eventually tied to what Hobbes (1998: 302) himself called for in terms of 'an uniformity of public worship', tied to national narratives and symbols, but beyond that, there has been a complex dispersal and fragmentation of 'sacred orientations' and related activities.

While Schmitt's emphasis on sacred 'bracketing' in a spatial sense has been appreciated by recent scholarship on sovereignty (cf., for example, Brown 2010: 46–7), I think we may push the point further: the sacred and corresponding categories partly function by withdrawing certain domains, both spatial and temporal – be it natural objects, artefacts, sites, temporal intervals, animals or people – from ordinary usage and circulation. Furthermore, such domains tend to be surrounded by reverence, respect, wonder and awe. Thus, the sacred transcends a typical liberal democratic focus on individual and human rights and even wider concerns of contemporary moral philosophy. As Singer (2009: 7–8) puts it, 'It would be nonsense to say that it is not in the interests of a stone to be kicked along the road by a schoolboy. A stone does not have interests because it cannot suffer'. And yet there are indeed, as we all know, sacred stones, and some people would react violently if we attempted to kick those along the road. Why, however, is that so?

The answer provided by Durkheim (1995) goes a long way to explaining this: some domains are assigned a special status because they symbolize a human community in its entirety and provide a structure to its existence. As a consequence, to violate that status is to disrespect that community as a whole. Furthermore, while Durkheim's primary subject of study was socalled primitive societies, contemporary liberal democracies, too, incorporate such artefacts, persons, sites, symbols and temporal intervals. Finally, while subsequent critics – Evans-Pritchard (1965) and Lukes (1973), to name two of the more prominent, came to question the accuracy of Durkheim's approach in describing 'primitive societies' and 'religion' – simply put, Durkheim arguably generalized far too much out of too flimsy empirical investigations – he surely says something of relevance to modern politics and its analogies with the Christian churches, about the withdrawing and 'bracketing' of certain domains associated with a community as a whole. Whether to call those domains sacred or, perhaps, to point to significant differences in the narratives and practices tied to them, pseudo-sacred, or some other term, is a matter of terminological preference.

Either way, the structural similarities are there, as has been noted repeatedly, primarily relating to nationalism (by Hayes 1960: 15; Parker 1984: 231; Anderson 1991: 5; and Smith 2001: 35, to name a few). One should beware, however, of taking the notion of nationalism replacing religion too literally. I merely argue that it did so, pertaining to collective rituals, shared by the political entity as a whole. In other ways, national narratives complemented, sometimes competed and, at other times, fused with or appropriated elements from, religious rituals. Still, the nation is constantly reproduced symbolically in grand occasions and at a more everyday or banal level (cf. Billig 1995).

It might be said that the 'political idea' of the EU clashes with the rites and symbols tied to its member states. Furthermore, concerning postnational as well as transnational and cosmopolitan proposals, it may be asked what the status of symbols and rituals ought to be. Ought the rituals and symbols of the nation be replaced by others or simply be rejected not to be replaced, or ought they to remain, while other layers of democratic governance are simply added on top of them and, if so, ought these latter to be associated with their own symbols and rituals? Indeed, Kant, a great source of inspiration for cosmopolitan projects as well as advocates of deliberative democracy, claimed that:

> The oft-repeated solemn ritual of renewal, continuation, and propagation ... under the laws of equality (communion) ... has in it something great which expands people's narrow, selfish and intolerant cast of mind, especially in religious matters, to the idea of a cosmopolitan moral community.
>
> (Kant 2001: 213–14)

There is no strong intrinsic reason to abolish shared symbols and rituals – to the extent that they support a regime we deem desirable, they are not problematic. If there are no strong reasons in favour of them being mandatory, they ought not to be, but they could still remain publicly supported. Perhaps Benjamin (1969: 242) ought not have countered the aestheticization of politics by fascism with the politicization of art by communism, but rather with the aestheticization of politics by democratic movements, which, luckily, took place in some countries. In either case, the major question is not whether there should be shared symbols and rituals – the empirical evidence suggests that all political entities have them, and it would be unwise by that reason alone to leave such a potent tool the exclusive domain of other projects than one's own – but rather at which level they ought to be located, and, if they are found on several levels at once, how those could and should interact. This problem is visible in, for example, the removal of explicit recognition of European Union state-like symbols in the shift from the rejected Constitutional Treaty to the Lisbon Treaty. Furthermore, as events of recent years have shown, anti-authoritarian, pro-democracy movements may effectively use symbols and rituals, too (often inspired by Sharp 2011: 125).

Communal rituals and the patterns observed by many in relation to feasts and festivals in several societies entail what we could call a *collective oscillation*; that is, the community as a whole oscillates between the activities serving the survival and reproduction of human beings, implying a division of labour, and the 'bracketing' of ordinary life associated with shared rituals and festivals, where people come together as a community beyond those divisions. This can even, in a hierarchical society, entail a temporary reversal of its hierarchies, the irony being that even that reversal serves merely as the exception proving the rule.

Now, it may be observed that in the complex societies of contemporary European liberal democracies, there does exist a kind of collective worship around shared symbols and rituals, tied to the narratives of the nation. But this collective worship involves people to a lesser extent, participation is less frequently mandatory in any sense, and the interpretation of symbols and narratives is more open to contestation and renegotiation, than is the case in those types of communities studied by Durkheim, or in many religious communities. Thus, Alexander (2006) labels contemporary rituals as 'ritual-like'. Furthermore, practices of a collective oscillation between the separation of work and the coming together in rituals and festivals are much more fragmented. There are countless examples of such an oscillating movement in late industrial societies, involving numerous constellations of people, from religious to countercultural communities, to the simple 'after work' beer at a pub, to the coming together of the family in front of the television screen, and so on. So the pattern is not one of a sharp dichotomy between 'religious' and 'secular' in this respect, but rather one of an increasing fragmentation.

Rituals and symbols, then, may be tied to a collective oscillation encompassing the community as a whole, or there may be the political rituals of the nation, the interpretation of which are open to contestation and besides which there are many other oscillating movements between the domains of a separation of work in the pursuit of survival and reproduction, on the one hand, and the coming together in the feast or some other element of play or relaxation, on the other.[1]

---

1   Bellah (2011), Gadamer (1986), Huizinga (2001) and Schechner (1993) all resort to the not unproblematic concept of 'play'. Bellah also speaks of a 'relaxed field', as opposed to the dispositions associated with the struggles for survival and reproduction.

Furthermore, in complex, fragmented societies, an abundance of competing ideological as well as commercial narratives may be tied to such symbols and practices. These may comprise distinct, but parallel experiences of temporality. On the one hand, there is the stereotypical image of an ideological horizon of time, entailing that eschatological visions have migrated directly or indirectly into ideological contexts, where they take on an immanent form bereft of any metaphysical, transcendent ties and where hopes for human action replaces the fears and anticipations of divine intervention (cf., for example, Koselleck 2004 and Voegelin 1997). On the other hand, there are the observations that consumer societies entail yet another type of experience of time, as consisting of increasingly disconnected fragments, moments of intense experiences lacking of any overarching interpretation – a view Schmitt criticized in terms of an 'immanent occasionalism' and tied to a German romantic heritage, and which, for example, Bauman describes in terms of a more general 'pointillist' experience of time (cf. Schmitt 2011: 78; Bauman 2007: 32).

Finally, however, there is the even more general question of the sacred as implying, on the one hand, behavioural commands and restrictions, calling for a disposition of reverence and respect in relation to certain objects and artefacts, animals or people, sites and temporal intervals, and on the other, an openness to a phenomenological spectrum of experiences of wonder and awe (cf., for example, Otto 1950; Eliade 1987). The sacred can be seen as an ambiguous category, not only because it includes experiences of both wonder and awe or even terror, but also because it seeks to fuse certain behavioural dispositions with a certain phenomenological spectrum of experiences. Those ties are often there, but not necessarily so. Thus, ascribing a sacred status to certain domains can be seen as – often successful – attempts at 'capturing' experiences of wonder and awe, thus rendering them socially useful, rather than disruptive.

Conversely, and by way of conclusion, this also suggests that processes of de- and re-sacralization may render this relational aspect of the sacred visible as such. Movements of secularization as well as de-secularization thus provide an opportunity for a deepened reflection concerning the desirable role of the functions outlined above, in relation to both techniques of domination as well as processes of appropriation, distribution and production, within the confines of a global *nomos*, and Schmitt's penetrating if problematic thoughts on the matter remain relevant to such a reflection. This is not a matter of trying to fashion an unambiguous and universally valid concept of the sacred. On the contrary, Schmitt's rather obscure treatment of 'bracketing' and the sacred actually invite us to explore a diversity of themes, without being bogged down in the attempt to construe a descriptive concept, allegedly correctly translating a host of categories from natural languages into one single division of sacred and profane. Instead, we would do well, as Schmitt reminds us, to look at concrete practices.

When we simply accept, without further thought, a combination of what we may call nationalist political theology and the immanent occasionalism of capitalist consumerism, we fail to politicize the ambiguity of the sacred and to perceive it in its very concreteness. Schmitt, whatever we may think of his ideological or theological affiliations, can help us to wake up to a greater awareness, so that these domains may indeed be *politicised*: transformed into domains of collective, publicly recognized challenges. That is, I think, the greatest potential legacy of his critique of nihilism.

Bibliography

Alexander, J. (2006) 'Cultural pragmatics: social performance between ritual and strategy', p. 29–90, in J. Alexander, B. Giesen, and J. Mast (eds), *Social Performance: Symbolic Action, Cultural Pragmatics, and Ritual*. Cambridge: Cambridge University Press.

Anderson, B. (2002) *Imagined Communities: Reflections on the Origin and Spread of Nationalism*. London: Verso.

Bauman, Z. (2007) *Consuming Life*. Cambridge: Polity.

Bellah, R. (2011) *Religion in Human Evolution: From the Paleolithic to the Axial Age*. Cambridge, MA: Harvard University Press.

Benjamin, W. (1969) 'The Work of Art in the Age of Mechanical Reproduction' [1936], p. 217–52, in W. Benjamin, *Illuminations: Essays and Reflections*. Trans. H. Zohn. New York: Schocken Books.

Billig, M. (1995) *Banal Nationalism*. London: Sage.

Brown, W. (2010) *Walled States, Waning Sovereignty*. New York: Zone Books.

Durkheim, É. (1995) *The Elementary Forms of Religious Life* [1912]. Trans. K. E. Fields. New York: Free Press.

Eliade, M. (1987) *The Sacred and the Profane: The Nature of Religion* [1959]. Trans. W. R. Trask. Orlando, CA: Harcourt.

Evans-Pritchard, E. (1965) *Theories of Primitive Religion*. Oxford: Clarendon.

Fichera, M. (2016) 'Carl Schmitt and the New World Order: A View From Europe', Chapter 11 in M. Arvidsson, L. Brännström and P. Minkkinen (eds), *The Contemporary Relevance of Carl Schmitt. Law, Politics, Theology*. Abingdon: Routledge.

Gadamer, H.-G. (1986) 'The Relevance of the Beautiful' [1977], in H.-G. Gadamer, *The Relevance of the Beautiful and Other Essays*. Trans. N. Walker. Cambridge: Cambridge University Press.

Hayes, C. (1960) *Nationalism: A Religion*. New York: Macmillan.

Hobbes, T. (1998) *Man and Citizen (De Homine and De Cive)* [1651/1658]. Indianapolis, IN: Hackett.

Hooker, W. (2009) *Carl Schmitt's International Thought: Order and Orientation*. Cambridge: Cambridge University Press.

Huizinga, J. (2001) *Homo Ludens: A Study of the Play-Element in Culture* [1938]. London: Routledge.

Kant, I. (2001) 'Religion within the boundaries of mere reason' [1793], p. 39215, in I. Kant, *Religion and Rational Theology*. Cambridge: Cambridge University Press.

Koselleck, R. (2004) *Futures Past: On the Semantics of Historical Time* [1979]. New York: Columbia University Press.

Lukes, S. (1973) *Emile Durkheim: His Life and Work*. Harmondsworth: Penguin.
Otto, R. (1950) *The Idea of the Holy: An Inquiry into the Non-Rational Factor in the Idea of the Divine and its Relation to the Rational* [1917]. Trans. J. W. Harvey. Oxford: Oxford University Press.
Parker, W. (1984) *Europe, America and the Wider World: Essays on the Economic History of Western Capitalism, Volume 1: Europe and the World Economy*. Cambridge: Cambridge University Press.
Schechner, R. (1993) *The Future of Ritual: Writings on Culture and Performance*. London: Routledge.
Schmitt, C. (1988) *Der Nomos der Erde im Völkerrecht des Jus Publicum Europaeum* [1950]. Berlin: Duncker and Humblot.
Schmitt, C. (1995) 'Völkerrechtliche Großraumordnung mit Interventionsverbot für raumfremde Mächte' [1939], p. 269–371, in C. Schmitt, *Staat, Großraum, Nomos: Arbeiten aus den Jahren 1916–1969*. Berlin: Duncker and Humblot.
Schmitt, C. (1997) *Land and Sea* [1954]. Trans. S. Draghici. Washington, DC: Plutarch Press.
Schmitt, C. (2003) *The Nomos of the Earth in the International Law of the Jus Publicum Europaeum* [1950]. Trans. G. L. Ulmen. New York: Telos.
Schmitt, C. (2005) *Political Theology: Four Chapters on the Concept of Sovereignty* [1922]. Trans. G. Schwab. Chicago, IL: University of Chicago Press.
Schmitt, C. (2007a) *The Concept of the Political* [1932]. Expanded edn. Trans. G. Schwab. Chicago, IL: University of Chicago Press.
Schmitt, C. (2007b) *Theory of the Partisan: Intermediate Commentary on the Concept of the Political* [1963]. Trans. G. L. Ulmen. New York: Telos.
Schmitt, C. (2008) *Political Theology II: The Myth of the Closure of Any Political Theology* [1970]. Trans. M. Hoelzl and G. Ward. Cambridge: Polity.
Schmitt, C. (2011) *Political Romanticism* [1919]. Trans. G. Oakes. New Brunswick, NJ: Transaction.
Sharp, G. (2011) *From Dictatorship to Democracy: A Conceptual Framework for Liberation*. London: Serpent's Tail.
Singer, P. (2009) *Animal Liberation: The Definitive Classic of the Animal Movement* [1975]. New York: HarperCollins.
Smith, A. (2001) *Nationalism: Theory, Ideology, History*. Cambridge: Polity.
Voegelin, E. (1997) *Science, Politics and Gnosticism* [1968]. Washington, DC: Regnery.

Chapter 14

Beyond the jurist as a theologian of legal science

The question of Carl Schmitt and the international legal order

Peter Langford and Ian Bryan

Introduction

The question of the contemporary relevance of Carl Schmitt involves the acknowledgement that the distinctiveness or singularity of his work is, in part, determined by its consciously confrontational stance with regard to the phenomena which it seeks to comprehend. The engagement with the work of Schmitt is, therefore, seemingly one in which the reader or interpreter is confronted with the choice of complete adherence (see, for example, de Benoist 2013) or immediate rejection (see, for example, Rawls 2005: lx). In accordance with these two extremes, this interpretative closure would, effectively, confer upon Schmitt, or a certain Schmittian style, the capacity to determine the meaning and purpose of his work.

The prospect of opening a space for interpretation beyond Schmitt's authorial intention emerges by exploring the question of Schmitt's contemporary relevance from the standpoint of his characterization and identity as jurist. Beginning with Schmitt's self-conception as a theologian of legal science, we proceed to place into question the possibility not only of Schmitt's self-ascription but also his position and identity as jurist and, furthermore, his legal thought. It will be seen that the difficulties and limitations revealed by way of this questioning flow from Schmitt's conceptualization of the international legal order. This questioning is, however, preparative to a transition to the delineation of an altered concept of the identity and position of the jurist. The transition entails a reconception of the primacy that Schmitt accords to the ordering of space, through the notion of law as *nomos*, through the interrogation of its dependence upon a theology of history. In this interrogation, the non-negatable negativity, presented by this theology of history, is rethought, through the introduction of the notion of the common. With the introduction of this notion, negativity is detached from a theological framework, and situated in relation to a notion of justice which is predicated upon a common experience of injustice.

The opening and development of the space for interpretation presupposes that behind the purported 'occasionalism' of Schmitt's work, there is a structure or system which can be entered into and comprehended, in order to think beyond it (for other approaches to an internal critique of Schmitt, see Galli 2010a; Hooker 2009; Kervégan 2011; Marder 2012; Ojakangas 2006; Ruschi 2008; Ruschi 2012; Legg 2011; Odysseos and Petito 2008). The process of entry and comprehension, at an initial philological level, acknowledges the internal modification of this structure in the chronological progression of Schmitt's thought. The modification is apparent in Schmitt's self-designation as a theologian of legal science,[1] which reflects the shift in the conceptualization of 'the orientation of order and the political unity' in both his own thought and that of 'modern political theory' (Galli 2010b: 1). The shift concerns the character of the conceptualization of the 'crisis of the state' (Galli 2010b: 3). In place of the predominance of 'decision, exception, sovereignty, political theology, the "political," constituent power, and concrete order' (Galli 2010b: 4), Schmitt emphasizes 'the spatial dimension of politics, the opposition between land and sea, the concept of *nomos*, and the *jus publicum europaeum*' (Galli 2010b: 4). This shift in conceptualization coincides with the post-World War II work of Schmitt in which the position and identity of the jurist concerns the possibility of global order and political unity. It is in this period of Schmitt's work that the question of the position and identity of the jurist in relation to the international legal order is given one of its clearest articulations.

The return to political theology from the collapse of National Socialism

The self-designation which Schmitt offers – of a jurist who is also a theologian of legal science – finds its first textual expression in the immediate post-World War II works of *Ex Captivitate Salus* (Schmitt 2002) and *Glossarium* (especially, Schmitt 1991: 23 [2.10.47], 224 [6.3.49], 311 [4.10.50]; on the *Großraum*, see Meier 1994) and accompanies Schmitt's experience of the collapse of National Socialism, including his arrest, transfer to and interrogation at Nuremberg and his subsequent release.[2] These experiences, then, become the basis for a revised representation of the role of jurist in Schmitt's thought, replacing the preceding variants he propounded of the role and its interconnectedness with National Socialism (for example, Schmitt 2001a; Schmitt 2001b; Schmitt 2011a; Schmitt 2011b).

1   For Taubes, this self-designation is itself problematic, as 'Carl Schmitt was a jurist not a theologian; but a legal theorist who entered the scorched earth that theologians had vacated' (Taubes 2013: 1).
2   His release also marks his withdrawal from formal participation in the post-War War II German university system, reinforced by the loss of his university position and accompanied by his refusal to participate in the post-War de-Nazification programmes in Germany.

The suggestions in the *Glossarium* and *Ex Captivitate Salus* as to the character of the position and identity of the jurist find a concise and important articulation in Schmitt's short response to Löwith's book, *Meaning in History* (Löwith 1949). In the *Three Possibilities for a Christian Conception of History*, Schmitt accepts the importance of Löwith's 'results and conclusions' (Schmitt 2009: 168) and then elaborates upon them, to rework the notion of 'meaning in history' from the perspective of a theologian of legal science. Löwith presents 'historical self-understanding of the last century' as one which consists of 'creating a historical parallel between its own time and … a wholly other time that dates back two thousand years' (Schmitt 2009: 168). This, for Schmitt, is an untranscendable form of historical self-understanding which, in turn, renders it 'important to understand why it is especially this time of early Christianity that seems so plausible to us' (Schmitt 2009: 168).

The plausibility of this time, for Schmitt, rests upon 'the question of whether eschatological faith and historical consciousness can coexist' (Schmitt 2009: 169). The possibility of their simultaneity 'consists in the conception of a force, which defers the end and suppresses the evil one. This is the *kat-echon* of the mysterious passage of Paul's second letter to the Thessalonians' (Schmitt 2009: 169), which is not to be reduced to 'a generalized designation of simply conservative or reactionary tendencies' nor to exemplars of a 'typological collection of historicism' (Schmitt 2009: 169).

Schmitt's concern is to maintain a thought which retains the 'original historical force of the figure of the *kat-echon*' (Schmitt 2009: 169).[3] The force entails an understanding of Christianity as 'historical event of infinite, non-appropriable singularity' (Schmitt 2009: 169–70) and as engaging in an 'active contemplation of' events from which emerges a continuous source of 'the dark meaning of our history' (Schmitt 2009: 170). The importance, here, is less Schmitt's critical appropriation of the German poet, Konrad Weiss's work, the *Christian Epimetheus* (Weiss 1933), but more the insistence that this original historical force enables a conception of history 'which grows through strong creations, which insert the eternal in the course of time. It is a striking of the roots in the space of meaning of the earth. Through scarcity and impotence, this history is the hope and honour of our existence' (Schmitt 2009: 170).

With this form 'self-understanding' (Schmitt 2009: 167), the parallels between the present and early Christianity enables the passage between eschatological faith and historical consciousness to distinguish themselves from 'the philosophy of history or a utopian self-dislocation' (Schmitt

---

3   We leave aside the difficulty of the interpretation of St Paul which this represents, which was to become one of the central features in the exchanges between Jacob Taubes and Carl Schmitt (see Taubes 2013; on the relationship of Schmitt to Rudolf Sohm, see Falk 2016, Chapter 12 in this volume; on the figure of the *katechon*, see also Arvidsson 2016, Chapter 15 in this volume, and Rech 2016, Chapter 10 in this volume).

2009: 167). The passage, as force, is simultaneously, the connection between this form of 'self-understanding' and legal science: a theology of legal science in which the notion of the *nomos* of the earth is the juridical equivalent of the insertion of 'the eternal in the course of time'.

The parameters of the political theology which encompass the position and identity of the theologian of legal science are only rendered explicit in Schmitt's final book, *Political Theology II* (Schmitt 2008). In the response that this text offers to Erik Peterson's *Monotheism as a Political Problem* (Peterson 2011) and Hans Blumenberg's *The Legitimacy of the Modern Age* (Blumenberg 1999), Schmitt articulates and defends the possibility of a political theology. Within this articulation, political theology originates in the relationship between the Roman Empire and the Catholic Church, from whose combination it emerges in its original political form. One of the essential elements of Schmitt's critique of Peterson is the philological dissociation of the Trinitarian form of Christian monotheism from the impossibility of a political form. The critique is an aspect of the wider demonstration that Peterson 'has not transcended the abstract and absolute disjunction between pure theology and impure politics' (Schmitt 2008: 95). This origin of political theology attests to the necessary interpenetration of the theological and the political which, for Schmitt, in the current conjuncture, renders redundant all projects of 'the absolute *purity* of the theological' (Schmitt 2008: 97). This extends to those projects, exemplified by Peterson, which attempt to reinvigorate the Augustinian distinction, in *The City of God* (Augustine 1998),[4] between the two kingdoms and its separation of 'the concept of "peace"' (Peterson 2011: 103) from the political order of the Roman Empire. The Augustinian peace is a purely theological concept in which 'the peace that the Christian seeks is won by no emperor, but is solely a gift of him who "is higher in all understanding"' (Peterson 2011: 105). It is also the counterpart, for Peterson, of the Greek fathers of the Church who, 'in relation to the concept of God', enabled the 'linkage of the Christian proclamation to the Roman Empire [to be] *theologically* dissolved' (Peterson 2011: 103). For Schmitt, this separation is incapable of being achieved as:

> [u]ntil the Day of Judgment, the Augustinian teaching on the two kingdoms will have to face the twofold open question: *Quis judicibat? Quis interpretabitur?* ['Who will decide? Who will interpret?'] Who answers *in concreto*, on behalf of the concrete, autonomously acting human being, the question of what is spiritual, what is worldly and what is the case

---

4 Peterson's text is dedicated to Augustine and, in the 'Prefatory Note', is invoked as the spiritual guide: 'May St. Augustine, whose impact has been felt in every spiritual and political transformation of the West, help with his prayers the readers and author of this book!' (Peterson 2011: 68).

with the *res mixtae*, which, in the interval between the first and the second coming of the Lord, constitute, as a matter of fact, the entire early existence of this spiritual-worldly, spiritual-temporal, double-creature called a *human being?*

(Schmitt 2008: 115)

The rejection of a depoliticized theology is the corollary of the rejection of a detheologized politics which, Schmitt considers, arises from Blumenberg's *The Legitimacy of the Modern Age.*

The response to Blumenberg concerns the reaffirmation of secularization as the historical process of transposition of theological categories into political categories.[5] For Schmitt, Blumenberg challenges the pertinence to modernity of two of the 'most developed constellations of "western rationalism": the Catholic *church* with its entire juridical rationality and the state of the *ius publicum Europaeum*: which was supposed to be Christian in even Thomas Hobbes' system' (Schmitt 2008: 117). In this challenge, the distinctive juridical acquisition of modernity[6] – the notion of the state and the notion of war between states – is dissolved through the Blumenbergian distinction between legality and legitimacy. The juridical, and the process of secularization, as the transposition and systematization of the theological into legal categories, thereby becomes mere legality: 'it cannot count as legitimacy' (Schmitt 2008: 118). The deflation of the juridical acquisition of modernity to mere legality is itself, for Schmitt, the expression of an underlying orientation to 'the self-empowerment of human beings and the thirst for human knowledge' (Schmitt 2008: 120). The 'pretentious and totally new, purely secular and humane humanity', which develops from a 'completely de-theologized and modern scientific closure of any political theology', leads to 'the immanent aggression of the unfettered new' (Schmitt 2008: 128, 121).[7]

In the confrontation with Peterson and Blumenberg, Schmitt insists that modernity cannot be dissociated from theology. The juridical acquisition of modernity – the juridical categories which enable the installation of a durable form of political order – become the repository of a counter tendency. This cannot resolve the chaos and evil of the human world, but which can only be sustained by this juridical acquisition as 'a *Katechon*, a power that arrests or slows down history' (Hohendahl 2008: 24).

---

5   The response derives from Blumenberg's presentation of Schmitt's *Political Theology* of 1922 as the exemplification of the flawed conception of modernity as the process of secularization.
6   For Schmitt, this juridical acquisition is co-extensive with modernity; 'it indicates the paradigm shift in modernity' (Schmitt 2008: 118).
7   The character of this immanent aggression is formulated in the four points of the final pages of the text (Schmitt 2008: 128–30).

The passage from political theology to the international legal order

The connection between Schmitt's *Three Possibilities for a Christian Conception of History* and the position and identity of the theologian of legal science becomes evident if one considers Schmitt's *The Nomos of the Earth* (Schmitt 2003a). The insistence in this text, and its concluding corollaries, upon tracing the etymological origin and derivation(s) of the Greek word *nomos* relates to the constitution of a specific form of juridical 'self-understanding'.

This juridical 'self-understanding' seeks to break with an analogous phenomenon of 'levelling' in the understanding of law and the legal order promoted by the predominant traditions of legal positivism (Kelsen 1926; 1932; 1942; 1944; 2002) and the resurgence of contemporary forms of natural law theory (centred upon notions of humanity and/or human rights). The origin of a legal order is to be understood from the essential dependence of the noun *nomos* upon the verb *neimen*:

> Such a noun is a *nomen actionis*, i.e., it indicates an action as a process whose content is defined by the verb. Which action and process is indicated by *nomos*? Quite obviously, it is the action and the process of *nemein*.
>
> (Schmitt 2003b: 326)

From this dependence, the meaning of *nomos* flows from the meaning of *nemein*, which for Schmitt contains three essential elements or aspects: appropriation, distribution and production. These are present in 'every stage of social life, in every economic order, in every period of legal history' (Schmitt 2003b: 327). The juridical expression of the original historical force, outlined in *The Three Possibilities for a Christian Conception of History*, is that of appropriation:

> Initially, there was no basic norm [contra Kelsen and the methodology of legal positivism], but a basic appropriation. No man can give, divide, and distribute without taking. Only a god, who created the world from nothing, can give and distribute without taking. It is noteworthy that the Greek *neimen*, after its meaning was broadened by good linguists to include distribution and production, even came to mean, first and foremost, appropriation, and to have the same linguistic root as the German word *nehmen*. *Nomos* then became a *nomen actionis* also for *nehmen*, and meant 'appropriation'.
>
> (Schmitt 2003c; 345–6)

The connection between the eternal and the historical is the force of appropriation which produces a history of 'the sequence of these processes' (Schmitt 2003b: 328). The presence of this connection between the eternal and the historical, within the international legal order, or, as the full title of Schmitt's work formulates it, *The Nomos of the Earth in the International Law of the Jus Publicum Europeaum*, is represented by a specific form of land appropriation which 'uproot[s] an existing spatial order and establish[es] a new *nomos* of the whole spatial sphere of neighbouring peoples' (Schmitt 2003a: 82).

The position and identity of the jurist is, then, an attempt to combine legal history and legal philosophy, in the phrase of Jacob Taubes, as 'a way of thinking in intervals [*Fristendenken*], that time itself is a duration with a definite ending' (Taubes 2013: 45). These intervals are the 'in-between-times' which Schmitt's later, *Political Theology II*, will situate within

> a single long waiting, a long interim between two simultaneities, between the coming of the Lord at the time of the Roman Caesar Augustus and the Lord's return at the end of time. Within this long interim, there emerge continually numerous new worldly interims, larger or smaller, which are literally between times.
>
> (Schmitt 2008: 86)

The intervals, from a juridical perspective, are the *nomoi* instituted by appropriation and reproduced through distribution and production.

The jurist, then, is situated as a theologian of legal science who demarcates and analyzes these intervals. The rise and fall of these *nomoi* becomes the fundamental orientation of the jurist who recognizes and experiences both the intensity of their creation and the inevitability of their decline. The attunement to the emergence of a new *nomos* is accompanied by the nostalgia for their decline.[8] Those works, which, after the Third Concluding Corollary of *Nomos* – 'The New *Nomos* of the Earth' – are the principal expression of this attunement, have as their object 'the earth, the planet on which we live, as a whole, as a globe, and [Schmitt] seek[s] to understand its global division and order' (Schmitt 2003b: 351).

This universal legal history, from which the international legal order arises, enables the present to be linked to the past and, in this linkage, to unmask and expose the suppression of this historical understanding in the existing theories of international law. The effect of unmasking – the revelation of the etymological origin and historical sequence of appropriation, division and production – is also the presentation of a fundamental and radical negativity which can never itself be negated. The intensity of each appropriation is already marked by its inevitable future decline – the *nomos*

---

8   This combination continues to underlie Schmitt's thinking until his very last essay, in 1978, entitled, 'The Legal World Revolution' (Schmitt 1987; on Schmitt's post-World War II work as 'imperial ruin gazing', see Hell 2009).

exists only as that which restrains (on the further development, see Schmitt 1958; 2012; also Ragazzoni 2013).

The limits of the jurist as a theologian of legal science

Schmitt's thought defines a particular position and identity for the jurist with regard to the international legal order. It situates the jurist as perpetually detached from a simple identification with, and thematization of the international legal order as an autonomous normative order. The question of normative coherence – the emergence and co-ordination of normative systems within an international or global legal order – is a fundamentally derivative question. To define the question of the international legal order as a question of normative coherence is to obscure its dependence upon a more originary process of global division and order.

Global division and order is spatial in the more primordial sense of its forcible constitution through appropriation: the installation of a *nomos* from which the attendant aspects of division and production then emerge and develop through their normative expression. The jurist concentrates upon, and is rendered acutely attentive to, the possibilities and potentialities of global division and order. The global is, then, the repository of these *nomoi* of spatial appropriation, division and order: it is a negative unity whose planetary surface contains the particular configurations of global division and order. The globe or the planet has no specific juridical sense other than through these possibilities and potentialities of global division and order. The legal science of the theologian of legal science is the rendering intelligible of the configuration[s] of the *nomos* of the earth. It is the parameters of this configuration which constitute the object of this legal science.

The limits and difficulties of this position and identity of the jurist become evident if one considers the origin of an international legal order as spatial appropriation. The intertwining of force and space entails its necessary personification and particularization. Schmitt will designate this etymologically, in footnote three of the First Concluding Corollary to *The Nomos of the Earth*, as the presence of *nomos* in the Homeric proper names of:

> *Amphinomos* [one who rules externally], *Ennomos* [one who rules internally], and *Eyryvnomos* [one who rules over vast expanses] [and] *Astynomos* [one who rules over a city]. All these proper names designate space and location: they indicate the concrete parcel of land that the bearer of the name has acquired through appropriation and division. In such a context, proper names have more evidential validity than do other words.
>
> (Schmitt 2003b: 325)

Force and space are also combined in the power to name a space which, for Schmitt, in the Second Concluding Corollary to *The Nomos of the Earth*, is the 'tendency to visibility, publicity and ceremony' of power inherent in 'a name and name-giving' (Schmitt 2003c: 349).

True Space – the space of a *nomos* – is the space of appropriation and command. Space begins, finds it cause, in leadership and command. Prior to this, there is only either space which has not known appropriation – *terra incognita* – or the space of the preceding *nomoi* and, theologically, the single period of long waiting initiated by 'the coming of the Lord at the time of the Roman Caesar Augustus' of *Political Theology II* (Schmitt 2008: 86).

In relation to this space of a *nomos* and the global space of order and division in which it is situated, the common cannot be conceived other than as an always already suspect universalism of humanity, humanism and human rights – a position which remains resolutely unchanged, and is forcefully repeated, in Schmitt's final article, in 1978, 'The Legal World Revolution' – or an empty legal formalism: a pure legality without a name. The object of legal science, therefore, results from a self-understanding of the jurist whose position and identity can only be one of the active and constant re-articulation or re-thematization of the history, and historical sequence, of appropriation, division and production against all the possibilities, in contemporary legal science, of their occlusion or neutralization.

Beyond the jurist as a theologian of legal science

The possibility of thinking beyond the parameters of this self-understanding of the jurist, as a theologian of legal science, is contained in the notion of the common. The conceptualization of the common, acknowledging existing work on the notion of the common (Coccoli 2012; Dardot and Laval 2014; Hardt and Negri 2011; Mattei 2012), commences from something other than the simple reaffirmation of the contemporaneity of the universalism of human rights or of a legal positivism predicated upon the primacy of international law (legal monism) over all other systems of legal norms.

A thought of the common is, here, the thought of space as that which is already common and is situated without relation to the theological period of waiting pronounced by Schmitt's *Political Theology II*. This enables space to be detached from its theological determination and for the common to become conceivable outside its reduction to the form of negative unity of Schmitt's globe. The common can then be placed into relation with a notion of justice which is not deferred and confined to 'the Lord's return at the end of time' (*Political Theology II*): the Day of Judgment. The globe becomes the common space for the immediate articulation of claims of injustice whose resolution is now the underlying purpose of the normative and institutional development of the international legal order.

The notion of the common is predicated upon the experience of injustice, and the production or creation of justice from injustice. The experience of injustice encompasses and transforms the Schmittian notions of evil and chaos as the underlying determinants of the human world. The essentially negative character of the human world is reconceived through the reorientation of the:

> articulation of negativity and subjectivity. The experience of injustice (which of necessity is a *lived experience*, which is not to say a purely *individual* experience; on the contrary, it must involve an essential dimension of 'mutuality', sharing, identifying with others, and witnessing the unbearable in the person and the figure of the other) is a necessary condition for the *recognition* of the reality and existence of institutional injustice.
>
> (Balibar 2012: 26–7)

The rearticulation of negativity and subjectivity reopens the question of the political and its relationship to a legal order. The primacy accorded to the common experience of injustice is 'the experience of the *repetition* of identical injustices, which itself testifies [to] their institutional and structural character' (Balibar 2012: 27). It is this experience of repetition which simultaneously redefines the Schmittian 'period of waiting' and displaces the combination of faith and endurance with the passage 'from the experience of injustice to the project of institutional justice itself' (Balibar 2012: 27).

In this displacement, the juridical systems of canon law and the *Jus Publicum Europeaum* cease to be co-extensive with the 'paradigm shift in modernity' (Schmitt 2008: 120) and are detached from their expression in the figure of the *katechon*. The *katechon*, as the theologically informed response to prevent the descent of the 'period of waiting' into complete chaos and evil, introduces a figure of negative thought which 'restrains evil by containing it, by keeping it, by hosting it and welcoming it, to the point of binding its own necessity to the presence of evil' (Esposito 2011: 63). The *katechon* is 'the positive *of* a negative' (Esposito 2011: 63) and has the form or structure of exclusionary inclusion of the negative. Order is maintained and endures, through the existence of the *katechon* but it is an order predicated upon 'containing iniquity'. The *katechon* protects, as protection through the restraint of evil, and, in this restraint 'the *katechon* forbids its annihilation, removing it from the final battle: the *katechon* nurtures and is nurtured by iniquity' (Esposito 2011: 64).[9] The experience of injustice

---

9 Esposito transposes the theological figure of the *katechon* into the biomedical discourse of immunization in order to characterize this figure as an example of the paradigm of immunization. The body, as the Christian body, is immunized by the *katechon* analogously to the manner in which 'the body is nurtured by the antidote necessary to its survival' (Esposito 2011: 64; see also Gunneflo 2016, Chapter 3 in this volume).

situates the thought of the negative externally to the form or structure of exclusionary inclusion; that is, the *katechon*, and the question of order, as 'the question about the legitimation of any reformation or revolution' (Schmitt 2008: 115), is no longer accorded the determinate role. For the experience of injustice – 'the reality of injustice and the necessity of justice' (Balibar 2012: 29) – 'is made *visible* and *audible* only by the "void" that the victims create or perform within the "plenitude" of the social fabric' (Balibar 2012: 29). This experience remains outside the figure of the *katechon* through its representation '*in displacements new beginnings*': 'the *forms and contents*, the *institutions of justice*, that are not imposed from outside the effort (the struggle), not "remembered" like a lost ideal but rather "discovered" like an insurrection without models' (Balibar 2012: 28).

The seemingly ineluctable historical sequence of appropriation, division and production is interrupted by the potential for claims of injustice to arise in any element of this sequence. This avoids simply characterizing appropriation as illegitimate and confining the legitimate global order to division and production. Hence, thereby avoiding Schmitt's critique, in the Concluding Corollaries of *The Nomos of the Earth*, of anti-imperialism as an essential confluence of socialism and 'classical political economy and its liberalism' (Schmitt 2003b: 331). In other words, that the question remains within, not outside this sequence, as it is one of re-distribution.

The claim of injustice is not simply and exclusively one of redistribution because the common, as a space of articulation, is constituted by the history of the development of the definition of injustice, beyond the economic claims of distributive justice, to the distinctive human claims of racial, sexual and linguistic justice and, the qualification of the primacy of the human, with the recognition of the non-human. The extension and internal diversity of the history of the definition of injustice is accompanied by the capacity for the experience of injustice to arise both within a particular part of the international legal order and between particular parts of the international legal order. The common has, in distinction from Schmitt's etymology of *nomos*, no intrinsic relation to appropriation and command. It arises from the speaking or expression of an intensity which falls outside the Schmittian logic of the proper name: it speaks of intensity as the infliction of a harm or the endurance of a suffering.

Conclusion

The contemporary relevance of Schmitt, as jurist, to legal theory is the insistence that the position of the jurist commence from a notion of negativity. The limits and difficulties of Schmitt's position concern the conception of negativity, as fundamental and radical negativity, according primacy to violence and confining law, as *nomos*, to appropriation and preservation. The limits and difficulties of Schmitt's position derive from the presumption that this negativity creates and perpetuates a history of world disorder which is itself the product of a (heterodox) theology of history.

To proceed beyond these limits and difficulties, the position and identity of the jurist is reconceived as the site for the interrogation of law in relation to the experience of injustice which, in turn, concerns the conceptualization of law and its critique.[10] In this conceptualization, the thinking beyond Schmitt recognizes the potential to transform the thought of the negative, as injustice, into the repetition of a reductive legal realism. The drift towards legal realism involves the simplification of the thought of the negative into the opposition between 'crisis and innovation' (Negri 2005: 33).[11] This opposition would underlie and structure 'the claim that law is a living and progressive superstructure of an economic, social, or, at any rate, collective structure' (Negri 2005: 35). Law, as legal realism, would be the dissolution of the experience of injustice into 'the rigidity of historical continuity': the 'product of the [legal] system's evolution' (Negri 2005: 34). The drift is interrupted by the introduction of the thought of negativity into law itself – 'justice appears as the internal lacuna, or the void of law' (Balibar 2012: 15) – in which justice is 'an internal excess: it does not affect the realm of law from the outside (from some theological or social other realm that, by nature, would be *nonlegal* or *illegal*)' (Balibar 2012: 28–9). This, in turn, conceives law in its permanent 'insufficiency' and contingency in relation to the experience of injustice as intimately intertwined with 'practices, vindications, protests, claims' (Balibar 2012: 15). It thereby demarcates itself from the contemporary discourse of governance and regulation which has become the prevailing theoretical framework for the thought of the international ordering of global space. The discourse of governance is the recognition of injustice through its management: the reformulation of the experience of harm and suffering into the 'regulation and administration of conflicts' (Balibar 2012: 28).

The insufficiency and contingency of law are the preconditions for the shift from the essentially spatial conception of Schmitt's ordering of international legal system (Schmitt 1958; 2003; 2012) to the notion of the common as the experience of injustice and the production of its possible juridical recognition. The notion of the common redefines the discourse of governance and regulation as the critique of 'traditional forms of law and sovereignty' (Negri 2010: 16), which prefigures, but cannot articulate,

---

10 Negri refers to this as the problem of 'the epistemological protocols of critique' (Negri 2005: 41).
11 The recognition of this potential for the drift towards legal realism also bypasses the potential for the Schmittian characterization of legal realism as an aspect of the 'progressive use of three freedoms (neutrality, use and objectivity [*Wert-Ververtungs-und-Bewertungsfreiheit*])' (Schmitt 2008: 129).

a notion of the common (Negri 2010: 20). The passage to the notion of the common and its 'law' requires the fundamental reconsideration of the adequacy of existing legal categories which, in turn, places into question, the interrelationship of the jurist, injustice and the international legal order.

Bibliography

Arvidsson, M. (2016) 'From Teleology to Eschatology: The Katechon and the Political Theology of the International Law of Belligerent Occupation', Chapter 15 in M. Arvidsson, L. Brannstrom and P. Minkkinen (eds), *The Contemporary Relevance of Carl Schmitt: Law, Politics, Theology.* Abingdon: Routledge.

Augustine (1998) *The City of God against the Pagans* [426AD]. Trans. R. W. Dyson. Cambridge: Cambridge University Press.

Balibar, E. (2012) 'Justice and Equality: A Political Dilemma? Pascal, Plato, Marx', p. 9–32, in E. Balibar, S. Mezzadra and R. Samaddar (eds) *The Borders of Justice.* Philadelphia, PA: Temple University Press.

Blumenberg, H. (1999) *The Legitimacy of the Modern Age* [1966]. Trans. R. M. Wallace. Cambridge, MA: MIT Press.

Coccoli, L. (2012) 'Idee del Comune. Un quadro storico-filosofico', p. 31–42, in M. R. Marella (ed.), *Ottre il Pubblico e il Privato. Per un dritto dei beni communi.* Verona: Ombre Corte.

Dardot, P. and C. Laval (2014) *Commun. Essai sur la révolution au XXIe siècle.* Paris: La Découverte.

de Benoist, A. (2013) *Carl Schmitt Today: Terrorism, Just War, and the State of Emergency.* London: Arktos Media.

Esposito, R. (2011) *Immunitas: The Protection and Negation of Life.* Trans. Z. Hanafi. Cambridge: Polity.

Falk, H. (2016) '"Im Kampf um Rom": Carl Schmitt's Critique of Rudolph Sohm and the Post-Secular Turn', Chapter 12 in M. Arvidsson, L. Brannstrom and P. Minkkinen (eds), *The Contemporary Relevance of Carl Schmitt: Law, Politics, Theology.* Abingdon: Routledge.

Galli, C. (2010a) *Political Spaces and Global War.* Trans. E. Fay. Minneapolis, MN: Minnesota University Press.

Galli, C. (2010b) 'Carl Schmitt and the Global Age', *CR: The New Centennial Review,* Vol. 10, No. 2: 1–25.

Gunneflo, M. (2016) 'Political Community in Carl Schmitt's International Legal Thinking', Chapter 3 in M. Arvidsson, L. Brännström and P. Minkkinen (eds), *The Contemporary Relevance of Carl Schmitt. Law, Politics, Theology.* Abingdon: Routledge.

Hardt, M. and A. Negri (2011) *Commonwealth.* Cambridge, MA: Harvard University Press.

Hell, J. (2009) '*Katechon*: Carl Schmitt's Imperial Theology and the Ruins of the Future', *Germanic Review,* Vol. 84, No. 4: 283–326.

Hohendahl, P. U. (2008) 'Political Theology Revisited: Carl Schmitt's Postwar Reassessment', *Konturen,* Vol. 1: 1–28.

Hooker, W. (2009) *Carl Schmitt's International Thought: Order and Orientation.* Cambridge: Cambridge University Press.

Kelsen, H. (1926) 'Les rapports du système entre le droit interne et le droit international public', *Recueil des cours de l'Académie de droit international de La Haye*, Vol. 14: 227–32.
Kelsen, H. (1932) 'Théorie générale du droit international public. Problèmes choisis', *Recueil des cours de l'Académie de droit international de La Haye*, Vol. 42: 117–352.
Kelsen, H. (1942) *Law and Peace In International Relations. The Oliver Wendell Holmes Lectures 1940–41*. Cambridge, MA: Harvard University Press.
Kelsen, H. (1944) *Peace Through Law*. Chapel Hill, NC: University of North Carolina Press.
Kelsen, H. (2002) *Introduction to the Problems of Legal Theory* [1934]. Trans. B.L. Paulson and S.L. Paulson. Oxford: Oxford University Press.
Kervégan, J.-F. (2011) *Que faire de Carl Schmitt?* Paris: Gallimard.
Legg, S. (ed.) (2011) *Spatiality, Sovereignty and Carl Schmitt: Geographies of the Nomos*. London: Routledge.
Löwith, K. (1949) *Meaning in History: The Theological Implications of the Philosophy of History*. Chicago, IL: Chicago University Press.
Marder, M. (2012) *Groundless Existence: The Political Ontology of Carl Schmitt*. London: Continuum.
Mattei, U. (2012) *Beni comuni. Un manifesto*. Rome: Laterza.
Meier, H. (1994) 'The Philosopher as Enemy: On Carl Schmitt's *Glossarium*', *Graduate Faculty of Philosophy Journal*, Vol.17, No. 1–2: 325–32.
Negri, A. (2005) 'Postmodern Global Governance and the Critical Legal Project', *Law and Critique*, Vol. 16, No. 1: 27–46.
Negri, A. (2010) 'The Law of the Common', *Finnish Yearbook of International Law*, Vol. 21: 16–25.
Odysseos, L. and F. Petito (2008) *The International Political Thought of Carl Schmitt: Terror, Liberal War and the Crisis of Global Order*. Abingdon: Routledge.
Ojakangas, M. (2006) *A Philosophy of Concrete Life: Carl Schmitt and the Political Thought of Late Modernity*. 2nd edn. Bern: Peter Lang.
Peterson, E. (2011) 'Monotheism as a Political Problem: A Contribution to the History of Political Theology in the Roman Empire' [1935], p. 68–105, in E. Peterson, *Theological Tractates*. Trans. M. J. Hollerich. Redwood City, CA: Stanford University Press.
Ragazzoni, D. (2013) 'Carl Schmitt and Global (Dis)Order at the Twilight of the *Jus Publicum Europeaum*', *Journal of Intellectual History and Political Thought*, No. 2: 170–91.
Rawls, J. (2005) *Political Liberalism*. New York: Columbia University Press.
Rech, W. (2016) 'Eschatology and Existentialism: Carl Schmitt's Historical Understanding of International Law and Politics', Chapter 10 in M. Arvidsson, L. Brannstrom and P. Minkkinen (eds), *The Contemporary Relevance of Carl Schmitt: Law, Politics, Theology*. Abingdon: Routledge.
Ruschi, F. (2008) 'Space, Law and Power in Carl Schmitt', *Jura Gentium. Journal of Philosophy of International Law and Global Politics*, Vol. 4: 44–53.
Ruschi, F. (2012) *Questioni di spazio. La terra, il diritto secondo Carl Schmitt*. Torino: Giappichelli.
Schmitt, C. (1958) 'Gespräch über den neuen Raum', p. 263–82, in A. Miaja de la Muela and C. Trelles (eds), *Estudios de derecho internacional. Homenaje al profesor*

Camilo Barcia Trelles. Santiago de Compostela: Universidad de Santiago.
Schmitt, C. (1987) 'The Legal World Revolution' [1978], *Telos*, No. 72: 73–89.
Schmitt, C. (1991) *Glossarium: Aufzeichnungen der Jahre 1947–1951*. Berlin: Duncker and Humblot.
Schmitt, C. (2001a) 'State, Movement, People: The Triadic Structure of Political Unity' [1933], p. 3–52, in C. Schmitt, *State, Movement, People; The Triadic Structure of Political Unity; The Question of Legality*. Trans. S. Draghici. Oregon: Plutarch.
Schmitt, C. (2001b) *Four Articles 1931–1938*. Trans. S. Draghici. Oregon, UT: Plutarch.
Schmitt, C. (2002) *Ex Captivitate Salus: Erfahrungen der Zeit 1945/47* [1950]. Berlin: Duncker and Humblot.
Schmitt, C. (2003a) *The Nomos of the Earth in the International Law of the Jus Publicum Europaeum* [1950]. Trans. G. L. Ulmen. New York: Telos.
Schmitt, C. (2003b) 'Appropriation/Distribution/Production: An Attempt to Determine from *Nomos* the Basic Questions of Every Social and Economic Order' [1953], p. 324–35, in C. Schmitt, *The Nomos of the Earth in the International Law of the Jus Publicum Europaeum*. Trans. G. L. Ulmen. New York: Telos.
Schmitt, C. (2003c) 'Nomos-Nahme-Name' [1957], p. 336–50, in C. Schmitt, *The Nomos of the Earth in the International Law of the Jus Publicum Europaeum*. Trans. G. L. Ulmen. New York: Telos.
Schmitt, C. (2008) *Political Theology II: The Myth of the Closure of Any Political Theology* [1970]. Trans. M. Hoelzl and G. Ward. Cambridge: Polity.
Schmitt, C. (2009) 'Three Possibilities for a Christian Conception of History' [1950], *Telos*, No. 147: 167–70.
Schmitt, C. (2011a) 'The Turn to the Discriminating Concept of War' [1937], p. 30–74, in C. Schmitt, *Writings on War*. Trans. T. Nunan. Cambridge: Polity.
Schmitt, C. (2011b) 'The *Großraum* Order of International Law with a Ban on Intervention for Spatially Foreign Powers: A Contribution to the Concept of *Reich* in International Law' [1939–1941], p. 75–124, in C. Schmitt, *Writings on War*. Trans. T. Nunan. Cambridge: Polity.
Schmitt, C. (2012) *Gespräch über die Macht und den Zugang zum Machthaber* [1954]. Stuttgart: Klett-Cotta.
Taubes, J. (2013) *To Carl Schmitt: Letters and Reflections*. Trans. K. Tribe. New York: Columbia University Press.
Weiss, K. (1933) *Der christliche Epimetheus*. Berlin: Edwin Runge.

Chapter 15

From teleology to eschatology

The *katechon* and the political theology of the international law of belligerent occupation

Matilda Arvidsson

Introduction

This chapter seeks to address the existence of a paradox within the international law of belligerent occupation (hereafter the laws of occupation) – the coexistence of preservation and transformation – through an enquiry into the political theology of international law and that of occupation. The chapter draws on Carl Schmitt's famous claim that 'all significant concepts of the modern theory of the state are secularized theological concepts' (Schmitt 2005a: 36), suggesting that the field of laws of occupation embodies the figure of the *katechon* within the eschatology of international law. While the chapter does not share Schmitt's eschatological vision – neither his theological and consequently nor his political – Schmitt's claim is helpful in thinking about the form and structure of the laws of occupation as part of that of international law.[1] The reading involves an enquiry into the wider theological implications of the embodiment of the katechonic figure: how we must not understand international law in terms of teleology (Koskenniemi 2012) but as an eschatology with an *eschaton* at its horizon, a proximate end of the world, and law's political force as bound to faith, promise and redemption pursued as a bond embedded within international law (Beard 2007; Noll 2014).

The chapter starts with the figure of the *katechon*. It then moves to consider Schmitt's employment of the *katechon* as it figures in the eschatology of his theology and in his scholarship. After briefly noting on Schmitt and the laws of occupation a reading of the field of law is pursued. Drawing on other fields and disciplines the essay aims to contribute to debates on the laws of occupation (for example, Stirk 2004; 2005; 2009; Bhuta 2010; Cohen 2012; Gunneflo 2014) as well as general international law (for

---

1 The intrinsic Christian character of international law, as well as the development and theoretization of the laws of occupation as pursued within an emphatically western Christian hemisphere and ideology is well established and deliberated elsewhere (for example, Beard 2007; Arvidsson 2010; Arvidsson 2012) why the suggestion in this essay focuses on Schmitt's claim through an analogy.

example, Koskenniemi 2004; Orford 2011; McLouglin 2013; Noll 2014; 2015) concerning the contemporary relevance of Schmitt's scholarship.

The *katechon*

The figure of the *katechon* appears in St Paul's eschatological teachings in the Christian Bible, the Second Letter to the Thessalonians (2:6–7) as 'that which withholds' and 'he who withholds'. The two appearances often translate as 'the *katechon*' or 'the restrainer'. The Biblical context is one of eschatological expectation: St Paul instructs the Thessalonians on the *parousia*, the second coming of Christ and the fulfillment of time and promise of redemption.[2] Within this eschatology the *katechon* appears as a restraining force holding back *anomos* – Antichrist or 'the man of lawlessness' (2 Thess 2:3) and 'the secret power of lawlessness already at work' – until the *katechon* is 'taken out of the way' (2 Thess 2:7). The *katechon* is thus a provisional figure and only after its removal will 'the lawless one be revealed' in its full power and the Lord return in splendour to fulfill the promise (2 Thess 2:8).

Theologians approach the *katechon* as an 'enduring exegetical enigma' (Nicholl 2008: 225) and exegesis from St Augustine (Augustine 2003) and onwards fail at providing a conclusive answer as to the *katechon's* identity. Interpretations include the order of the Roman Empire, the Catholic Church and Christian faith as such (see, for example, Peerbolte 1997: 141–4; Nicholl 2008: 30–1). It is a figure commonly understood as lending itself to embodiment in the world throughout its historical progression towards the End. Common to theological and philosophical interpretations is the identification of a paradox: battling *anomos* and working to uphold a *status quo* within an enduring eschatological 'now' the *katechon* is neither empowered to defeat *anomos*, nor can it deliver redemption. It rather 'embodies the principle of defense from evil through its preliminary internalization' (Esposito 2011: 11), thus temporarily governing the world and progression of time (*chronos*) until the *eschaton*: the End. The figure of the *katechon* defends and deals with the concrete and worldly here and now; our human – and indeed corporeal – condition, and the political of each given moment until the return and fulfilment of the promise it ultimately serves and simultaneously infinitely defers. The *katechon* functions as an exceptional and provisional form of governance, which enables as well as explains the prolongation and progression of time (*chronos*) within time

---

2   *Parousia* literally means 'presence' and does not imply a second messianic event but the second coming of Christ. The *parousia* in St Paul's teaching is not another *kairos* but, rather, the messianic already present by ways of *kairos* which does not coincide with a specific instance of chronos but which 'seizes hold of this instance and brings it forth to fulfillment' (Agamben 2005: 71).

(*kairos*) (on *kairos*, see, for example, Agamben 2005: 70). Without the *katechon*, there can be no world as we know it. Conversely, with the *katechon* at work in the world, *anomos* cannot become unleashed in its full power, nor can the day of the Lord arrive and the promise of redemption be fulfilled. For the latter to take place, the *katechon* must be taken out of the way. The *katechon* thus functions within a larger system of faith and order to bring into check two terrifying states of instability and entropy: that of *anomos* and that of the *eschaton* (Virno 2008: 60).

The *katechon* in Schmitt's political theology

The *katechon* figures prominently both in Schmitt's world and in contemporary commentary on his scholarship (for example, Fornari 2010; Meyer *et al.* 2012; Prozorov 2012; Falk 2014; Noll 2014; 2015; see also Langford and Bryan 2016, Chapter 14 in this volume). In *Glossarium*, Schmitt maintains that the *katechon* has occupied his thoughts since 1932 (Schmitt 1991: 80). However, the figure enters significantly into Schmitt's writing in the post-World War II setting (for example, Schmitt 1958; 1991; 2003; 2008; 2009), lending its form to his thinking explicitly (for example, Schmitt 2003), as well as implicitly (for example, Schmitt 2007; 2011; Meyer *et al.* 2012.). Schmitt exegesis tends to mystify the *katechon* and Schmitt's understanding of it (for example, Hell 2009). However, although it is certainly true that Schmitt argues outside of theological orthodoxy (Meier 1998:158–64; Hohendahl 2008; Prozorov 2012) – Schmitt is not shy of lending from heretical as well as Lutheran and Catholic theological sources so as to ground his Catholic theological identity – he is far from obscure in his employment of the *katechon*.

For Schmitt the *katechon* restrains *anomos* and keeps the world from plunging towards its End. It explains and instils meaning for the Christian in this world and prevents apostasy. Schmitt's world is not haunted by eschatological anxieties related to an afterlife. Rather, it is an emphatically worldly world as opposed to a utopian 'paradise on earth' (Schmitt 1996; Meyer *et al.* 2012: 689). Schmitt worries about 'eschatological paralysis' (Schmitt 2009: 3; 2003: 60): that we (as Christians) might lose our sense of historical meaningfulness *in this world* and thus lose our dedication to the political as we are awaiting the proximate *parousia*. Schmitt's *katechon* functions as an antidote: 'I believe in the *katechon*', Schmitt maintains, 'for me he is the sole possibility for a Christian to understand history and find it meaningful' (Schmitt 1991: 68; see also Maschke 2005: 852–3; Noll 2015). While the Christian in Schmitt's understanding must always put his faith in the historical progression towards the *parousia* and the End the *katechon* 'forges a link between eschatological faith and the consciousness of "historicity"' (Meier 1998: 162; Schmitt 2009). Schmitt embraces the *katechon* because once embodied the *katechon* brings about a concrete order

(Prozorov 2012: 486), which holds back the end of (Christian) history (Schmitt 2003: 59–66). The God of Schmitt's theology is not present and at work in this world through its inhabitants, in particular the Christians. A negative anthropology like Schmitt's would not be able to invest humans with such agency. It is against this void of positive forces active in the world that the *katechon* emerges as a form capable of containing evil and invigorating faith. Schmitt transforms, as it were, the eschatology of Christianity into a 'katechology' where the role of the Church is to contain *anomos* and infinitely postpone rather than preach and embrace the End (Björk 2012: 153). Schmitt in this vein transposes the role of the Church to ground (the Christian doctrine of) state power (Prozorov 2012: 483) as a katechonic embodiment to which he attaches the modern, secular nation state (see, for example, Schmitt 2003: 59–62; see also Falk 2014: 228). Historically, Schmitt identifies the *Respublica Christiana* as an example of the repetitive rise and fall of empires embodying the katechonic figure (Schmitt 2003: 59–60; Hell 2009), appearing within history as 'a complement and correction of "the genuine, ever present, and necessary eschatology"' (Meier 1998: 162).

Schmitt's negative anthropology (for example, Schmitt 1996: 58–68; 2008) is thus situated within an eschatological vision which traces the original sin towards humanity's proximate end, finding a temporary refuge and faith in a figure that restrains and contains rather than supersedes and annihilates its negative. In this, Schmitt leaves the question of redemption unanswered or at least out of sight and emphatically out of this world. This is not a *lapsus* of Schmitt's but rather follows from his personal and heretical theological position, one in which the Christ has an uneasy position.

Schmitt and the international law of belligerent occupation

Before turning to the reading of the laws of occupation as embodying the katechonic figure, I offer a few notes on Schmitt's ventures into the former (Schmitt 2003; see also 1991; 2005b; 1940; Rasch 2008). Schmitt's analysis of the field of law is brief and suggestive (Schmitt 2003: 199–209). Being an exception by and though law (Benvenisti 2012: vii), as well as an exceptional form of non-sovereign international territorial governance, the laws of occupation lend themselves well to Schmitt, as well as to contemporary Schmittian analysis, especially in terms of grounding non-sovereign authority (for example, Schmitt 2003; Stirk 2004; Bhuta 2005; Cohen 2012; Gunneflo 2014).

Schmitt approvingly invokes the field of law as the 'last achievement of the international law of the *jus publicum Europaeum*' (Schmitt 2003: 207), emerging as a legal concept distinct from *debellatio*, regime change and change of sovereignty though constitutional change (Schmitt 2003: 205).

Schmitt finds 'striking parallels' between the laws of occupation and the state of exception in domestic constitutional law (Schmitt 2003: 206–7; see also Benvenisti 2012: vii: 'Occupation is a state of exception for international law'). He does not expand on these parallels but the analogy pursued in *Political Theology* on the theological figure of the exception is noteworthy: that of the miracle (Schmitt 2005a: 36). The nature of sovereignty is put to the forth in both analyses. During belligerent occupation, Schmitt contends, we are faced by 'effective state power over a foreign state area ... against the will of the foreign sovereign without a change of sovereignty' (Schmitt 2003: 206). Legal title is curiously drawn directly from international law and establishes, Schmitt points out, a direct political relationship between occupier and occupied. This relationship is defined by, on the one hand, protection afforded by the occupying power and, on the other hand, obedience by the occupied people (Schmitt 2003: 206; Bhuta 2005: 727). Belligerent occupation in Schmitt's analysis becomes a moment of 'undifferentiated, self-defining power' (Stirk 2004: 534).

The contemporary international law of belligerent occupation embodying the katechonic figure

The law of Schmitt's analysis is by and large the law of the current: belligerent occupations are as a matter of law defined, formed and structured primarily by the Hague Regulation of 1907. The relation between occupier and occupied is further set out in the Fourth Geneva Convention of 1949 and its First Additional Protocol of 1977, pursuant to the protection of the individual. Specific United Nation Security Council Resolutions details the form of governance for specific cases of – although far from all – belligerent occupations (see, for example, United Nations Security Council Resolution 1483 on the administration of the belligerent occupation of Iraq). Customary international law proscribes additional legal norms.

The laws of occupation are configured through a particular kind of temporality. Its time is that of *kairos* rather than *chronos*, which is to say that it operates within law's time (*chronos*) yet is configured as apart from while still residing within it. International law, through its universality, claims to apply everywhere and to all times, while that of belligerent occupation applies in specific times and territories only (Article 42, the Hague Regulation), temporarily suspending international and domestic laws alike. It is a time that has its own notion of an enduring 'now'. This 'now' has a beginning, as defined in Article 42, the Hague Regulation, fixed and fixable in terms of time within history (*chronos*). Although the return of sovereign rule marks the end of occupation, law cannot fix such an end in terms of time (*chronos*) (see, for example, Ferraro 2012). The time of the laws of occupation rather stretches and bends towards itself in a perpetual repetition of the enduring 'now'. The temporal configuration of the law can thus be understood as neither static nor teleological and taking place in a material sense yet being irreducible to historicity.

This time paradoxically hosts two opposing notions: preservation and transformation. Preservation or 'the conservationist principle' (Benvenisti 2008: 632) is a notion and a direction of withholding, remaining, restraining and keeping a *status quo* (Glahn 1957: 27–37; Nabulsi 2005: 6; Bhuta 2005: 723; Fox 2008: 235). This notion is closely aligned with that of the restraining force of the *katechon* and the function of containment of the negative. Following the notion of preservation, the occupation power is to act as a 'temporary custodian' (Fox 2005: 199) in and of occupied territories, temporarily governing occupied territory and people until the return of sovereignty. The notion of preservation also stipulates that the occupying power must refrain from taking advantage of its power position in relation to the occupied territory and people made vulnerable by it. The role of the occupying power is to 'restore, and ensure, as far as possible, public order and safety, while respecting, unless absolutely prevented, the laws in force in the country' (Article 43, the Hague Regulation). To this end, the law maintains an equilibrium which contains – restrains as well as legalizes – the lethal force of the belligerent power(s) as well as the ambition to 'liberate' peoples from governing themselves or being governed by 'evil powers' in the form of persons or institutions such as religious, legal, economical, or political systems. The notion of preservation and its *status quo* principle is firmly emphasized in international legal scholarship (Fox 2012). Transformation, on the other hand, aligns itself with teleology and the fulfilment of international law's promise (Roberts 2006; Fox 2008: 228–34; Stirk 2009: 203–26). It often addresses pressing humanitarian concerns of the 'here and now', and it aims to work with the legal form provided by the laws of occupation to align it with international secular, legal, political and economic standards of the day. The notion of transformation is embedded in the positive obligations directed at the occupation power (for example, Article 43, the Hague Regulation, and Article 64, Paragraph 2, the Geneva Convention). It is also embraced in contemporary discourses on the application of human rights in occupied territories and the demand for processes of democratization and economic, political and legal development during occupation. The notion of transformation brings the laws of occupation closer to general international law than that of preservation does. Transformation is thus sometimes seen by international legal scholars as a means to update a seemingly outdated field of law. Yet, it is misleading to think of preservation as the old principle and transformation as an innovative means to pursue international law's ends (for example, Fox 2008: 228–34; Stirk 2009: 203–26). Apart from (mis)reading transformation as a modern phenomenon, existing interpretations of the two notions often aim at reading one or the other as being the 'true' intention of the law: its *telos*.

Transformation can be understood as the notion which the *katechon* as a form of governance has always had to encompass given its emplacement within *chronos*, within the world. If the notion of preservation takes the laws of occupation apart from international law's narrative of progress – and in particular the progression of time – the notion of transformation brings it into relation to the very same. Drawing on Schmitt's friend theologian Erik Peterson's criticism of Schmitt's political theology (Peterson 2011), an analogy can be made between the Christian (Catholic) Church as a katechonic figure and that of the laws of occupation. Just as the Church in Peterson's reading *acts in the world* and therefore must take part in worldly problems, the katechonic figure of the laws of occupation acts within the practical reality of belligerent occupation: it must face the problems specific to that situation and time. However the Church is *not of this world* but draws its particular political force from its other-than-this-worldliness, from it being part of a divine order (see Peterson 2011; Hoelzl and Ward 2008: 9; Björk 2012: 157, 160). Similarly, the laws of occupation are not borne out of specific belligerent occupations – although it must be noted that praxis is an important feature of customary international law of belligerent occupation – but draws its particular force from its emplacement within international law as an order which legitimizes its existence and which purpose it ultimately serve.

From this, it follows that the katechonic figure, and its embodiment, does not only imply a restraining force in the world, an exceptional temporary form of governance, the coexistence of paradoxical notions of preservation and transformation and containment of the negative, but importantly, that the figure for its particular force relies on promise, faith and a bond binding subjects in expectation of deliverance in a time/space which lies beyond the 'now'.

To feel ambiguous about the nature of the laws of occupation and the katechonic configuration of the law is to join a significant strand of critical thinkers. Indeed, how are we to conceive of a field of law which contains a seemingly overpowering, harmful and inhumane force, but which does not aim to overthrow or annihilate it? The law embraces the often abhorrent and exceptional, although not anomalous (Dinstein 2009: 1), state of belligerent occupation and makes it lawful. To respond to the field of law and its inherent paradoxical notions without arguing the primacy of preservation – often part of the criticism pursued from the left – or to promote transformation through the implementation of human rights in particular – a common basis for liberal interventions – is to join the few. The risk of eschatological paralysis – which is Schmitt's concern – is embedded in arguments for a strict adherence to the principle of *status quo*. Yet, there is an equally haunting risk of the normalization of the legal form of belligerent occupation, of turning the exception into a permanent rule in occupied as well as in other territories, when arguing for substantive transformational measures (Benvenisti 2012: 79). Both lines of argument risk embracing the *katechon* as a figure in which we are to put our faith: law as the means to contain disorder and chaos, lawlessness and 'evil'. Law in this vein is reduced to a katechology without an eschatology, a figure taken apart from the order it serves and out of which it is born.

Emplacing the katechonic figure within the eschatology of international law

The reading of the laws of occupation pursued in this chapter is one which understands the pervasive coexistence of preservation and transformation as being that which signifies the particular configuration of the law: its embodiment of the figure that encompasses both notions; that is, the *katechon*. It is a reading aiming to understand the laws of occupation and its contemporary scholarly debates beyond mere apology and utopia (Koskenniemi 2006) and beyond mere teleology (Koskenniemi 2012).

With Schmitt we understand the laws of occupation as an exception within the international legal order, one which might be productively diagnosed as part of a political theology and as an exception through which the norm might be studied (Schmitt 2005a: 15). In contrast to readings of political theology which investigate particular legal *concepts* (or rather *Begriffe*) often dislocated from their theological context (see Slotte 2010), this chapter finds it necessary to consider the emplacement of the laws of occupation as a katechonic figure within the wider political theology of international law. Such a consideration brings forth the questions of faith, force, redemption, the Christ and the coming of the End as intrinsic to international law as opposed to a concern primarily with and for the *katechon* at work in the world. The latter would be a concern closely aligned with that of Schmitt's. The chapter thus embraces Gregor Noll's observation that any argument for the existence of universal norms, such as international law, 'presupposes a doctrine on the meaning of history. In other words, it presupposes eschatology' (Noll 2014: para. 26).

To say that the laws of occupation embody the figure of the *katechon* is to suggest that the field of law operates in relation to an *anomos* without which it cannot exist and has no purpose. The suggestion might appear obvious and simplistic. Yet, if we consider the historical emergence of the legal concept as, for example, Schmitt does in *The Nomos of the Earth* (Schmitt 2003; see also Bhuta 2005; Benvenisti 2008), we find it to be an outcome of state praxis. Historically, the state praxis through which the specific legal concept of belligerent occupation emerged, has not only served to contain abhorrent acts of belligerents – although the argument has certainly been prominently pronounced (see, for example, Nabulsi 2005): state praxis can also be understood as an articulation of a desire for a legal form through which non-sovereign governance of territories is possible to pursue as precisely *legal*. State praxis, and the way in which the legal concept of belligerent occupation historically emerges from it, can be understood as an articulation of the desire for (to decide on and in) the exception of international law. Consequently, the *katechon* lends itself as a legal form to contain the *anomos* and yet, at the same time, its form emplaces it in a theological economy of desire. To embody the *katechon* is to govern – and indeed to contain – the bodies and souls of the masses in an unmediated relation sanctioned within a divine eschatological legal order. To perform such a figure is a powerful and at certain junctures highly desirable mission. Belligerent occupation is not a 'state of nature' but a historical invention *de facto* as well as *de jure* closely aligned with the emergence of the nation state within a European space and Christian ideology as these relate to their 'Other'. The embodiment of the figure of the *katechon* as a powerful position to perform easily lends itself as an end in itself. Why, we might ask ourselves from the position of the occupying power, unleash the *anomos* in its full power and further the end of our own time and power if law lends itself to us as a way of furthering it within history? The time to exercise this power is ours if we literally take territory apart in an act of belligerency, if we refrain from entering into a mediated, even democratic and/or equal, relationship with the people we govern.

The *katechon* of the Second Letter to the Thessalonians restrains the *anomos* whereas its full power and ultimate destruction is postponed to a final battle coinciding with the return of the Christ. Theological as well as philosophical interpretations keep those functions apart: the force that restrains – the *katechon* – and another and greater force that will ultimately defeat the *anomos*. The greater force is that of the Christ in which we put our faith as Christians. It is adamant to keep these two powers apart when contemplating the *katechon*. It is also instructive to remember where faith lies. The Biblical *anomos* translates as 'lawlessness', 'the lawless one' or 'Antichrist' whereas the *katechon* translates as 'the restrainer' – *not as the Christ*. The implications of this for law and jurisprudence must not be overlooked. The *katechon* promises a provisional governance for the 'now', but the greater force – that of the Christ – promises individual redemption through a logic of submission, faith and a personal bond through which the Christian as well as the legal subject is formed (Beard 2007: 7, 18–22). The power of that bond, as Beard makes clear, lends to international law its alluring and persistent force (Bead 2007: 181). The bond reaches beyond the world as we know it, beyond the End, and leashes the heart of each person to the power that can overcome and not only contain the *anomos*. It taps into the desire for redemption and it infuses faith. This faith resides with the 'after' the End whereas action is hosted in the enduring 'now'. The particular power with which the faithful is able to act in this world draws in this way, as Peterson has argued (Peterson 2011), on hopes and expectations of that which lies beyond this world.

In embodying the figure of the *katechon*, the laws of occupation do not deliver any redemptive promise beyond the 'now' for people under belligerent occupation. Instead, it superimposes a temporary and emphatically non-democratic form of governance while an end and a return of, or a turn towards, law and sovereignty in its full sense is awaited. This locates the promise of international law and the repository of faith *elsewhere* and *elsewhen* than with the katechonic figure, as seen from the perspective of the occupied. While faith in the *katechon* might serve as an antidote to eschatological paralysis and can invigorate political struggle and resistance during occupation, such faith simultaneously invests the *katechon* with a power intrinsic to the other and greater force of international law's eschatology. The (Christian) bond of submission, faith and promise of redemption translates into a desire for and faith in legal entitlements and legal rights accessible *elsewhere* and *elsewhen* in and through international law – infinitely differed yet eschatologically present though international law's promise – not the least pronounced during belligerent occupation as the right to self-determination and individual human rights. The political force of international law thus resides neither with the military power of the occupation forces nor with the figure of the *katechon* but, rather, with the power of a bond of faith and promise of fulfillment in that which lies beyond the End (see also Noll 2014: para. 27).

The End

International law is often thought of and argued in terms of teleology (Koskenniemi 2012), closely aligned with notions such as progress, development and prosperity for all of human kind (Beard 2007). The laws of occupation appear as an anomaly within such teleological thinking and use of legal argument. It is the exception of international law which instils an enduring 'now' governed by a provisional and spatially delimited legal order. It does not deliver progress or prosperity but instils, instead, a non-democratic and non-sovereign arrestment of time and territory.

To read the laws of occupation as katechonic locates the law as embracing the paradoxical coexistence of preservation and transformation. The laws of occupation serve to restrain and contain – and thus embrace and internalize – the *anomos* within an equilibrium of *status quo*. It does not serve to supersede the *anomos* but feeds from it to nourish its own existence. At the same time, the law, taking place within history, must and does relate to the progression of time (*chronos*) within time (*kairos*) through embracing transformation. The figure of the *katechon* thus provides a form, historically as well as conceptually, for the laws of occupation as an exception and its temporal configuration as one which explains its taking place in time and history (*chronos*) and yet being a 'now' (*kairos*) with a temporality of its own. The theological emplacement of the figure of the *katechon* as part of international law's eschatology reminds us that its figuration is rendered legitimate precisely because of its relation to *a power which it is not* but whose proximate return the continuous existence of the laws of occupation announces yet infinitely defers. Emplacing the katechonic figure within international law's political theology reminds us that there is no *katechon* without an eschatology and there is no eschatology without an *eschaton*: an End. The theological emplacement of the laws of occupation also positions the promise of redemption as located *elsewhere* and *elsewhen* within international law's eschatology.

This chapter has invoked Schmitt not without certain concerns. Schmitt's thinking and employment of the *katechon* as well as his notes on the laws of occupation are topical and it has proven fruitful to draw on Schmitt's claim on political theology, although in a rather unfaithful way. Faith, promise, redemption and the implications of the End are *topoi* which Schmitt's political theology does not provide a particularly helpful platform for to think through. But perhaps it is precisely in that realization that something important can be learned about the problem of being a theologian of legal science, another concern of Schmitt's (see Langford and Bryan 2016, Chapter 14 in this volume). What is the purpose of one's exegesis as a jurist? How does one embody containment, faith, desire, and promise as a legal scholar? Where does one's faith lie if we, unlike Schmitt, find that we cannot have faith in the figure of the *katechon*?

Perhaps the belief in a figure which defers the End is the true role of the jurist that Schmitt both identifies and identifies with: to tend to and believe in the *katechon* so that we, as jurists, in the enduring 'now' might repress the implications of our own proximate carnal Ends, the end of anthropocentrism, and the end of our physical world, while still finding meaning in the historical progression of time. Or, better still, to refrain from pronouncing hope and faith. Or, rather to have no faith at all, but to carry on as if.

Bibliography

Agamben, G. (2005) *The Time that Remains: A Commentary on the Letter to the Romans.* Trans. P. Dailey. Redwood City, CA: Stanford University Press.

Arvidsson, M. (2010) '"How long is "now"? The Christian eschatological concept of time within international laws of, in, and after war: a critique of law and of our Nordic societies', p. 365–90, in L. Christoffersen, S. Andersen, and K. Modéer (eds), *Law and Religion in the 21st Century – Nordic Perspectives: New Life in the Ruins – Pluralistic renewal in the Lutheran setting.* Copenhagen: DJØF.

Arvidsson, M. (2012) 'Ockupationsrättens politiska teologi', p. 199–222, in J. Wittrock and H. Falk (eds), *Vän eller fiende? En antologi om Carl Schmitts politiska tänkande.* Göteborg: Daidalos.

Augustine, St. (2003) *The City of God* [5th century AD]. Trans. H. Bettenson. London: Penguin.

Beard, J. (2007) *The Political Economy of Desire: International Law, Development and the Nation State*. Abingdon: Routledge-Cavendish.

Benvenisti, E. (2008) 'The Origins of the Concept of Belligerent Occupation', *Law and History Review*, Vol. 26, No. 3: 621–48.

Benvenisti, E. (2012) *The International Law of Occupation*. 2nd edn. Oxford: Oxford University Press.

Bhuta, N. (2005) 'The Antinomies of Transformative Occupation', *European Journal of International Law*, Vol. 16, No. 4: 721–40.

Bhuta, N. (2010) 'New Modes and Orders: The Difficulties of a Jus Post Bellum of Constitutional Transformation', *University of Toronto Law Journal*, Vol. 60, No. 3: 799–854.

Björk, M. (2012) 'Att älska sin fiende', p. 145–72, in J. Wittrock and H. Falk (eds), *Vän eller fiende? En antologi om Carl Schmitts politiska tänkande*. Göteborg: Daidalos.

Cohen, J. L. (2012) *Globalization and Sovereignty: Rethinking Legality, Legitimacy, and Constitutionalism*. Cambridge: Cambridge University Press.

Dinstein, Y. (2009) *The International Law of Belligerent Occupation*. Cambridge: Cambridge University Press.

Esposito, R. (2011) *Immunitas: The Protection and Negation of Life*. Trans. Z. Hanafi. Cambridge: Polity.

Falk, H. (2014) *Det Politisk-teologiska komplexet: Fyra kapitel om Carl Schmitts Sekularitet*. Gothenburg: Gothenburg University.

Ferraro, T. (2012) 'Determining the beginning and end of an occupation under international humanitarian law', *International Review of the Red Cross*, Vol. 94, No. 885: 133–63.

Fornari, G. (2011) 'Figures of Antichrist: The Apocalypse and Its Restraints in Contemporary Political Thought', *Contagion*, Vol. 17, No.1: 53–86.

Fox, G. (2005) 'The Occupation of Iraq', *Georgetown Journal of International Law*, Vol. 36, No. 2: 195–297.

Fox, G. (2008) *Humanitarian Occupation*. Cambridge: Cambridge University Press.

Fox, G. (2012) 'Transformative occupation and the unilateralist impulse', *International Review of the Red Cross*, Vol. 94, No. 885: 237–66.

Glahn, G. (1957) *The Occupation of Enemy Territory: A Commentary on the Law and Practice of Belligerent Occupation*. Minneapolis, MN: University of Minnesota Press.

Gunneflo, M. (2014) *The Life and Times of Targeted Killing*. Lund: Faculty of Law.

Hell, J. (2009) 'Katechon: Carl Schmitt's Imperial Theology and the Ruins of the Future', *The Germanic Review*, Vol. 84, No. 4: 283–326.

Hoelzl, M. and G. Ward (2008) 'Editors' Introduction', p. 1–29, in C. Schmitt, *Political Theology II: The Myth of the Closure of any Political Theology* [1970]. Trans. M. Hoelzl and G. Ward. Cambridge: Polity.

Hohendahl, P. (2008) 'Political Theology Revisited: Carl Schmitt's Postwar Reassessment', *Konturen*, No. 1: 1–28.

Koskenniemi, M. (2004) 'International Law as Political Theology: How to Read *Nomos der Erde*?', *Constellations* Vol. 11: No. 4: 492–511.

Koskenniemi, M. (2006) *From Apology to Utopia: The Structure of International Legal Argument*. Cambridge: Cambridge University Press.

Koskenniemi, M. (2012) 'Law, Teleology and International Relations: An Essay in Counterdisciplinarity', *International Relations*, Vol. 26, No. 3: 3–34.

Langford, P. and I. Bryan (2016) 'Beyond the Jurist as a Theologian of Legal Science: The Question of Carl Schmitt and the International Legal Order', Chapter 14 in M. Arvidsson, L. Brännström and P. Minkkinen (eds), *The Contemporary Relevance of Carl Schmitt. Law, Politics, Theology.* Abingdon: Routledge.

McLouglin, D. (2013) 'A tale of two Schmitts: authority, administration and the responsibility to protect', *London Review of International Law*, Vol. 1, No.1: 141–7.

Maschke, G. (ed.) (2005) *Carl Schmitt. Frieden oder Pazifismus? Arbeiten zum Völkerrecht und zur internationalen Politik 1924–1978.* Berlin: Duncker and Humblot.

Meier, H. (1998) *The Lesson of Carl Schmitt: Four Chapters on the Distinction between Political Theology and Political Philosophy.* Trans. M. Brainard. Chicago, IL: University of Chicago Press.

Meyer, R., C. Schetter and J. Prinz (2012) 'Spatial contestation? The theological foundations of Carl Schmitt's spatial thought', *Geoforum*, Vol. 43, No.4: 687–96.

Nabulsi, K. (2005) *Traditions of War*, Oxford: Oxford University Press.

Nicholl, C. (2008) *From Hope to Despair in Thessalonica: Situating 1 and 2 Thessalonians.* Cambridge: Cambridge University Press.

Noll, G. (2014) 'IS – a threat to the structure of international law?', Trans. S. Bengtsson, *Open Democracy*, 27 November. Available at https://www.opendemocracy.net/gregor-noll/is-%E2%80%93-threat-to-structure-of-international-law (accessed 18 April 2015).

Noll, G. (2015) 'What Moves Law? Martti Koskenniemi and Transcendence in International Law', in W. Werner, A. Galan and M. de Hoon (eds), *The Law of International Lawyers; Reflections on the Work of Martti Koskenniemi.* Cambridge: Cambridge University Press (forthcoming).

Orford, A. (2011) *International Authority and the Responsibility to Protect.* Cambridge: Cambridge University Press.

Peerbolte, L. (1997) 'The Katéxon/Katexωn of Thess. 2:6–7', *Novum Testamentum*, Vol. 39, No.1: 138–50.

Peterson, E. (2011) 'Monotheism as a Political Problem: A Contribution to the History of Political Theology in the Roman Empire' [1935], p. 68–105, in E. Peterson, *Theological Tractates.* Trans. M. Hollerich. Redwood City, CA: Stanford University Press.

Prozorov, S. (2012) 'The katechon in the age of biopolitical nihilism', *Continental Philosophy Review*, Vol. 45, No. 4: 483–503.

Rasch, W. (2008) 'Anger Management: Carl Schmitt in 1925 and the Occupation of the Rhineland', *New Centennial Review*, Vol. 8, No. 1: 57–79.

Roberts, A. (2006) 'Transformative Military Occupation: Applying the Laws of War and Human Rights', *American Journal of International Law*, Vol. 100, No 3: 580–622.

Schmitt, C. (1940) *Begriffe im Kampf mit Weimar – Genf – Versailles 1923–1939.* Hamburg: Hanseatische Verlagsanstalt.

Schmitt, C. (1958) *Verfassungsrechtliche Aufsätze aus den Jahren 1916–1969.* Berlin: Dunker and Humblot.

Schmitt, C. (1991) *Glossarium: Aufzeichnungen der Jahre 1947–1951.* Berlin: Dunker and Humblot.

Schmitt, C. (1996) *The Concept of the Political* [1927]. Trans. G. Schwab. Chicago, IL: Chicago University Press.

Schmitt, C. (1997) *Land and Sea* [1957]. Trans. S. Draghici. Washington, DC: Plutarch.
Schmitt, C. (2003) *The Nomos of the Earth in the International Law of the Jus Publicum Europaeum* [1950]. Trans. G. L. Ulmen. New York: Telos.
Schmitt, C. (2005a) *Political Theology: Four Chapters on the Concept of Sovereignty* [1922]. Trans. G. Schwab. Chicago, IL: University of Chicago Press.
Schmitt, C. (2005b) 'Die Rheinlande als Object internationaler Politik' [1925], p. 26–50, in C. Schmitt, *Frieden oder Pazifismus? Arbeiten zum Volkerrecht und zur internationalen Politik 1924–1978*. Berlin: Duncker and Humblot.
Schmitt, C. (2007) *Theory of the Partisan: Intermediate Commentary on the Concept of the Political* [1963]. Trans. A. C. Goodson. New York: Telos.
Schmitt, C. (2008) *Political Theology II: The Myth of the Closure of Any Political Theology* [1970]. Trans. M. Hoelzl and G. Ward. Cambridge: Polity.
Schmitt, C. (2009) 'Three Possibilities for a Christian Conception of History' [1950]. Trans. M. Wenning. *Telos*, No. 147: 167–70.
Schmitt, C. (2011) 'The *Großraum* Order of International Law with a Ban on Intervention for Spatially Foreign Powers: A Contribution to the Concept of *Reich* in International Law (1939–1941)' [1941], p. 75–124, in C. Schmitt, *Writings on War*. Trans. T. Nunan. Cambridge: Polity.
Slotte, P. (2010) 'Political Theology within International Law and Protestant Theology', *Studia Theologica*, Vol. 64, No. 1: 22–58.
Stirk, P. (2004) 'Carl Schmitt, the Law of Occupation, and the Iraq War', *Constellations*, Vol. 11, No. 4: 527–536.
Stirk, P. (2005) *Carl Schmitt, Crown Jurist of the Third Reich: On Preemptive War, Military Occupation and World Empire*. Lewiston: Edwin Mellen.
Stirk, P. (2009) *The Politics of Military Occupation*. Edinburgh: Edinburgh University Press.
Virno, P. (2008) *Multitude: Between Innovation and Negation*. Trans. I. Bertoletti, J. Cascaito and A. Casson. Los Angeles, CA: Semiotext(e).

Legislative Acts

Convention (IV) respecting the Laws and Customs of War on Land and its annex: Regulations concerning the Laws and Customs of War on Land. The Hague, 18 October 1907.
Convention (IV) relative to the Protection of Civilian Persons in Time of War. Geneva, 12 August 1949.
Protocol Additional to the Geneva Conventions of 12 August 1949, and relating to the Protection of Victims of International Armed Conflicts (Protocol I), 8 June 1977.
United Nations Security Council Resolution 1483 (2003) The situation between Iraq and Kuwait, S/RES/1483 (2003), May 22, 2003.

Index

absolute freedom 108
absolute hostility 141
acceleration, social *see* social acceleration
Acheron 135, 137–40
Acheronta movebo 138
Adams, Henry 95
administrative state 36
AFSJ (area of freedom, security and justice) 166, 167
Agamben, Giorgio 5, 108, 181
Age of Neutralizations and Depoliticizations, The 110, 198–9
Alexander, J. 204
al-Qaeda 60
American-Soviet dualism 149
amity lines 196
Amphinomos 215
anarchy 121–2, 129–31; of general causes 65
anomos 224, 225
Anschütz, Gerhard 38
apolitical life of the masses 127–8
apolitics 79–81
appropriation 213–14, 214–15, 216, 218
Article 2 (4) UN Charter 55
Article 48 (Weimar Constitution) 43, 44
Article 51 UN Charter 56
assembly, representative 36
association 50
Astynomos 215
Augustinian distinction 211
Augustinian peace 211
authority: and charisma 185; downward delegation of 97–100, 102; hierarchy of 30; and sovereignty 26; ultimate 29; unrestricted 28

authorized subject 21
autochthonism 136

Balakrishnan, Gopal 1, 182
Balibar, Étienne: sovereign decision 51
Barion, Hans 184
basic rights 65
Bauman, Z. 204
Beard, Jennifer 54, 231
belligerent occupation 227–30, 231
Benjamin, W. 203
Bible, the 154
Bichsel, Peter 82
bipolarity 157
Bismarck, Otto von 138
Blumenberg, Hans 211, 212
Böckenförde, Ernst-Wolfgang: on constitutional law 52
Bodin, Jean 108, 190
Bolz, Norbert 186
borders 53
Bosnia 58
bourgeois society 42
Brännström, Leila: sovereign decision 51
Brazil: economic fragility of 158
British Empire 197
brother as double 140–2
Bruderkampf 140–2

capital 31
capitalist world-view 150
Catholic Church 53; political role of 3
Catholicism 182–4; and charisma 187–9; and the post-secular age 189–91; visibility against neutrality 187–9
challenge and response theory 152
character, defining 111–12

charisma 184–7; charismatic
  organization 186
charismata 185, 186
China: economic growth 159;
  harmonious universal society 160;
  increased military budget 159;
  peaceful rise 147; potential for
  conflict with the USA 158–9;
  superpower status 158
Chinese Journal of International Law 147
choice: and necessity 109
Christian Epimetheus 210
Christian eschatology 151–5
Christianity: historical consciousness
  154; sacred history 155
chronos 227
Churchill, Winston 153
Church law 188
City of God, The 211
civil war 60
Clausewitz, Carl von 138
Clinton, Hillary 159, 160
Cold War 148, 149; endurance of
  157–8; multipolar constellation 155;
  unipolarity outcome 155
collective oscillation 202, 204
colonialism 54
colonies 201
Common Foreign and Security Policy
  (CFSP) 166, 167
common, notion of 216–17, 218
communication: speedier 92
communists 42
community: identification with a
  property 51; leadership and moral
  decision-making 29; preservation of
  27–8
Concept of the Political, The 55
conceptual sociology 182, 184
concrete orders 20–1, 22–3; Catholic
  Church 73; isolated 27; leadership
  principle 22, 25; legal substance of
  22, 25; role of the state 23;
  sustaining a 'normal situation' 22
conduct, norms of 22
Confucius 160
Congress of Vienna 140
conservative revolution 120
constitution: all-encompassing 51;
  defence by the executive 43;
  democratic 40; executive
  guardianship of 44–7; identity
  39–40; infringement of provisions
  43; positive concept of 39–40, 40, 44;
  safeguarding of rights 35; social and
  political ordering 39; suspension of
  provisions 43
constitutional guardianship: concept of
  41–4; by the executive 44–7;
  protection against constitutional
  change 34; protection of
  constitutional rights 35; protection
  of social and political ordering 35;
  reserved for president of the
  Weimar Republic 42–3
constitutional laws 39
constitutional liberalism 19
constitutional monarchy 36
Constitutional Theory 39, 41–2; liberal
  constitutional state 51
contingent sovereignty 54
co-progressiveness 147–8
Court of First Instance 173
Court of Justice 173
Croce, M.: concrete-order perspective
  20n1
cultural hegemony 184

Dahlheimer, Manfred 188
Dai Bingguo 160
decision: active impulse towards
  correctness 115; arbitrary instance
  of the sovereign's will 113; basic 67;
  constitutional review 66; distinction
  72, 73; and necessity 108, 109–12;
  rightness of 114
decisionism 19; revolutionary 28n8;
  sovereign response to emergency 31
decrees 94
deflation 96
delegation: downward 97–100;
  legislative 94, 96; of powers 94, 102
democracy: election of Parliament 36;
  identity of ruler and ruled 45; and
  motorized legislation 95;
  representative assemblies 36
democratic constitutionalism 40
democratic deficit 102
democratic legitimacy 44–7
democratic politics: slow process of 101
demos 29
Der Arbeiter 121, 125
Der Hüter der Verfassung 66
Derrida, Jacques 117; brother enemy
  140–2; dehumanized desert 143;
  philosophy and the Acheron

137–40; quasi-psychoanalytical reading of Schmitt 134; telluric autochthonism 136
Der Weltstaat 125, 126
Der Wert des Staates und die Bedeutung des Einzelnen 129
An der Zeitmauer 125
de-secularization 205
Die Einheit der Welt 95–6
Die Schere 129
dire emergency 107
disenchantment 185, 189
dislocated partisan 59–60
division 213, 214, 215, 218
division of powers 66
domestic law: protection of political community 50–2
double, figure of 140–2
downward delegation of authority 97–100, 102
Dulles, John Foster 153
Durkheim, Émile 202
Dürrenmatt, Friedrich 78, 81–2; themes of law and justice 82n4

economics: and value 70
economic state intervention 95, 96
Economy and Society 185
Elden, Stewart 54
élites 75
emergency 19; dire 107; executive decision-making powers 46–7; overriding individual rights 44; sovereign decision in response to 31
Empire 58
Enabling Acts 94, 96
enclosure 174
enemy *see* foe, and friend
Engels, Friedrich 139
England: marine-based existence 123
Enlightenment 149
enmity 174
Ennomos 215
Entscheidung 67; decision 72
Environmental Protection Act 98
eschatology: Christian 151–5; emplacing the katechonic figure of international law 230–2; and the *katechon* 224
Esping, Hans 99–100
Esposito, Roberto 51, 53
ethics of conviction 116
ethics of responsibility 116

EU (European Union): enlargement 165, 174; expansion by regional integration 167; fundamental values 174; identity 165; internal and external dimensional security 172–5; project of integration 165, 166; security-identity continuum 166; security zone 165; transnational security entrepreneur 172, 174
Eurocentric global order 200
European Council 173
European international law 52–5; borders 53; disintegration 58; equality of states 53; Eurocentric 53–4; protection of political community 53; war as duel 53
European Security Defence Policy (ESDP) 166, 167
Evans-Pritchard, E. 202
exacting moral decision 29
Ex Captivitate Salus 209, 210
exception 25–8; legal norms 24–5; meaning of 25–6; repression of 199; *see also* state of exception
Execution of Justice, The 78; critique of juridical romanticism 82; overlapping levels of politics in 82; *see also* Kohler, Isaak (fictional character); Spät, Felix (fictional character)
executive: blurring of role with legislature 96; and constitutional change 46; defence of the constitution 43; dictatorship 45; guardian of rights 42; guardianship of the constitution 44–7; political control of 46; role of 97
exigency 107
existential history 151–5
existentialism 161–2
existential threat 110, 111
Eyryvnomos 215

Federal Constitutional Court 40
Feur und Blut 120
field of law 226
final judgement 117
Finalreihen 68
First Additional Protocol (1977) 227
First World War 52–3; collapse of European hegemony 197
foe, and friend 72, 74, 110; criteria for the enemy 110

Forest Passage, The 121, 122, 128
formal legality 71
Foucault, Michel 161
Fourth Geneva Convention (1949) 227
framework legislation 97–100, 101–2, 103; characterization of 98
franchise 36
fratricidal war 140–2
French revolution 138
Freud, Sigmund 135, 138
Freundschaftliche Begegnungen 121
friend and foe 72, 74, 110
friend-enemy distinction 50, 57
Frisch, Max 82

Geltung 67
general laws 36
Geneva Convention (1949) 60, 137
Germany: constitutional theory in 37
Gesetzesvorbehalt 37, 38
Gesetz und Urteil 24n5, 114
global civil war 52
global division and order 215
global dualism 149
global hegemony 148
globalization 168–70
global order: Eurocentric 200; original 196; post-First World War 197
global partisan 59–60
Glossarium 120, 209, 210
Gnosticism 188, 189
goal-rules 98
golden age 126
Gottman, Jean 124
greater-space assertion 56–8
Großraum 56
Gruppe Olten 82
Guevara, Ernesto 'Che' 59
Gulf War 58

Hague Convention (1907) 137, 227
Haiti 58
Harbermas, Jürgen 191
Hardt, Michael 58
Hartmann, N. 67–8, 69
Health and Medical Services Act 98
Hegel, Georg Wilhelm Friedrich 129
hegemony: collapse of 197; correlation with progressivism 150; cultural 184; global 148; legalised in international law 54; and progressivism 150; superpower 148–51
Heliopolis 121

Hesiod 126
Hetzler, Antoinette 99, 102
high-speed society 92, 100–3
historical consciousness 153, 154
historical events 161; contextual significance 151–2
historical existentialism 152
history: existentialist account of 152
Hitler, Adolf 56, 120, 185
Hobbes, Thomas 64, 122, 190
Hohendahl, Peter 125
Holy Roman Empire 53
Holy Spirit 187
holy wars 54
Homo sapiens 125, 128, 129, 130
Hooker, W. 197
hostility: absolute 135, 136, 141; and Lenin 139; *see also* telluric partisan
human dignity 65, 70, 72, 73
humanity: material content 73; protection from itself 30
Hydén, Håkan 99

illegitimate constitutional identity 39–40
imperialism: spaceless 57, 58
India: economic fragility of 158
Industrial Revolution 123
inflation 96
injustice 217–18, 219
institutional guarantees 42
integration: EU project 165
international equilibrium 157
international law: ban on war 55–6; eschatology of 230–2; European 52–5; greater space assertions 56–8; legalised hegemony 54; political self-determination 170–1; prophecies on the future of 155–8; rhetoric of universalization 171; self-defence exception 55–6; spaceless imperialism 56–8
international legal order: passage from political theology 213–15
international order 149; historical context 157
intervals 214
ius publicum Europaeum 212

judicial review 40–1
judicial rule 35
judiciary: decisions of judges 114; devious lawgiver 66; and the division

of powers 66; illusionary power 66; notion of safeguarding values 65; role of 97
Jünger, Ernst: anarchical life of the species 129–31; golden age 126; the political 128; relationship with Schmitt 120; singular exemplar 129; world of the tale 126; world of the worker 121–2, 125
juridical decision 23
juridical romanticism 79–81, 87
juridical self-understanding 213
jurisdictional competence 25
jurist, the 209; beyond the jurist as a theologian of legal science 216–18; limits as a theologian of legal science 215–16; position and identity of 214; situated 214
jus ad bellum 53
jus in bello 53
jus publicum europaeum 169
justa causa 169
justice: breach of the constitution 66; and romanticism 81; *see also Execution of Justice, The*
justice of exchange 70
justus hostis 53
just wars 116, 168

Kadi case 173–4
kairos 227
Kant, Immanuel 203
katechon 153, 154, 210, 217–18, 224–5; eschatology of international law 230–2; identity 224; and the laws of occupation 226–30; paradox 224; and political theology 225–6; and transformation 228–9
Kellogg–Briand Pact (1928) 55
Kelsen, Hans 47, 183
Khan, Paul W. 29, 181
Kierkegaard, Søren A. 152
Kohler, Isaak (fictional character) 82–3, 83–4, 85
Koselleck, Reinhart 91
Koskenniemi, Martti 150

Laband, Paul 2
Land and Sea 148
land appropriation 54, 200, 214
Landnahme 200
large spaces theory 155–6; definition 169–70; and the EU 174

large space theory: Third Reich 198
law: concrete-order approach 20; constitutional 39; domestic 50–2; general 36; and the Gospel 186; increasing statutorification of 93; as legal realism 219; and necessity 109; open-ended 97, 100; overall goals 100; in *Political Theology* 23–5; reflexive 102, 102n9; and romanticism 79–81; rule of 88; science of 190
law of acceleration 95
law of nations 148–9
laws of occupation 226–30; belligerent occupation 227
leadership principle 22, 25; function of 29–30; prevention of political contestation 30
League of Nations 56
Lebensform 50
leerlaufend 38
legal norms 23–4; atypical cases 24–5, 25n6; exception 24–5; presupposes order 26; routine cases 24; validity of 24
legal order: indirect effect of values 74; international 53; principles and norms 71; protection of concrete orders 22; subjective valuations 69; threat to 31
legal positivism 95
legal realism 219
legal science 215–16
legal system: need for clear and stable rules 67
legal title 227
legislation 66; delegation of powers 94; framework 97–100, 101–2, 103; motorized 91, 92–7; secondary 100
legislative delegations 94, 96
legislative state 36–9; obsolescence of 36; pluralism of 42
legislature: blurring of role with executive 96; role of 97
legitimacy 185
Legitimacy of the Modern Age, The 211, 212
legitimate constitutional identity 39
legitimate force 60
Lenin, Vladimir Ilyich 136, 139, 140
Leviathan 122, 124, 131
Leviathan, The 122
liberal constitutionalism 23; political

relativism 30; *see also* legislative state
liberal democracy 41–2; basis of 71n14; and formal legality 71; separation of powers 39, 96, 97
liberalism: avoidance of political antagonisms 87; depoliticizing and neutralizing conflict 171; and political romanticism 87
liberal society 42
Lidbom, Carl 98
Lievens, Matthias 191
Lomax, Harvey 107
Löwith, Karl 112, 114, 152–3, 210
Lukes, S. 202
Luther, Martin 186

majority rule 35
Mao Tse-tung 139, 140, 141
Marxism 149
Marx, Karl 139
Maschke, Günter 95
masses: apolitical life of 127–8; Unknown Soldier 127
Maxima – Minima 125
McCormick, John P. 181
Meaning in History 152–3
Mearsheimer, John 158–9
Meier, Heinrich 116–17, 139n8, 182
Milbank, John 181, 189–90
minority groups 47
mobility 136
modernity 211, 212
modern partisan 136–7
Monotheism as a Political Problem 211
Monroe doctrine 56, 57, 170, 197
moralism 172
Morgenthau, Hans 151
motion picture 92
motorized legislation 91, 92–7; increasing statutorification of law 93–4; laws responding to social change 95; market economy and state intervention 95; structural transformation of the legislative process 94
Mouffe, Chantal 5
Müller, J-W. 135
multipolar *nomos* 157
multi-tasking 92

Nachwort 67
Napoleon 135, 140
nationalism 203

Nationalist Socialist German Workers' Party 120
National Socialism: collapse of 209; revolutionary decisionism 28n8
necessity: absence of choice 109; and the decision on the exception 109–12; definition 109; and the political 107–8; and political existence 110–12
negativity 208, 214, 217, 218–19
Negri, Antonio 58
neutrality: of values 72
New World 53, 54; order of Central Europe 54
new world order 168–70
nihilism 198; emergence of 201; sacred orientation 203–6
Noll, Gregor 230
nomos 53–4; definition 168, 200, 213; of the earth 123, 125; just war 168; multipolar 157; of the sea 123–5; state control of recourse to violence and economic resource 168–9
Nomos of the Earth, The 4, 53
normal conditions 74–5
normality 22; sovereign as guarantor of 27–8
normative coherence 215
norms *see* legal norms
norms of conduct 22
Nuremberg 209
Nuremberg trials 4

objectified spirit 68–9
objective necessity 108
occasionalism 114
occidental rationalism 188, 190, 199
Occupational Safety and Health Act 98
occupying power 228
On the Three Types of Juristic Thought 4, 20; concrete-order thinking 50–1
open-ended laws 97
order: plural 112; and sacred orientation 201–2
order thinking 183
orientation 113–15

Parliament: battleground for competing social groups 36; democratically elected 36; social diversity 36
parliamentary debate 36
parliamentary democracy 95

parliamentary majorities 35
parousia 224, 224n2
partisan: criteria for identification of 135–7; modern 136–7; origin of 135; and philosophy 139–40; Prussian Edict 138; revolutionary 134, 136; telluric 58–60, 134, 136; woman as absolute 142–3
partisan, theory of 58–60; definition of partisan 59
Peace, The 122
people, the: apolitical side of the masses 127–8; concrete subjects 128; exercising constituent power 39; high-speed society 92, 100–3; politicization of 128
perfect gift 135
personal ends 68
Persson, Göran 101
Peterson, Erik 211, 229
philautía 142
philosophy: and the Acheron 137–40; of history 148–9; and the partisan 139–40
plenty, world of 126
Plight of European Jurisprudence, The 91, 92–3
pluralistic systems 169
plural order 112
pneumocracy 186
political: action 108
political community: enclosure 174; existential understanding of 170, 174–5; force in international law 60–1; greater space assertions of 56–8; and partisanship 59; protection by European international law 53; protection in domestic law 50–2
political, concept of: decisions oriented towards war 107; definition of 108; exclusion of the woman 143; form of public representation 123–4; freedom of decision 107; necessity 107–8; political existence 110–12; restructured 144; rethinking 134–44; revolutionary war of parties 139
political conflict 30
political entities 196; German European large space 197
political existence 110–12, 112
political existentialism 171, 173

political ideas 197–8
political identity 34
political order: and constitution 39; constitutional protection of 35
political relativism 30
political romanticism 81, 87
Political Romanticism 2, 79, 87
political theology 64n2, 182–4; and charisma 187–9; *katechon* in 225–6; originating 211; passage to international legal order 213–15; and the post-secular age 189–91
Political Theology 3, 5, 108, 199; characteristic of sovereignty 26; definition of sovereignty 19; law in 23–5; paradox in 20; relation of order and decision 27; understanding of law 20
Political Theology II 184
politicians: and responsibility 116
politics: of the land 124; reactive 101; situational 101; of spatiality 124–5
Politics as a Vocation 115
Politics of Friendship 117, 141
Popitz, Johannes 93
Posner, Eric 46, 47
possibility 83–4
Post Card, The 144
post-secular turn 181–2
praxis, state 230–1
preservation 228, 229
presidency: plebiscitary legitimacy of 47
presidential dictatorship, theory of 3, 45
presidential guardianship 41, 44
president (Weimar Republic): power to protect public security 43
primitive societies 202
production 213, 214, 215, 218
progressivism 147; as advocated by China 147, 148; belief in by the USA and the Soviet Union 149–50, 151; Chinese 160; correlation with hegemony 150; international financial and trade institutions 161; philosophy of 148–51; of the superpowers 150
Protestantism 184–5
Prussia 138
pseudo-sacred symbols 202
psychologization 185
public security: presidential protection of 43

Putin, Vladimir 158

Quixote, Don 86

radical evil 117
Rasch, W. 54; decisions of judges 114; responsibility 115
rationality 199
realist school 171
reality 83–4
reflexive law 102, 102n9
regional iconography 124
religious wars 116
representation 187–8; of anarchy 121–2; making the invisible visible 124; *nomos* of the earth 123; *nomos* of the sea 123–5; of the political 123–4; the ship 122–5, 125; Unknown Soldier 127, 128
representative assemblies 36
repression of the exception 199
responsibility 115–17
Respublica Christiana 226
revolutionary decisionism 28n8
revolutionary partisan 134, 136
Rhodes Declaration 166
rights: basic 65; institutional guarantees 42; minority, threat to 47; overridden in state of emergency 44; safeguarding under a constitution 35; under the Weimar Constitution 37, 42
rituals 203–5
Roman Catholic Church: public character 188
Roman Catholicism and Political Form 3, 150, 187
Roman Empire 153, 211
romantic genius 80
romanticism: and law 79–81; simplistic notion of 87; suspension of reality 80; *see also Execution of Justice, The*
romantics 2
Roosevelt, President Theodore 57
Rosa, H.: slipping slopes syndrome 92
rule: judicial 35; majority 35
rule of law 65, 88
ruler and ruled 45
Russia: economic dependence on exports 158; *see also* Soviet Union

sacred orientation 201–2, 203–6
sacred symbols 202

Salvatore, A.: concrete-order perspective 20n1
Santner, Eric L. 181
Schachter, Oscar 55–6
Scheuerman, W. E.: delegation 102; motorized legislation 95
Schmitt, Carl: army duties 2; early years 2; imprisonment in America 4; joining the Nazi party 4; marriage 3; publications during Weimar era 2–3; returns to academia 2
Schopenhauer, Arthur 129
Schwab, George 107
science of law 190
sea: Industrial Revolution in England 123; *nomos* of 123–5
secondary legislation 100
Second Vatican Council 187
secularization 205
secular law 186
secular, the: autonomous existence 190; creation of 190
security: leading the security discourse 172–3; notion of 165; rhetoric 173
security entrepreneurship 172
security-identity continuum 166
security, public: presidential protection of 43
sedimented norms of conduct 22
self-defence 55–6; and international law 56
self-determination 40
self-understanding, juridical 213
Senkaku Islands dispute 159
separation of powers 39, 96, 97
Shapiro, Kam 123
Sienho Yee 147, 160
Simpson, Gerry 54
Singer, Pete 202
singular exemplar 129
site, the 200
situational politics 101
slipping slopes syndrome 92
Slomp, G.: partisans 59
Smith, David Norman 189
social acceleration 91–2, 95–7; definition of 92; forms of 92
social democrats 42
social order: and constitution 39; constitutional protection of 35
Social Services Act 98, 102
social welfare 99
society *see* people, the

sociopolitical world 31
Sohm, Rudolph 184, 185, 186, 188
Sollen 68
Somalia 58
South African Truth and Reconciliation Committee 87
sovereign decision 25–8
sovereignty: absolute authority 30–1; agenda 28–30; and authority 26; competition between political actors 29; concept of 19; contingent 54; decisionism 19; limitations of possible actions 27; and responsibility 115–17
Soviet Union: assistance to minor powers 155; implosion 158; and progressivism 149–50, 151; *see also* Russia
space: contests in 195; discontinuity 195; and force 216; spaciality of 195; spatial exception 200
spaceless imperialism 57, 58
space revolution 96
Spanish Civil War 59
Spät, Felix (fictional character) 78, 82, 83, 84–5, 85–6
spatial exception 200
species: anarchical life of 129–31
state intervention, economic 95, 96
state of exception: authority of the sovereign 26; frame of normality 31; restoring normal order of a political community 28; state's right of self-preservation 108
state praxis 230–1
state, the: administrative 36; economic rationality 73–4; emerging dominance of 195; goodness of the offices 129–30; guarantor of social order 27; man as a legal person 131; monopoly on legitimate force 60; overarching institution 23; production of man as a political animal 130–1; representation of individual positions and roles 73; and technology 125; transcendentalism of 130, 131
statutorification 93, 93n3
statutory positivism 2, 37–8
St Augustine 224
Steiner, Gary 107
Stellenwert 70
Sterzel, Fredrik 98

St Paul 73, 153, 224; and charisma 185
Strauss, Levi 107
Strong, Tracy 113
A Study of History 152
superpower hegemony 148–51
Sweden: framework laws 98; framework legislation 97–100
symbols 203–5
systemic determination 108

tale, the 126
Taubes, Jacob 214
technicity 198–200
techniques of domination 201
technological acceleration 92, 96
technology: and the modern partisan 136–7; and the state 125
telluric partisan 58–60, 134, 136
tempo of life 92
Termitisierung 93
Theology and Social Theory 189–90
The Theory of the Partisan *see* partisan
Theory of the Partisan 58
Thessalonians 224
Third Reich 198
Three Possibilities for a Christian Conception of History 210, 213
Toynbee, Arnold 148, 152
transformation 228–9
transitional justice 87
transnational security entrepreneur 172, 174
transportation: speedier 91–2
travel: speedier 91–2
Trawny, Peter 125
Treaty of Maastricht 166
true peace, concept of 157
True Space 216
two-kingdom theory 186
tyranny of values: basic rights 65; radical conflict 68
Tyranny of Values, The 65

Überfluß 126
Ukraine: dependence on Russian gas supplies 57; Russian military intervention in 57
Ulmen, G. L. 57
UN Charter 55
union 50
unipolarity: characterization of 157
United Nations Security Council Resolutions 227

United Nations (UN) 169
United States of America (USA): assistance to minor powers 155; international policeman 58; paradox of becoming the true Europe 170; potential for conflict with China 158–9; and progressivism 149–50, 151; religious aspects of political narrative 151
universal humanity 72–3
universalism 157
universalization: rhetoric of 171
Unknown Soldier 127
unrepresentable 126–7
UN Security Council 58, 173
unurban life 126–7
Urgemeinde 186
utilitarianism 70
utopia 73–5

values: conflicts 68–9; directly applied 67; in economic exchange 70; legal framework for 67; and points 67–71; safeguarded by the judiciary 65; universal neutralization 72; validity of 67; value appropriation 173; *see also* tyranny of values
Vermeule, Adrian 46, 47
Vinx, Lars 52
völkischer Großraum 56
Vries, Hent de 190

war: ban on 55–6; bracketing of 196; existential necessity of 110; fratricidal 140–2; guilt 52–3; justification for 111; logic of 125–6; making life serious 112; necessitation of 107; self-defence 112; universal values 112; value of the enemy 112
Weber, Max 115–16, 184; and charisma 185–6, 186–7; disenchantment 185, 189
Weber, Samuel 55
Weber, Werner 93
Weimar Constitution 36–7; list of basic rights 37; moving beyond the legislative state 37; people's demand for democracy 39; protecting public security 43; protection of rights under 42; statutory positivism 38
Weimar Republic 38; constitutional guardianship 42–3
Weiss, Konrad 210
Wertphilosophie 67, 67n8, 70
Westphalia 53
Williams, Bernard 110, 111
Wilsonianism 57
Wilson, President Woodrow 52, 57
woman, as absolute partisan 142–3
worker, world of 121–3, 125; apolitical life of the masses 127–8; unurban life 126–7; and war 125–6
world order 148
world revolution 59

Yelle, Robert 185
Yugoslavia 141

Zhao Tingyang 160
Žižek, Slavoj 113
Zwischenlage 190, 191